G. W. M. REYNOLDS

G.W.M. Reynolds from *Reynolds's Miscellany*, 7 November 1846, p. 1

G. W. M. Reynolds
Nineteenth-Century Fiction, Politics, and the Press

Edited by

ANNE HUMPHERYS
Lehman College, City University of New York, USA

LOUIS JAMES
University of Kent, UK

Routledge
Taylor & Francis Group

LONDON AND NEW YORK

First published 2008 by Ashgate Publishing

2 Park Square, Milton Park, Abingdon, Oxfordshire OX14 4RN
52 Vanderbilt Avenue, New York, NY 10017

Routledge is an imprint of the Taylor & Francis Group, an informa business

First issued in paperback 2019

British Library Cataloguing in Publication Data
Humpherys, Anne
  G.W.M. Reynolds: Nineteenth-Century Fiction, Politics, and the Press. –
  (The Nineteenth Century)
  1. Reynolds, George W. M. (George William MacArthur), 1814–1879 2. Reynolds,
  George W. M. (George William MacArthur), 1814–1879 – Criticism and interpretation.
  3. Reynolds, George W. M. (George William MacArthur), 1814–1879 – Political and
  social views. 4. Authors, English – 19th century – Biography. 5. Periodicals –
  Publishing – Great Britain – History – 19th century. 6. Literature publishing –
  Great Britain – History – 19th century. 7. Politics and literature – Great Britain – History
  – 19th century. 8. Authors and publishers – Great Britain – History – 19th century.
  9. Narration (Rhetoric) – History - 19th century.
  I. Title II. James, Louis, Dr.
  823.8

Library of Congress Cataloging-in-Publication Data
Humpherys, Anne.
  G.W.M. Reynolds: Nineteenth-Century Fiction, Politics, and the Press / Anne Humpherys and
  Louis James.
     p.   cm. – (The Nineteenth Century Series)
  Includes bibliographical references and index.
  1. Reynolds, George W. M. (George William MacArthur), 1814–1879. 2. Authors, English –
  19th century--Biography. 3. Reynolds, George W. M. (George William MacArthur), 1814–1879 –
  Criticism and interpretation. 4. Reynolds, George W. M. (George William MacArthur), 1814–1879
  – Political and social views. 5. Periodicals – Publishing – Great Britain – History – 19th century.
  6. Literature publishing – Great Britain – History – 19th century. 7. Politics and literature –
  Great Britain – History – 19th century. 8. Authors and publishers – Great Britain – History –
  19th century. 9. Press – Great Britain – History – 19th century. 10. Narration (Rhetoric) – History
  –19th century. I. James, Louis, Dr. II. Title.
  PR5221.R35Z56 2008
  823'.8–dc22
  [B]   2007049840

ISBN 978-0-7546-5854-2 (hbk)
ISBN 978-0-367-88796-4 (pbk)

Contents

Illustrations

General Editors' Preface

The aim of the series is to reflect, develop and extend the great burgeoning of interest in the nineteenth century that has been an inevitable feature of recent years, as that former epoch has come more sharply into focus as a locus for our understanding not only of the past but of the contours of our modernity. It centres primarily upon major authors and subjects within Romantic and Victorian literature. It also includes studies of other British writers and issues, where these are matters of current debate: for example, biography and autobiography, journalism, periodical literature, travel writing, book production, gender, non-canonical writing. We are dedicated principally to publishing original monographs and symposia; our policy is to embrace a broad scope in chronology, approach and range of concern, and both to recognize and cut innovatively across such parameters as those suggested by the designations 'Romantic' and 'Victorian'. We welcome new ideas and theories, while valuing traditional scholarship. It is hoped that the world which predates yet so forcibly predicts and engages our own will emerge in parts, in the wider sweep, and in the lively streams of disputation and change that are so manifest an aspect of its intellectual, artistic and social landscape.

Vincent Newey
Joanne Shattock
University of Leicester

Notes on Contributors

Sucheta Bhattacharya is a Senior Lecturer in the Department of English, Serampore College, University of Calcutta. She is completing her dissertation on 'Cultural Hybridity: A Study of the Translations and Adaptations of G.W.M. Reynolds in Nineteenth-century Bengal' at Jadavpur University, University of Calcutta.

Stephen James Carver is a Lecturer at the Norwich School of Art and Design. He has previously taught Victorian literature at the University of East Anglia and the University of Fukui, Japan. He is the author of *The Life and Works of the Lancashire Novelist William Harrison Ainsworth 1850–1882* (Edward Mellen, 2003).

Berry Chevasco is a graduate of the University of California, Berkeley, Université de Paris, Sorbonne, and INSEAD, and holds a PhD from University College, London. She is the author of *Mysterymania: The Reception of Eugène Sue in Britain 1838–1860* (Peter Lang, 2003). She is an Honorary Research Fellow of University College, London.

Michael Diamond spent most of his working life with the World Service of the BBC. Since retirement his publications have included *Victorian Sensation* (Anthem, 2003). His contribution on Reynolds and Dickens to the 2000 conference on Reynolds at the University of Birmingham was published in 2002 in the *Dickensian*.

Helen Hauser is finishing her PhD at the University of California, Santa Cruz. Her dissertation work focuses on linking the popularity of Reynolds's penny dreadful fiction with the shift from endemic to organic notions of disease. She reads popular fiction as a type of social physic paralleling new medical theories of cure.

Ian Haywood is Reader in English at Roehampton University, London. His publications include *Bloody Romanticism: Spectacular Violence and the Politics of Representation 1776–1832* (Palgrave, 2006), *The Revolution in Popular Literature: Print, Politics and the People 1790–1860* (Cambridge University Press, 2004) and a three-volume edition of Chartist fiction published by Ashgate (1996–2001).

Anne Humpherys is Professor of English at Lehman College and the Graduate Center, City University of New York. She is the author of *Travels into the Poor Man's Country: The Work of Henry Mayhew* (University of George Press, 1977) and has published on G.W.M. Reynolds, Dickens, Tennyson and the divorce novel in nineteenth-century Britain.

Louis James first wrote on G.W.M. Reynolds's life and work in *Fiction for the Working Man, 1830–1850* (Oxford University Press, 1963) and has remained actively involved, through his writing and lecturing, in the various strands of Reynolds scholarship that culminate in this volume. He wrote Reynolds's entry in the *Oxford National Dictionary of Biography*. He is presently Emeritus Professor in Victorian and Modern Literature at the University of Kent, Canterbury, England.

Sara James wrote her doctoral thesis on the urban mystery novels of Eugène Sue and G.W.M. Reynolds at the University of Birmingham. She is the author of articles on Sue, Reynolds and French literature and on nineteenth-century women's writing in France. She is a Lecturer in French at Somerville College, Oxford. Her monograph, *G.W.M. Reynolds in France: Readings and Rewritings in French Literature, 1830-1848* is forthcoming.

Juliet John is a Reader in English Literature at the University of Liverpool and Director of the Gladstone Centre for Victorian Studies in Wales and the northwest of England. She is the author of *Dickens's Villains: Melodrama, Character, Popular Culture* (Oxford University Press, 2001), editor of *Charles Dickens's Oliver Twist: A Sourcebook* (Routledge, 2006) and *Cult Criminals: The Newgate Novels*, 6 vols (Routledge, 1998). She is also co-editor (with Alice Jenkins) of *Rethinking Victorian Culture* (Palgrave, 2000) and *Rereading Victorian Fiction* (Palgrave, 2000). Her monograph *Dickens and Mass Culture* is to be published by Oxford University Press in 2008.

Andrew King is a Senior Lecturer at Canterbury Christ Church University. He is the author of *The London Journal 1845–1883* (Ashgate, 2004) and, with John Plunkett, has edited *Victorian Print Media* (Oxford University Press, 2005) and *Popular Print Media 1820–1900* (Routledge, 2004).

Graham Law is Professor in Media History at the School of International Liberal Studies, Waseda University, Tokyo. In addition to a wide range of articles on nineteenth-century literary and publishing history, he is the author of *Serializing Fiction in the Victorian Press* (Palgrave, 2000) and *Indexes to Fiction in the 'Illustrated London News' and the 'Graphic'* (Queensland Community Press, 2002). He has produced scholarly editions of a number of popular Victorian novels, including David Pae's *Lucy, the Factory Girl* (Sensation Press, 2001). He is also co-editor of *The Public Face of Wilkie Collins: The Collected Letters* (Pickering and Chatto, 2005) and of the *Wilkie Collins Society Journal*.

Rohan McWilliam is Senior Lecturer in History at Anglia Ruskin University, Cambridge, and the author of *Popular Politics in Nineteenth-century England* (Routledge, 1998) as well as *The Tichborne Claimant: A Victorian Sensation* (Hambledon Continuum, 2007). He co-edited *The Victorian Studies Reader* with Kelly Boyd (Routledge, 2007).

Brian Maidment is Professor of English at the University of Salford. He has a long-standing interest is mass-circulation Victorian literature, especially periodicals and prints. His most recent book is *Dusty Bob: A Cultural History of Dustmen 1790–1870*

(Manchester University Press, 2007). Current work includes a book called *Comedy, Caricature and the Social Order 1820–1850* and editorial work on the Victorian volume of *The Oxford History of Popular Print Culture*.

Ellen Bayuk Rosenman is a Professor of English and an affiliate of the Gender and Women's Studies programme at the University of Kentucky. She is the author of *Unauthorized Pleasures: Accounts of Victorian Erotic Experience* (Cornell University Press, 2003). Her current project is a study of popular working-class fiction.

Michael H. Shirley earned his PhD in British History from the University of Illinois at Urbana-Champaign in 1997, and teaches at Eastern Illinois University. He has published articles on various topics, including G.W.M. Reynolds, and, with Todd Larson, edited *Splendidly Victorian: Essays in Honour of Walter L. Arnstein* (Ashgate, 2001).

Antony Taylor is Senior Lecturer in History at Sheffield Hallam University. He has written widely in the field of nineteenth- and twentieth-century popular politics in Britain. His most recent books are *'Down with the Crown': British Anti-monarchism and Debates about Royalty since 1790* (Reaktion Press, 1999) and *'Lords of Misrule': Hostility to Aristocracy in Late Nineteenth- and Early Twentieth-century Britain* (Palgrave, 2004).

Acknowledgements

Professor Humpherys wishes to thank Lehman College of the City University of New York for a Scholar Incentive Award, and especially the Leverhulme Trust for awarding her a Visiting Professorship at Birkbeck College, University of London, during which appointment this book was developed. It has been a united effort, and the editors are grateful to individual contributors for help and advice beyond the writing of essays. They also wish to thank John Adcock; Maha Atal; Dick Collins; Guy Dicks; Harold Gough; Jean Guivarc'h, and Monica North for generously contributing information from their own research into Reynolds's life and work; and Tony Heathcote of the Royal Military Academy, Sandhurst, and Paul Sterne of the National Archives, Kew, who have helped to access archival documents. The editors also thank David Bowman and the Cooperative Press, Ltd, Hanover Street, Manchester, for kind permission to use posters advertising *Reynolds's News* from the Cooperative Movement archive. For assistance in the book's production, the editors are grateful to Spencer Scott of the Templeman Library Photographic Unit at the University of Kent; Sara Cuervo of the Graduate Center, City University of New York, who helped with the primary bibliography and illustrations, and Louise McConnell who read parts of the book and offered very helpful editorial suggestions. Finally, the editors wish to thank Brigitte Lee for her excellent services in the final preparation of the manuscript.

Whilst every effort has been made to trace the owners of copyright material, we take the this opportunity to offer our apologies to any copyright holders whose rights we may have unwittingly infringed.

Dating Reynolds's Serial Publications

Reynolds habitually published his fiction without giving dates of publication, presumably so that he could continue republishing novels without his titles ever appearing out of date. As they were not listed in standard trade periodicals, the first appearance of some works can only be estimated using magazine advertisements. These problems are complicated by the fact that Reynolds's longest serials were gathered both into individual 'volumes' and into 'series'. The following is offered to help clarify the issues.

Reynolds considered *The Mysteries of London* and *The Mysteries of the Court of London* to be one continuous work. The penny publication of *The Mysteries of London* (London: George Vickers) began in or around October 1844. The volumes were: volume 1 (vol. 1, first series), 1845; volume 2 (vol. 2, first series), 1846; volume 3 (vol. 1, second series), 1847; volume 4 (vol. 2, second series), 1848. The series ended on 16 September 1848. (Vickers continued to publish a two-volume third series written by Thomas Miller and E.L. Blanchard, but Reynolds had nothing to do with this.)

The Mysteries of the Court of London (London: John Dicks) overlapped with its precursor, starting on 9 September 1848 and finishing in either December 1855 or January 1856. The dates of the volume publication are as follows: volume 1 (vol. 1, first series), 1849; volume 2 (vol. 2, first series), 1850; volume 3 (vol. 1, second series), 1851; volume 4 (vol. 2, second series), 1852; volume 5 (vol. 1, third series), 1853; volume 6 (vol. 2, third series), 1854; volume 7 (vol. 1, fourth series), 1855; volume 8 (vol. 2, fourth series), 1856. The series was first issued weekly in penny issues, monthly in sixpenny parts, and finally in single volumes of 52 numbers. The 12 volumes were paired into six individual 'series', with the chapters in each series numbered consecutively across both volumes as a single story. This massive enterprise was frequently reprinted, with different editions using the original stereotype plates, so that dates the title pages may indicate later publication, although the chapter and page numbers remain unchanged. *In this book, notes refer to the first volume issue, citing the volume number and date, but not the series.*

Reynolds's Miscellany began as *Reynolds's Magazine of Romance, General Literature, Science and Art* on 7 November 1846. The word '*Magazine*' in the title was changed to '*Miscellany*' with the fifth issue. The first series ran for two volumes until 6 November 1847; the second ran for 42 volumes until 14 June 1869. All references to this serial are given as '*RM*'.

Reynolds's Political Instructor was begun on November 10, 1849 as a weekly offshoot of *Reynolds's Miscellany*, and was enlarged to become *Reynolds's Weekly Newspaper, a Journal of Democratic Progress and General Intelligence* running from 5 May 1850 to 9 February 1851; it continued as *Reynolds's Newspaper* from 16 February 1851 to 25 September 1924; *Reynolds's Illustrated News* from 21 September 1924 to 23 February 1936; *Reynolds's News* from 4 March 1936 to 13 August 1944; *Reynolds's News and Sunday Citizen* from 20 August 1944 to 16 September 1962; and *the Sunday Citizen* from 23 September 1962 to 18 January 1967, when it was discontinued. All references to this journal are given as '*RN*'.

See also the 'Bibliography', p. 271

Abbreviations

The following abbreviations are used in the footnotes for the most frequently cited works by G.W.M. Reynolds.

LJ	*London Journal*
MOCL	*The Mysteries of the Court of London*
MOL	*The Mysteries of London*
RM	*Reynolds's Miscellany*
RN	*Reynolds's Newspaper*
RPI	*Reynolds's Political Instructor*

Introduction

Anne Humpherys and Louis James

G.W.M. Reynolds has remained a tantalizingly shadowy presence in mid-Victorian culture. He was hailed by *The Bookseller* as 'the most popular writer of his time,'[1] an author whose works outsold those of Dickens; he was an influential pioneer in the field of modern popular journalism; his radical newspapers were valued by many British working-class readers untouched by mainstream politicians. His influence spread to the United States, where he was pirated and plagiarized, and to India, where many of the emergent reading public considered him an English 'classic'. Yet until very recently, he has remained absent from standard histories of the period. His attitude towards his contemporaries in both literary and political culture is hard to determine with certainty, which makes him difficult to place in the overall picture of nineteenth-century society and culture. This volume is the first book-length effort to remedy this neglect; it brings together a range of authoritative scholars, from different disciplines, to create a coherent study of a major figure that the Victorian 'respectable' public conspired to ignore.

A Turbulent Life

George William McArthur Reynolds was born in Sandwich, Kent, on 23 July 1814, the son of George Reynolds, a post-captain in the Royal Navy, and Caroline Frances (née) Dowers, daughter of a Royal Navy captain. The family had a proud tradition of military service, which, as the eldest son, Reynolds was expected to follow. His father died in 1822, leaving him and his brother Edward under the guardianship of a Dr McArthur, who entered him, aged 13, into the Royal Military Academy, Sandhurst,[2] in July 1828. Little is known of Reynolds's family relationships, but autobiographical elements of Reynolds's first published novel, *The Youthful Impostor* (1835) significantly retitled *The Parricide* (1847), indicate that he was at odds with his father and the naval tradition to which he belonged: the story's characters include a monstrous Lord Fanmore who had been brutalized by commanding a Royal Navy man-of-war, 'on board of which a captain can be as despotic a tyrant as he pleases'.[3] Shortly after his mother died in 1830, the young Reynolds rejected his father's wishes that he should follow a military career, and on 13 September he summarily left Sandhurst, 'withdrawn by his friends' according to the College Register (a

---

1   'G.W.M. Reynolds' [obituary] *The Bookseller*, 3 July 1879, pp. 600–601.

2   Register of Gentleman Cadets at the Royal Military Academy, Sandhurst (RMAS), courtesy of the Curator, RMAS Collection.

3   G.W.M. Reynolds, *The Parricide* (1847), ch. 44. It is tempting to see the later title as prophetic of a life dedicated to destroying the restrictive paternal tyranny embodied in state institutions.

phrase used to indicate an irregular departure from the Academy), and without a commission. All previous accounts of this episode have stated that Reynolds left Sandhurst with a considerable family inheritance. Dick Collins, however, has examined the legal documents,[4] and found that Reynolds would have received a meager £400 from his mother's will, and he would only have received this in 1835. A modest £1,200 from his father's estate was also due, but not until in 1837. The fact that he left the Academy virtually penniless left Reynolds to live off his wits. Some time later, in 1848, a Captain Walmer Vincent sent a retrospective 'Statement' made by Dr. McArthur, Reynolds's erstwhile guardian, to the Home Office. This reported that the young Reynolds had become 'guilty of every species of fraud and immorality.'[5] He had run up a large bill at Long's Hotel in Bond Street, London, which he attempted to pay with the proceeds of stolen jewellery: discovered, he narrowly escaped transportation. In Paris, he got into trouble with the French police for 'swindling and playing with loaded dice'. In a Calais hotel he masqueraded as 'Master' to his younger brother Edward's servant, who acted as a decoy when he absconded without paying his bill. These accusations, not made until Reynolds was under attack as a Chartist leader, appear to be malicious. Reynolds was arrested for debt in May, 1839, and may have been seized by bailiffs in Long's Hotel, in a scene he then (re)created in *Grace Darling* (1839). But there is no implication of committing theft, either then or in 1830.[6] The accusation may have drawn on the gambling scams in *The Mysteries of London*, and Reynolds's fascination with the French underworld. It is however possible the young George, in revolt against authority, and radicalized by a youthful reading of Thomas Paine's *The Rights of Man*,[7] felt justified in flouting the laws of a corrupted society, and ran amok.

Reynolds's Radicalism helped draw him from England to France,[8] where he found a Paris that was heady with excitement just after the Revolution of July 1830 had toppled Charles X. If he had found himself in the bloody proletarian upheavals of the late eighteenth century, he might have had a different reaction, but the 1830 Revolution had been a revolt of the middle classes, led by radical intellectuals who aimed to create a literate culture without social boundaries, an objective he could enthusiastically embrace. In *The Modern Literature of France* (1838) he wrote that the 1830 Revolution had opened up a new era for French literature, making

---

4   Dick Collins, 'George William McArthur Reynolds: a biographical sketch', in G.W.M. Reynolds, *The Necromancer* (Kansas City, Missouri: Valancourt Books, 2007), pp. vii-lv. Collins includes other important new information on Reynolds life.

5   Captain Walmer Vincent of the Royal Navy to Sir George Grey, 9 April 1848, National Archives, HO 45/2410, Box 1, 337–4. I am grateful to Michael H. Shirley for pointing out this document. See Shirley, 'On Wings of Everlasting Power: G.W.M. Reynolds and "Reynolds's Newspaper", 1848–1876' (PhD thesis, University of Illinois at Urbana-Champaign, 1997); Rohan McWilliam, 'The Mysteries of G.W.M. Reynolds: Radicalism and Melodrama in Victorian Britain', in Malcolm Chase and Ian Dyck (eds), *Living and Learning: Essays in Honour of J.F.C. Harrison* (Aldershot: Scolar, 1996), p. 184.

6   I am grateful to Dick Collins for pointing out this connection. However Rohan McWilliam among others accepts Vincent's story: see below, pp. 33–4.

7   *RM*, 6 April 1850; cited in Shirley, 'On Wings of Everlasting Power', p. 6.

8   Collins, 'George William McArthur Reynolds: a biographical sketch', p. viii.

possible the creative writing of Victor Hugo and Alexandre Dumas, George Sand and Paul de Kock. In Paris (while in gaol, according to McArthur, although there is no evidence of this) he met a young Englishwoman Susannah Frances Pierson (also written Pearson), and on July 23 1835 they were married in the English Embassy chapel.[9] The wedding may have been hasty, for their first child was christened there the following January, but the event may also have been prompted by Reynolds, now 21, receiving his mother's legacy, and so being able to finance a family. By all accounts their marriage was a happy one. The couple shared interests in literature and politics. Susannah was a minor novelist with radical leanings, and later wrote domestic features for Reynolds's periodicals. Over Susannah's lifetime they were to have four sons, George Edward, Frederick, Kossuth Mazzini and Ledru Rollin, and five daughters, Blanche, Theresa Arabella, Joanna Frances, Louise Clarisse and Emily. In Paris, at 55 rue Neuve St Augustine, Reynolds ran Le Librairie des Étrangers, a small bookshop, reading room and publishing house[10] and from this address G.G. Bennis published Reynolds's first novel, *The Youthful Impostor*, in 1835. Reynolds became literary editor of the *Paris Literary Gazette*, in which role he gave the young W.M. Thackeray, then a struggling art student in the city, his first earnings as a writer.[11] Maha Atal writes that Reynolds's 'acquaintances in Paris included leaders in [the city's] nascent literary culture like Baudry and the Renouard brothers as well as prominent English expatriates.'[12] Reynolds was to claim that shortly after his marriage, on 2 November 1835, he became a French citizen, and served for two years in the cavalry regiment of the Thirteenth Legion of the Paris National Guard. He also claimed that he 'enjoyed the friendship of several of the most eminent authors of France', and, according to Cyril Pearl, met Eugène Sue.[13]

A (hostile) Home Office Report repeats the details of Reynolds's French naturalization and National Guard service.[14] But these facts have been contested. Maha Atal, working from research in Paris, writes that Reynolds attempted to buy the lease on 55 rue Neuve St Augustine 'as a *foreigner*'. Reynolds's National Guard service is also dubious: the National Guard regiment was prestigious, its members having to provide their own horses and uniforms, and so was unlikely to include a young English outsider of limited means. Reynolds may have made these claims partly as a stinging snub to his patriotic family, who had intended him for *British*

---

9   International Genealogical Index, Family Research Centre, London; cited in Shirley, 'On Wings of Everlasting Power', p. 7; Collins, 'George William McArthur Reynolds: a biographical sketch', p. xx.

10   See Maha Atal, 'G.W.M. Reynolds in Paris 1835-6: a New Discovery', in *Notes and Queries* (forthcoming).

11   Jean Guivar'ch, 'Deux journalistes anglais à Paris: G.W.M. Reynolds et W.M.T.', *Etudes Anglaises*, 28/2 (1975): 203–14.

12   Private communication, 11 March 3008. Collins however questions Reynolds's acceptance by the English expatriate community. 'George William McArthur Reynolds: a biographical sketch', p. xxii.

13   *The Modern Literature of France*, 2nd edn (London: George Henderson, 1841), vol. 1, pp. ii–iii; Cyril Pearl, *Victorian Patchwork* (London: William Heinemann, 1972), p. 73. Maha Atal however considers it unlikely that Reynolds met Sue.

14   W. Weston to Sir George Grey, 18 April, 1848, HO45. OS 2410, p. 345.

military service. If the facts were fantasy, they were true to Reynolds's aspirations. He was to remain unwavering in his devotion to the ideals of the 1830 Revolution, believing that reform in England could come only through the overthrow of a parasitic aristocracy and corrupt state institutions. But any dreams of life in France were to be dashed. Reynolds was impractical with money. For all his Radical attitudes, he had an aristocratic taste for good living, and a cavalier attitude to the claims of tradesmen. Reportedly, he invested heavily in an English newspaper, *The London and Paris Courier*, of which he was to be a co-editor.[15] There is no evidence this ever appeared. In the Autumn of 1837 Reynolds declared himself bankrupt, and returned with his family to England.

There, living in cramped, impoverished quarters in Bethnal Green[16], he set about supporting his growing family by his pen. From 1837 to the end of 1838 he edited the long-running *Monthly Magazine of Politics, Literature and the Belles-Lettres*, serializing the first chapters of his *Pickwick Abroad; or the Tour in France* (1837–38) in its pages. This picaresque novel greatly increased the journal's circulation, and the work itself remained in print throughout Reynolds's lifetime, but the racy 'continuation' of Dickens's original offended the managers, who terminated his editorship. In May 1840, after a chance encounter with the temperance lecturer J.H. Donaldson, Reynolds began an impassioned involvement in the teetotal movement.[17] That year he became chairman of the London United Temperance Association, started publishing *The Anatomy of Temperance*, and edited the *Teetotaller* (1840–41), which featured 'Pickwick Married', a serial in which the Pickwickians took the pledge. Then, in a typically impulsive change of heart, the following year he quarrelled with the movement's leaders and became director-general of the United Kingdom Anti-Teetotal Society.

In October 1844 he launched *The Mysteries of London*, published in penny weekly numbers by George Vickers from Holywell Street, a street previously notorious for pornographic and radical publications. It was to run for two series, making up four annual volumes, until September 1848 when Reynolds and Vickers fell out, and Vickers hired Thomas Miller and Edward Leman Blanchard to write a continuation. Reynolds turned to his own printer, John Dicks (see below), and continued his serial as *The Mysteries of the Court of London* (four series in eight annual volumes, 1848–56). The sequence, with its startling dramatization of the conflict between wealth and poverty, became a central feature of mid-Victorian popular fiction, and provides the focus for several essays in this volume. In March 1845 the illustrator and publisher George Stiff appointed Reynolds to be the first editor of the *London Journal* (1845–1912); the following year Reynolds left Stiff to start his own *Reynolds's Miscellany*

---

15   See *The Paris Literary Gazette*, 27 October, 1835, p. 13. I am grateful to Jean Guivarc'h for this reference.

16   Collins, 'George William McArthur Reynolds: a biographical sketch', p. xxvii-xxvii.

17   See P.T. Winskill, *The Comprehensive History of the Rise and Progress of the Temperance Reformation* (Warrington: privately printed, 1881); *The Temperance Lancet and Penny Trumpet*, 1/2 (25 September 1841), cited by Guy Dicks, *The John Dicks Press* (published by the author, 2005), p. 9.

(1846–69). In spite of his journalistic success, Reynolds had been dogged by an inability to manage his financial affairs. He pleaded bankruptcy in 1838, 1840 and again in 1848, provoking furious accusations of accounting dishonesty.[18] However justified these might be, Reynolds's fortunes were about to change. In 1847 he had been fortunate to hire a young printer, John Dicks, into his service. Dicks was to prove the astute business manager Reynolds needed to put his affairs in order and to ensure that he profited from his prodigious literary output. From 1848 John Dicks's name appeared as Reynolds's publisher, and in 1863 Reynolds and Dicks became formal partners.[19]

Reynolds had never abandoned his passionate involvement in his once-adopted nation, France. On 23 and 24 February 1848, radicals in the streets of Paris clashed bloodily with troops in the popular uprising that was to overthrow Louis-Philippe. In London ten days after the rioting in Paris, a crowd estimated at between 10,000 and 15,000 gathered in Trafalgar Square to demonstrate its solidarity with the French uprising, workers being joined by middle-class radicals protesting against income tax. Charles Cochrane, the scheduled chairman, had not appeared, and police with placards were attempting to close down the meeting, which, being less than a mile from the Houses of Parliament, was illegal. The event was saved when Reynolds impulsively scrambled onto the platform and, recognized as a radical novelist, was voted to the chair. Although this was his first public address, he spoke eloquently in favour of Louis Blanc, and the meeting closed with a massive vote of support for the French radicals. When the crowds dispersed, Reynolds was followed down the Strand to his house at 7 Wellington Street by cheering demonstrators, and continued his speech from his balcony. He was never to forget that moment of glory, and vividly recounted the experience at the annual festival held for his and Dicks's employees in 1875.[20]

The episode launched his career in Chartist politics. He was invited to speak at Chartist meetings on Kennington Common a week later, and, most importantly, at the great meeting on 10 April 1848.[21] Reynolds found an ally in Bronterre O'Brien, and in 1850 presided over the first meeting of O'Brien's National Reform League.[22] In 1851 he was elected with the largest vote onto the Chartist executive, and between 1851 and 1853 was invited to stand as a Chartist Member of Parliament for Finsbury, Bradford and Lambeth. But nothing came of this, and he resigned from the executive in under a year. Several reasons have been offered as to his marginal role in the Chartist movement, including poor health, the burden of his debts and his

---

18 *The Times*, 13 October 1837, p. 4; 17 May 1846, p. 6; 27 May 1848, p. 7; 2 June 1848, p. 7; 23 August 1848, p. 7; 7 September 1848, p. 7; 30 September 1848, p. 7; 3 October 1848, p. 6. See also *The Examiner*, 16 September 1848.

19 Dicks, *The John Dicks Press*, p. 32.

20 'The Festival of Messrs Reynolds's and Dicks's Establishment', *RN*, 11 July 1875, p. 1.

21 The one objective report on the meeting was by W.M. Thackeray in the *Morning Chronicle*, 14 March 1848.

22 R.G. Gammage, *A History of the Chartist Movement 1837–54*, 2nd edn (Newcastle: Brown and Brown, 1894); reprinted with an important introduction by John Saville (London: Frank Cass, 1964).

demanding workload of novel writing and editing. But Reynolds was also obstinate in his opinions and quick to take offence, making him a divisive committee member. He quarrelled intemperately with other members. In 1850 Thomas Clark published his *Letter*, a comprehensive attack on Reynolds's duplicitous financial dealings and the immorality of his novel writing,[23] and in 1859 Ernest Jones successfully sued Reynolds for libel. Chartist leaders suspected Reynolds's motives, refusing to believe that he could be sincere in his political radicalism while writing scandalous fiction.

Rohan McWilliam has argued that the loss was largely that of the Chartist movement.[24] Focused on their six-point political agenda, and split between middle-class radicals and workers, the industrial north and the metropolitan south, Chartism lost the opportunity Reynolds's journalistic enterprise offered to engage culturally with the mass of the common people. When the Chartist movement broke up, its dynamic moved into the development of trades unions, radical movements that led to the formation of the Socialist League of 1885, and the Cooperative Movement, both movements that were to rely largely on Reynolds's periodicals. In 1850 his *Political Instructor*, begun in 1849 as a weekly offshoot of his *Miscellany*, was enlarged to become *Reynolds's Weekly Newspaper, a Journal of Democratic Progress and General Intelligence*. By 1850 it changed its name to *Reynolds's Newspaper*, with a circulation of nearly 50,000, rising in 1872 to over 300,000.[25] It continued, with variations in its title from 1924 to 1962.[26] The periodical became the main channel of information for British socialist activities, and in 1862 Karl Marx grudgingly noted that it was the 'one surviving mass circulation working-class organ in Britain'.[27] From 1862 Reynolds also edited *Bow Bells*, successfully projected by Dicks as a more 'genteel' companion to *Reynolds's Miscellany*, which it absorbed in 1869.

With his financial affairs managed by the able John Dicks, Reynolds settled down as a secure (though never socially accepted) member of the mid-Victorian society. His writing became increasingly popular in the colonies,[28] across Europe and in the United States, where he was widely pirated, plagiarized and imitated. From 1851 to 1876 he was fêted at the annual dinners given for the employees of *Reynolds's Newspaper*, at which, in 1853, Edward Reynolds spoke with pride of being brother to one 'whose works had obtained a larger circulation than that [of] any other living

23 Thomas Clark, *A Letter addressed to G.W.M. Reynolds reviewing his conduct as a professed Chartist* (London: Thomas Clark, 1850), BM microfilm Dex 251.

24 McWilliam, 'The Mysteries of G.W.M. Reynolds', pp. 189–90.

25 H.R. Fox Bourne, *English Newspapers: Chapters in the History of Journalism*, 2 vols (London: Chatto and Windus, 1887), vol. 2.

26 See Editors' Note for the successive name changes.

27 'A London Workers' Meeting', *Die Presse*, 2 February 1862; republished in Karl Marx and Friedrich Engels, *On Britain* (Moscow: Progress Publishers, 1971), pp. 459–63, cited in Dicks, *The John Dicks Press*, p. 10.

28 On his 'classic' status in India, see Priya Joshi, *In Another Country: Colonialism, Culture, and the English Novel in India* (New York: Columbia University Press, 2002), ch. 2, and Chapter 15 in this volume by Sucheta Bhattacharya, 'G.W.M. Reynolds: Rewritten in Nineteenth-century Bengal'.

author'.[29] In 1854 he and his family moved to Herne Bay, Kent. But their rural idyll ended when Susannah died in 1858, and Reynolds moved back to London, living at 41 Woburn Square. He became a warden of St Andrew's Church, Wells Street. Although he may have continued to edit material for Dicks's publications, his last recorded published fiction was the short story 'The Young Fisherman; or, The Spirits of the Lake', which appeared in *Reynolds's Miscellany*.[30] When he died on 17 June 1879, leaving an estate of £28,000, London radical clubs came together at a memorial meeting to honour Reynolds's contributions to the progress of socialism from its Chartist days. As McWilliam has noted, Reynolds's entry in the *Dictionary of National Biography* had the distinction of being written by the future Labour Prime Minister, Ramsay McDonald.[31]

The Reception of Reynolds and his Work

In his own time, G.W.M. Reynolds was widely known as a Chartist politician, the publisher of a popular Sunday newspaper, *Reynolds's Newspaper*, and author of the most widely read bestseller of the century, *The Mysteries of London* and *The Mysteries of the Court of London*. While all of these works were in print for the whole of the second half of the century in various forms and had a very wide circulation in cheap formats, the largely middle-class commentators and reviewers who wrote for the press were without exception overtly hostile to Reynolds's politics and works, though there is indirect evidence that his readership was wider than his 'respectable' readers would admit and his novels had an unacknowledged influence on Dickens and Thackeray.[32] His death in 1879 produced some more balanced evaluations, but his reputation as a 'red republican' and writer of scandalous fiction remained into the twentieth century.

Reynolds's work essentially disappeared from critical view after the first two decades of the twentieth century. Then, at mid-century as interest in 'history from below' and a recognition of the importance of popular literature and the periodical press to an understanding of Victorian history and culture began to emerge, Reynolds and his works slowly began to enter into critical discussions. The 1990s saw a significant increase in scholarly work on Reynolds, and by 2000 this development was highlighted in the first academic conference on his works at the University of Birmingham, England. At the same time, interest in postcolonial approaches to the study of literature and culture brought an investigation of Reynolds's influences abroad. The current collection of essays, the first study solely devoted to Reynolds

---

29   Dicks, *The John Dicks Press*, p. 23.

30   *RM*, 5 October–9 November 1861.

31   McWilliam, 'The Mysteries of G.W.M. Reynolds', p. 195.

32   Trefor Thomas begins his essay 'Rereading G.W.M. Reynolds's *The Mysteries of London*' (in Alice Jenkins and Juliet John [eds], *Rereading Victorian Fiction* [New York: Macmillan, 2000], p. 59) by noting that he worked from a finely bound 12-volume set of the novels from the library of Almeric Hugh Paget, first Baron of Queensborough. Robert Colby notes Thackeray's high regard for Reynolds in *Thackeray's Canvass of Humanity* (Columbus: Ohio State University Press, 1979), pp. 252–9 and p. 272, nn. 65 and 67.

and his works, is both a culmination of this growth of interest and, we hope, a foundation for further investigation.

Contemporary Responses

Most of the contemporary responses published during Reynolds's lifetime were dismissive, though some recognized his immense popularity among the working and lower middle classes, and even his literary skill. In 1848, *The Man in the Moon*, a comic weekly edited by two *Punch* writers, Albert Smith and Angus Bethune Reach, published an illustrated satire on Reynolds's pretensions as a political leader after his appearance at the Kennington Common meeting which they titled 'Dips into the Diary of Barrabas Bolt, Esq. (Late Delegate from Smokely-on-Sewer to the National Convention)'[33] and which parodied his heightened rhetorical style. Dickens referred indirectly to Reynolds as a writer of scandalous fiction as well as a purveyor of radical politics in the first number of *Household Words* in March 1850, denouncing him as one of the 'Bastards of the Mountain, draggled fringe on the Red Cap, Panders to the basest passions of the lowest natures – whose existence is a national reproach'.[34] Karl Marx was also dismissive of Reynolds's political pretensions – he called him a 'scoundrel' – though Marx grudgingly recognized the importance of *Reynolds's Newspaper*.[35] In 1868, one of the first attempts to assess Reynolds's work appeared in *The Bookseller*, a journal for the trade. Entitled 'Mischievous Literature', the essay concluded that: 'In too many instances this clever writer has, we regret to say, administered the poison and forgotten the remedy – pandered to his readers' morbid love of excitement, without attempting to point the moral that should always accompany the descriptions of successful vice or splendid villainy.'[36] But the article nonetheless closed with the first effort to compile a bibliography of Reynolds's fiction.

---

33   *The Man in the Moon*, vol. 3, no. 17 (1848), pp. 235–44. But, as noted above, Thackeray wrote a broadly respectful report of the speech in the *Morning Chronicle* of 14 March 1848.

34   'Preliminary Word', *Household Words*, vol. 1 (30 March 1850), p. 1.

35   Letter to Ferdinand Lassalle, 28 April 1862, in *Letters of Karl Marx*, ed. Saul K. Padover (Englewood Cliffs, NJ: Prentice Hall, 1979), p. 465.

36   *The Bookseller*, 1 July 1868, p. 448.

THE MAN IN THE MOON.

DIPS INTO THE DIARY OF BARRABAS BOLT, ESQ.

(Late Delegate from Smokely-on-Sewer to the National Convention.)

PRIL 1.—This day I left that cradle of infant freedom, the city of Smokely-on-Sewer, to proceed to London, there to help in the glorious work of overthrowing the tyranny which holds to the grind-stone the flattened face of merry England. I was accompanied to the station by a band of patriots, who, as I paid the three pewter half-crowns, destined by the local association for my third-class fare, knelt upon the earth and solemnly swore never to wash their faces until the Charter became the law of the land. For my own part, I vowed to return with the glorious tidings, or be brought back pickled in a cask, a corpse to the cause of freedom. In a moment I was on the platform. There stood the train, its

Fig. 0.1   Caricature of G.W.M. Reynolds from *The Man in the Moon*, vol. 3, no. 17 (1848), p. 235.

When Reynolds died in 1879, there were a handful of obituaries – one in *Reynolds's Newspaper* of course, though none in *The Times*. *The Bookseller* again was neither flattering nor dismissive. The article called him 'the most popular writer of our time' while acknowledging that *The Mysteries of the Court of London* was the most objectionable of his publications in its sensationalism and sensuality. But the writer went on to say, rather ruefully, that 'their very excellence, as specimens of literary work, is one of the main elements of their danger',[37] echoing a judgement made in the above-mentioned attack by Thomas Clark, who noted that the 'aesthetic skill' and the 'gusto' of *The Mysteries of the Court of London* denote 'the diseased, corrupt, and sink-like mind from which it emanated'.[38] These negative judgements continued through the rest of the nineteenth century. In 1886 the *Saturday Review* published a satiric piece which attacked both Reynolds's fiction and his journalism for their critique of the ruling classes, particularly in his novels *The Seamstress*, which called attention to the miserable conditions of seamstresses, and *The Soldier's Wife*, a condemnation of flogging in the army.[39] Two years later Robert Louis Stevenson referred to him as 'un-utterable Reynolds' and claimed that when given a copy of *The Mysteries of London*, he fell back 'revolted'.[40]

After the 1880s, for the most part, though Reynolds's fiction remained in print into the beginning of the twentieth century and *Reynolds's Newspaper* thrived under the editorship of his brother Edward, his literary works were no longer of much critical or scholarly interest. On 27 May 1900, *Reynolds's Newspaper* issued a jubilee issue celebrating 50 years of publication, which contained information about the start of the newspaper and about Reynolds himself. Reynolds appeared in some memoirs of his contemporaries, and Frank Jay's series of articles, 'Peeps into the Past' (1918–21), added important biographical and bibliographical information.[41]

Early Twentieth-century Responses

A piece on Reynolds for the *Times Literary Supplement* in 1924 marks a shift in evaluation of his work. The anonymous author concluded that if Reynolds's works 'did no great good, they did no great harm, and unquestionably relieved a world which was somewhat drab at its best … his skill in developing a plot was undeniable'.[42] In 1931 Q.D. Leavis championed Reynolds in her pioneering study *Fiction and the Reading Public*, commending the 'impressive decorum' of *Reynolds's Miscellany*, including in this praise Reynolds's serials *Wagner the Wehr-Wolf* and *Faust*. Although she did not discuss the journal at any length, she found it an example of the

---

37   *The Bookseller*, 3 July 1879, p. 601.

38   Clark, *Letter*, p. 21.

39   'G.W.M. Reynolds', *Saturday Review*, 6 February 1886, p. 199.

40   Robert Louis Stevenson, 'Popular Authors', *Scribner's Magazine*, vol. 4 (April 1888), p. 126.

41   Frank Jay, 'Peeps into the Past', published as a supplement to *Spare Moments*, 26 October 1918; 23 November 1918; 30 November 1918. This work is accessible from the website edited by Justin G. Gilbert: www.geocities.com/justingilb/texts/PEEPS.

42   'G.W.M. Reynolds', *Times Literary Supplement*, 24 January 1924, p. 56.

'considerable achievement' of mid-Victorian working-class culture, whose quality the pulp press that followed it 'can hardly understand'.[43]

From this point on Reynolds and his works again disappear from critical view for a decade. The recovery began with bibliographical work. In 1941 Montague Summers issued his impressive *Gothic Bibliography*, containing an extensive bibliography of Reynolds's works, which is still valuable in efforts to sort out the tangled history of the issue and reissue of Reynolds's fiction in its penny weekly, sixpenny monthly and volume form, as well as some of the pirated editions in the United States. This was followed in 1947 by J.V.B. Stewart Hunter's bibliography, though the 'old view' remained as Hunter quoted a critic saying that Reynolds had a 'talented pen to poison the minds of boys and girls'.[44]

Re-evaluation at Mid-twentieth Century

The beginning of the revival of critical interest in Reynolds and his work is marked by the centenary edition of *Reynolds's News* in 1950, which celebrated Reynolds as political figure, editor and journalist, as well as fiction writer, with the top half of the front page of this issue devoted to an article entitled 'IT ALL STARTED WITH – A Young Man in Revolt'.[45] The growing interest in 'history from below' and popular culture as well as the beginnings of research into the vast field of Victorian periodicals are heralded by Margaret Dalziel's groundbreaking *Popular Fiction One Hundred Years Ago*, in which Reynolds and his works figure considerably.[46] One of the major early scholars who both recovered much information about Reynolds and started the first wave of critical re-evaluation was Louis James with his book *Fiction for the Working Man, 1830–1850*, published in 1963. James's evaluation of Reynolds was measured, recognizing his canny ability to judge the popular taste, his innovative periodical work and his middle-class attitudes.

This was followed in 1972 by Cyril Pearl's *Victorian Patchwork*. Pearl summed up his 19-page chapter on 'Mr Dickens and Mr Reynolds' by saying that Reynolds's 'neglect by the pundits of his time is easily explained: he was a violent republican and radical and he wrote of sex with a lusty and exuberant freedom unique in the popular fiction of his time. His neglect today is less understandable. No other novelist, not even Dickens, gives as good a picture of some aspects of London life in the 'forties and 'fifties.'[47]

---

43   Q.D. Leavis, *Fiction and the Reading Public* (Harmondsworth: Peregrine Books, 1979), pp. 143–5.

44   J.V.B. Stewart Hunter, 'George Reynolds', *Book Handbook*, 4 (1947): 234.

45   The centenary issue of *RN* is the subject of Chapter 16 in this volume by Ian Haywood, 'Modernity, Memory and Myth: *Reynolds's News* and the Cooperative Movement'.

46   Margaret Dalziel, 'The Most Popular Writer of Our Time', in Margaret Dalziel, *Popular Fiction One Hundred Years Ago: An Unexplored Tract of Literary History* (London: Cohen and West, 1957), pp. 35–45.

47   Pearl, *Victorian Patchwork*, p. 71.

Fig. 0.2   G.W.M. Reynolds, reproduced in Cyril Pearl, *Victorian Patchwork* (London: Heinemann, 1972), p. 72.

Recovery and re-evaluation grew steadily. A year after Pearl's book, Donald Kausch produced yet another bibliography.[48] Two years later the reprint publishing house Dover Publications introduced the first – but not the last – reprint of a complete Reynolds work, *Wagner the Wehr-Wolf* (1846–47), with an extensive introduction by E.F. Bleiler which gave both biographical and critical material followed by what is

48   Donald Kausch, 'George W.M. Reynolds: A Bibliography', *The Library*, 5th series, 28/3 (December 1973): 319–26.

today still the fullest bibliography of Reynolds's work, though, as Bleiler himself admitted, it is incomplete and not without errors. In 1976, Virginia Berridge wrote the first dissertation that incorporated material on *Reynolds's Newspaper* (followed in 1978 by her influential article on content analysis of that newspaper along with two others[49]). The next year Robert Maxwell published the first modern scholarly article about *The Mysteries of London*, which was followed in 1992 by his book *The Mysteries of London and Paris*, which might be said to mark the beginning of the new wave of scholarly interest in Reynolds. In 1981, Louis James compared Reynolds with Dickens and Thackeray in his article 'The View from Brick Lane: Contrasting Perspectives in Working-class and Middle-class Fiction in the Early Victorian Period'.[50] Anne Humpherys published her first article on Reynolds's *Mysteries of London* in 1983.[51] The Reynolds revival then began to expand dramatically with new scholars, new interests and new takes on 'the most popular writer' of the nineteenth century.

Reynolds Redux: The 1990s and Early 2000s

Critical evaluations of Reynolds and his works continued the re-evaluation of his political influence through his journalism and the literary importance of his bestsellers, *The Mysteries of London* and *The Mysteries of the Court of London*. In addition, there was recognition of Reynolds's influence outside Britain. Trefor Thomas in 1994, recognizing that *The Mysteries of London* was now being taught in university classes, produced a one-volume selection from *The Mysteries of London*, the first reprint in nearly 75 years. He also included an introduction. (A part of *Mysteries of London* is currently being reproduced on the Internet.[52]) The first dissertation written solely on Reynolds was finished by Michael Shirley in 1997, followed by that of Sara James in 2001; these two new Reynolds scholars organized and convened the above-mentioned academic conference on Reynolds and his work at the University of Birmingham. Priya Joshi published *In Another Country* in 2002 which included discussion of Reynolds's large influence on the development of the modern Indian novel. Rohan McWilliam contributed two essays, one on Reynolds's work, politics and melodrama in 1996 and another on Reynolds's novel *The Seamstress* in 2006.[53] Books on politics and literature that made use of both Reynolds's works and the recent critical work on him followed: Berry Chevasco, *Mysterymania: The Reception of Eugène Sue in Britain, 1838–1860* (2003) and Ian Haywood, *The Revolution in Popular Literature: Print, Politics, and the People, 1790–1860* (2004).

---

49   Virginia Berridge, 'Popular Sunday Papers and Mid-Victorian Society', in George Boyce, James Curran and Pauline Wingate (eds), *Newspaper History from the Seventeenth Century to the Present Day* (London: Constable, 1978), pp. 247–64.

50   *Yearbook of English Studies*, 2 (1981): 87–101.

51   'The Geometry of the Modern City: G.W.M. Reynolds and *The Mysteries of London*', *Browning Institute Studies*, 11 (1983): 69–80.

52   www.victorianlondon.org/mysteries/mysteries-01.htm.

53   McWilliam, 'The Mysteries of G.W.M. Reynolds' and 'The Melodramatic Seamstress: Interpreting a Victorian Penny Dreadful', in Beth Harris (ed.), *Famine and Fashion: Needlewomen in the Nineteenth Century* (Aldershot: Ashgate, 2005), pp. 99–114.

The current volume, with essays by most of the older and newer scholars who have contributed to this expansion of interest in Reynolds and his work, is thus a culmination of this flowering of interest in the last decade and a half and, at the same time we hope, a foundation for new work.

New Directions

The volume is divided into five sections that highlight the major elements in Reynolds's life and work: France, editing and journalism, the writing of fiction, popular culture and Reynolds's later influence. In Part I, Sara James and Rohan McWilliam trace the influence of France on Reynolds's early career as well as his use of his French experience to try to change anti-French sentiments in England. In Part II, Andrew King and Michael Shirley trace the development and importance of Reynolds's two major journalistic ventures, *Reynolds's Miscellany* and *Reynolds's Newspaper*, while Michael Diamond demonstrates through references from his historical novels and journalism how Reynolds writes 'an alternative history' of Britain from a radical political perspective. Antony Taylor analyses the importance of *Reynolds's Newspaper* after Reynolds's death and while under the editorship of his brother Edward on attitudes towards the British Empire.

Part III focuses on the work for which nearly all later readers and scholars know Reynolds – *The Mysteries of London*. Anne Humpherys provides an introduction to the larger 12-volume work made up of the two series of the *Mysteries of London* and the four series of *The Mysteries of the Court of London*. Following on from Sara James, Berry Chevasco analyses the relationship between Eugène Sue and Reynolds, challenging the common assumption that Reynolds was only imitating the French text. Stephen James Carver shows how *The Mysteries of London* develops the tropes and genres of other popular writers, while Juliet John places the work in the broad context of the popular culture of mid-nineteenth-century Britain.

The chapters in Part IV delve into material that most readers will not know – the massive amount of fiction that Reynolds wrote in addition to *The Mysteries*. Louis James traces the fiction published in the *London Journal* and *Reynolds's Miscellany*, arguing that it follows a generic pattern of 'social melodrama'. Graham Law charts another generic movement in Reynolds's fiction, that of the first-person fictional memoirs of working- and lower-middle-class lives. Ellen Bayuk Rosenman takes one of the memoirs and uses it, along with a very popular text by another writer, James Malcolm Rymer ('Malcolm J. Errym'), to demonstrate how stories of illegitimacy can chart the rewards of natural goodness. Brian Maidment closes this section with a chapter on the illustrations of Reynolds's fictions and ways to read them.

Finally, Part V contains two essays on the afterlife of Reynolds's work which demonstrate what rich material still waits to be explored. Sucheta Bhattacharya analyses the translations and adaptations of Reynolds in Bengali, and Ian Haywood, concentrating on the 1950 centennial edition of *Reynolds's News*, shows how Reynolds's brand of politics emerges into the mid-twentieth century.

It is our hope that this collection of new studies into 'the most popular writer of our time' will generate a new burst of investigation. Though the authors in this volume have been on Reynolds's trail for a decade or more, we have only begun to analyse or even to understand Reynolds's career, his place in his own culture and history, and his influence. We look forward to the work that is to come.

PART I
Beginnings: France

Chapter 1

G.W.M. Reynolds and the Modern Literature of France

Sara James

Throughout his career, G.W.M. Reynolds flaunted his associations with France. He lived in France for six years, from 1830 to 1836. He claimed to have served in the Thirteenth Legion of the Paris National Guard and to have witnessed the three glorious days of revolution in July 1830, and anecdotes in his early fiction hint at youthful escapades across Northern France with his younger brother Edward. He wrote his first polemic there, *The Errors of the Christian Religion Exposed, by a Comparison of the Gospels of Matthew and Luke* (1832); his first novel, *The Youthful Impostor* (1835); and the first of several translations, *Songs of Twilight* (1836), an ambitious verse translation of Victor Hugo's *Chants du Crépuscule* (1835).[1] He was married and became a father in Paris, and was naturalized as a French citizen in 1835. His first involvement with the press was as editor of the shortlived *Paris Literary Gazette*, which ended in his first lawsuit, bankruptcy and subsequent return to England in 1836. Back in London, he was keen to affiliate himself with France at every opportunity, from the pseudonym 'Parisianus' he used in the late 1830s to the fact that he proudly announced his membership of the Historical, Statistical and Agricultural Societies of France on the title-page of many of his works. Much of his early fiction has a French flavour: *Pickwick Abroad; or the Tour in France* (1837–38), *Alfred de Rosann, or the Adventures of a French Gentleman* (1838–39) and *Robert Macaire in England* (1839–40).[2] He also wrote a guide to the *Modern Writers of France*, serialized in the *Monthly Magazine* in 1838 and published in two volumes as *The Modern Literature of France* (1839) and a *French Self-Instructor* (1846) teaching grammar and pronunciation.[3] He even named one of his sons after the French politician Ledru Rollin.

Reynolds's involvement in politics and radical journalism in England following the 1848 uprisings in France associated him indelibly with revolutionary France

---

1   G.W.M. Reynolds, *The Errors of the Christian Religion Exposed, by a Comparison of the Gospels of Matthew and Luke* (London: R. Carlile, 1832); *The Youthful Impostor*, 3 vols (Paris: G.G. Bennis, 1835); Victor Hugo, *Songs of Twilight*, trans. G.W.M. Reynolds (London: French, English and American Library, 1836).

2   G.W.M. Reynolds, *Pickwick Abroad; or the Tour in France* (Philadelphia, 1838; London: Thomas Tegg, 1840); *Alfred de Rosann, or the Adventures of a French Gentleman* (London: J.W. Southgate, 1839); *Robert Macaire in England* (London: Thomas Tegg, 1840).

3   G.W.M. Reynolds, *The Modern Literature of France*, 2 vols (London: George Henderson, 1839); *The French Self-Instructor* (London: George Vickers, 1846).

and tends to overshadow the impact French literature had on him, both as reader and writer. Yet few Victorian writers had as wide a knowledge of contemporary French literature and particularly of French fiction as he did. So what can Reynolds's writings tell us about the modern literature of France and what can the modern literature of France tell us about Reynolds? Answers to both these questions can be explored through analysis of his first novel, *The Youthful Impostor*, and of his examination, translation and assessment of French writers in *The Modern Literature of France*. Understanding Reynolds's relationship with French letters is, as this chapter will demonstrate, central to our understanding of his attitudes to literature, his development as a writer and his later fiction.

The Youthful Impostor

Written when he was 18 and published three years later, *The Youthful Impostor* tells us a great deal about Reynolds's early aspirations and models as a writer. It was a three-volume novel, aimed at the readers of circulating libraries. It signalled its literary aspirations through epigraphs and frequent allusions to a diverse range of writers – from Spinoza to Descartes, Horace to Silvio Pellico, Ainsworth to Shakespeare – and it was eclectic, promising in the Preface to 'vary the sameness so incidental to modern novels'.[4] It was translated into French in 1836 by Auguste-Jean-Baptiste Defauconpret, who was well known for his translations of Sir Walter Scott and James Fenimore Cooper, and whose name thus bestowed considerable prestige.[5] In presentation, if not in content, it is distinct from his subsequent fiction in its evident pursuit of an educated readership from the middle classes.

For all this, many stylistic as well as plot elements of the novel indicate some of the avenues he was to follow in *Robert Macaire in England* and *The Mysteries of London*. There are frequent authorial digressions on matters as diverse as love, beauty, prostitution and the afterlife; flowery apostrophes to the spirits of great men; songs; slang; and references to present-day events in France.[6] Large sections of the narrative concern life in the city and the possibility of practising deception on unsuspecting visitors to the metropolis; and as the title suggests, duplicity and its exposure is the theme that unites the otherwise rather rambling central plot. The

---

4   Reynolds, *The Youthful Impostor*, 'Preface', unpaginated [iii].

5   G.W.M. Reynolds, *Le Jeune Imposteur*, trans. A.-J.-B. Defauconpret, 2 vols (Paris: E. Renduel, 1836).

6   One such reference suggests a possible reason for Reynolds's application to become a French citizen: 'A foreigner … not naturalized in France, cannot enter into any process to recover money lent to another individual, however aggravated the circumstance' (*The Youthful Impostor*, vol. 3, p. 225). A letter from Reynolds dated 22 December 1835 and held in the Bibliothèque Nationale de France sets out the particular terms of these aggravating circumstances as they relate to his court case against John Wilks (G.W.M. Reynolds, *Circular*, 22 December 1835, Bibliothèque Nationale de France, FP-5540). Reynolds also alludes to tensions between France and England: one character complains of the French authorities shipping refugees to England 'as if our country were the Botany Bay of France' (*The Youthful Impostor*, vol. 3, p. 221).

epigraph from Shakespeare's *Twelfth Night*, 'Disguise, I see thou art a wickedness, / Wherein the pregnant enemy does much' (II, ii), was repeated on the title-page of *Robert Macaire in England* and the theme of disguise was reworked time and again in *The Mysteries of London*.

The Youthful Impostor is particularly interesting in its frank acknowledgement of the debts it owes to other writers. The Preface explicitly stated that the inspiration for a central character was taken directly from Alexandre Dumas's play *Angèle*, which Reynolds had no doubt seen at the Théâtre de la Porte Saint-Martin where it played from December 1833 to early 1834.[7] Authorial intercalations throughout the novel also point out other borrowings, for example from two works he later translated, Victor Hugo's *Le Dernier Jour d'un condamné* and Paul de Kock's *Soeur Anne*.[8] Comparing Reynolds's novel with Dumas's stage play allows us to see which elements of *Angèle* Reynolds chose to develop and how he modifies them; it also foregrounds his anxieties about his ability to generate completely new material and his hesitation over what constituted plagiarism.[9]

Angèle

Initially entitled *L'Echelle des femmes* (The Ladder of Women), *Angèle* is set in the latter half of 1830 and follows the fortunes of Alfred d'Almivar, an opportunistic Don Juan who established his financial and social position through amorous conquests, lost it in the aftermath of the July Revolution, and is determined to regain it by marrying the 15-year-old heroine. Watched by a jealous rival, the melancholic and tubercular doctor Henri Muller, Alfred seduces Angèle while she is taking a water cure in the Pyrenees chaperoned by an elderly aunt, promising to secure her mother's agreement to their marriage. He quickly changes his plans when Angèle's widowed mother, the Comtesse de Gaston, reveals she intends to marry again herself to further her political influence. She takes him back to Paris as her lover. The night their engagement is to be announced and Alfred's promotion to Minister assured, his plans are frustrated by the political influence of a former lover, Ernestine de Rieux, and by the arrival of Angèle in Paris, heavily pregnant and seeking his help. Fortunately for Angèle, Henri Muller has followed her to Paris and is at hand to deliver the baby, kill Alfred in a duel and marry her himself. The play is a fast-paced and light-handed *drame bourgeois* that employs various theatrical commonplaces – soliloquy, asides, dramatic irony, disguise and coincidence – to explore the causes and effects of the political, social and sexual fortunes of both men and women. Dumas's unnamed collaborator, Anicet Bourgeois, added a more sombre, proto-

---

7   Alexandre Dumas, *Angèle. Drame en cinq actes* (Paris: Charpentier, 1834).

8   Victor Hugo, *The Last Day of a Condemned*, trans. G.W.M. Reynolds (London: George Henderson, 1840); Paul de Kock, *Sister Anne*, trans. G.W.M. Reynolds (London: George Henderson, 1840).

9   See, for example, the following footnote: 'The idea of a condemned malefactor listening to the song of another in a similar predicament, is borrowed from *Le dernier jour d'un condamné*, of Victor Hugo; but I fancy the plagiarism is so trivial, it was scarcely necessary to acknowledge it' (*The Youthful Impostor*, vol. 3, p. 145).

naturalist tone by limiting Henri's social aspirations not only by his social standing but also by his genetic inheritance of tuberculosis.[10] The play was an immediate success when it opened at the Théâtre de la Porte Saint-Martin on 28 December 1833 and the following day a review in the *Gazette des Théâtres* proclaimed Dumas the leader of the modern dramatists.[11]

Reynolds borrowed two major elements from *Angèle* for *The Youthful Impostor*. The first he acknowledged directly, explaining in an Advertisement preceding the opening chapter that 'the original idea of the young Surgeon's character is taken from that of *Henri Muller* in M. Dumas's excellent melo-drama, *Angèle*'.[12] The idea underwent very few modifications: Reynolds's Henry Hunter no longer suffers from tuberculosis but simply from the effects of his undeclared passion for the heroine, Emily Crawford. The second, a suitably anglicized seduction plot, was signalled indirectly by one of the two epigraphs to the novel, taken from the first scene of Act IV: 'Assez loin d'ici pour qu'il n'y ait pas un instant à perdre, monsieur – une jeune fille – en ce moment – une jeune fille dont le déshonneur rejaillirait sur toute une famille, une jeune fille va devenir mère!'[13] Emily, seduced by Stanley Arnold whilst staying with her aunt and tricked by him into believing they will be married once her mother consents, becomes pregnant; Hunter mopes his way through some nine hundred pages before delivering her baby and killing Arnold in a duel. This time Reynolds kept the bare bones of the action but expanded the character of the heroine, her family and in particular her brother, the impostor of the title, whose descent into crime is also brought about by Arnold. Numerous borrowings from English Newgate and silver fork novels, particularly those of Ainsworth and Edward Bulwer-Lytton, were also evident in this criminal plot, as were certain tongue-in-cheek references to his own life.[14]

Several things become apparent in this reworking. Reynolds rejects the interplay between the sexes where, with the exception of Angèle, women are equally implicated in sexual and political power struggles. He later explained that this was 'a striking illustration of the sway which women invariably exercise in France'.[15] He is more interested in developing and embellishing the melodrama, sentiment, coincidence and adventure of the plot. This is not to say that he abandoned the

---

10 On Dumas's plays in general and the collaboration of Anicet Bourgeois, see Daniel Zimmermann, *Alexandre Dumas le Grand* (Paris: Juillard, 1993).

11 '[L]e véritable chef de l'école dramatique moderne' (Zimmermann, *Alexandre Dumas le Grand*, p. 312).

12 Reynolds, *The Youthful Impostor*, 'Advertisement', unpaginated [i].

13 'Far enough from here that there is not a moment to lose, sir – a young girl – this very moment – a young girl whose dishonour would rebound on her entire family, a young girl is about to become a mother!' Here and elsewhere in this chapter, all translations are my own unless otherwise indicated.

14 The novel is set in Bagshot and one of the heroes, Captain Stewart, relates details about his youth that exactly parallel Reynolds's: his grandfather was a post-captain in the Navy and he was educated at Ashford, then at Sandhurst. Captain Stewart, however, subsequently takes up a commission in the Army bought for him by one Col. Mac— (*The Youthful Impostor*, vol. 1, ch. 9).

15 Reynolds, *The Modern Literature of France*, vol. 1, p. 148.

underlying concern with money, class and duplicity: far from it. The novel anticipates the obsession with appearance, documents and debt displayed in *The Mysteries of London*, just as it dramatizes sexual inequality and foregrounds the injustice of the marriage laws. Yet Reynolds does so through adding layer upon layer of new action and is constantly drawn to the striking tableau, the whispered tête-à-tête, to theatrical gestures and to dramatic irony as ways of progressing the narrative. His appreciation of the play was evidently derived in large part from the performance, particularly that of the actor who played Henri Muller. Like Muller, Hunter presents an exaggerated picture of *le mal du siècle*, constantly questioning the value of his life in melancholic outbursts that in some cases echo word for word the original script. Of course, using the techniques and subject matter of popular melodrama for a novel was nothing new; the commercial success of melodrama made it a source of inspiration for many novelists, and theatres relied equally on stage adaptations of popular novels. Nonetheless, it shows how *The Youthful Impostor* anticipates both *Pickwick Abroad* and *Robert Macaire in England* in its extraction of a memorable character who was someone else's idea and in exploiting that character for comic or dramatic effect. It is noticeable, for example, that Reynolds's Robert Macaire remains to a large extent the witty, dramatic scoundrel created by actor Frédéric Lemaître in the popular French melodrama *L'Auberge des Adrets*, in comparison to the caricaturist Honoré Daumier's transformation of the character into a cypher for the greed of July Monarchy France. Illustrations often reinforced this link with drama: Ellen Rosenman has remarked that the woodcut of Eliza Stanley that illustrated the opening chapter of *The Mysteries of London* depicts the character in an acting pose typical of stage manuals of the period.[16]

The Reception of *The Youthful Impostor*

The Youthful Impostor did not do well in England. Nor did *Le Jeune Imposteur* do any better in France, despite the draw of Defauconpret's name, which was printed in letters far larger than that of the author's. It did, however, attract one review, of which Reynolds was obviously aware. This was in Joel Cherbuliez's *Bulletin littéraire et scientifique*, an annual journal that presented all new books. M.G. Devonshire noted in 1929 that Cherbuliez reproached the novel with 'prolixity of detail, a hero who was already a criminal, an intrigue carried through without skill, and a set of characters all of whom were rogues'.[17] Yet this is something of a distortion of the complete review, which also had plenty to encourage the young author: four earlier paragraphs set Reynolds above his French rivals for the simplicity of his writing, the fast pace of the narrative and for his residual respect for *vraisemblance*:[18]

---

16 Ellen Bayuk Rosenman, 'Spectacular Women: *The Mysteries of London* and the Female Body', *Victorian Studies*, 40 (1996): 48–50.

17 M.G. Devonshire, *The English Novel in France 1830–1870* (London: University of London Press, 1929; repr. London: Cass, 1967), pp. 220–21.

18 On the importance of *vraisemblance* to the historical novel and the *roman d'aventures*, particularly as it affected the critical reception of books in France, see Fiona McIntosh, *La Vraisemblance narrative en question* (Paris: Presses de la Sorbonne Nouvelle, 2002).

Mr Reynolds, it must be said, is not afraid to draw frequently from the arsenal of terror, murder and crime exploited so extensively by today's novelists; but we must do him the justice of saying that at least he never departs too far from the appearance of truth and that he always stays within the bounds that, on this earth, and in our social surroundings, even the most reckless passions and the most audacious criminals never cross.[19]

Cherbuliez was not a man to mince his words, frequently rejecting books as mediocre or refusing to comment on them at all, so his criticisms appear far less a dismissal of the novel than a direct, quasi-editorial opinion of the Englishman's weaknesses and strengths. He advised him to cut descriptions of characters in favour of letting their actions speak for themselves; to introduce more honest characters and to pay attention to the direction and denouement of his plot; moreover, he suggested that the interest of the novel would be better served by a protagonist who began honest and embarked step by step on a life of crime:

> There is no clear focus for our attention, and above all it is a great mistake to show the hero, from the beginning of the novel, already guilty of a heinous crime. It would have been better, I think, to depict him still honest, and gradually succumbing to the lures held out to his vanity and weakness.[20]

It is precisely in this detailed attention to style and characterization that the review's significance lies, for the evidence of Reynolds's later novels suggests that he took these points extremely seriously. He did, after all, aspire to the 'deserved success as a novelist' that Cherbuliez's closing comments predicted.[21] It may then be no coincidence that some of Reynolds's later characters, such as Ellen Monroe in *The Mysteries of London*, noticeably follow a similar trajectory to the one Cherbuliez describes.

From *The Youthful Impostor* to *The Parricide*

By the time Reynolds revised the novel in 1847 as *The Parricide, or, A Youth's Career of Crime*,[22] he had established his reputation and was targeting his fiction

---

19   'M. Reynolds ne craint pas, il est vrai, de recourir souvent à l'arsenal de terreur, de meurtres et de crimes si généralement exploité par tous les romanciers du jour; mais on lui doit la justice de dire que du moins il ne s'écarte jamais trop de la vraisemblance et demeure toujours dans les limites que, sur cette terre, au milieu de notre état social, on ne voit jamais franchir par les passions même les plus désordonnées, par les criminels les plus audacieux' (Joel Cherbuliez, '*Le Jeune Imposteur*, traduit de l'anglais de G.W.M. Reynolds par A.-J.-B. Defauconpret', *Bulletin littéraire et scientifique* [Paris: Cherbuliez, 1836], pp. 206–7).

20   'L'intérêt ne sait sur qui s'arrêter, et c'est surtout un grand tort de nous montrer, dès le début du roman, le héros déjà coupable d'un grand crime. Il aurait mieux valu, je crois, nous le peindre encore honnête et succombant graduellement aux appâts tendus à sa faiblesse vaniteuse' (Cherbuliez, '*Le Jeune Imposteur*', p. 207).

21   '[U]ne juste renommée comme romancier' (Cherbuliez, '*Le Jeune Imposteur*', p. 208).

22   G.W.M. Reynolds, *The Parricide, or, A Youth's Career of Crime* (London: John Dicks, 1847).

at a markedly different audience. This recycling of his earlier work was no doubt suggested by the labour-saving and time-saving opportunities it presented; certainly the inconsistent chapter numbers indicate that composition was hasty. Yet the Advertisement explicitly offered the tale as a 'completely remodelled' and 'it is hoped, *improved*' version of *The Youthful Impostor*,[23] emphasizing that the original novel had been written when he was only 18 and only published when he was 21. The changes he made to the plot follow to the letter the improvements suggested by Cherbuliez and result in a far tighter narrative than the rambling original. He omitted all authorial digressions and self-conscious narration, and made numerous cuts: all songs, inessential dialogue and descriptions and a lengthy episode set in a debtors' prison that had been suggested to him by a scene in Paul de Kock's *Soeur Anne* (1825). In their place he added a new narrative thread revolving around Sophia Maxwell, a love interest for the youthful impostor who becomes suspicious of his activities and discovers his guilty secrets by disguising herself as a boy. Other changes demonstrate his awareness of his target audience and subsequent downgrading of literary elements: with the exception of a few epigraphs, he suppressed all literary allusions, and in its new form, the general tone of the narrative was simplified and sensationalized, while the language was deliberately vulgarized.[24] Sophia Maxwell, for all her pluck and deviant cross-dressing, succumbs to a decidedly sticky end, tricked, raped, mugged and finally confined in a lunatic asylum by the two criminal protagonists.

The 11 years that passed between *The Youthful Impostor* and *The Parricide* enable us to trace Reynolds's gradual renunciation of his serious literary ambitions and his decision to embrace 'economic literature', publishing in newspapers and in the penny weekly format.[25] If the guaranteed audience and pecuniary success of *Pickwick Abroad* suggest straightforwardly mercenary motives, Reynolds's persistence with translation and frustration at slow sales tell a different story. Translating Hugo's *Chants du Crépuscule* of 1835 (*Songs of Twilight*, 1836) was a labour of love. He was resolved to turn his admiration of Hugo's poetry into something concrete even though Hugo's talents had been 'depreciated in England by reviewers and critics'.[26] He found this no easy task, writing in the translator's preface that 'the

23   Reynolds, *The Parricide*, 'Advertisement', unpaginated [i].

24   For example, in one chapter of *The Youthful Impostor* comically satirizing celebrity culture, news about a significant government bill is ignored in favour of celebrity gossip; this is replaced in *The Parricide* by news of a horrible murder; 'prostitutes' become 'harlots'; minor villains are upgraded from 'Mr' and 'Sir' to 'Lord', suggesting the calculated lashing of the aristocracy that Henry Mayhew found Reynolds's working-class readers enjoyed (Henry Mayhew, 'The Literature of Costermongers', in selections from *London Labour and the London Poor* [London, 1861–62], ed. Victor Neuberg [Harmondsworth: Penguin, 1985], p. 25).

25   The term 'economic literature' is used by John Wilson Ross in his essay on 'The Influence of Cheap Literature' in *LJ*, vol. 1 (1845), p. 115. Ross heralded the increase of cheap or economical publications as the dawning of a new epoch in literature and alluded to Reynolds as an example of a writer who assisted in moulding and fashioning the tastes of the lower classes.

26   Reynolds, *Songs of Twilight*, pp. v–vi.

difficulties contingent to the translation of French Poetry, are not inconsiderable, either in magnitude or in number ... That which is beautiful in French, is frequently nonsense in English.'[27] Although he managed to turn the French into often quite elegant and apt English verse, the *Songs of Twilight* were no more successful than *A Youthful Impostor* and the promised second half of the translation never materialized. Reynolds had nonetheless learned a valuable marketing lesson and he used the slim volume both to respond to criticism of his novel and to advertise his other projects.

Chief among these was his editorial participation in the *Paris Advertiser*, or *Paris Literary Gazette*, which he describes as 'my Literary Journal'. At the time of writing, January 1836, he tells us that it had 'emerged from its former insignificance as a simple advertising paper to its present consequence as a literary one'.[28] He was confident that the journal would topple the monopoly on English newspapers held by Galignani; and with contributors like William Makepeace Thackeray he had reason to be hopeful.[29] Its failure was crushing to his literary ambitions and forced him to return to England. In the subsequent years, which saw his success with *Pickwick Abroad* and his energetic editing of the *Monthly Magazine*, Reynolds continued to be puzzled by the lack of success for his second translation of Hugo, *The Last Day of a Condemned* (1840), and for his translation of *Sister Anne* (1840) by the popular author Paul de Kock, a staple of the circulating libraries. This was one of the factors, together with his increasing fury at conservative prejudice against French fiction, that led him to write *The Modern Literature of France*.

The Modern Literature of France

The Modern Literature of France provides not only a comprehensive guide to Reynolds's opinions of different French writers, but also a clear indication of the beliefs and concerns that were to inform his future career. The two volumes, each of nine chapters, tackled between them 18 authors, finishing with a selection of national airs, songs and poetry.[30] Each chapter was structured very simply: an introduction and commentary on the writer, his work and critical opinion, followed by an extract from a recent publication which Reynolds translated himself and which he hoped would offer readers the chance to form their own opinions. The most controversial parts of the work were his Introduction to the guide, which undertook a spirited defence of French realism, and the Preface, in which he attacked prejudiced views of French fiction:

---

27   Reynolds, *Songs of Twilight*, p. vi.

28   Reynolds, *Songs of Twilight*, p. 124.

29   Jean Guivar'ch identifies Reynolds as Thackeray's first editor in 'Deux journalistes anglais à Paris: G.W.M. Reynolds et W.M.T.', *Etudes Anglaises*, 28/2 (1975): 203–14.

30   The first volume presented and discussed the work of George Sand, Honoré de Balzac, Eugène Sue, Frédéric Soulié, Lamartine, Alexandre Dumas, Auguste Ricard, Prosper Mérimée and Paul de Kock; the second volume focused on Victor Hugo, Jules Lacroix, Jules Janin, de Béranger, de Tocqueville and Michel Chevalier, de Jouffroy, Charles Nodier and Michel Raymond, ending with a chapter on the National Airs, Songs and Poetry of France.

Prejudice, which a celebrated political writer very happily denominated 'the spider of the mind', has done much to depreciate the value of foreign systems and institutions in the minds of the English. Hence it is that we daily hear even men of most liberal opinions expressing sentiments anything but impartial and just in reference to the French. This is more to be regretted, inasmuch as it is only by comparison, emulation, and research, that we can perfect or improve any system of laws, morals, literature, science or arts. But when we find the leading journals and periodicals of the English press still leaguing together against the French, with all the bitterness and hate which characterized the sentiments of the nation in those times when Napoleon rolled his war-chariot from the gates of Madrid to the palace of the Kremlin, and when our armies and household troops were called forth to protect the coasts against the menaced invasion of the imperial hero, – we feel our regret at such injustice commingled with a sentiment of pity, or indeed of contempt, for the narrow-mindedness of our fellow-countrymen.[31]

Reynolds's contempt was directed principally at J.W. Croker, whose lengthy denunciation of 'French Novels' had appeared in the *Quarterly Review* of April 1836.[32]

'French Novels'

Croker's condemnation of French novels followed his earlier attack on the profligacy of French drama and rehearses arguments typical of conservative criticism of literature from France in this period. Full of hyperbole from the outset, the essay openly avowed the author's aim to stigmatize French novels as a brand of poison, which acted as 'conductors of contagion' to 'infect' the dwellings of their readers.[33] His alarm was clearly linked to political fears following the July Revolution, which he saw as exciting and inflaming immorality in the population at large, and which probably reawakened in his mind the spectre of 1789 and the Terror; but no doubt also to the proliferation of French novels serialized in British newspapers for the increasingly literate lower classes. He saw fiction as an index of revolutionary feeling and considered novels to be both the cause and consequence of a spirit that threatened the whole fabric of European society.[34] In particular, he attacked the work of authors who claimed to present a picture of real life, setting their novels in contemporary society, copying their characters from the existing population and yet, in his view, presenting an exaggerated view of society as riddled with crime and

---

31 Reynolds, *The Modern Literature of France*, pp. i–ii.

32 J.W. Croker, 'French Novels', *Quarterly Review*, 56 (April 1836): 65–131. (The article is also reprinted in John Charles Olmsted, *A Victorian Art of Fiction: Essays on the Novel in British Periodicals* [London: Garland, 1979], pp. 167–80.)

33 Croker, 'French Novels', p. 66.

34 The metaphor of literature as miasma was itself to propagate and spread throughout conservative criticism of the French novel in England in the following decade as French fiction became a staple ingredient of newspapers and miscellanies like the *London Journal* and *London Pioneer*. See Louis James, *Fiction for the Working Man, 1830–1850: A Study of the Literature Produced for the Working Classes in Early Victorian Urban England* (London: Oxford University Press, 1963), pp. 136–45; Berry Chevasco, *Mysterymania: The Reception of Eugène Sue in Britain, 1838–1860* (Oxford: Peter Lang, 2003), pp. 72–3.

adultery. Although he singled out seven contemporary authors to illustrate his point – Paul de Kock, Victor Hugo, Alexandre Dumas, Honoré de Balsac (*sic*), Michel Raymond, Michel Masson and George Sand – the majority of his objections lay with the novels of Balzac and Sand.

Balzac was targeted on two accounts: firstly for claiming to be the most accurate painter of private life in contemporary France, and secondly for claiming his books were moral. The title *Etudes de moeurs*, in Croker's view, was a misleading designation for 'a series of unconnected tales of the vulgarest and most licentious character'.[35] His principal objection was to the adulterous relationships embarked upon by so many of Balzac's heroines and to the exaggerated characters of *Le Père Goriot* (1835) and, worse still, the secret societies, melodrama and violence of *Histoire des Treize* (1833–35). The fact that his writing had literary qualities to commend it merely compounded the offence.

The fiction of George Sand constituted for him the apotheosis of all these evils combined, carrying 'to the most pernicious excess this species of the demoralizing novel'.[36] What he considered the wickedness of novels like *Indiana* (1831) and *Valentine* (1832), let alone the vague and vicious *Lélia* (1833), was doubly offensive given that Sand was a woman. Her attacks on the institution of marriage, several of which he quoted, led him to fire the final salvo in his armoury: his conviction that novelists like Balzac and Sand were the '*instruments* and *organs*' (his italics) of a decline in female morality, in league with the St Simonists, whose doctrines 'relieve[d] women from the obligations of personal continence and matrimonial fidelity'.[37] He sealed the argument with a quotation from the *Revue des Deux Mondes* lamenting a loss of reserve in the representation of morals in fiction and, more alarmingly still, in the language used by women since July 1830.[38] 'This admission', he concluded, 'that the July Revolution has worked a great and sudden change in the moral condition of women in France, by *emancipating* them from "*etiquette* and *reserve*" – that is, in one word, from morality, is all that we require.'

Reynolds's Response

Reynolds systematically refuted all Croker's arguments. He ridiculed the assumption of a circular link between literature, political revolution and weakening morality, laughed at the notion that a woman might turn to adultery because her imagination was fired by the contents of a circulating library, and queried the claim that most French novels were by definition licentious and abandoned. He accused the author of giving false and misleading information. The major sticking point was, however, the view the article propounded of the July Revolution and its effects on the population:

---

35   Croker, 'French Novels', p. 81.
36   Croker, 'French Novels', p. 99.
37   Croker, 'French Novels', p. 129.
38   '[Their] language has become coarser' ('l'on a parlé plus crûment'); this and subsequent quotations, Croker, 'French Novels', p. 130. Croker quotes from the French; the translation is mine.

The predilections and passions of individuals are not subject to variation on account of the secession or expulsion of one dynasty and the succession of another. An extension of political liberty does not implicate a *decrease* of moral rectitude and social order; it rather encourages an *increase*.[39]

In fact, however outraged he might be at the suggestion that emancipation had undermined the moral fibre of French citizens, both men and women, the main sweep of his Introduction agreed with Croker in finding a distinct change of character in the literature written after 1830:

A sudden impulse was given to the minds of men by the successful struggle for freedom which hurled the impudent Charles from his regal seat; and all aims – all views – and all interests underwent a vast and important change. Ages of progressive but peaceful form could not have accomplished so much, in reference to the opinions and tastes of a mighty nation, as those three days of revolution and civil war.[40]

Reynolds's own appetite for change (still, at this stage, relatively moderate in comparison with his later views; he does not reject the new monarch) can be clearly read in his opposition of Charles X as a 'superstitious and encroaching despot' hurled like Milton's Satan underground, and Louis-Philippe as the Christian family man who would lead the country from slavery into comparative freedom. Even eight years into the July Monarchy, he massively overestimates the scope of change, seeing the 1830 Revolution as a defining moment in French civilization, a sudden leap from old to new, from censored thought to soaring imagination, from the hidebound past to glorious modernity. Fiction, for Reynolds as for Croker, was the embodiment of these new ideas and freedoms, the visible face of a rapidly changing France.

Yet neither was mistaken in identifying a sea change in the world of French letters. This was after all the decade that saw the battles between Romantics and Classicists over Hugo's play *Hernani* (1830) and the introduction of the *roman-feuilleton*. Ever the champion of progress and change, Reynolds's analysis offers, in the words of one surprised French critic a century on, 'a real and full defence of our Romantic literature'.[41] It is simply, perhaps, unfortunate that he chose the word 'nudity' to describe the progress he saw:

Now the French author paints the truth in all its nudity; and the development of the secrets of Nature shocks the English reader, because he is not yet accustomed to so novel a style. To depict truth, in all its bearings, consistently with nature, is a difficult task; and he who attempts it must occasionally exhibit deformities which disgust the timid mind.[42]

By nudity, or what he characterized elsewhere as a 'bold and naked display of truth', he meant not simply the depiction of sex or 'downright indecency', although he was prepared to concede that might be found in the works of Paul de Kock and

---

39 Reynolds, *The Modern Literature of France*, vol. 1, p. xi.
40 Reynolds, *The Modern Literature of France*, vol. 1, p. xiii.
41 '[U]ne véritable apologie de notre littérature romantique' (Marcel Moraud, *Le Romantisme français en Angleterre, 1814–1848* [Paris: Champion, 1933], p. 344).
42 Reynolds, *The Modern Literature of France*, vol. 1, p. xii.

Auguste Ricard; but rather the reversal of the traditional denouement of moral tales to show virtue crushed and vice triumphant. Modern French writers were abandoning impossible fictions in favour of portraying the 'rocks' and 'quicksands' of urban life in nineteenth-century France.

This argument was nuanced further in his comments on Sand, Balzac and Hugo. Sand was revolutionary in her ideas concerning domestic society; revolutionary too in defying gendered conceptions of men's and women's writing and in her scrutiny of the human mind and emotions, both male – *Jacques* (1833) and *Simon* (1835) – and female – *Rose et Blanche* (1831). What Reynolds admired particularly in these novels was the detailed psychological realism of Sand's characterization of her protagonists: '[e]very fibre is dissected, scrutinised, tested and examined: every vein – every nerve is laid bare: in all its nudity is that mind unfolded to the curious observer'.[43] Balzac, meanwhile, with his wide field of vision, acute observation and detailed description of ordinary people and places, unveiled an uncomfortable picture of society that examined humble lodgings and princely hotels alike:

> [But] how true are his descriptions! How full of reality his delineations! ... Simple and unadorned, they stand before the world in their primitive state of nudity, and the tears, which are shed during a contemplation of those paintings, must be real and heart-wrung indeed![44]

Hugo's portrayal of human society in *Notre-Dame de Paris* was contrasted with that of Walter Scott: no longer benevolent and kind, but like Balzac sometimes painful to read, 'the offspring of uncompromising and stubborn truth'.[45]

Given their innovation and diagnosis of the state of society, Sand and Balzac in particular perfectly illustrated Reynolds's idea of a revolutionary writer, and he attributed the popularity of their works to the new impulse the July Revolution had given them. Sand was the ideal illustration of Reynolds's introduction. He portrays her as indifferent to prejudice, successful and a political writer of no mean ability; as a daughter of revolution, a baroness transformed into a writer, formed and fashioned by the study of the events of July 1830. In many other respects, however, Reynolds's response to Sand's fiction is highly conventional. If he was bewitched and bewildered in equal parts by the 'strange' morals and potent magic of *Indiana* (1832) and *Valentine* (1833), he was not alone in finding *Lélia* (1833) devoid of a single redeeming feature, nor unusual in thinking it a 'hellish compound of poisonous drugs'.[46] His modelling of Sand as a campaigner for sexual equality and for revolution in domestic society is matched by his unease at her blurring of 'masculine' and 'feminine' styles of writing, and he is content to end by praising the 'vast powers of her masculine mind' even as he explains away her affairs as a justifiably feminine need for consolation.[47]

43 Reynolds, *The Modern Literature of France*, vol. 1, p. 4.
44 Reynolds, *The Modern Literature of France*, vol. 1, p. 31.
45 Reynolds, *The Modern Literature of France*, vol. 2, p. 9.
46 Reynolds, *The Modern Literature of France*, vol. 1, p. 6.
47 Reynolds, *The Modern Literature of France*, vol. 1, p. 7.

'De la littérature industrielle'

Reynolds is unusual not only in defending French realism, but also in setting forth his perception of the economic changes afoot in France. As twentieth-century literary historians have shown, the increasing dominance of the novel that so discomfited Croker followed, and to some extent provoked, social change, developments in print, radical cuts in the price of reading matter and, thanks to the primary education acts of 1833, an increase of literacy.[48] Writers began to split into two camps, those determined to push forward new literary frontiers (*l'art véritable*) and those whose writing was primarily a matter of earning money (*le métier*). The judgements of Sainte-Beuve in his influential article on this phenomenon, 'De la littérature industrielle' (*Revue des Deux Mondes*, 1839), are often quoted in relation to the growth of the literary marketplace in France. Sainte-Beuve predicted the establishment of a new democracy of letters with trepidation, fearing that the *roman-feuilleton* would degrade the novel to the level of the lowest common denominator.[49] Reynolds's judgements offer us an alternative perception written that same year: his detailed observations of what authors earned and in some cases what the circulation figures were for their work illustrate how the relationship between reader and writer was placed increasingly on an economic footing. The picture he offers us is – as we might expect from his later career – far less pessimistic about the consequences of this change and shows far more faith in the judgement of individual readers.

The examination Reynolds presented to readers of *The Modern Literature of France* was, then, if not impartial, in many respects remarkably accurate. Despite the lukewarm reception it initially received on both sides of the Channel, it is a text posterity has recovered for its considered views and factual detail, its account primarily of a reader's experience of revolutionary France.[50] This, of course, makes

---

48 I am thinking particularly here of Christopher Prendergast's analysis of Balzac's relations with the reading public in *Balzac: Fiction and Melodrama* (London: Edward Arnold, 1978); see also John Lough, *Writer and Public in France: From the Middle Ages to the Present Day* (Oxford: Clarendon Press, 1978).

49 Sainte-Beuve, 'De la littérature industrielle', *Revue des Deux Mondes* (Paris, 1839), pp. 675–91.

50 A reviewer in the *Athenaeum* complained of its lax morality and could not say anything in favour of Reynolds's volumes other than finding that 'its mischievous tendency is neutralized by its dulness [*sic*]' (*Athenaeum* [London, 1839], p. 721). Notwithstanding this, Reynolds refused to take back any of his words and published the second edition unabridged and in a cheaper format so that more readers could afford it. At the other end of the spectrum, the *Glasgow Examiner* thought it far inferior to *Pickwick Abroad*, although not altogether without merit, seemingly judging them comparable if only as regards the revenue they brought him (despite going through two editions, *The Modern Literature of France* only earned the author the sum of £300 in comparison to the £800 he earned for *Pickwick Abroad* and £375 for *Robert Macaire*) ('Mr G.W.M. Reynolds', *Glasgow Examiner*, 8 November 1845; repr. *LJ*, vol. 1 (1845), p. 191). Compare E.F. Bleiler's description of it as 'superior to *Pickwick Abroad*, although it has now been completely forgotten' (Introduction to G.W.M. Reynolds, *Wagner the Wehr-Wolf* [New York: Dover, 1975], p. ix) and Berry Chevasco's praise for its judicious and dispassionate comment (*Mysterymania*, p. 135).

it a singularly important document for our understanding of Reynolds himself, not just as a reader and thinker but as a writer. The view it offers us of 'industrial' or 'economic' literature, of imitations and of the merits and pitfalls of originality, shows a new respect for the craft of fiction, for literature as *métier* as well as *art véritable*. Together with his translations of the 18 authors this goes a long way towards explaining the apparent discrepancy between the measured discourse we find here and *The Mysteries of London*. Like his published translations of Hugo and de Kock, these translated extracts bridge the gap chronologically between the literary allusions and aspirations of *The Youthful Impostor* and the coarser, tighter plotting of novels like *The Parricide*. In addition, they give us chapter and verse for many of the sources of his plots and a yardstick by which to measure how he uses them in his fiction.[51] If this evidence hidden within *The Modern Literature of France* proves beyond a doubt that many of Reynolds's plots were not original, his arguments query the validity of judging solely on that merit. His readers – as Reynolds would no doubt approve – must simply judge for themselves.

---

51   See, for example, his translation and skilful reworking of Jules Janin's short story, 'Elle se vend au détail', which is clearly a source for the narrative of Ellen Monroe in *The Mysteries of London* and which I analyse in a forthcoming article, 'G.W.M. Reynolds and Jules Janin: The Politics and Practice of Imitation'.

Chapter 2

The French Connection: G.W.M. Reynolds and the Outlaw Robert Macaire

Rohan McWilliam

'Tis laughable to see John Bull affect
Profound contempt for all things Gallican;
And yet we universally detect
Him borrowing from the French when'er he can.

G.W.M. Reynolds[1]

After the defeat of Napoleon in 1815, France remained a source of fascination for the British. Its fashions, styles, political movements and restaurants were the subject of lavish accounts if only to explain the peculiarities of the national character of each nation. Paris was an obvious tourist destination and playground of pleasure but the plays and literature of the French were eagerly followed, reproduced and pirated within British popular culture.[2] Nor was the trade one way. The French Romantics, for example, gobbled up Shakespeare, Sir Walter Scott and the gothic. London and Paris represented two paths to urban modernity, cities that dealt with comparable problems in different ways. Tales of the two cities were not unusual, whether it took the form of comparing their respective sanitary achievements or exploring their underworlds and their treatment of prostitution. When George W.M. Reynolds first came to the attention of the mass reading public, it was essentially as an interpreter of France to the British.

We know that Reynolds's life was transformed by his sojourn in France between 1830 and 1836. Employing an inheritance, he arrived in the wake of the 1830 Revolution and the formation of the July Monarchy. There is relatively little information available about his time there. He was apparently punished for gambling with loaded dice and, at one point, he and his brother Edward booked into a hotel in Calais, pretending to be master and servant, ran up a huge bill and decamped without paying.[3] In 1830, Reynolds was only 16 and was clearly seduced by the promise and

---

1   G.W.M. Reynolds, *A Sequel to Don Juan* (London: Paget, 1843), p. 234.

2   On the Anglo-French relationship, see Robert and Isabelle Tombs, *That Sweet Enemy: The French and the British from the Sun King to the Present* (London: William Heinemann, 2006).

3   Captain Vincent to Sir George Grey, 9 April 1848: Home Office Papers 45/2410 A f. 337 (National Archives); Rohan McWilliam, 'The Mysteries of G.W.M. Reynolds: Radicalism

charisma of the literary life that Paris offered. He became an enthusiast for radical politics. His first published work (a secularist tract in a Paineite vein) appeared in English two years after he arrived and his first novel came out in 1835. He took over the Librairie des Etrangers in 1835, the same year he became literary editor of the *Paris Literary Gazette*. Reynolds apparently became a French citizen, served in the National Guard and met his wife, Susannah. By 1836, he was back in London, bankrupted by his attempts to live by his pen.

France shaped his literary and political career. When he stepped onto the political stage as a leading Chartist in 1848, it was as a defender of that year's French Revolution. His best-known work, *The Mysteries of London* (1844–48), was an appropriation of the French author, Eugène Sue. Much of Reynolds's early literary output (particularly in the half-decade after 1836) was devoted to the elaboration of French themes. His first bestseller was *Pickwick Abroad* (1837–38), which dispatched Boz's character to France. He translated a number of French works including novels by Victor Hugo and Paul de Kock. In *The Modern Literature of France* (1839), he anthologized writings by Hugo, Sue, George Sand and other French authors both to show off their literary merit and to demonstrate the appeal of French civilization. The novel *Alfred de Rosann*, first published in the *Monthly Magazine* (July–December 1838), was set in France and featured praise for Louis-Philippe as a model monarch that sits oddly with Reynolds's increasingly republican tastes. Reynolds commences *Alfred* by stating that after 1789, 'ambitious rulers had changed the principles of a glorious revolution into the hateful tyranny of murderous despots', but the novel ends in the 1830s when a 'virtuous monarch' has introduced 'national freedom' and 'just laws'.[4] Reynolds's imagination was based around two cities, Paris and London, which were sources of attraction and repulsion (he is not dissimilar to Dickens in this respect). They were spaces that degraded rich and poor alike. We can find this landscape in his 1840 novel, *Robert Macaire in England*, based on the popular fictional character who had emerged on the French stage in the 1820s.[5]

In an earlier work, I described Reynolds as 'a sponge, absorbing the radical and romantic elements of his culture'.[6] As with *Pickwick Abroad, Robert Macaire in England* displays Reynolds's bare-faced cheek in ripping off other people's ideas. Literary piracy was rife in the early Victorian years.[7] The stage and the popular fiction market were part of a culture geared up to appropriating and reproducing anything that would sell. However, Reynolds's use of the popular character Robert Macaire was not just an example of his commercial instincts. The novel alerts us to the interpenetration of English and French popular culture in this period.

---

and Melodrama in Victorian Britain', in Malcolm Chase and Ian Dyck (eds), *Living and Learning: Essays in Honour of J.F.C. Harrison* (Aldershot: Scolar, 1996), p. 184.

4   G.W.M. Reynolds, *Alfred, or the Adventures of a French Gentleman* (London: Willoughby and Co., 1839), pp. 1, 237.

5   G.W.M. Reynolds, *Robert Macaire in England* (London: Thomas Tegg, 1840).

6   McWilliam, 'The Mysteries of G.W.M. Reynolds', p. 184.

7   Louis James, *Fiction for the Working Man, 1830–1850: A Study of the Literature Produced for the Working Classes in Early Victorian Urban England* (London: Oxford University Press, 1963), ch. 4.

Much of the literature on Reynolds has understandably concentrated on *The Mysteries of London*, a text that allowed the author to become a leading Chartist. By focusing on *Robert Macaire*, we can see much of his later radicalism prefigured even though, at around this time, he was anti-Chartist as he believed mass education had to precede universal suffrage.[8] France clearly provided Reynolds with a literary and political voice, but he also drew on indigenous English elements such as the culture of the gothic and the Newgate novel. He combined this with the values of radical Grub Street, which created an ambiguous and complex moral position that contrasted with the certainties and forms of narrative closure normally found in melodramatic fiction.[9] *Robert Macaire in England* contains only hints of the political radicalism that became Reynolds's trademark in later writings. However, Reynolds was always distinctive in presenting radical themes alongside conservative and ostensibly non-political elements.[10] This is a study of the peculiarities of Reynolds's imagination and the ways that French melodrama and satire made possible a form of fiction that could combine romance and politics.

Robert Macaire was a fictional character and symbol who charmed Britain and France in the nineteenth century, although he did not prove to be an enduring figure, unlike some contemporary characters in the novels of Victor Hugo or Alexandre Dumas. Technically, Macaire was the creation of Benjamin Antier, Jean Armand Lacoste and Alexis Chapponier, who introduced the character in their 1823 stage melodrama, *L'Auberge des Adrets*. In most other respects, Macaire was the creation of the great actor Frédéric Lemaître, who played Macaire in the original production. Macaire, as written, was a villain who, alongside his faithful but cowardly accomplice Bertrand, escapes from prison and arrives at an inn where a wedding is about to take place. The young groom, it transpires, is actually Macaire's abandoned son. Macaire kills the father of the bride and steals the dowry. The villain's former wife (who by chance turns up) is accused of the murder by the police, but eventually Macaire is identified as the culprit and is killed trying to escape.

The opening night of the play at the Ambigu-Comique has become part of theatrical folklore.[11] Lemaître disliked the play and refused to stick to the script, which was intended as a straightforward melodrama of the sort that had been pioneered on the Boulevard du Temple in the 1790s. Instead he sent the action up, introduced all sorts of comic business for Macaire and delivered such a flamboyant performance that the character took over the play. In the script, Macaire was a conventional villain. By playing the part for laughs, Lemaître not only made him charming but got the audience on his side. He seemed to be acting in a different play from the one that the other actors thought they were appearing in, although he got Firman (who was cast

---

8   Reynolds, *A Sequel to Don Juan*, p. 35.

9   See Rohan McWilliam, 'The Chartist Gothic: Radicalism and the Romantic Element, 1830–1850' (forthcoming).

10   See also Rohan McWilliam, 'The Melodramatic Seamstress: Interpreting a Victorian Penny Dreadful', in Beth Harris (ed.), *Famine and Fashion: Needlewomen in the Nineteenth Century* (Aldershot: Ashgate, 2005), pp. 99–114, which examines Reynolds's *The Seamstress* (1850).

11   Robert Baldick, *The Life and Times of Frédéric Lemaître* (London: Hamish Hamilton, 1959), ch. 3.

as Bertrand) to play along. The audience found themselves laughing with Macaire and therefore became at one level complicit in his crimes (a feature that Reynolds would later employ in his novel). The actors and the authors were unhappy about being upstaged in this way but there was nothing they could do as the play was an instant hit because of what Lemaître had done with his part. With each performance Lemaître extemporized further and introduced new stage business, such as a snuff box that creaked every time it was opened, which audiences found immensely funny because of the strange noise it made. The following year the play was forbidden by the Ministry of the Interior on the grounds of taste (Macaire was too proud of his crimes), but it was revived at the Porte Saint-Martin in 1832.[12]

Macaire was a villain who proved to be both charming and lovable. Even Lemaître's stage costume stressed his liminal personality. When he first appeared at the back of the stage, he seemed to be wearing the fine clothes of a gentleman. As Lemaître advanced towards the front of the stage, it became clear that his costume was made up of bits of cloth, patches and rags that merely simulated the appearance of a gentleman.[13] He was betwixt and between, moving frequently between different worlds, an ironic character in that least ironic of genres, melodrama.

L'Auberge des Adrets turned Lemaître into one of the most popular actors of his day and Macaire into one of the most popular fictional characters of the time. Such outlaws are often transformed into heroes by popular culture: they become symbols of popular longing and defiance of the rich, although they are mainly found in agrarian societies.[14] Macaire was perhaps particularly cherished by the common people who loved the man made of rags and adored Lemaître's extemporizations and wisecracks (although he appealed to all audiences). One evening, Lemaître apologized for not killing a gendarme as the actor was ill but offered the following evening to kill two.[15] Macaire became a powerful, demotic symbol, exposing the fact that the powerful were no different from anyone else. A novel about Macaire appeared in 1833 as did another play, which presented Macaire and Bertrand on the eve of their execution. Although Balzac did not write the novel about the character that he contemplated, elements of Macaire can be found in his fiction.[16] Lemaître returned to the role in 1834 in a sequel that he helped write, called simply *Robert Macaire*. In the new play, Macaire goes to Paris and founds a company that deals in insurance against theft. He attracts the attention of 'Baron de Wormspire' (in reality a conman) and his daughter, Eloa (in reality, a prostitute). Macaire and Wormspire try to cheat each other. In the play's most famous scene, the pair play cards and each realizes the other is an experienced card-sharper when both produce nothing but kings. Lemaître had liberal sympathies, and his play was seen as an attack on

---

12 Catherine Coeuré (ed.), *L'Auberge des Adrets/Robert Macaire* (Grenoble: Roissard, 1967), p. 14.

13 Charles Selby, *Robert Macaire, or, The Two Murderers: A Melodrama in Two Acts* (London: Samuel French, 1890), p. 3.

14 Eric Hobsbawm, *Bandits* (London: Weidenfeld and Nicolson, 1969, 2000).

15 Frederick Brown, *Theater and Revolution: The Culture of the French Stage* (New York: Viking, 1980), p. 116.

16 Coeuré, *L'Auberge des Adrets/Robert Macaire*, p. 17.

the climate of corruption and speculation that had become integral to the regime of Louis-Philippe. The gambling scenes also emerged from the popular critique of aristocratic gaming that was widespread. After considerable success on both sides of the Channel, the play was banned by the French censors.[17]

Macaire also became the central character in a series of satirical prints drawn by the great French cartoonist Honoré Daumier. The series was commissioned by Daumier's co-author, Charles Philipon, who wrote the captions and published the pictures in his comic periodical *Le Charivari* between 1836 and 1842.[18] The series sent up the corruption of life under the July Monarchy by presenting Macaire in a series of shady, get-rich-quick schemes. Amongst other guises, Macaire becomes a banker, a restaurateur, a pharmacist, a quack doctor, an animal magnetizer and an architect. The character was often shown amongst the rich and the powerful. In this sense, he was not dissimilar to the British figures of Mr Punch or (later) of Ally Sloper, two demotic characters who are often presented hobnobbing with the elite despite their lowly origins and attitudes.[19] The point of the cartoons was that modern France had become the kind of place where crooks like Robert Macaire could take over. Daumier published over a hundred cartoons about Macaire and the series became a popular response to the speculation mania of the mid-1830s.[20] Macaire was appropriated for political purposes. In 1848, he became a socialist emblem but could also be employed by conservatives to attack the pretensions of socialism. Macaire so dominated the popular imagination that even Karl Marx found himself describing Louis-Philippe as 'Robert Macaire on the throne'.[21]

In England, the character proved equally popular. Versions of *L'Auberge des Adrets* and *Robert Macaire* were regularly performed in London throughout the 1830s and 1840s. Macaire was even the subject of a comic ballet at Drury Lane in 1845.[22] When Lemaître brought a production of *L'Auberge des Adrets* over to London in 1835, *The Times* commented:

> The subject of the melodrame is sufficiently familiar to the frequenters of theatres in London. It has been translated and played under various titles at several of the minor theatres, and very recently at the Victoria Theatre.[23]

---

17 Baldick, *The Life and Times of Frédéric Lemaître*, ch. 10.

18 David S. Kerr, *Caricature and French Political Culture, 1830–1848: Charles Philipon and the Illustrated Press* (Oxford: Clarendon Press, 2000).

19 On Punch and Judy see Robert Leach, *The Punch and Judy Show: History, Tradition and Meaning* (London: Batsford, 1995); Rosalind Crone, 'Violence and Entertainment in Nineteenth-century London' (unpublished DPhil thesis, University of Cambridge, 2006), ch. 1. On Ally Sloper see Peter Bailey, '"Ally Sloper's Half-Holiday": Comic Art in the 1880s', in Peter Bailey, *Popular Culture and Performance in the Victorian City* (Cambridge: Cambridge University Press, 1998), pp. 47–79.

20 *Les Cent et Un Robert-Macaire* (Paris: Aubert, 1839–40).

21 Karl Marx, *The Class Struggles in France, 1848–1850* (New York: New York Labor News Company, 1924), pp. 37–8.

22 *The Times*, 25 March 1845, p. 5.

23 *The Times*, 26 January 1835, p. 3.

On another occasion, it complained that the play was devoted to 'that violent and vulgar class which our neighbours on the other side of the Channel have of late so strangely encouraged'.[24] Amongst other things, this was probably a reference to the popularity of the memoirs of the French criminal and police investigator Vidocq, which had been available in English since 1828. When Lemaître (a not unfamiliar figure on the London stage) revived his Macaire in London in 1847, one reviewer noted: 'Everybody knows who is Robert Macaire, and how Lemaître plays; and we need not dilate on the imperturbable assurance, the ceaseless scintillation of eccentricities, the inimitable costume, and the unapproachable waltz, that go towards the completion of his attributes'.[25] The *Illustrated London News* saw Lemaître's performance as the realization of Daumier's cartoons.[26] Although (as we have seen) the influence was probably the other way round, it is likely that Lemaître and Daumier/Philipon fed off one another.

In its early years, *Punch* employed the Macaire figure in ways analogous to the Daumier version in which the powerful are seen as crooks. Sir Robert Peel was presented in a cartoon as Macaire and, on another occasion, 'Louis-Philippe Macaire' instructed counsel for the defence in the English House of Lords.[27] In the later nineteenth century, Henry Irving enjoyed great acclaim in the role, performing it on a number of occasions and emphasizing the gentlemanliness of the villain.[28] Robert Louis Stevenson even wrote a one-act farce (with William Ernest Henley) about Macaire, although it was not a success.[29] There were also novelizations of the Macaire plays.[30]

It was only in the twentieth century that the Macaire character slipped out of the popular imagination and audiences lost their familiarity with the figure. Even Irving's later portrayals of the figure were not so successful as audiences found much of the stage business (such as the squeaking snuff box) to be unintelligible or just unfunny.[31] There has, however, been considerable interest in the Daumier cartoons as examples of satirical art, and in Marcel Carné's great film, *Les Enfants du Paradis* (1945), there is a scene showing Frédéric Lemaître, one of the three central characters in the film, playing Macaire.

---

24 *The Times*, 19 January 1835, p. 3.

25 *The Times*, 25 January 1847, p. 5.

26 *Illustrated London News*, 6 February 1847, p. 85.

27 *Punch*, vol. 1 (1841), p. 199; Richard D. Altick, *Punch: The Lively Youth of a British Institution, 1841–1851* (Columbus, OH: Ohio State University Press, 1997), pp. 251–2, 391, 397–8.

28 Jeffrey Richards, *Sir Henry Irving: A Victorian Actor and his World* (London: Hambledon, 2005), pp. 30–33.

29 William Ernest Henley and Robert Louis Stevenson, *Macaire: A Melodramatic Farce in Three Acts* (Edinburgh: R. and R. Clark [privately printed], 1885).

30 E.g., *Robert Macaire* (London: George Routledge, 1888).

31 Percy Fitzgerald, *Sir Henry Irving: A Record of Over Thirty Years at the Lyceum* (London: Chatto and Windus, 1895), pp. 112–13.

We know that Charles Dickens was fascinated by Lemaître's version of Macaire.[32] It is therefore poetically appropriate that Reynolds, who was shadowing Dickens at this time with his literary piracies, should have turned to the Macaire character in 1840. Reynolds may himself have seen Lemaître's Macaire. He was in Paris when Lemaître's second Robert Macaire play was performed in 1834 and there are hints of Lemaître's performance in the presentation of the character in Reynolds's novel. It is, however, a mistake to think that Reynolds was merely importing a French idea. Even at the time, it was noted by Thackeray that the world of *L'Auberge des Adrets* was very similar to that of *The Beggar's Opera*.[33] In other words, Macaire was a reworking of MacHeath, John Gay's dissolute but romantic highwayman. Macaire was also a version of the conman or confidence trickster who was a not uncommon figure in European and American literature, including Mr Jingle in *The Pickwick Papers*, which Reynolds had pirated. Macaire was not a remarkably original creation but offered a version of the romantic and charming villain for a modern audience. Unlike Lemaître's character, Reynolds's Macaire is not intended to be comic in any way. Instead, he is roguish, dangerous and also romantic. The comic moments are left to the cowardly Bertrand. Reynolds did, however, identify with some of the elements in the Macaire figure, which pointed towards political radicalism.

Robert Macaire in England was published in 1840 by Thomas Tegg, known for his cheap reprints of major works and for remainders, although he also published gothic stories and improving educational volumes.[34] We cannot be certain about the impact of Reynolds's novel, but it is likely that it proved popular as it was reprinted in 1845, 1849, 1870 and 1884; there was also an edition published in 1924 in Madras. The original edition was illustrated by 'Phiz', although the 1849 revised edition published by John Dicks employed pictures by Reynolds's frequent illustrator Henry Anelay (many of which reworked the 'Phiz' drawings). The latter edition also added a subtitle, 'The French Bandit in England'.

At the beginning of the story, Macaire and Bertrand rob a stagecoach in France and take the money and papers of an English gentleman, Charles Stanmore, en route to London. Macaire decides to use the money to pass himself and Bertrand off as gentlemen in London. They use the stolen papers to insinuate themselves into the home of a London City merchant called Lumley Pocklington. Bertrand is made out to be one Count Bertrandi de Bertrand whilst Macaire claims to be a French financier, M. Lebeau, who had been expected. When the real Lebeau is about to show up, Macaire kills him. Macaire uses his sexual magnetism to seduce Pocklington's niece, Maria Leslie, as a way of obtaining her wealth. Once she is in his power, he reveals that he is a famous bandit, wanted by the police for terrible crimes, but she is so drunk with love that she promises not to reveal his secret. Her suitor, Charles Stanmore, has to cope with the information that Maria does not love him. Stanmore (whose father had

32   Juliet John, *Dickens's Villains: Melodrama, Character, Popular Culture* (Oxford: Oxford University Press, 2001), pp. 79–80.

33   'Mr Titmarsh' [William Makepeace Thackeray], *The Paris Sketch Book* (London: John Macrone, 1840), vol. 2, pp. 26, 29.

34   James J. Barnes and Patience P. Barnes, 'Reassessing the Reputation of Thomas Tegg, London Publisher, 1776–1846', *Book History*, 3 (2000): 45–60.

disappeared in mysterious circumstances in France) does not recognize Macaire and Bertrand as the criminals who robbed him but becomes suspicious of the hold that Macaire exerts over Maria.

In a chance encounter, Stanmore obtains Bertrand's pocket book, which makes him decide to go to Paris to discover more about the mysterious arrivals in the Pocklington household. He finds Bertrand's mother living in poverty, having been robbed of all she possessed by her son when he went off to follow Macaire. Having established that 'Lebeau' is Macaire, Stanmore leaves Paris. In a wood outside the city, he rescues a young lady, Blanche de Longueville, who is living among thieves. After dispatching them he realizes that Macaire, in league with these villains, had murdered his father. Stanmore falls in love with Blanche, who is the illegitimate daughter of parents she never knew. Her guardian, however, turns out to be Macaire, who returns to France to protect his new identity and to acquire Blanche's inheritance. He is confounded when Blanche is claimed by her grandfather, the Count de Moranval. Macaire is subsequently identified and arrested by the police.

Imprisoned, Macaire employs his connections in the Parisian underworld to stage a daring escape. However, when he returns to London, he is confronted by Stanmore, who reveals Macaire's identity to Lumley Pocklington. The rogue is able to announce that he has succeeded in seducing Maria before being thrown out.

The Pocklingtons move to Canterbury to escape the shame of her seduction. Maria, now pregnant with Macaire's child, still has feelings for him and the scoundrel is able to smuggle letters to her suggesting that they run away together. The attempt is frustrated but Macaire does succeed in secretly marrying Maria. Travelling back to London, Macaire is set upon by thieves at Shooter's Hill. He kills one of his assailants, who turns out to be Bertrand, and Macaire is beside himself with grief. In the meantime Maria herself is gravely ill, apparently dying of a broken heart. Pocklington finds Macaire and brings him to Maria. As she dies, Macaire is stricken with remorse and agrees to renounce his life of crime. He returns to Paris and discovers that Stanmore and Blanche have married. Macaire is arrested for the murder of Stanmore's father and at the trial is found guilty. He manages to stage another escape and goes to Blanche, confessing to her that he is actually her father. Blanche persuades Stanmore to save him from the gendarmes once more and he travels to Switzerland to live out his repentance. In an epilogue added to the 1849 edition, Reynolds tells how Macaire, a changed and contrite figure, dies a few years later.

Robert Macaire in England is not a political book. Yet in some respects it prefigures Reynolds's later writings and contains themes that would be developed in *The Mysteries of London* and in his journalism. Reynolds conceives the story as a dark romance and employs an urban gothic landscape that is reminiscent of Hogarth and Pierce Egan, Sr, but also of some of the authors he celebrated in *The Modern Literature of France* (1839), written at approximately the same time. We find similar kinds of settings that are present in his later work, ranging from aristocratic gaming tables to the criminal underworld of thieves and prostitutes, as well as the imagery of dirt, disease and degeneracy. The book trades on the fear of gambling that was a marked feature of English and French society and fiction, since it exposed the insubstantial and possibly evanescent nature of wealth, a form of affluence based not on hard work but on speculation.[35] This should lead us to rethink any notion that Reynolds was simply imitating Eugène Sue when he came to write *The Mysteries of London* a few years later. Instead, both authors were appropriating common themes about the perils of city life that a range of authors and commentators were deploying to make sense of metropolitan society.[36] These tales represented the city as a place of fear but also as one of adventure and romance. In that sense, Reynolds and Sue updated the world of Walter Scott. Reynolds was what we might call today a *Zeitgeist* surfer, rethinking and reusing diverse elements in the culture.

In *Robert Macaire* he wrote about a bandit but he was himself a bandit. He engaged in literary piracy, employing other people's visions to create something of his own and to fashion a version of the Macaire character that was in some respects different from the others available. Reynolds's theft of Macaire was a cynical exercise in making money. The year before he wrote his novel, Reynolds had appeared in the bankruptcy court and was even reduced to allowing his name to be used in an advertisement for a headache cure.[37] The tendency to pirate literary works in early Victorian Britain was undoubtedly a form of opportunism, but we might also see such publications as generated by a feeling that a fictional character was simply too important to be the property of one author alone, that there are other stories to be told, that existing characters serve to create new possibilities in a reader's imagination. Whether we think of Tom Stoppard's *Rosencrantz and Guildenstern are Dead* or slash fiction on the Internet, this is easy to see. As an author, Reynolds relished the opportunity to put other people's characters in new situations.

The novel does not flinch occasionally from taking on political issues. *The Mysteries of London* is distinctive for the way in which Reynolds frequently breaks from the narrative and employs the novel as a platform or pulpit from which to lecture about the evils of the day. There are only intimations of this style in *Robert Macaire*, but they are there. Reynolds complains about the failures of the legal process and the way the rich could use their station to avoid punishment:

Alas! Even in these times of civilization, how many acts of turpitude are committed and never detected by justice – how many terrible deeds lie concealed in the darkness in which they are done! ... And how true is the adage that 'one man escapes after having stolen a horse, while another is hanged for only looking over the hedge'.[38]

---

35   Michael Flavin, *Gambling in the Nineteenth-century Novel* (Brighton: Sussex Academic Press, 2003).

36   John Marriott (ed.), *Unknown London: Early Modernist Visions of the Metropolis, 1815–1845* (London: Pickering and Chatto, 2000); Louis Chevalier, *Labouring Classes and Dangerous Classes in Paris during the First Half of the Nineteenth Century* (London: Routledge and Kegan Paul, 1973). See also Chapter 8 in this volume by Berry Chevasco, 'Lost in Translation: The Relationship between Eugène Sue's *Les Mystères de Paris* and G.W.M. Reynolds's *The Mysteries of London*'.

37   *The Times*, 13 November 1839, p. 7; 21 March 1839, p. 8.

38   Reynolds, *Robert Macaire*, ch. 9, p. 23. All page references are to the 1849 edition published by John Dicks.

The difficulties for the working class in obtaining justice would be a common theme in *Reynolds's Newspaper*. Another example of Reynolds's use of the novel as a platform is his opposition to flogging in the army (he came from a military background and briefly attended Sandhurst). He celebrated the French approach:

> Corporal punishment is not permitted in any institution throughout France, and the French army, navy, and houses of incarceration, do not contain a number of individuals whose flesh has been lacerated by the terrible scourge beneath which the poor English soldier has been known to expire, while his comrades stood looking on without even uttering a yell of execration, much less raising a hand to rescue him![39]

Later, his 1853 novel *The Soldier's Wife* contained such a vehement attack on flogging that the army banned sales of *Reynolds's Newspaper* to soldiers.[40]

The lifestyle of the wealthy is represented as an imposition on the lives of the common people.[41] Pocklington is informed by one character:

> Oh! Dear sir, you little know the misery and crime which destitution produces in this accursed country – a country where everything is for the rich few, and nothing for the toiling millions.[42]

On the whole, the rich in this story (in the shape of Pocklington and Stanmore) are represented fairly sympathetically. There are only a few of the aristocrats who normally serve as villains for Reynolds. However, the aristocracy feature in a Hogarthian scene in London's Haymarket (then notorious for the presence of prostitutes), which contains echoes of Pierce Egan's portraits of gentlemen slumming it among low life. Bertrand enters a pub where two fashionable toffs, the Marquis of Brandyford and Lord Augustus Mirliflor, pay a man to drink as much beer as he can for their amusement. After extensive imbibing, the man falls to the floor and is found to be a corpse.[43] *Robert Macaire* was written at the moment when Reynolds enjoyed his short-lived relationship with the temperance movement. He briefly edited the *Teetotaller*, led the London United Temperance Association and produced a novel, *The Drunkard's Progress*, before becoming director-general of the United Kingdom Anti-Teetotal Society and editor of the *Anti-Teetotaller*.[44] The episode in the novel barely advances the plot but it provides a moment when rich and poor are seen degrading one another.

Reynolds's Robert Macaire features some of the characteristics of the Lemaître and Daumier/Philipon versions of the outlaw (although he jettisons his distinctive eyepatch early in the story when Macaire disguises himself as the financier Lebeau). While many of Reynolds's characters have a cardboard quality, like figures in a Pollock's toy theatre, his Robert Macaire is a more complex creation that pushes

39   Reynolds, *Robert Macaire*, ch. 47, p. 106.
40   McWilliam, 'The Mysteries of G.W.M. Reynolds', p. 187.
41   Reynolds, *Robert Macaire*, ch. 25, p. 62.
42   Reynolds, *Robert Macaire*, ch. 36, p. 88.
43   Reynolds, *Robert Macaire*, ch. 10, pp. 25–6.
44   Rohan McWilliam, 'The Mysteries of G.W.M. Reynolds', p. 185.

against the limits of propriety, which helps explain why Reynolds was never considered to be respectable.

In the novel, Macaire robs, cheats and seduces with abandon. Reynolds describes him as a 'cool – calculating – selfish wretch'.[45] Yet Reynolds constantly refers to him as 'our hero'.[46] By positioning him as the central character, Reynolds is effectively making the reader complicit in the villain's crimes, although Macaire does repent after Maria's death. Reynolds thus attempted the same sleight of hand that Lemaître had pulled off on stage. We need, however, to go further in explaining the moral ambiguity of the novel and the construction of Macaire as anti-hero. At one level, we might see the novel as a product of radical Grub Street, the underworld of journalists, satirists and pornographers who had turned their backs on respectability and embraced a libertine tradition.[47] This kind of counter-culture had become increasingly unacceptable in the 1830s and 1840s. Reynolds constantly walked a narrow line between propriety and what some considered to be pornography. *Robert Macaire* presents a vision of a world turned upside down in which the villains are the heroes and private debauchery is offered to the public gaze (we will find the latter in his fiction and journalism).

We might also see Reynolds's work and especially this novel as an example of the absorption of Byron into popular culture. One absence in Reynolds scholarship has been any discussion of his relationship to Byron, an influence that clearly infuses a lot of his work. Byron wrote about romance and passion but was also associated with liberal politics and with nationalism. The life and writings of Byron shaped the Victorian world and challenge us to rethink ideas of conventional Victorian respectability.[48] He influenced the development of the gothic, an integral part of Reynolds's narrative. Most parts of society read Byron. Notoriously, he was the favourite reading of many working-class radicals. We should consider Reynolds's Byronism in this light. Macaire is in some respects a romantic outlaw who possesses a personality that refuses to be bound by the conventional social rules as well as a remarkable sexual charisma. We might also view him as a version of Byron's Don Juan. Three years after *Robert Macaire*, Reynolds penned *A Sequel to Don Juan* in verse that was a deliberate imitation of Byron. There are a number of references to Byron in the novel, although they are insignificant. Lumley Pocklington's wife, we discover, reads only Scott and Byron.[49] On another occasion, Reynolds writes:

---

45 Reynolds, *Robert Macaire*, ch. 7, p. 20.

46 Reynolds, *Robert Macaire*, ch. 2, p. 12; ch. 7, p. 21; ch. 19, p. 46; ch. 37, p. 92; ch. 42, p. 108.

47 Iain McCalman, *Radical Underworld: Prophets, Revolutionaries and Pornographers in London, 1795–1840* (Cambridge: Cambridge University Press, 1987); Vic Gatrell, *City of Laughter: Sex and Satire in Eighteenth-century London* (London: Atlantic, 2006).

48 Andrew Elfenbein, *Byron and the Victorians* (Cambridge: Cambridge University Press, 1995).

49 Reynolds, *Robert Macaire*, ch. 2, p. 7.

'Like Byron, we choose to be particular in dates' (the novel is set in 1834).[50] Byron's characters set precedents for the figure of Macaire.[51]

At another level, Macaire is a reworking of the figures of the romantic highwayman and the gentleman outlaw. There is a Robin Hood dimension to Reynolds's Macaire, although he is emphatically not one of Eric Hobsbawm's 'social bandit' types who steal from the rich, give to the poor and are generally prized by the working class.[52] The gentleman outlaw could be politically neutral or even conservative rather than subversive. When he attacks the stagecoach at the beginning of the novel, Macaire is glad that he has only stunned the courier because he likes to be 'economical of life: good people are precious'.[53] His assassinations serve a purpose although, as the murder of Lebeau shows, he is prepared to kill innocent people when necessary. We learn that Macaire (like Reynolds himself) was born a gentleman but, having squandered his inheritance, resorted to crime.[54] Reynolds notes his 'air of faded dandyism' and his politeness when holding up the stagecoach at the beginning of the novel.[55] The robber had been a figure of romance going back to the Middle Ages; by the eighteenth century there was a complex repertoire of images propagated by the expanding print culture, which included the figure of the polite, gentlemanly robber.[56] By the 1830s, highway robbery was a thing of the past. The last recorded incident involving a highwayman took place in Taunton in 1831. The expansion of banking and credit meant that fewer travellers had sufficient money to make highway robbery worthwhile and the emergence of railways in the early Victorian years made highwaymen an anachronism.[57] Figures such as Dick Turpin (or Macaire) could therefore be reimagined as dashing, romantic and embodying a kind of personal liberation because they no longer posed a threat. Harrison Ainsworth's *Rookwood* (1834) helped construct the modern image of the romantic highwayman and the attack on the coach at the beginning of Reynolds's novel is presumably an allusion to Dick Turpin. Whilst Macaire is not a proletarian, part of his popularity may come from his identity as a gentleman who lives among the working classes. In this sense, he is characteristic of a particular social type identified at this time in Paris by Henri Murger and others: the bohemian.[58] In retrospect, Reynolds's sojourn in Paris and

---

50 Reynolds, *Robert Macaire*, ch. 9, p. 23.

51 Gustave Flaubert considered Macaire the greatest popular symbol since Don Juan (although he did not necessarily mean Byron's version): Brown, *Theater and Revolution*, p. 120.

52 Hobsbawm, *Bandits*.

53 Reynolds, *Robert Macaire*, ch. 1, p. 6.

54 Reynolds, *Robert Macaire*, ch. 6, p. 18.

55 Reynolds, *Robert Macaire*, ch. 1, p. 6.

56 Gillian Spraggs, *Outlaws and Highwaymen: The Cult of the Robber in England from the Middle Ages to the Nineteenth Century* (London: Pimlico, 2001).

57 James Sharpe, *Dick Turpin: The Myth of the English Highwayman* (London: Profile, 2004), pp. 159–60; R.B. Shoemaker, 'The Street Robber and the Gentleman Highwayman: Changing Representations and Perceptions of Robbery in London, 1690–1800', *Cultural and Social History*, 3/4 (2006): 381–405.

58 Jerrold Siegel, *Bohemian Paris: Culture, Politics and the Boundaries of Bourgeois Life, 1830–1930* (New York: Viking, 1986).

his deployment of French themes represent an early engagement with bohemianism (although the mythology of artistic bohemianism in Paris and elsewhere was only just coming into existence).

It should also be clear that *Robert Macaire* is in effect a Newgate novel, belonging to the cycle of fiction that dealt with urban crime in the 1830s and 1840s. Oddly, Reynolds is not often discussed as part of the Newgate tradition, but his work is clearly meant to be part of it.[59] Novels such as Ainsworth's *Jack Sheppard* (1839) and its penny dreadful equivalents generated a moral panic because they were believed to cause crime. They were also disturbing because they caused confusion about how their heroic criminals should be read; they were as fascinating as they were worthy of condemnation.[60] *Robert Macaire in England* was part of a wave of imitations of Ainsworth, combining the dashing highwayman of *Rookwood* with the daring prison escapes of *Jack Sheppard*, published the year before Reynolds's novel. *Jack Sheppard* was an evocation of Hogarth's London that Reynolds clearly appreciated.[61] However, unlike Ainsworth, Reynolds found he could use these gothic narratives to talk about the necessity of social reform.

Reynolds in *Robert Macaire* relishes the underworld in both Paris and London, a feature of Newgate fiction. Crime, he shows, observes no national boundaries. Reynolds is clearly indebted in part to Vidocq, who is invoked when Macaire plans an escape from prison and who is identified in a footnote as '[t]he celebrated thief-catcher, whose memoirs are doubtless familiar to all our readers'.[62] In Paris, Macaire visits a crooks' convention in a secret underworld location. The room is full of thieves, bosomy prostitutes, desperadoes and assorted low life who applaud Macaire as a 'king and a patron', whilst he salutes them as '[w]orthy and excellent bretheren of the same craft'.[63] On another occasion we learn about a similar establishment in the Borough in London 'at which thieves and vagabonds congregated at night to partake of the meals procured by the earnings of the day'.[64]

Macaire is represented as a conman able to gain the confidence of wealthy dupes like the Pocklingtons in order to get his way. The ease with which he is accepted by the rich suggests that wealth itself is a form of performance, a characteristic device that emerges from many impostor narratives.[65] Macaire is frightening because of his ability to transform himself through a variety of disguises. Nineteenth-century

59 Keith Hollingsworth, *The Newgate Novel, 1830–1847: Bulwer, Ainsworth, Dickens, and Thackeray* (Detroit: Wayne State University Press, 1963). Anne Humpherys has connected Reynolds with the Newgate novel in her unpublished article, 'Who's Doing It?: The Construction of Crime in the Newgate Novel', which also examines *Robert Macaire in England*.

60 Juliet John (ed.), *Cult Criminals: The Newgate Novels, 1830–1847* (London: Routledge, 1998), vol. 1, p. v.

61 Reynolds went on to write *The Days of Hogarth, or The Mysteries of Old London* (London: John Dicks, [1850]), which was originally serialized in *RM* in 1847–48.

62 Reynolds, *Robert Macaire*, ch. 46, p. 117.

63 Reynolds, *Robert Macaire*, ch. 21, p. 51.

64 Reynolds, *Robert Macaire*, ch. 36, p. 89.

65 This is explored further in Rohan McWilliam, *The Tichborne Claimant: A Victorian Sensation* (London: Hambledon Continuum, 2007).

popular culture placed great emphasis on the value of transparency. In melodrama the motivations of all characters are easy to discern; yet Macaire is a dissembler and a cheat who refuses to play by the rules. This is the significance of the gambling scene (also a feature of Lemaître's second Macaire play) where Macaire uses Bertrand to help him cheat at cards at a party hosted by the Pocklingtons.[66] Macaire makes great play of the fact that he is a 'philosopher', although this is an ironic justification of his wicked conduct. However, when he accidentally kills Bertrand, there is a strong sense towards the end of the book of the villains being devoured by their own conduct and a conventional morality begins to assert itself.

The outlaw hero is historically complex but can be employed both as an object of condemnation and as an agent of human freedom. Cloaking outlaws with gentlemanly origins or behaviour is a way of linking them to the aristocracy, the one group in society that is perceived as truly free. Figures such as Macaire are both conservative and libertarian. The liminality of the gentleman outlaw makes him paradoxical but also fascinating because of his ironic detachment from society.

The anti-heroism and disguises of Macaire expose hypocrisy. Macaire appealed to Reynolds's imagination on the fringes of literary life but also enabled him to draw on his French experience. The novel allows Reynolds to interpret France and in particular Paris for an English audience. When Macaire is about to return to the city, Reynolds writes:

> Macaire was in high spirits at the prospect of visiting his own country once more – that country which he emphatically described to be the land of prospectuses, programmes, projects, philanthropic ideas, useful plans, and vast combinations, all directed towards one grand aim – the improvement of mankind![67]

It is difficult not to feel that the author is writing in his own voice here. France allowed Reynolds to uncover a space that embraced political and sexual radicalism as well as republicanism. Reynolds was an enthusiast for the French Revolution. He describes a chapel in the prison of the Conciergerie as having once been inhabited by 'that depraved and licentious woman, Queen Marie Antoinette'.[68] We are told on a number of occasions that Macaire is a republican.[69] It might be possible to argue that republicanism was a bad thing if it was supported by criminals like Macaire, but that does not seem to be Reynolds's meaning here. Republicanism becomes a commitment to freedom. Macaire also declares himself to be 'a citizen of all nations', which makes him sound like Thomas Paine, whom Reynolds admired.[70] Describing the Palace of Justice, Reynolds trumpets that the 'days of despotic splendour have passed; and Republicanism has introduced changes which have entirely annihilated the remnants of feudal magnificence and King-craft in regenerated France'.[71] He

---

66 Reynolds, *Robert Macaire*, ch. 4, p. 14.

67 Reynolds, *Robert Macaire*, ch. 18, p. 44.

68 Reynolds, *Robert Macaire*, ch. 27, p. 59.

69 Reynolds, *Robert Macaire*, ch. 21, p. 51; ch. 24, p. 60.

70 Reynolds, *Robert Macaire*, ch. 24, p. 60.

71 Reynolds, *Robert Macaire*, ch. 43, p. 109. This reference to 'King-craft' is an addition to the 1849 edition and an example of how the text shifted in the wake of the 1848 French

became increasingly disillusioned with Louis-Philippe. For the 1849 edition of *Robert Macaire*, Reynolds added a footnote to the description of a young man Macaire meets in the Parisian underworld: 'This young man attempted the life of the tyrant, Louis Philippe, who has, however, since met a more righteous doom at the hands of the brave French nation.'[72] This is a clear reference to the 1848 Revolution, which Reynolds supported. Thus whilst there is a conservative dimension to the novel (the romanticized gentleman outlaw), Reynolds also turns the story towards an explicit commitment to an unspecified form of liberal politics inspired by France.

One of the features of this form of popular fiction is that the city becomes a character in the action. Reynolds always sets his novels in very specifically described locations so as to increase verisimilitude, even though he also offers a gothic rendering of the city. London is described as a 'mighty Babylon'.[73] However, Reynolds breaks the action at several points to extol the virtues of Paris:

> There is an air of gaiety and joyousness about Paris which is found in no other metropolis in the world. All the faces that you meet seem to wear an aspect of pleasure; and although the myriads of shops and marts teem with the choicest productions of the world, in all their perfection, and of all kinds, Paris still seems rather a city of pleasure than business.[74]

Shortly afterwards we find ourselves in more familiar Reynolds territory when Charles Stanmore goes to the Marais, allowing the author to provide descriptions of dirt and grime (similar to those a few years later in Sue's *Les Mystères de Paris*). Stanmore finds Bertrand's mother living in the filthiest street of the Marais where people keep pigs indoors.[75] On another occasion Reynolds sets a scene on the Pont Neuf, which he describes as the frequent site of suicides and robberies, but he also reassures the reader:

> Instances of assassination upon the bridge are, however, now rare: and the bad fame of the Pont Neuf is rather borrowed from the deeds of the past than from the events of the present.[76]

The city is therefore a theatrical and mesmerizing presence, the site of attraction and repulsion, a place where the reader and traveller have to negotiate the possibility of criminal encounter. The use of occasional footnotes with factual information (more evident in the 1849 edition) heightens the reality effect of the novel. As in *The Mysteries of London*, Reynolds provides glossaries of thieves' slang both to assist the reader and to increase the feeling of an invisible underworld of crime.[77] These

---

Revolution.

72 Reynolds, *Robert Macaire*, ch. 21, p. 51.
73 Reynolds, *Robert Macaire*, ch. 11, p. 21.
74 Reynolds, *Robert Macaire*, ch. 12, p. 30.
75 Reynolds, *Robert Macaire*, ch. 12, p. 30.
76 Reynolds, *Robert Macaire*, ch. 21, p. 50.
77 Reynolds, *Robert Macaire*, ch. 24, p. 59.

kind of images of the city were, of course, not new but were becoming part of the repertoire of melodrama.[78]

Robert Macaire should be understood partly as a novelization of the kind of plays that were filling cheap theatres.[79] Macaire was not an unusual figure in nineteenth-century theatre, which had developed a sub-genre around bandits or outlaws. Reynolds seems aware of Macaire's theatrical origins. Although, as we have seen, he creates his own version of Macaire, Reynolds effectively refers back to the Lemaître version, adopting the gestures of the figure on stage:

> 'We will go to England, my boy!' ejaculated Macaire, starting from the ground and throwing himself into an imposing attitude, by placing his left hand on his hip, and extending his right arm, while he eyed his friend with a glance of the most perfect satisfaction.[80]

Later on, Macaire strikes 'one of his favourite attitudes by throwing forward his right leg, placing his left hand upon his hip, leaning his body backwards, and extending his right arm'.[81] Bertrand is very close to the buffoon that he was on stage. He retains his catchphrase from *L'Auberge des Adrets*, exclaiming 'oh, my poor nerves' when anything bad is happening. Lemaître's creaking snuff box frequently appears, making Bertrand hysterical. Reynolds presumed that many readers would be familiar with the device from the stage and laugh. We do not think of Reynolds as a comic writer (although that was clearly how he saw himself at this time, especially when he was still imitating Boz). Even the use of songs in the narrative echoes the use of musical interludes on stage, although one song employing underworld slang also echoes Ainsworth's *Jack Sheppard*.

The novel is also true to its melodramatic roots in its portrait of women. The two main female characters are Maria Leslie and Blanche de Longueville. Neither is as fleshed out as Macaire, although, as Janice Radway points out, readers will often appropriate and identify with apparently wooden characters by investing them with characteristics derived from their own imaginations.[82] Blanche is an archetypally good woman who is told by Charles Stanmore that her 'pure and unsophisticated mind cannot comprehend the nature of men's bad feelings'.[83] Reynolds informs the reader how to view his character when she is first introduced by pointing out that 'Blanche' means 'white'.[84] Maria is also good but a slave to passion. She is trapped by Macaire once she surrenders to her love for him and dies of a broken heart, although she is not cast out of her family in the manner of other representations of fallen women in this period. At the same time, Reynolds is often prepared to describe

---

78   Michael Booth, 'The Metropolis on Stage', in H.J. Dyos and Michael Wolff (eds), *The Victorian City: Images and Realities* (London: Routledge and Kegan Paul, 1973), vol. 1, pp. 211–24.

79   Reynolds, *Robert Macaire*, ch. 12, p. 30.

80   Reynolds, *Robert Macaire*, ch. 2, p. 7.

81   Reynolds, *Robert Macaire*, ch. 2, p. 11.

82   Janice Radway, *Reading the Romance: Women, Patriarchy and Popular Literature* (Chapel Hill, NC: University of North Carolina Press, 1984).

83   Reynolds, *Robert Macaire*, ch. 28, p. 122.

84   Reynolds, *Robert Macaire*, ch. 12, p. 35.

these female characters in sexual ways, reminding us that he was sometimes viewed as a pornographer. When Maria is first introduced, Reynolds resorts to voyeurism: 'The undulations of her beautiful form were almost visible through the virgin-white gown, which concealed it.'[85] Subsequently, Maria is described thus:

> She was clad in a morning wrapper which was as yet open at the breast; and her young and beauteous bosom, which the garment only half-concealed, heaved with frequent sighs.[86]

Whilst this is not the extreme pornography available elsewhere in the 'radical underworld' of the period, it is clear that this has become the novel of a libertine. The conventional morality of some parts of the novel does not efface Reynolds's male gaze.

This has been a study of republican romanticism. In *The Modern Literature of France*, Reynolds championed French civilization and argued that after the 1830 Revolution, the French people 'felt their ideas expand' and their literature became marked by the spread of liberal ideas. He also defended French literature from charges of indecency, which he argued was actually uncommon.[87] In *Robert Macaire*, however, he chose to take the low road, invoking the liberal but also libertine aspects of French culture. France contained both possibilities in the British imagination.

Reynolds's novel is about a man of disguise. At the same time it allowed the author to adopt his own disguise, presenting himself in effect as Harrison Ainsworth just as, a few years later, he would turn himself into Eugène Sue. A cultural sponge, his novels were grand pastiches of Romanticism, which he deployed in a commercial and commodified form. Reynolds is significant because of the way he acknowledged the radical possibilities of these narratives. It would be too much to say that Reynolds subverted the values of the Victorian public sphere, but his writings always inhabited the edge of respectability. Macaire was similarly liminal, living on the fringes, combining republican ideals with the morality of the underworld.[88] From the first night of *L'Auberge des Adrets*, the Macaire figure refused to follow the script that was written for him and would not be contained by conventional morality. It made sense for Reynolds to bring this dangerous figure to England.

85 Reynolds, *Robert Macaire*, ch. 2, p. 8.
86 Reynolds, *Robert Macaire*, ch. 5, p. 16.
87 G.W.M. Reynolds, *The Modern Literature of France* (London: George Henderson, 1839), vol. 1, pp. xiv, xix.
88 Brown, *Theater and Revolution*, p. 114.

PART II
Politics and the Periodical Press

Chapter 3

Reynolds's Miscellany, 1846–1849: Advertising Networks and Politics

Andrew King

In the mid-1850s *Reynolds's Miscellany* (1846–69) was one of the four penny fiction weeklies that served most to inform the cultural imaginary of Britain. Together, these four – the *Miscellany*, the *Family Herald*, the *London Journal* and *Cassell's Illustrated Family Paper* – reached at least 50 per cent of the population of Britain, a social penetration far exceeding that of canonical works and usually associated with twentieth-century mass media, or the 1890s at the earliest.[1] This chapter, however, is concerned with examining the particularities of *Reynolds's Miscellany* in the late 1840s, when its circulation was low. Rather than challenging head on the orthodoxies of either literary or media history by focusing on mass-consumed texts several decades before they are supposed to occur, this chapter has two, less ambitious, purposes.

First, it tests some of the descriptive framework outlined in my book on one of the four periodicals mentioned above, the *London Journal*. This is appropriate not only because the *Miscellany* is located in a cultural zone contingent to the *Journal*, but also because Reynolds was the *Journal*'s first editor, only leaving it to launch his *Miscellany*.[2] In order to accomplish my purpose, it has been necessary to create a bibliographical map of the entire contents of *Reynolds's Miscellany* to provide the data against which to test the theory. Its first issue is dated 7 November 1846 and its last 19 June 1869, when it merged with *Bow Bells* (another fiction weekly from the same publisher, John Dicks). Twenty-three years of a weekly publication generates far too much material to be contained within a single chapter such as this. As a result, I have chosen to concentrate on the first five volumes, comprising the three of its first series (7 November 1846–1 July 1848) and the first two of its second (14 July 1848–21 July 1849). This run was published just before Reynolds started his famously pro-

---

1   See Andrew King, *The London Journal 1845–1883: Periodicals, Production and Gender* (Aldershot: Ashgate, 2004), p. 89. On the rise of the mass media, see, e.g., Alison Chapman, *Comparative Media History* (Cambridge: Polity, 2005); Martin Conboys, *Journalism: A Critical History* (London: Sage, 2005); James Curran and Jean Seaton, *Power without Responsibility: The Press and Broadcasting in Britain*, 6th edn (London: Routledge, 2003); Lyn Gorman and David McLean, *Media and Society in the Twentieth Century* (Oxford: Blackwell, 2003); Kevin Williams, *Get Me a Murder a Day! A History of Mass Communication in Britain* (London: Hodder Arnold, 1998).

2   See *LJ*, vol. 2, p. 191 and vol. 3, p. 384 (which suggests that Reynolds left the *Journal* towards the end of July 1846).

Chartist *Political Instructor* (10 November 1849–11 May 1850), a weekly which was shortly to become *Reynolds's Newspaper*, one of the main organs of working-class radical political thought for over a century (5 May 1850–16 September 1962).[3] If 1846–49 are not the years of the *Miscellany*'s prodigious circulation nor coincident with Reynolds's major involvement with political publication, they do constitute an important period straddling Reynolds's sudden emergence as a Chartist leader. They can be regarded as a murky solution out of which precipitates not only Reynolds's success in the mass market but also his more direct engagements with the political public sphere. As such, they enable my second purpose: to think through how the *Miscellany* may shed light on Reynolds's much debated relation to politics. 'Politics' is a slippery term in discussions of this sort and so I shall define it here as referring to the organization of social relations. I shall think through Reynolds's relation to this politics not only by discussing the discourses recorded in the *Miscellany*, but also by analysing Reynolds's relationships both with fellow producers and with consuming readers.

The first section outlines the descriptive framework that underlies the present study. Some of the elements are discussed at much greater length than others: one, the organization of Reynolds's network – an element that will emerge as key to my definition of politics – is so complex as to require a separate section at the centre of this chapter. The last section comprises a discussion of one of the most cited aspects of the *Miscellany*, the series of 'Letters to the Industrious Classes'. It is this section that brings to the fore how Reynolds projects his political engagement in his magazine, and allows the clearest comparison between what is preached and what is practised.

What Can We Do with Periodicals?

In my *London Journal* book I was concerned to think through the implications of a periodical considered as a commodity fetish, to outline the prestidigitatory tricks of a mass-market periodical in a specific area of the literary field over a particular timeframe, designed to create and sustain as wide a readership as possible. I broke down these tricks into categories. Not all are discussed here given the constraints of the chapter format, and most of those that are will be returned to and refined several times.

One category I labelled 'textual practices', relating them to genre as leading to the reader's identification of the periodical's particular character within the wider notion of periodicals. This category allows the reconstruction of the 'implied reader' of a periodical against which evidence concerning 'real readers' can be compared. A second was 'title', which I took to imply a kind of brand for a consumer, both

---

    3   *RN* continued until 1967 (as the *Sunday Citizen*). See Donald Kausch, 'George W.M. Reynolds: A Bibliography', *The Library*, 5th series, 28/3 (December 1973): 322. On *RPI*, see Anne Humpherys, 'G.W.M. Reynolds, Popular Literature and Popular Politics', *Victorian Periodicals Review*, 16 (1983): 78–89; on *RN*, see Virginia Berridge, 'Popular Journalism and Working-class Attitudes, 1854–1886: A Study of *Reynolds's Newspaper*, *Lloyd's Weekly Newspaper*, and the *Weekly Times*' (PhD dissertation, University of London, 1976).

familiar and yet always new.[4] New brands must create a genealogical relation to previous products and the title is a potent way of doing this. *Reynolds's Miscellany* started off as *Reynolds's Magazine* but switched to its more familiar title without warning in its fifth issue.[5] While the change of title was once adverted to in a reply to a reader's query, it was never explained.[6] Indeed, the reason for the change remains unclear when one considers that the term 'magazine' was already established in the field of penny periodicals through the *Penny* and *Saturday*. Furthermore, it was common to combine the term with that of a proper name: *Ainsworth's*, *Douglas Jerrold's*, *Tait's*, *Hood's* all attest to the regularity of its usage. 'Miscellany' was less often used at this time: in the previous 20 years we find only *Chambers's* (1845) and *Bentley's* (1837–68) amongst publications generally available, and it may be by reason of its comparative rarity that Reynolds chose it. What is more significant is the title's reliance on Reynolds's own name as what modern-day marketing calls the product's unique selling proposition. Reynolds no doubt believed in the saleability of his name after the successes of *Faust* in the *London Journal* and of the *Mysteries of London*, both of which carried his signature. When he advertises his products in the *Miscellany*, he treats his name as more important than their titles: one strategy is to announce a new serial by him – or by his wife, usually called 'Mrs G.W.M. Reynolds' – but only reveal its title the week it actually appears.[7] This only confirms how it is his name that carries the brand promise. Just like other periodicals such as *Ainsworth's*, *Reynolds's* was a focal point to which the author's other work was attached, containing the core values of the more general brand. The individual works are less important than the name.

What I termed 'demographics' comprises the social locations of real readers who overlap to various degrees with the 'implied reader' suggested by the generic practices. 'Notices to Correspondents' might in theory help here, as several critics have noted.[8] Patricia Anderson, who based her mapping of readers on the analysis of 18 pages of 'Notices' gleaned from three penny fiction weeklies between 1845

---

4   On the paradox of the new commodity's having to appear as both new and familiar, see Judith Williamson, *Decoding Advertisements* (London: Marion Boyars, 1978), pp. 24ff. The anachronistic-sounding term 'brand' in the sense of trademark was in fact already in use by 1827 (see *OED*).

5   Reprint editions replace the original headpieces with the later ones.

6   See *RM*, vol. 2, o.s., p. 80. Here and in further references 'o.s.' refers to volumes in the first (old) series; 'n.s.' refers to those in the second ('new'). See Editors' Note.

7   See, e.g., *RM*, vol. 1, o.s., pp. 128, 144, 416, 432; vol. 2, o.s., pp. 16, 32, 208, 256; vol. 1, n.s., pp. 144, 160, 176.

8   Humpherys ('G.W.M. Reynolds') devotes several interesting pages to 'Notices to Correspondents', suggesting, I think rightly, that Reynolds wrote most of the 'Notices' himself. Richard Altick (*The English Common Reader: A Social History of the Mass Reading Public, 1800–1900*, 2nd edn [Columbus, OH: Ohio University Press, 1998]), Patricia Anderson (*The Printed Image and the Transformation of Popular Culture, 1790–1860* [Oxford: Clarendon Press, 1991]) and Teresa Gerrard ('New Methods in the History of Reading: "Answers to Correspondents" in *The Family Herald* 1860–1900', *Publishing History*, 43 [1998]: 51–69) have all analysed replies to correspondents' queries, continuing a practice dating back at least to 1847 (see King, *The London Journal*, p. 25).

and 1859, includes amongst them five from the *Miscellany* in the period under study here. She found a preponderance of 'clerks, shopkeepers and the more prosperous strata of the working classes'.[9] However, she does not distinguish between the readerships of the different periodicals nor changes in the nature of the pages over time. My charting of 'Notices' throughout the first five volumes of the *Miscellany* reveals much less than a study of pages from later periods or from other comparable periodicals. Most signatures I found comprise initials followed by a geographical location in brackets (from all over the British Isles, with no significant bias towards one area) or designations that declare a correspondent's loyalty to the periodical or to the editor either through assertion of economic constancy ('A Constant Subscriber') or through declaration of identification with a character in one of the editor's serials ('Faust', 'Wagner', 'Otto Pianalla', 'Nisida', 'Jem Ruffles').[10] Far fewer signal their insertion into literary culture in general with pseudonyms such as 'Hamlet', 'Menelaus', 'Sam Weller', or 'Amy Robsart'. Fewer still use classical tags (e.g., 'Philo-Chroma', 'Senectus', 'Sigma'). Most answers to correspondents' queries are so opaque or general as to prevent any social classification of the enquirer. Indeed, there are very few social indicators at all, even of gender (what genderable replies there are – only around 15 per cent of the total – suggest men wrote in over three times as often as women). I have identified just four indicators of ethnicity, all Jewish.[11] What jobs are mentioned confirm Anderson's conclusions as regards apprentices and clerks (though there are very few schoolteachers). I can add a few tradesmen, soldiers and aspirants to naval midshipman posts (who are always recommended to rethink their ambition).

However, to me these markers designate less the social position of the *Miscellany*'s core readership than a declaration of class consciousness on the part of a very few correspondents, a class consciousness that is not necessarily deep-seated, but contingent on the nature of the question posed. For example, 'An Architect' wants to know about how to make varnish, 'A Young Author' offers contributions or enquires about plays, 'A Clerk' wonders about the grammar of something he has written, 'A Newsman' asks how much the prints cost that are sold as optional extras to certain numbers of the *Miscellany*.[12] From April 1848, the title 'A Working Man' appears more often than before, along with a sprinkling of 'Chartists', 'Friends of Freedom' and 'Patriots'.[13] These radical labels perhaps suggest a stronger assertion of class identity (or at least solidarity), but we must remain cautious about claiming too much. First, these signatures are outweighed almost three to one by just 'Constant Subscribers' and 'Subscribers from the First' in the same set of pages, let alone any other category of signature. Second, many of the 'Notices' seem to me invented.

9   Anderson, *The Printed Image*, p. 140.

10   The last three are characters in Reynolds's *Faust, Wagner the Wehr-Wolf* and *The Days of Hogarth*.

11   Reynolds was declaredly philosemitic and the correspondents are all responding to his writings on the subject. There is one reply to 'A Black Boy' but this signature may refer only to someone with black hair – the reply is ambiguous.

12   *RM*, vol. 1, o.s., p. 144; vol. 2, o.s., p. 80; vol. 3, o.s., p. 192; vol. 1, n.s., p. 96; vol. 3, o.s., p. 336.

13   See, e.g., *RM*, vol. 3, o.s., pp. 336, 352, 384, 431–2.

Some signatures and replies appear an inordinate number of times: 'A Mechanic' is recommended A. Peck's *Mechanics* 27 times over the five volumes, for example.[14] It would have been all too easy to fill up space with material such as the following.

S.N. (London). – Apply at Carvalho's, Fleet-street.

MECHANICUS. – Procure No. 1 of the Park-house Catechism – 'MECHANICS,' price 9d, published by Rolfe and Fletcher, Cloak-lane. It is an admirable little work.

A.B.M. – Eve's 'Catechism', price 1s. 6d., published by Darton and Clark, Holborn-hill, is an excellent work for youthful students of both sexes.

'FAUST: A HISTORICAL ROMANCE OF THE SECRET TRIBUNALS,' is now publishing, in Weekly Penny Numbers and Monthly Sixpenny Parts, by George Vickers, 3, Catherine-street, Strand.

S.J. (Lark-hill). – Your first question shall be answered next week. – To your second, we reply, it is lawful. – Major Beniowski's System of Mnemonics has been pronounced good by many sensible people; but we know nothing of it. – There is a work called 'Songs of the Press,' published, we believe, by Fisher, Newgate-street.

'PAPERS ON POPULAR SCIENCE.' – Mr. Peck will commence 'Mechanics' in Volume II of the 'MISCELLANY.'

J.M.D. – All respectable firms keep books; the large houses chiefly by double entry. – Your handwriting would prove one good qualification to recommend you to a clerk's situation.

FAUST. – The book can be obtained at Mr. Vickers', 28 and 29, Holywell-street. – Roman cement.

SOLYMAN A. (Scarborough). – Yes.[15]

The typographical equivalence of correspondents' signatures and the titles of advertised texts make it difficult at times to distinguish an advertisement from a response to an individual query. As a result of all the above, the hard 'demographics' that 'Notices' seem to promise dissolves into something more akin to the hypothesized implied reader suggested by textual practices. Instead of locating readers in society, 'Notices' limn an implied reader's relationship with the periodical, one that gives priority to commercial imperatives. For the reader addressed in 'Notices' in the first three volumes is above all a *consuming* reader. He is not predominantly a political actor or even an actor genuinely seeking information independent of the commercial nexus Reynolds operated in. He is a (male) reader constructed as lacking in knowledge whose lack may be filled by consumption of texts he is directed to. What 'Notices' give is not a free gift of empowering information or knowledge but rather education into the structures of a still nascent consumer society. This is a point that will be elaborated below both in the discussion of the 'Letters to the Industrious Classes' and in the relationship of 'Notices' to advertisement. For the while, though, it is sufficient to note the unhelpfulness of the category 'demographics' in this particular study.

Another key descriptive category I used was circulation. This I linked to demographics but, for a commercial operation such as the *Miscellany*, it is just

---

14 Cf. also the notice to 'Mechanicus' in the following quotation, a recurrent variant I do not include in the figure quoted.

15 *RM*, vol. 1, o.s., pp. 415–16.

as closely wedded to my last two categories, credit (income generated) and debit (production costs). These latter two concern the financial viability of the media text. Advertising had been an important source of income for periodicals since the early eighteenth century.[16] The account books of *Reynolds's Miscellany* do not survive, and for the period in question we can calculate no figures at all for income from advertising. Unless there was a goodly number of adverts on the 'Illustrated Wrappers' on the sixpenny monthly parts – copies of which I have not been able to find – one has to assume that there was little advertising income. Most of the advertising space that survives (on the last page of each issue) promotes Reynolds's own publications or those of his circle. Reynolds may, indeed, have found it difficult to garner advertising contracts: only a few years later Mitchell's *Newspaper Press Directory* would be asserting that it was better to advertise in publications whose readers had spare cash for the products advertised: large circulation alone was no guarantee of advertising effectiveness.[17] Nonetheless, Reynolds behaved as though circulation were indeed the marker of financial and cultural success, publishing the *Miscellany*'s sales figures in 'Notices'. These claim that the magazine had reached what was considered the break-even point for penny magazines, a circulation of 30,000, as early as the sixth issue.[18]

There is, however, a more reliable source than this. Reynolds declared bankruptcy in the late summer of 1848 and an account of the hearing in *The Times* offers an important insight into the *Miscellany*'s economics.[19] In court Reynolds stated that he could make a profit only with a circulation of over 26,000 a week, but actual circulation never rose above 6,000 less than that. The figures in the *Miscellany* were then – unsurprisingly – exaggerated, no doubt with the intention of attracting advertisers and proving the financial viability of the enterprise to his creditors. Already in debt to the tune of £1,700 by January 1847, Reynolds confessed that he was losing between £8 and £10 a week on the *Miscellany*, and by the time of the hearing owed 'upwards of £2,000'. The reason that he became bankrupt even though he was earning around £500 a year from his writing was that he spent all his income on his family rather than using some to subvent his periodical. In the end, he found himself able to pay his creditors only a small percentage of what he owed.

It is clear, then, that what we are dealing with is an operation run with the imperative need either to generate income by means other than cover price or to

---

16 Jeremy Black, *The English Press 1621–1861* (London: Sutton, 2001), pp. 60–65.

17 Diana Hindley and Geoffrey Hindley, *Advertising in Victorian England, 1837–1901* (London: Wayland, 1972), p. 25.

18 For claimed circulation figures in *RM*, see 'W.J.T.', 12 December 1847; 'Quaesitor', 16 January 1847, 'over 30,000'; 'N.V.Z.', 13 March 1847, 30,000, and with back numbers, 40,000; 'Notices', 12 April 1847, 34,000; 'H.K', 23 October 1847, 38,000; 'Notices', 26 February 1848, 32,000. I give dates rather than volume and page numbers here as dates are more important in tracing the claimed sales curve. For 30,000 as the break-even point, see Sally Mitchell, *The Fallen Angel: Chastity, Class and Women's Reading 1835–1880* (Bowling Green: Bowling Green University Popular Press, 1989), p. 4.

19 See *The Times*, 7 September 1848, p. 7; 29 September 1848, p. 6; 3 October 1848, p. 6. Accounts in the *Weekly Times* (10 September, 1 October and 8 October 1848) exaggerate Reynolds's expenditure.

reduce costs. The need to keep costs down is visible in the meagre format and the small numbers of contributors, which I shall detail below. And if it is impossible to give figures for income in the absence of precise circulation or advertising revenue, it is nonetheless possible to trace an economic *system* in which advertising – in an extremely extended sense – plays a vital part.

What I have been claiming above contradicts the statements of previous historians of the field who have remarked on the *Miscellany*'s early success. Circulation indubitably rose in the 1850s – we have some figures that suggest this, corroborated to the extent that Reynolds became wealthy – but throughout the period covered here, the *Miscellany* remained on the margins of survival.[20] That it did survive is a tribute to Reynolds's projected belief in himself and his canny manipulation of his network, both enabled, no doubt, by his upper-middle-class background documented elsewhere in this collection.

The Economics of Networks

When Reynolds left the *London Journal*, he took with him several of his contacts, most obviously the French publishers Galignani (who appear in the colophons of the *Miscellany* over the entire period under study here). More contentiously, he also took a set of practices (which comprise part of the *Reynolds* brand). An important one of these was social exposé. His introductory 'To Our Readers' in the first issue uses Whiggish tropes typical in prospectuses for periodicals of its kind (flattery of the reader by praising the moral 'progress' of the reading public and its insatiable curiosity in the politically safe areas of 'Science, Art, Manufacture', followed by the customary promise of a singularly appropriate mixture of the *utile* and *dulce*). But it makes two exceptional additions. First, the *Magazine* will cover 'the various matters of social or national importance', a promise that opens the way for social exposé, and second, it is careful to defuse any possible tension with rivals.

> Appearing in opposition to no existing Cheap Publication, – started without the least idea of rivalry, – and issued in the full belief that there is room for its being, without displacing any other, this MAGAZINE is established to supply a desideratum which has for some time been acknowledged. The remark on one side has been that certain Cheap Publications contain too much light matter, while on the other side it has been observed that another set of Periodicals are too heavy. To steer the medium course is the object of 'REYNOLDS'S MAGAZINE'.[21]

---

20   Charles Knight estimated sales of 200,000 by 1854 (Alice Clowes, *Charles Knight: A Sketch* [London: Bentley, 1892], p. 226). For 1855, Anderson (*The Printed Image*, p. 14) gives a figure of 250,000, though on pp. 91 and 181 gives 200,000. Athanase Cucheval Clarigny (*Histoire de la presse en Angleterre et aux Etats-Unis* [Paris: Amyot, 1857], p. 228) states at least 100,000 in 1856. Figures from booksellers suggest that *RM* was always a poor relation of the *Family Herald* and *LJ*, selling between a third and half as many as these periodicals in the mid-1850s. This still meant around 200,000: see representative figures in Altick, *The English Common Reader*, pp. 351, 394; King, *The London Journal*, pp. 85–7.

21   'To Our Readers', *Reynolds's Magazine*, vol. 1, o.s., p. 16.

The passage was almost certainly addressed to George Stiff, who owned the *London Journal*, as a public placatory gesture. For Reynolds did not start up his *Magazine* as a result of a quarrel with Stiff as has been claimed: rather, the quarrel came later, when he began the second series of the *Miscellany*. This second series was much closer in format to the *Journal* than the first, and it may have been this formal similarity that incited Stiff to set up his own *Reynolds's Magazine* the moment the second series appeared at the end of June 1848. Stiff even wrote a 'wretched travestie' of *The Coral Island* (Reynolds's new tale in the *Miscellany*) under the title of 'The Corral Island' and duplicated other features 'to mislead the public'.[22] If Reynolds dared imitate Stiff's *Journal*, then Stiff would reciprocate by carrying imitation to the point of disruptive parody. Reynolds, however, quickly took out an injunction, and Stiff was almost immediately forced to cease publication. This was the origin of the quarrel between Reynolds and Stiff.[23]

In the context of rivalry, format was clearly regarded as the key, since otherwise there was little immediate change in the content or tone of the new *Miscellany*. While it was a 16-page stereotyped penny fiction weekly like the *Journal*, the page size of the first series had been much smaller and it had fewer, and considerably less stylish, illustrations (usually just two per issue). It would have been hard to confuse the two publications, the *Miscellany* coming across as decidedly worse value for money – no doubt a factor in its limited appeal.

Most of the illustrations in the *Miscellany* were drawn by the artist Henry Anelay and engraved by the obscure and short-lived firm of Griffin & Duvergier.[24] Anelay had provided pictures for the *Journal* but, since March 1846, its brand image had been strongly associated with the work of one of the most popular illustrators of the nineteenth century, John Gilbert. Although, like Gilbert, Anelay also drew for the *Illustrated London News*,[25] he was far less accomplished in high-status pictorial styles and was less central to the brand promise of the *Journal*. Sharing Anelay with Reynolds would not therefore have been a great loss to Stiff. Importantly for Reynolds, Anelay almost certainly commanded a lower fee than Gilbert.

Others who contributed images included, from 29 May 1847, the firm of Gorway who engraved the illustrations for Reynolds's serial *The Days of Hogarth, or The Mysteries of Old London*, a narrative intended to explain and link various pictures of Hogarth's drawn from throughout his career in no particular order other than that provided by Reynolds's imagination. Reynolds's publicly declared intention was to educate the public in the 'national' and 'immortal pictures' of Hogarth with their 'mighty morals … and an ever changing succession of social phases', presenting his readers with a gift 'of what may be termed the "HOGARTH GALLERY OF

---

22   'Address to the Public', *RM*, vol. 1, n.s., p. 48. Note that actual publication occurred on the Wednesday morning ten days before the date on the headpieces 'in time for all the parcels sent into the country by the London Booksellers': see *RM*, vol. 1, o.s., p. 191; vol. 3, o.s., p. 48. This was usual practice at this time (see King, *The London Journal*, p. 81).

23   For a fuller account of this episode, see King, *The London Journal*, pp. 71–3.

24   Rodney K. Engen (*Dictionary of Wood Engravers* [Cambridge: Chadwyck Healey, 1985], p. 109) has only one reference to them (from 1848).

25   See Simon Houfe, *The Dictionary of British Book Illustrators and Caricaturists 1800–1914*, 2nd edn (Woodbridge: Antique Collectors Club, 1981), p. 219.

PICTURES"'.[26] However, while promising both art education and more exposé of the 'social phases' of the city, he may have been trying to save money. By relying on already extant pictures, he could cut out an artist's fees altogether: the engraver could take the images directly from any of the several books of reproductions of Hogarth's complete works then available.[27] This would have left more money to pay a decent engraving firm such as Gorway. Like Anelay, Gorway did regular work for the *London Journal*. Again, this did not cause a rupture with Stiff, confirming how Stiff considered the network far less important than the set of repeated visual practices that constitute the brand image of a periodical.

Other engravers' signatures that appear from time to time on the *Miscellany*'s illustrations are Edwin Brett, A. Miles and H. Carter. None of these did work for the *Journal*. Miles is not even listed in Engen's *Dictionary of Wood Engravers*, and Brett is but an obscure reference there, rendering all the more curious the appearance of such a luminary as Carter. Having risen through the ranks to become head of the engraving department at the *Illustrated London News*, in 1848 Carter emigrated to America where, seven years later, he founded the phenomenally successful *Frank Leslie's Illustrated Newspaper*.[28] In the body of the *Miscellany* his work appears first in small, delicate illustrations to single episode tales by Gabriel Alexander.[29] Later, he engraved a series of illustrations to Reynolds's translation of Hugo's *Last Day of a Condemned*, a six-parter on the inside pages of volume 3.[30] Reynolds had originally published the translation in 1837 with an edition three years later that added a substantial Preface arguing against the death penalty. A commentary on the Hugo in the *Miscellany* comprises a collage of material taken from that Preface.[31] In recycling an old publication, Reynolds was liberating time to spend on writing other material and so generate income. Perhaps he thought that freed time would free money to spend on an expensive engraver (though it is significant that the illustrations are small and would have been correspondingly priced). Much flashier than these small engravings, though, was Carter's rendition of Wilkie's *Rent Day*, drawn by George Standfast, 'no less than seven months in preparation … the *finest* as well as the *largest* ever presented to the Public … the exact size of the Original, printed on fine paper', and only a penny halfpenny with number 68 of the *Miscellany*. In the advert for this optional extra, Carter's name, like Standfast's, is given in small

---

26 Advert for *The Days of Hogarth, or The Mysteries of Old London, RM*, vol. 2, o.s., p. 32. Ignoring Reynolds's stated intentions, Anderson (*The Printed Image*, pp. 117–18) regards this series as part of the trivializing of Art.

27 E.g., those issued by Baldwin, Craddock and Joy in 1822 or by John Major in 1831. Similar economics may be at work in series such as 'The Beauties of the Court of Charles II' and 'Napoleon Bonaparte' (both in vol. 2, n.s.), whose illustrations are also based on paintings.

28 See Joshua Brown, *Beyond the Lines: Pictorial Reporting, Everyday Life, and the Crisis of Gilded-Age America* (Berkeley: University of California Press, 2002), pp. 17–22, 25–31 and passim.

29 *RM*, vol. 2, o.s., pp. 113, 116, 152, 154, 177 (this last, exceptionally, on the front page of a number).

30 11 December 1847–15 January 1848.

31 See 'The Punishment of Death', *RM*, vol. 3, o.s., pp. 167–9.

capitals, marking his high status even to those who had no idea of status relations in the field.[32] Almost immediately, another penny halfpenny print is offered, of Wilkie's *Blind Man's Buff*, but in this case there is no indication of engraver or copyist.[33] Both engravings were popular, having to be reprinted several times. Later optional engravings, always available with certain numbers only, were produced in series such as 'The Seasons'. But these would cost only halfpence each, would be engraved by the much less prestigious firm of W. Williams and drawn by Anelay.[34] The later, cheaper, prints coincided with the start of adverts for patent remedies: it is tempting to think that the prints were funded by the adverts, each working to promote the other.

If the artists and engravers overlapped to some extent with those of the *London Journal*, Reynolds used the same printer only once. The *Miscellany* migrated from printer to printer with alarming rapidity over its first two volumes, suggestive of financial instability. The first, Thoms of 12 Warwick Street, was a medium-sized operation (it had employed ten men and five boys in 1839).[35] They printed just the first three numbers before the tiny firm (just one boy) of White (79 Great Queen Street) took over the following 16. The large company (37 men and ten boys) of W.H. Cox, which had a steam press, printed numbers 20 to 37, after which Reynolds got the obscure Wilkinson to take over the job. It is this last which the *Miscellany* shares with the *Journal*, though not at the same time.

It was not until the first number of volume 3 (6 November 1847) that the association of Reynolds and the printer John Dicks began. Thereafter, the colophons declare that the *Miscellany* was 'printed and published for the PROPRIETOR by JOHN DICKS, at the Office, No. 7, Wellington Street North, Covent Garden'. This was exactly the moment when *The Days of Hogarth* became the lead serial with its cost-cutting circumvention of an artist's fees. At the time of the Wilkie reproductions, Reynolds was heavily engaged in Chartist activities; Dicks may have therefore had a freer hand, perhaps taking the idea of circulation-boosting optional extra prints from the *Illustrated London News*. Likewise, for all Stiff's parodic assault on the *Reynolds* brand, it may have been Dicks, rather than Reynolds, who lay behind the redesign of the *Miscellany* for the second series so that it looked more like the *London Journal*.[36]

As far as the verbal contents of the *Miscellany* are concerned, the network involved was both more limited and more extensive than the *Journal*'s: more limited

---

32 *RM*, vol. 3, o.s., pp. 224, 240, 256.

33 *RM*, vol. 3, o.s., pp. 304, 320.

34 See *RM*, vol. 1, n.s., pp. 176, 192, 320, 352, 368, 384; vol. 2, n.s., pp. 608, 640, 672, 688, 704, etc. I have seen none of the prints I describe here as they are not bound in with the British Library run, the only copy I have had access to.

35 The information on printers is taken from the table printed in Ellic Howe (ed.), *The London Compositor: Documents Relating to Wages, Working Conditions and Customs of the London Printing Trade 1785–1900* (London: Oxford University Press, 1947), pp. 299–302.

36 On Dicks's business acumen, see Anne Humpherys, 'John Dicks', in Patricia J. Anderson and Jonathan Rose (eds), *British Literary Publishing Houses, 1820–1880*, vol. 106 of the *Dictionary of Literary Biography*, (Detroit: Gale Research, 1991), pp. 126–8.

in that Reynolds's 'staff' (if such we may call regular contributors) was smaller and yet also wider in that in order to fill pages he exploited more extensively the general field of magazines. Despite its title and the portrait of Reynolds on the very first front page, the *Miscellany* was not the work of one man alone, though it more or less consistently stuck to the brand values associated with his name. Rather, Reynolds was the core of a network of workers in a particular area of the literary field, rather than the visual or printing fields, where Dicks emerges as more dynamic.

At first, the *Magazine* comprised the serialization of *Wagner the Wehr-Wolf* by Reynolds, which occupied between six and seven of its 16 pages. An illustrated (but never sexualized) *Anatomy and Physiology of Ourselves Popularly Considered* by James Johnson comprised another two. Another page or less was composed of an unsigned series called 'The Provincial Press of the United Kingdom'. It is clearly modelled on a series on the metropolitan press in the *London Journal* under Reynolds and both series were probably written by him.[37] The rest is made up of extracts from other publications, 'Notices to Correspondents', which, to begin with, consisted of less than one column (though it later grew to around a page), and a column or so of adverts. The extracts constitute over a third of the whole, a proportion considerably greater than in the *London Journal* or the *Family Herald*.

Excluding signatures that appear just once – which means the piece might be lifted from elsewhere – the circle of contributors of original written material to the *Miscellany* was very small and inconstant. James Johnson never became established, appearing only as the author of the anatomy series in the first two volumes (though his other publications continue to be advertised). His abilities were too specialized. John Taylor Sinnett, a translator who worked for the *London Journal*, contributed several pieces to the *Miscellany*. He never became a major presence either. Even though Anthony Peck's *Park House Catechism* (on electricity) is frequently referred to both in 'Notices' and in adverts, he wrote only a few articles and some single episode tales for the *Miscellany*. More curiously given her own literary work, which is extensively advertised and, indeed, defended from attack, Reynolds's wife Susannah has no prose and just two poems printed in the five volumes studied here – unless she wrote anonymously or pseudonymously. This chapter can unfortunately shed little light on this overshadowed woman.[38]

Only two writers even remotely approach Reynolds's luminous centrality over the period I have mapped here: Gabriel Alexander and Edwin F. Roberts. Alexander was a Scottish advocate born in 1793 who moved to London to gain access to publishing circles. The 1841 Census lists him as a writer in Southwark, though by 1851 when living alone in Westminster, he defines himself as an 'advocate'. The earliest work I

---

37 I recommend both series for the detail they provide regarding staffing, politics and finances of individual titles: see 'The Newspaper Press of London', *LJ*, vols 1 and 2 (1845–46); *RM*, vol. 1, o.s. (1846–47) with an updated account in *RM*, vol. 2, n.s., p. 496.

38 Her named work comprises just 'The Man-of-war', *RM*, vol. 1, o.s., p. 377; 'The Belle of the Village', *RM*, vol. 2, o.s., p. 9. Writing as 'Mrs G.W.M. Reynolds', Susannah also contributed a novel, *The Poacher's Daughter*, to volume 1 of the *Weekly Magazine*, a halfpenny journal that was being published simultaneously from the same office as *RM*, from no. 9 (26 February 1848) to no. 24 (10 June 1848). On Reynolds's defence of Susannah's *Gretna Green*, see *RM*, vol. 3, o.s., pp. 46–7, 95.

have found by him is the 24-page tale *Fair Maid of Wyoming*, published by Steward of the Strand in 1846. In its introduction Alexander claims to have visited the United States, which puts him amongst the bohemian group who sought to turn experience into money. He wrote regularly for *Reynolds's Miscellany* from 6 March 1847, when a medieval tale with allegorizing commentary entitled 'Woman's Mission' appeared. Thereafter hardly an issue appeared without a one-episode tale by him.

Edwin Roberts was born in Liverpool in 1819 and marks himself as a writer in the Census reports of both 1841 and 1851 (and 'journalist' in 1861). The earliest publication by him I have found comprises *Essays and Poems*, published in 1844 by the respectable house of Saunders and Otley. A collage of commonplaces gleaned from high-status sources mixed with an enthusiasm for *amplificatio* renders him an excellent choice for writing in the late 1840s mass market with its demands on writing fixed amounts to a fixed schedule.

> Where are they all? Where have these emperors vanished? Power combined, and wrought, and linked, and interwoven, that they would seem to end only with the world – they are gone – swept away into some soundless sea, that tells not when or how they were lost, scattered into infinite elements – stones, and old chronicles are alone left to us. Babylon is no more, and the satyrs are dancing among the broken walls, and foul things nestle where princely heads were wont to lay …[39]

Roberts's name first appeared as an author in the *Miscellany* on 15 April 1848, with a biography of the opera singer Marietta Alboni on its front page, a decidedly tame subject when Reynolds was busy with Chartism. Thereafter Roberts took over as main contributor and editor, concentrating on literary and artistic (i.e., safe) topics. When Reynolds returned for the beginning of the new series on 15 July, Roberts continued to contribute single-episode tales and a set of six-part serials.

The early years of the *Miscellany*, then, although dependent upon a circle of writers, were very much centred upon Reynolds. This meant that he could afford neither illness nor holiday: he had to become a perfectly oiled machine. That this was impossible to sustain is evident from 'Notices'. First, there are announcements that the editor has mislaid correspondents' 'Letters'.[40] Second, there are complaints about his fiction published both inside and outside the *Miscellany*: several correspondents wrote to complain of how *The Parricide* ended too abruptly, for instance – they wanted to know what happened to Catherine Crawford and Captain Stuart. Reynolds possibly forgot to tie up this story arc, but he replied that he did not need to do so for it was obvious that the couple got married.[41] Sometimes episodes of his serials are short or missing altogether, or the words do not match the illustrations. One week Reynolds had to omit episodes of both *Wagner* and *Days of Hogarth* because he is 'indisposed' (as James Johnson did with his *Anatomy* series).[42] At other times, it is

---

39   E.F. Roberts, 'Time', in *Essays and Poems* (London: Saunders and Otley, 1844), p. 17.

40   See, e.g., *RM*, vol. 1, o.s., p. 431; vol. 2, o.s., pp. 96, 384; vol. 3, o.s., p. 144.

41   *RM*, vol. 2, o.s., p. 143.

42   *RM*, vol. 1, o.s., p. 197; vol. 2, o.s., p. 128.

clear that Reynolds has simply been too busy to fulfil his writing quota.[43] This is especially common around the time of his political involvements, and culminates in a rather peevish self-justification:

> We do not pledge ourselves to give a specific quantity each week; and when you consider that in a period of nineteen months you have had two complete Tales from our pen, you surely can allow *us* a little holiday now and then. If we pause at times, it is only to gather energy for a renewed application to our literary duties.[44]

Reynolds identified his *Miscellany* as a production of his own body. In this, the periodical was by now old-fashioned: neither the *Family Herald* nor the *London Journal* make public justifications of the kind just quoted, nor are they so publicly dependent on individuals even while exploiting the Star Name of the individual author. Even if they underwent similar vicissitudes, they simply did not admit it. Rather, they projected an identity based on the regular, reliable, smoothly operating steam press, a conception where bodies were replaceable just like the spare parts of a machine. If somebody were 'indisposed' for whatever reason, their functions could be taken up by somebody else. This is a radical alienation of labour in the face of industrial production and demands by the consumer. It is a split of body and name which in the 1840s Reynolds was resolutely refusing to submit to – he identified his 'brand' with the products of his labouring body, not with a disincarnate name. By the late 1860s, however, he had come to accept such alienation, selling to Dicks not only his copyrights but also the right to use his name.[45]

Further conclusions about how Reynolds negotiated the gruelling demands of periodical production can be drawn from a study of the relationship between the adverts, 'Notices' and the extracts. In my study of the *London Journal* I sought to determine whether networks could be revealed through higher concentrations of extracts from certain publishers or authors. I found none. But the same technique produces striking results in the case of the *Miscellany*, demonstrating very clearly that 'network' does not only mean a set of contributors who produce material expressly for a publication.

What I discovered was a marked seepage between adverts, 'Notices' and extracts, extending the typographic blurring between advert and reply to correspondent that I have already described. A common practice in the *Miscellany* was for a work to be advertised, for an extract or two to be printed in the main body (often praised in a footnote), and a couple of weeks later, for readers to be referred to it in 'Notices'. These referrals would be repeated over an extended period as providing answers to queries. The *Miscellany* in this light becomes not only a showcase for Reynolds's own products but a rolling advertisement for those of his network (who are not necessarily contributors) as well.

---

43   See *RM*, vol. 1, o.s., p. 192; vol. 3, o.s., pp. 16, 111, 288, 400.

44   J.H.R.G., *RM*, vol. 3, o.s., p. 400 (29 April 1848).

45   Anne Humpherys, 'Generic Strands and Urban Twists: The Victorian Mysteries Novel', *Victorian Studies*, 34 (1991): 455–72, quoting Montague Summers, 'John Dicks, Publisher', *Times Literary Supplement*, 7 November 1942, p. 552.

At times, it is possible to trace the links between the members of the network quite specifically. In one case, a publisher seems the tie. James Gilbert of 49 Paternoster Square published Reynolds's *Master Timothy's Bookcase*, the *Household Book of Practical Receipts* by 'Mrs Pierson' (i.e., Reynolds's wife)[46] and James Johnson's *Ready Remedies in Cases of Poison and Other Accidents*. From the first number, all three texts are regularly advertised on the last page of each issue of the *Miscellany*; in almost every issue, 'Notices' direct readers to the last two for information. Soon Reynolds would refuse to answer any more queries in 'Notices' that he felt might be better dealt with – or already had been dealt with – in his wife's book, instead referring readers to that publication in almost every number.[47] Furthermore, besides being mentioned in adverts and 'Notices', an extract from Johnson's *Ready Remedies* appeared in the main body of the periodical, in addition to his series on anatomy.[48]

Reynolds's relationship with the *Weekly Dispatch* constitutes another interesting case. This newspaper was the second to be described in the *London Journal*'s series on metropolitan newspapers (after *The Times*), its editor, Mr Wrightson, and its other contributors highly praised. This was just confirming what the market already knew: it is recorded that the *Dispatch* had the highest circulation of all newspapers between 1843 and 1845, weekly or daily. After *The Times*, it had the highest number of advertisements, indicating its elevated status as a space for public communication.[49] In the *Miscellany*, praises for the *Dispatch* continue in adverts, in prose extracts in the main body and in many 'Notices'.[50] Furthermore, the *Miscellany* reprints poems by Eliza Cook taken from the *Dispatch*, always with footnotes commending the paper.[51] In an article lauding 'the most eminent female writers of the age' (Cook, Lady Blessington and Mrs Norton), Cook is described as '*par excellence* our national poetess', of 'almost unparalleled popularity'. The piece is also careful to include a celebration of the *Dispatch*, remarking its 'immense circulation' of 60,000.[52] What readers of the *Miscellany* outside Reynolds's immediate circle would not have known

46   Elsewhere her maiden name is spelled 'Pearson'. The publication came out in penny parts before appearing in volume form. Mrs Reynolds wrote it in collaboration with W.E. Hall, an author of non-fiction for *LJ* until January 1848.

47   Referrals to the *Household Book* begin in issue 2; from issue 20 notices appear informing correspondents that all relevant 'Letters' have been handed to the editors of the *Household Book* and will be dealt with there.

48   *RM*, vol. 1, o.s., p. 45.

49   *LJ*, vol. 1, p. 54 and cf. the circulations given of the other weeklies described in the series. On the *Dispatch*'s circulation in 1843, see [F.D.] Lewis and Lowe, *The Advertisers' Guide to the Newspaper Press of the United Kingdom*, 3rd edn (London: Lewis and Lowe, 1844), p. 13.

50   See, e.g., *RM*, vol. 1, o.s., p. 144; vol. 2, o.s., p. 48; vol. 3, o.s., pp. 313–17; vol. 2, n.s., p. 496, where the *Dispatch*'s (i.e., Reynolds's own) are singled out as the best accounts of France.

51   *RM*, vol. 2, o.s., pp. 151, 398; vol. 3, o.s., pp. 233, 371; vol. 1, n.s., pp. 88, 335; vol. 2, n.s., pp. 471, 733, 767, 791, 847.

52   *RM*, vol. 1, o.s., pp. 233–4.

was that Reynolds had been the foreign editor of the *Dispatch* since 1842 and would continue to be so until after his bankruptcy in 1848.[53]

This interaction between advertising and extracting has a double, political, function which operates in the interest of both the network as a whole and the individual producer who organizes it: for the producer, it fills empty pages without costs beyond printing; for members of the network, it is an advertisement. Authors were willing to provide material from already published works free of charge (rather than take Reynolds to court for breach of copyright) in return for recommendation of the full-length work. What was essential for them was that the origins of the extracts be acknowledged and, preferably, praised. Such puffing, part of the general practice of 'reviewing' in many other magazines, can and should be seen as the result of cooperation in the face of economic adversity. Networks are drawn on to enable the economic survival of the individual or group, who in return supports the wider network.

It would be wrong to claim that all extracts in the *Miscellany* work in the same way, even if they partake in the system I have just described, for there seem to have been three levels of engagement in it. First of all, there are the works of Reynolds's immediate contacts, to which readers are adverted in the ways I have described. Second, at a greater distance from Reynolds, are the works advertised and then extracted, but which are not referred to constantly in 'Notices'. Third, and most distant from Reynolds in the field, are the magazines mined for extracts, column fillers or the 'Miscellaneous' section that made up the few pages before 'Notices'. In this case, there is little indication that Reynolds knew the producers personally. As in the *London Journal*, *Punch* was the carcass that the *Miscellany* picked at for the vast majority of its fillers, quoted over four times more frequently than its nearest rival in volume 1, the satirical monthly *Go-a-head Journal* – a confirmation of *Punch*'s immense cultural penetration beyond its immediate readership. From October 1847 *Punch*'s competitor *The Man in the Moon* started to be quoted almost as much, and in some issues much more.

In the new series, however, this dependence on the comic-satiric evaporated in favour of longer extracts from expensive magazines such as the three-shilling *Belle Assemblée* or the half-crown *Fraser's*. This was not a new practice but an intensification of one, suggesting that the implied reader of the *Miscellany* was becoming more genteel than he already was. These longer extracts are often accompanied by a footnote adverting the reader to 'this month's excellent issue'.[54] The small fillers, on the other hand, acted as advertisements for the original periodicals in their own right through the very frequency with which their titles were printed.

Almost all publications extracted would have been well beyond the pockets of clerks, shopkeepers and aspirant midshipmen, and one might conclude that

---

53 Louis James, 'Reynolds, George William MacArthur', in H.C.G. Matthew and Brian Harrison (eds), *Oxford Dictionary of National Biography: From the Earliest Times to the Year 2000* (New York: Oxford University Press, 2004), vol. 46, p. 537. At his trial Reynolds refused to divulge the name of the paper he worked for, saying he would be instantly dismissed were it known. It seems he was dismissed anyway.

54 See, e.g., *RM*, vol. 1, o.s., p. 61; vol. 3, o.s., p. 11; vol. 1, n.s., pp. 44, 123.

advertisements in them would be useless. However, the sycophantic footnotes, like the stated sources, should be read not only as addressing potential consumers but also as mantras, directed towards publishers, intended to ward off the threat of prosecution for piracy. As such, they constitute a declaration of belief in the system of private intellectual property, which is confirmed many times by other writing in the *Miscellany*. That Reynolds thought this prophylaxis would work (and there is no reason to think that it did not) suggests that he was exploiting the common fantasy of a unified literary market. In a direct contradiction of hard-headed marketing knowledge (legible in *Mitchell's Press Directory*), it was believed worthwhile being advertised throughout society, even if it meant that one's publications were dismembered. Underlying this was a Whiggish trope that 'good' material would drive out the bad – that the private property of certain businessmen would eliminate that of others according to the 'natural law' of the market.[55] Whether Reynolds himself subscribed to this belief in the natural law of the market rather than simply making use of it for his own ends remains to be seen.

'Letters to the Industrious Classes'

Of all the elements comprising *Reynolds's Miscellany*, amongst the most salient to a discussion of politics explicitly represented (as opposed to enacted or implied) is a series of seven 'Letters to the Industrious Classes' published at irregular intervals between 13 January and 14 May 1847.[56] After a 'General Address', there are 'Letters' to 'Cotton Spinners and Weavers', 'Needlewomen' (by 'Plain John'), 'Young Men Studying to become National Schoolmasters', 'Preceptors' (by Anthony Peck), 'Governesses' (by John Taylor Sinnett) and 'Agricultural Labourers'. Although the question of national consciousness is not raised in the course of the essays, all groups are addressed as belonging to 'the United Kingdom'. In the initial 'Letter', Reynolds reassures readers that he will 'not enter upon political disquisitions' (he knew that if he did the *Miscellany* would be liable to stamp duty). The 'Letters' will be 'moral, domestic and social. They will, therefore, offend no partisan or annoy the feelings of any sectarian'. In this, he is exploiting the familiar restrictive definition of 'politics' as 'party politics': that leaves open for analysis the organization of social relations and its concomitant, the distribution of resources.[57] It is this latter, indeed, that the 'Letters' are concerned to document and denounce.

Reynolds's support for the notion of private property and opposition to communism and socialism is made clear from the start:

> I do not say you should share the profits of your employer: I admit that he must be adequately recompensed for his outlay of capital, the interest on that capital, the risk he

---

55 On the strategic use of the concept of 'natural law' and nature in general in the justification of different economic systems, see Catherine Gallagher, *The Body Economic: Life, Death and Sensation in Political Economy and the Victorian Novel* (Princeton, NJ: Princeton University Press, 2006).

56 See Humpherys, 'G.W.M. Reynolds', p. 81.

57 Cf. King, *The London Journal*, p. 182.

incurs, the bad debts that may deteriorate his profits, and the anxiety of mind invariably attendant on the spirit of speculation. These reasons will show why his gains, my friends, should in justice be larger than your's [*sic*]; but they will not prove why they should be so much larger than they are. The proportion is not fairly adjusted: he has far too much – and you far too little.[58]

Reynolds is indeed very much in favour of free trade and against all forms of protectionism: free trade, he claims, brings benefits to the poor. This is confirmed by much of the writing in the *Miscellany*, though two particularly striking examples will suffice. The first is a piece on a front page celebrating a huge new bakery in south London that is able to undercut its rivals in the area, bringing cheaper bread to the poor. The piece fails to consider the wider economic and social fallout of the predicted collapse of small bakeries. Second, there is high praise for a publication by S.Y. Collins, *How to Get Money: or, Six Ways of Making a Fortune*, 'cleverly written ... most valuable to those who have spirit and enterprise sufficient to make a bold dash in either of the departments of speculation treated'.[59] The lengthy extract chosen for reproduction concerns advertising, the public communication of capitalism and a practice already fingered as central to this chapter. Patent medicines and cosmetics are the recommended products to sell because they cost next to nothing to produce and '[a]ll the capital that can be obtained, therefore, can be laid out in giving publicity. In this way Rowlands expends £30,000 a year. His profits must be immense'.[60] This puff in praise of advertising appears in the same issue as the letter to aspiring national schoolmasters who are warned that they will make only £40–£50 a year, not the £100 they are usually promised. Two years later, adverts will appear for Barker's Genuine Enamel, 'universally acknowledged to be the best discovery yet made, for curing Toothache', and for other such remedies, including cures for baldness.[61]

The fact that three of the six 'Letters' addressed to particular categories of workers are involved in education is very significant, for, besides free trade, the other cornerstone of Reynolds's strategy to improve the lot of the exploited is a national education system. This, he claims, will enable the industrious classes to know and understand their position in society and 'appreciate the relative condition of your employers and yourselves, treating them as they deserve to be treated, and still maintaining your own just rights and privileges'.[62] In an article by John Taylor Sinnett on 'How to Read' inserted between the 'Letters' in an analogous position,

58 'Letters to the Industrious Classes', 'Letter I – General Address', vol. 1, o.s., p. 199. See also a lengthy Notice in which Reynolds emphatically denies he is a socialist (vol. 2, n.s., p. 832, dated 7 July 1849).

59 *RM*, vol. 1, o.s., p. 283.

60 Rowland produced a variety of quack medicines and cosmetics, including the famous Macassar Oil. The firm was notorious for its extensive and confident advertising, claiming patronage from royalty of several nations (see E.S. Turner, *The Shocking History of Advertising* [London: Michael Joseph, 1952], pp. 57–8).

61 These quack medicines start appearing from September 1848 and evidently constitute a new source of revenue: see *RM*, vol. 1, n.s., pp. 160, 192, 268, 224, 240, etc. See above for their possible relation to the optional extra prints.

62 *RM*, vol. 1, o.s., p. 200.

reading is praised because '*the finest spirits in a country have always been diligent readers*', because it '*makes men better*' and because it is cheap.[63] This emphasis on free trade and education has particular resonance for a man who makes his living in the print industry: education is a prerequisite for the consumption of printed words, and the circulation of the latter is hampered by the taxes on knowledge, considered in the same way as the Corn Laws, as an artificial increase in the price of the commodity in order to maintain an oligopoly. If any political action is advocated in these 'Letters' beyond the formation of a very general group consciousness based on position in production, it is that deprived groups should be enabled to access the media to agitate for more resources. In other words, to end their oppression, these groups need to be educated and financially able to participate in the public sphere of print culture and gain the ability to self-represent. That most are not able to speak for themselves as yet – not even the governesses whose high educational standards are so extolled – is evident from the fact that only the 'Letter to Preceptors' is written by a 'Fellow Labourer', all the others being written by Reynolds himself, by 'Plain John' or by J[ohn] T[aylor] S[innet]. When oppressed groups do eventually speak, it is a 'law of nature' that they will correct the errors propagated about them and end their exploitation. The 'Letter to Governesses' (by Sinnett) concludes in typical fashion with an analogy drawn from nature and an assumption of a people's natural disposition:

> That your salaries would be increased, and that an ultimate provision would be made for you at the end of your professional career, provided you took measures to assert your claim, is as certain as that there is a sun above your heads. The British people are not naturally unjust, but they take a long time in seeing a grievance of which they are the cause. *They are also quite indisposed to help those who are too tame, too easy and compliant.*[64]

A different version of the same point is legible in 'Letter II', 'To the Cotton Spinners and Weavers of the United Kingdom', by Reynolds. After asserting the importance of this group through stressing its size, almost the whole of the piece comprises a criticism of publications about the industry for their lack of attention to the condition of the workers. Specifically marked for criticism are the entry 'Cotton' in the *Penny Cyclopedia* and the references to cotton in Geoffrey Richardson Porter's *Progress of the Nation*, both originally published by Charles Knight, one of Reynolds's inveterate competitors and indeed enemies.[65] The writers of these publications may laud innovations in machinery and the progress of the industry when considering national output, but because they are from the same 'Order' as the employers, claims Reynolds, they do not ask '*has the state of the cottonworker kept pace with the fortune of his employer?*' (italics in original). Nor do these texts enquire whether moral progress has been made amongst the workers. The 'Letter' ends by exhorting spinners and weavers to assert their rights as honest Englishmen.

---

63   *RM*, vol. 1, o.s., pp. 377–80, emphasis in the original.

64   *RM*, vol. 1, o.s., p. 367, italics in original.

65   *The Progress of the Nation, in its Various Social and Economical Relations, from the Beginning of the Nineteenth Century to the Present Time* came out first (in parts) from 1836. A new edition was published by Murray later in 1847.

How to do that exactly is not stated beyond that they should educate themselves. But Reynolds has shown by the example of the article itself how to use that education: to publish alternative accounts of industrial 'progress' from the point of view of the worker. In the same vein, the next 'Letter' offers as a solution to the exploitation of needlewomen the collection and publication of prices charged by employers for work and for the products of work – something Reynolds was to do for them in his 1850 *Miscellany* serial *The Seamstress, or The White Slave of England*.[66] This will right the wrongs done to them. In both cases, publication is the *natural* solution to exploitation. What prevents this natural communication in the public sphere is the absence of a free market for print and its necessary prerequisite, education for all.

However, as both the extract on advertising and Reynolds's printed circulation figures have shown, publication also allows for the dissemination of false claims. This includes false claims about false claims: for it is in fact untrue that the moral condition of workers is ignored in Porter's *Progress of the Nation*, although whether Porter calls for social intervention is ambiguous. What Reynolds has done in his critique is to simplify, implicitly comparing products from two rival firms, his own and Knight's. In ways typical of advertisement, he sets up a problem and offers a solution: his products offer a utopian answer to misery, fusing politics (in the sense of a call for the redistribution of resources) and commercialism in ways that the competition does not. As such, the 'Letter' remains very much within capitalist rhetoric and social processes.

The 'Letters' also lay themselves open to the criticism that they only deal with what was visible to the educated urban bourgeoisie: needlewomen were easy to see from this perspective, since they had already attained high visibility in the press since Hood's 'Song of the Shirt' in *Punch* in 1843.[67] However, three of the four occupations which David Vincent has called 'the vanguard of the Industrial Revolution' – potters, metal workers and miners – are not addressed at all.[68] The *Miscellany*'s final 'Letter to Agricultural Workers' seems a realization that there has been oversight. Interestingly, here the addressee is unstable: though there is an occasional second-person exhortation, most of the piece discusses agricultural workers in the third person, offering measures that Parliament (not workers themselves) can take to alleviate their plight. An article nine months later by John Taylor Sinnett about 'The Woollen Clothworkers of the United Kingdom' reads as another afterthought to the series. This does not address the clothworkers directly at all, although it again recommends publication of information as the answer to poor wages. Here too is rendered explicit what was only ambiguous before: the real enemy is idleness, not the masters. Whatever we may have liked to think in our attempts to claim ancestors

---

66 See Rohan McWilliam, 'The Melodramatic Seamstress: Interpreting a Victorian Penny Dreadful', in Beth Harris (ed.), *Famine and Fashion: Needlewomen in the Nineteenth Century* (Aldershot: Ashgate, 2005), p. 103.

67 On Hood's 'Song of the Shirt', see T.J. Edelstein, '"The Song of the Shirt": The Visual Iconology of the Seamstress', *Victorian Studies*, 23 (1980): 183–210 and '"Weary Stitches": Illustrations and Paintings for Thomas Hood's "Song of the Shirt" and Other Poems', in Harris (ed.), *Famine and Fashion*, pp. 13–39.

68 David Vincent, *Literacy and Popular Culture: England 1750–1914* (Cambridge: Cambridge University Press, 1989), p. 96.

of leftist thought, 'industrious' meant 'hard-working' after all; it was not, in this series anyway, a mid-Victorian synonym for 'industrial'. The Malthusian inflection and Whiggish politics are clear:

> The clothworkers of Great Britain should know that it is their duty to defend themselves. They must collect information; they must know the stock of their manufacture throughout the kingdom; they must compare their master's profits with their own labour, – what they get with what they do.... Their masters are not their real enemies, and very soon will be fellow-sufferers with them. A great battle between land and labour is approaching, and the large community of idle men ... are now conspiring together to stop the progress of trade and industry, and plunder the new generations. Every one feels that the increase of population must push the labourer and manufacturer against the proprietors of land, and that as the working man has been deprived of all he can spare, the new millions of human mouths, as they start into existence, must be fed some how or other out of the corn-lofts of the oppressors.[69]

What is perhaps more significant about all the non-addressed groups than their lack of visibility to a metropolitan bourgeoisie is their low literacy. They are not yet potential consumers of the *Miscellany*. Even if few schoolmasters and governesses actually wrote in and bought the *Miscellany*, at least those social groups had the ability to read and purchase. It was thus worthwhile addressing them to expand the circulation in those demographic areas. It could be argued that Reynolds did not address non-literate groups because, even though cases of one worker reading out loud to his or her colleagues are well documented, he did not realize that his message could be orally disseminated. But pleas of ignorance overlook how the need to raise circulation was at the core of Reynolds's strategy, however unsuccessful it was at this time. For the survival of the *Miscellany* and to keep him out of bankruptcy, he had to boost *sales*, not gifted dissemination of knowledge.

In the new series, after his involvement with Chartism had begun, Reynolds presented the reader with much more startling material than the 'Letters'. Especially striking is the illustrated series 'The Coal Mines of Great Britain', which comprises nine parts in volume 2, continued with three more pieces (unillustrated) on 'The Coal Mines of the Continent'. This is not addressed to miners but to readers whose awareness 'of the horrors endured by a great number of our fellow creatures' needs to be raised. One important incitement to action is the 'demoralisation' of the miners, the blame for which 'must not rest on the operatives themselves, but upon the Legislature which has adopted such trifling, tardy and ineffectual means to ameliorate the conditions, and improve the minds of the denizens of the coal pits'.[70] This was a common plea amongst liberal social critics. The implied reader Reynolds constructs here is much more specifically urban, educated and domestic, who nonetheless likes to feel outraged – and perhaps slightly titillated – by such examples of demoralization as an illustration which shows a woman in tatters cranking a pulley to lower into a mine shaft a semi-naked girl sitting astride the lap of an equally unclothed boy.

---

69 *RM*, vol. 3, o.s., p. 236.
70 *RM*, vol. 2, n.s., p. 456.

Edwin Roberts was now providing series which likewise thrilled and appalled, always according to the same pattern: *The Road to Transportation. In Six Steps*; *The Six Stages of Punishment, or The Victim of a Vitiated Society*; *The Life of a Labourer, or Six Episodes of Emigration*; *The Road to Happiness. In Six Steps*; *The Gamester's Progress. In Six Stages.* The fiction as a whole indeed (which also included at this stage the concluding episodes of Reynolds's *Coral Island* and his *Bronze Statue, or The Virgin's Kiss*) has a consolatory function: at the end of each, resources are redistributed according to moral worth – as *The Bookseller* was to point out in Reynolds's obituary, the novels in the *Miscellany* are 'admirable in their style and unexceptionable in their tendency'.[71] Utopian, they are thus unlike the documentary exposés of the mineworkers which call for redistributive action but do not imagine it possible in the present:

> Were the proprietors to set aside some small portion of their gains, – and to do so, even deprive themselves (if necessary) of some few luxuries, and devote a sum for the sole purpose of ameliorating the conditions of the men they employ, – their purse would not suffer much, and humanity would be a great gainer. Alas! their thoughts are generally directed to a balance-sheet ...[72]

If, then, I have been suggesting that the majority of words in the *Miscellany* are fundamentally inoffensive, conservative even, I also have to state that a new feature of 'Notices' is not. The first volume of the second series had headed many notices with lengthy puffs of new works such as a new edition of *Sketches of her Majesty's Household* or *The Emigration Circular*.[73] Large numbers of these works concerned social or political questions which Reynolds highlighted. From the middle of the second volume, however, Reynolds replaced the puffs with his own commentaries on topics of the day which directly asked the reader to notice some social outrage (a development of the social exposé aspect of the *Reynolds* brand). These could almost be leaders from his later *Political Instructor* (in fact they seem to have been suggested by a letter from a correspondent in response to the pieces on mines). Subjects covered include sinecures and pensions to aristocrats, the exploitation of needlewomen by 'emporiums' which sell cheap clothing, the recent reduction of factory workers' wages in Glasgow, the brutality of military discipline, and so on.[74] If there is any masquerade here where news pretends to be something else to avoid paying stamp duty, it is typographical, since these pieces adopt the same typeface as the rest of 'Notices' – which, it also has to be said, continue the mélange of advert and answer familiar from the old series. Politics is thus drawn into the personal and the commercial so that it is visually indistinguishable from them.

This intertwining of clashing strands is symptomatic of our difficulty in defining Reynolds today. In May 1848, bankruptcy looming, he declared in a notice, in larger

---

71 *The Bookseller*, 3 July 1879, p. 601.

72 'The Coal Mines of Great Britain II. – Accidents', *RM*, vol. 2, n.s., p. 471. In similar vein, Edwin Roberts was to publish a gloomy and rather shocked *Visit to the Environs and Ironworks of Merthyr Tydfil* (London: William Pointer, 1853).

73 *RM*, vol. 1, n.s., pp. 64, 175.

74 See *RM*, vol. 2, n.s., pp. 624, 688, 752, 784, 800, 816.

than usual type, addressed 'To My Late Constituents of Derby', that he could not take up the offer of representing them as his 'literary avocations occup[ied] nearly the whole of [his] time'. He went on:

> as my works are all weekly serials, any interruption to the issue of which on the appointed days would prove ruinous to them and most detrimental to my reputation as an author, I felt that if I sate [*sic*] in the National Assembly I must either neglect the interests of my constituents or the pursuits whereby I obtain a livelihood for myself and my family.
>
> Now as you *can* find a good and true man to devote his whole time in the National Assembly to the object of his vicarious mission – and as the nature of my profession is such that its duties must be discharged by myself, and *cannot* be performed by a substitute, – you will admit that while my withdrawal from the representation of Derby is absolutely required by my own affairs, it does not in any way militate against your interests ...
>
> With my pen I shall continue to labour arduously and enthusiastically in the good cause; and I hope to be able occasionally to attend public meetings, where I may raise my voice in behalf of the oppressed Millions, and against a vile and execrable oligarchy.[75]

The extract, in some way a summation of this entire chapter, shows Reynolds's refusal to separate his body from his name that I commented on earlier, as well as a tense entanglement of the personal and familial with commercial and political motives. That each pulled him in contrary directions is obvious. That each injured the other is certain. Hardly the 'able speculator' that Marx called him – Stiff and Dicks were far more able – Reynolds nonetheless exploited any technique he could to keep the leaky hull of the *Miscellany* afloat and, more importantly for him, his family in the circumstances he believed they deserved.

75　*RM*, vol. 3, o.s., p. 432.

Chapter 4

G.W.M. Reynolds, *Reynolds's Newspaper* and Popular Politics

Michael H. Shirley

Reynolds's Newspaper, founded in 1850 by George W.M. Reynolds in the aftermath of the last great Chartist demonstrations of 1848, was a radical newspaper in the tradition of earlier Chartist newspapers, most notably the *Northern Star*.[1] As with the *Northern Star*, reading *Reynolds's Newspaper* was in itself an act of political expression.[2] The context, however, was different. In the decades following the 'end' of the Chartist era, *Reynolds's Newspaper* stood alone as the most popular and stable radical weekly, espousing radicalism and reform with every issue.[3] As such,

---

1   Aled G. Jones, 'Chartist Journalism and Print Culture in Britain, 1830–1855', in Joan Allen and Owen R. Ashton (eds), *Papers for the People: A Study of the Chartist Press* (London: Merlin Press, 2005), p. 17.

2   See James Epstein, *Radical Expression: Political Language, Ritual, and Symbol in England, 1790–1850* (Oxford: Oxford University Press, 1994), pp. 148–9.

3   While scholars generally agree that *RN* was a successful, widely circulated publication, its real circulation numbers are not exactly known. Ellegard estimates that *RN* sold approximately 50,000 copies a week in 1855, a figure that increased to 60,000 by 1860, 150,000 in 1865 and 200,000 in 1870 (Alvar Ellegard, *The Readership of the Periodical Press in Mid-Victorian Britain* [Göteborg: Göteborgs Universitets Årsskrift, 1957], p. 20). The only other figures available are from *RN* itself, which claimed in 1851 that its circulation was over 20,000 weekly, and still growing (*RN*, 14 December 1851, p. 8). In 1857, circulation was estimated to be upwards of 100,000, and was said to be past 150,000 by 1858 (*RN*, 4 January 1857; 13 June 1858, p. 8). In 1870, when Ellegard claimed that it sold 200,000 copies per week, *RN* also claimed a guaranteed circulation of 200,000, but noted a steady increase in actual circulation: it claimed sales of 230,000 in February (*RN*, 27 February 1870, p. 4); 240,000 in May (*RN*, 22 May 1870, p. 4); 250,000 in July (*RN*, 24 July 1870, p. 4); 280,000 in August (*RN*, 28 August 1870, p. 4); and 300,000 in September (11 September 1870, p. 4). Even assuming that Ellegard was conservative in his estimations, and that *RN* was overly enthusiastic, it is clear that it had a very large circulation. Raw circulation numbers alone, however, do not tell the entire story of the size of its readership. Reading for the working classes was often communal in nature (Elizabeth Long, 'Textual Interpretation as Collective Action', in Jon Cruz and Justin Lewis [eds], *Viewing, Reading, Listening: Audiences and Cultural Reception* [Boulder, CO: Westview Press, 1994], p. 196). It was common for one man to read a newspaper aloud to others. Reynolds himself estimated that each copy of a weekly newspaper was read by at least five people (*RN*, 13 July 1862). Indeed, Sunday weeklies as a whole were more popular than daily papers, especially among members of the working classes. Raymond Williams asserts, convincingly, that Sunday weeklies were popular among the working classes as that was their only day of leisure, and they preferred

Reynolds's Newspaper acted as a national focus for radicals; it was essentially a national 'meeting in print' for Chartists and other radicals in the decades following the last great Chartist demonstrations. Reynolds himself assumed a leading role in the Chartist action of 1848, and would take a leading rhetorical position in the national radical community his newspaper helped keep alive.

Had Reynolds been a man of lesser gifts and luck, or had he been 'pure' in his political intentions, his career might well have paralleled that of Ernest Jones. They were both of fortunate birth, possessed literary talents, suffered financial setbacks and became noted figures in the world of working-class radical politics. But Jones never quite found a niche that would allow his talents to flourish in conjunction with his beliefs. In his *Newspaper*, Reynolds did. One reason for this may have been that Reynolds's radicalism was of longer duration, which means that his professional development was of a piece with his political development. Where Jones had converted to the side of the angels as an adult, Reynolds was a radical at a young age – he claimed he had been a republican since he was a boy – and never varied from his essential stance. While Reynolds has frequently been portrayed as an inadequate Chartist, he was actually a radical republican whose profession happened to be journalism. Despite his brief flirtation with the public political stage, he was a writer who was most effective in the medium he knew best. His favourite literary form, the melodrama, reflected his own melodramatic nature. A rich man who also laboured on behalf of the working classes, his life and his writing were extreme in tone. If he was volatile, egotistical and vituperative – as he surely was – he was also consistent in his beliefs; his message and his goal never changed. He wanted universal suffrage, the secret ballot and payment of Members of Parliament; these advances, he was sure, would lead inexorably to a republic in which all citizens would be free. This republican catechism of beliefs was at the core of his public positions. It would be the theme that organized the newspaper's narrative from its first issue.

In 1848, G.W.M. Reynolds was new to the world of public political action, but he had long been involved in publishing and it was natural that he would express his political beliefs in the context of a familiar system. *Reynolds's Political Instructor*, offered at the price of one penny, made its appearance on 10 November 1849. It was short – eight tabloid pages of three columns each – but as it was limited to opinion pieces rather than news, it was rich in argument beyond what *Reynolds's Newspaper* would be. The *Political Instructor* was overtly Chartist in tone and content from the start, but its polemic was expressed within the larger context of current European radicalism. As a commercial test vehicle for *Reynolds's Newspaper*, it was successful, but it was also an interesting newspaper in its own right and deserves some attention here.

Each issue of the *Political Instructor*, save the first, featured a brief front-page biography of a political hero or heroes.[4] The tone of these pieces was less

---

to read journals in a timely fashion (Raymond Williams, *Communications*, rev. edn [London: Chatto and Windus, 1966], p. 23). For the readers of *RN*, reading was both a social and a political activity.

4   Each of these biographies was illustrated with a portrait of the subject. The initial issue, however, seems to have caught Reynolds a bit short: portraits of Sir Joshua Walmsley,

hagiographic than might be expected. Although they were not inclined to include unflattering facts, they were for the most part straightforward accounts of the public career of the subject.

The newspaper, relying as it did on opinion rather than news, devoted most of its pages to several serials, one of them signed and the rest anonymous. Edwin Roberts, who would continue his association with Reynolds after the birth of *Reynolds's Weekly Newspaper*, offered 'A New History of England', which discussed the reign of each monarch since William the Conqueror. Roberts's argument was that English history, as it had hitherto been written, was a tapestry of lies, to which he offered correction. He wrote:

> We maintain, that the history of kings is the history of tyranny, and not the history of men or of humanity in any individual or aggregate shape. We hold that the lives of monarchs form the genealogy of crime. From their lust after power, their thirst for conquest, their avaricious grasping after the goods and the property of others, spring those misfortunes which a people lament generations after in tears and blood. From this bloated tyranny, which feeds upon human flesh, and which grows greater as the years roll by into centuries, has the whole race of mankind drawn its endless and fertile source of wretchedness, famine, massacres, and legal assassination.[5]

'The Rise, Progress, and Phases of Human Slavery: How It Came Into The World, And How It Shall Be Made To Go Out', a series of 21 articles by 'A National Reformer', almost certainly James Bronterre O'Brien,[6] attempted to show that, while chattel slavery had been abolished, the working classes were the equivalent of slaves. O'Brien went on to assert that the National Reform League offered the best hope for the working-class 'slaves' to free themselves. Reynolds himself contributed frequent signed leaders to *Reynolds's Political Instructor*, the first being an explanation of Chartism. 'Chartism', he stated, 'is a principle, and not a mere proposition. It contains within itself the evidence of its own truth.'[7] This bald assertion was typical of Reynolds's personal style; he preached to the converted as fellow men of intellect

---

MP, and Feargus O'Connor, the well-known Chartist leader, were printed, but no biography was offered. In printing the portraits, *RPI* seems to have marked a stylistic transition between *RM* and *RN*; the former was extensively illustrated and the latter was not illustrated for the first 20 years of its existence. The first illustrations to grace the pages of *RN* were prosaic: half-page maps of the 'seats of war', beginning on 7 August 1870, p. 4. Detailed etchings of the European countryside, they were designed to familiarize readers with the geography of the land on which the Franco-Prussian wars were being fought. The maps were continued throughout the month with notable results: circulation jumped by 30,000 (*RN*, 11 September 1870, p. 8).

5   *RPI*, 10 November 1849, pp. 3–4.

6   Alfred Plummer, *Bronterre: A Political Biography of Bronterre O'Brien, 1804–1864* (London: George Allen and Unwin, 1971), p. 194. O'Brien's connection with *RPI* and *RN* is unclear. Plummer asserts that he probably worked for *RN* for about three months, probably wrote leaders and may have helped with the editing (pp. 203–4). Whatever the details, *RN* would twice note that he was not working there after mid-August 1850 (*RN*, 15 September 1850, p. 4; 22 December 1850, p. 4).

7   *RPI*, 17 November 1849, p. 10.

and common sense. He did not seek to convince his readers with argument, but to instruct them with carefully selected facts. Given the normally assertive premise, the conclusions were self-evident: 'To those who have studied Chartism with an unbiased mind, there is no merit in becoming its proselytes – because such proselytism is only a natural adhesion which men of common sense give to principles of common sense.'[8] As interesting and provocative as the *Political Instructor* was, it did not seem likely to be stable enough to provide a long-term outlet for Reynolds's political ideas. It seems clear that his mind turned quickly to establishing a more permanent journal. *Reynolds's Weekly Newspaper* began life on 5 May 1850.[9]

The *Newspaper* continued some of the features the *Political Instructor* had contained, but was a markedly different publication. Whereas the *Political Instructor* had been overtly pedantic in tone and title, the *Newspaper* contented itself with maintaining a heated polemic, dropping the somewhat superior tone in which the *Political Instructor* had often addressed its readers, and including them within the gates of heaven. The reader assumed a rhetorical place beside the editor and writers, looking out at the horrors of society. The first issue of *Reynolds's Weekly Newspaper, a Journal of Democratic Progress and General Intelligence*, was published on 5 May 1850, at a single-copy price of fourpence.[10] Although the *Newspaper* would undergo several changes in content and layout during the first few years of its existence,[11] almost all of the elements that would mark it throughout Reynolds's active tenure as editor were in place from the start. The first item on the front page was the signed leader, written by Reynolds himself. His initial offering was hopeful. Entitled 'The Prospects of the Democratic Cause', it decried the depredations of the upper classes, while predicting that the working classes would triumph in their battle for equality. The front page's other notable feature would also become a staple. 'Foreign Intelligence' was a column (or two, depending on the state of the world) devoted to news from other countries, especially France.[12] If such news were pressing, more detailed stories were often included inside; in this first issue, an article entitled 'The Law and Order Party in France', which discussed French politics in some detail, was located on page four.

The column by 'Gracchus', which would be continued in the *Newspaper* long after Reynolds's death, was likewise present from the start.[13] Under the title 'Policy

---

8   *RPI*, 17 November 1849, p. 10.

9   Reynolds apparently considered *RPI* to have been essentially the same publication as *RN*, despite their differences in content and emphasis: in 1858 he asserted that *RN* had been launched in 1849 ('Notices to Correspondents', *RN*, 21 March 1858, p. 8).

10   The price was briefly raised to fivepence in July in response to Lord Ashley's bill prohibiting newspaper delivery on Sundays, and then lowered in mid-August to 2½d. It remained at that price until the repeal of the newspaper stamp regulations.

11   The paper was retitled *Reynolds's Newspaper* in February 1851 (see Editors' Note). In 1861 it went from 16 pages and four columns to eight larger pages and eight columns.

12   International affairs were a point of interest to the readers of *RN*; by December 1851, coverage of events in Paris had apparently resulted in a rise in circulation (*RN*, 21 December 1851, p. 8).

13   The identity of Gracchus in the first issues of *RN* is uncertain, but Edward Reynolds, G.W.M. Reynolds's younger brother, was Gracchus for many years until his death in 1894,

of Ministers: Wants and Duties of the People', Gracchus demanded the imposition of universal manhood suffrage. Other articles and leaders dealt with 'The Parliament and its Doings', 'Mr. Cobden's and Mr. Henley's Motions for Reductions in the Expenditure' and a day-by-day summary of parliamentary occurrences. Those parliamentary reports were not normally comprehensive, but tended to focus on debates concerning working-class issues, Irish questions and the like.

Most of the rest of the first issue was devoted to less overtly political concerns, while maintaining a political focus. 'Reviews of Books' discussed the merits of recent books, pamphlets and periodicals. These reviews were not neutral discussions of the merit of literary works; they almost always focused on politics in the context of the work under review. They either alerted the working classes to the existence of a helpful book, or warned them about trickery. Henry Mayhew's *London Labour and the London Poor* found favour, as did the second edition of Samuel Smiles's *Self-Help*.[14] A new edition of Kingsley's *Alton Locke*, on the other hand, was greeted with distaste. The author had added a new preface, in which he asserted that relations between the aristocracy and the working classes had improved significantly. *Reynolds's Newspaper* ascribed this change of heart to Kingsley's appointment as a professor at Cambridge and chaplain to the Queen.[15]

Sometimes the warnings about dangerous books would be more overt. *Advice to the Mariners of England, and Enterprising Youths Inclined for the Sea Service* was described as a propaganda piece published at the behest of the Lords of the Admiralty. It was designed, the reviewer asserted, to entice young men into naval service by describing the advantages inherent in being a sailor, while concealing the 'odious cat-o-nine-tails'.[16]

The emphasis on political argument as a form of book review occasionally overshadowed the contents of the book in question. Such was the case with the 'review' of Reynolds's own *Mysteries of the Court of London*, which used a description of a slum in Bermondsey contained in the book to decry the failure of progress in the British social system: 'The utter disregard manifested by the wealthy classes for the poorer orders is strikingly exhibited by the bare fact that such a plague-spot should be allowed to exist after the tremendous warning afforded by the ravages of cholera in the year 1849.'[17]

Virginia Berridge has asserted that this emphasis on politics tells us more about the *Newspaper*'s political ideology than about its readers' interests, but that argument

---

and it is quite possible that he was responsible for the column from its inception. In any case, he wrote for *RN* for more than 40 years, always under a pen name. Eric Smyth, Research Officer of *RN*, noted of Edward Reynolds in 1950 that 'he is probably the only journalist in newspaper history who had contributed articles and leaders regularly for the best part of half a century without once having had a by-line in his own name' (*Co-operative News*, 22 April 1950).

14   *RN*, 22 December 1850, p. 9; 10 June 1866, p. 2.

15   *RN*, 11 May 1862, p. 6.

16   *RN*, 12 February 1854. The evil of corporal punishment in the military was a frequent theme in the paper.

17   *RN*, 29 September 1850, p. 2.

is unconvincing.[18] *Reynolds's Newspaper* was an expressly political newspaper, and its readers would have had to be interested in the political views it expressed, else their purchase of it would have been irrational. Further, they would have looked to Reynolds and his paper to inform them of books relevant to that sphere of interest. The books reviewed, while they were not of a type, were carefully chosen for the stances they took. Both pro- and anti-working-class books allowed the *Newspaper* to make its point. The readers of *Reynolds's Newspaper* read culture through the prism it offered, and while they might not have done so consciously, it is unlikely that they would have considered a more 'objective' view to be more accurate.

Reynolds's attitude towards the business of covering news is difficult to discern. He was himself his paper's best and most prolific writer, and it is impossible to determine how many reporters he employed, and on what basis. He relied on reports from his readers for provincial news, and certainly was not in the business of aggressive investigation. He explained, in response to a reader's letter, that *Reynolds's Newspaper* did not send reporters to private political meetings unless specifically invited to, as to do otherwise might be seen as an intrusion.[19] The newspaper also devoted considerable space to 'police news', that is, reports of crimes and criminal trials. This concern with the lurid side of news would bring Reynolds considerable criticism, but it seems to have been a popular feature and was in any case no greater an example of prurience than that exhibited by many other newspapers of the day. Indeed, Reynolds would later claim that the *Newspaper* was more decorous than the leading establishment daily. In the 'Notices to Correspondents', he asserted that *The Times* was quite hypocritical in its calls for rectitude in connection with stories about the Palmer poisoning case of 1856. '*The Times*', he wrote, 'occasionally preaches morality by way of a change, but disseminates bestiality as a matter of profit.' *Reynolds's Newspaper*, he asserted, had veiled medical details in seemly language; *The Times* had been unnecessarily graphic.[20] Reynolds was not, however, averse to hooking readers with a prurient headline.[21]

The Palmer case is also instructive as an example of Reynolds's mingling of politics and sensation. Editors assured readers that the *Newspaper* would provide the fullest possible coverage of the trial, and later the execution, as extra reporters had been hired for just that purpose.[22] At the same time, however, that the *Newspaper* devoted much of its space to stories about the trial, Palmer's conviction was the

---

18   Virginia Berridge, 'Popular Journalism and Working-class Attitudes, 1854–1886: A Study of *Reynolds's Newspaper*, *Lloyd's Weekly Newspaper*, and the *Weekly Times*' (PhD dissertation, University of London, 1976), p. 183.

19   *RN*, 8 August 1852, p. 8.

20   *RN*, 31 August 1856, p. 8.

21   *RN* finally did attempt to take the high stylistic road completely, publishing a flier in which it proclaimed that it would henceforth eschew 'Cheesecake and Sensationalism'. This change of direction did not occur, however, until the next century, in 1956; *RN* was nothing if not persistent (Reynolds's News Collection, National Museum of Labour History, GS/Reynolds's Newspaper/15, Box 8).

22   *RN*, 11 May 1856, p. 8; 8 June 1856, p. 8.

occasion for editorial lamenting.[23] Palmer's trial had lasted so long, the third leader claimed on 1 June 1856, because he had been able to afford a good defence. A poor person would have been tried, convicted and hanged in less time than justice should allow. There are two laws, the leader concluded, one for the rich and one for the poor.[24]

Reynolds was well aware that for his newspaper to succeed he would have to amuse as well as inform, and so he devoted column space to entertainment beyond that inherent in police reports. Theatre reviews, court news and sports intelligence were constant features from the start. *Reynolds's Newspaper* gleefully reported salacious goings-on in palaces, country houses and the occasional brothel, while also demanding an end to the social and political system that made such things possible. This ability to make money from that which he decried has caused some scholars to denounce him as a hypocrite who was interested in the working classes solely for the profit they would bring him; Berridge is especially harsh.[25] But this call for purity of motive is naive; accusing people of being hypocrites is accusing human beings of behaving like human beings. Reynolds was no more hypocritical than were his readers, and he was realistic in recognizing that the news business was a business, and that breadth of coverage was essential.

Advertisements for political meetings and manifestos from political and quasi-political organizations were often given space, although there is no way of telling which were paid for and which were printed gratis. It seems likely that pleas for subscriptions to various causes were printed as news, especially when Reynolds himself was involved, but other types of political advertisements were probably not, and might occasionally be the source of comment within the *Newspaper* itself. In 1852, for example, during the struggle between the omnibus drivers and their masters, the masters' advertisement setting forth their position prompted the comment in the 'Notices' section that 'although a certain portion of our journal devoted to the advertisement department is, to a certain extent, public property, we nevertheless reserve the right of denouncing and exposing such monstrous misrepresentations as those contained in the omnibus masters manifesto'.[26] Despite these occasional comments, advertisements were generally printed without qualm. Picking and choosing advertisements for moral purity would quickly have put the newspaper into financial trouble.

The most interesting feature of *Reynolds's Newspaper*, and the one that provides the greatest insight into the character of its readers, was the 'Notices to Correspondents' column, which provided answers to readers' questions. The letters themselves were not printed, but the answers are often illuminating. They provide a unique glimpse

---

23 Stories about the trial occupied three full pages of the 18 May issue, four pages of the 25 May issue and three-and-a-quarter pages of the 1 June issue, exclusive of editorials.

24 *RN*, 1 June 1856, p. 8.

25 Virginia Berridge, 'Popular Sunday Papers and Mid-Victorian Society', in George Boyce, James Curran and Pauline Wingate (eds), *Newspaper History from the Seventeenth Century to the Present Day* (London: Constable, 1978), p. 54. See also Gertrude Himmelfarb, *The Idea of Poverty: England in the Early Industrial Age* (New York: Alfred A. Knopf, 1984), pp. 435–52.

26 *RN*, 29 February 1852, p. 8.

into the interests of the newspaper's readers; the sheer breadth of questions asked is indicative of the intellectual esteem in which its audience held it. The notices are also evidence of Reynolds's wide-ranging interests and of his attitude towards his readers. Anne Humphreys has asserted convincingly that Reynolds wrote most of the notices in *Reynolds's Miscellany* (indeed, responses to letters to *Reynolds's Political Instructor* were printed in the *Miscellany*) and it is likely that he continued the practice with the *Newspaper*, certainly in the first years of its operation.[27] To judge from the consistent style of the responses, he probably continued to answer most of the correspondents himself for some time thereafter.

The subjects mentioned in the 'Notices' were wide ranging. Reynolds's readers seemed to trust him to know the answer to any number of questions, from the best way to improve one's handwriting to the rules of chess. Occasionally, as in his response to 'a Countryman', he would also editorialize: 'Guano is a substitute for manure: we know of no better, unless it be a heap of the *Daily News*, or a cartload of John Cassell's "pure and unadulterated" coffee.'[28] He was also occasionally asked about the proper way to conduct a business. Given Reynolds's frequent financial troubles and questionable honesty in matters of money, this trust in his business acumen was probably misplaced. But, as Patrick Joyce has demonstrated, the 'Gentleman Leader' was a recurring player in working-class political culture, and Reynolds seems to have had and maintained the implicit trust of his readers.[29] Correspondents regularly requested advice on legal and medical matters, and Reynolds consulted doctors and lawyers before replying. On other matters, however, he was his own authority. Reynolds's self-proclaimed position as a well-educated man of letters prompted young people to write in for advice on how they might improve themselves. He was always willing to offer help, as in the following reply to 'C.E.':

> A 'Young man of sixteen' who wants to become well read should begin by reading the history of his own country, and the biography of his distinguished countrymen; then he should read history and biography generally, and the essays, reviews, and criticisms of the best writers in the English language; also, the works of the great novelists, poets, &c., &c., besides keeping up with the current literature of the day as far as possible.[30]

Although he was widely read in literature, Reynolds thought that history was the most fruitful subject for deep study, and attempted to pass that attitude on to his readers. He also informed them that education was a long-term process of careful discernment. His advice to 'L.F.' may have been a description of his own intellectual journey:

·

---

27   Anne Humphreys, 'G.W.M. Reynolds, Popular Literature and Popular Politics', *Victorian Periodicals Review*, 16 (1983): 86. See also Chapter 3 in this volume by Andrew King, '*Reynolds's Miscellany*, 1846–1849: Advertising Networks and Politics'.

28   *RN*, 19 December 1852, p. 8.

29   Patrick Joyce, *Visions of the People: Industrial England and the Question of Class, 1848–1914* (Cambridge: Cambridge University Press, 1991), p. 45.

30   *RN*, 26 August 1866, p. 4.

you will find that historians often disagree on important topics; and you must learn to judge for yourself. It would be a good plan for you to read every history of England you can get hold of, and compare the accounts and opinions of the different historians on disputed points, and see which most commend themselves to your own instincts and understanding. You must distrust every author, and distrust your own judgment also. After five years, or so, of industrious and conscientious reading and reflection, you will begin to be able to form some respectable opinion on historical matters; your information will crystallize into knowledge; your charity for poor humanity will be vastly expanded and deepened; and your faith in Providence and the destiny of the human race will become clear and steadfast.[31]

Eventually, the many requests for advice on self-education that he received prompted him to publish a series of 'Educational Columns' in the *Miscellany*, which were eventually put together in book form as *The Self-Instructor*. 'Persons of defective education', he announced in the *Newspaper*,

can improve themselves exceedingly by its use. Indeed it contains all the requisite lessons to constitute the groundwork of a really good education. The French language can be self-taught by its aid in a very short time, with the help of a dictionary and a grammar. All the requisite rules for composition, punctuation, &c., are given in this work, as well as the necessary instructions for poetical composition. Elegance of diction and correct manner of expression are to be acquired from the 'Self-Instructor'.[32]

It is clear that Reynolds saw himself and the *Newspaper*, in the days before the National Education Act, as the best school the working classes had available to them, particularly in the realm of politics. 'The cheap press', he wrote, 'is the sole real educator of the masses. It teaches them to know their rights and their wrongs, and is thus gradually effecting the silent revolution of the heart in this great country.'[33] Reynolds was occasionally blunt in his answers to correspondents. He advised one young man, for example, that '[a] person with knock-knees had better turn his attention to some other occupation than the stage'.[34] He could also be rude if a correspondent failed to meet his standards. He refused to answer any letters written in pencil, or if the writing were crossed.[35] And he was at his most haughty when asked for advice on how to write well. 'H.C.G.' wrote a request for help in composing letters that resulted in the following diatribe:

---

31 *RN*, 22 September 1867, p. 4.

32 *RN*, 16 February 1862, p. 5. He also had published earlier *The French Self-Instructor* (London: George Vickers, 1846). The new book, although it did not bear his name as author, apparently incorporated much of that work as part of its coverage of a greater number of subjects.

33 *RN*, 20 September 1857, p. 8. He was not alone in this assessment. The *New York Tribune* noted that Members of Parliament were frequently surprised by the depth of political knowledge held by members of the working classes in their constituencies, and cited the cheap Sunday newspapers as the source of that knowledge. *RN* was mentioned specifically. Quoted in *RN*, 9 January 1859, p. 6.

34 *RN*, 14 March 1852, p. 8.

35 *RN*, 22 July 1866, p. 4.

The reason you are such a 'poor composer of letters' is, probably, because you have but few ideas, and limited intelligence. In order to write a good letter, you must have something to say, and know how to say it. A 'Complete Letter-Writer' would not help you much, except temporarily. You would probably fall into the habit of copying passages from it, and would be apt at last to depend upon it altogether; whereby you would impair what meagre powers of composition you now possess.[36]

The 'Notices' were also used to promote the *Newspaper* as the voice of democracy,[37] to advertise upcoming events or to solicit funds for deserving workingmen who had fallen on severe times. Testimonial and aid solicitations were a regular feature in *Reynolds's Newspaper*, with Reynolds using his office as a receiving point for funds. Typical was the notice that appeared in 1859, during a dispute between the master builders and their workers:

> The master builders having pushed matters to extremities with their workpeople, thereby driving them to a general strike, it is the incumbent duty of every trade society and individual operative in the United Kingdom to afford prompt assistance to the builders, and continue that assistance until the dispute is brought to a triumphant conclusion. In furtherance of this object, subscriptions will be received at the office of *Reynolds's Newspaper*, and duly acknowledged – however small the amount – in the columns of this journal.[38]

Other events occasioned solicitations for funds and testimonials. When two soldiers were arrested at a Hyde Park political demonstration, Reynolds raised a subscription and hired counsel. On their release, he gave them what monies were left over.[39] Bronterre O'Brien's ill health in 1853 prompted the call for a testimonial dinner, so that workingmen might express appreciation for the 'great advocate for labour'.[40]

As might be inferred from his frequent bankruptcies, Reynolds was free with his money in what he thought was a good cause, and sometimes was taken advantage of. Following the Trafalgar Square demonstration of 1848, he received letters congratulating him on his actions. Two of his correspondents solicited funds for the 'Democratic Union of Sutherland' and the 'Republican Society of Newcastle-upon-Tyne'. Reynolds sent them two guineas each, and was later chagrined to discover that the societies in question did not actually exist.[41]

---

36 *RN*, 26 August 1866, p. 8.

37 For example, when the *Literary and Educational Year Book* named *RN* as the only 'Democratic' English newspaper, the following notice appeared: 'Suffice it to say that we are proud of our exceptional position' (*RN*, 18 March 1858, p. 8). Earlier, Reynolds had proclaimed that 'the immensity of our circulation places us beyond the possibility of entertaining a feeling of envy [for another paper]. No newspaper in existence has ever experienced such success as ours' (*RN*, 2 January 1852, p. 8).

38 *RN*, 21 August 1859, pp. 3–4. Reynolds himself, the article noted, pledged £3, 8s.

39 *RN*, 29 July 1854, p. 8.

40 *RN*, 17 July 1853, pp. 8, 13.

41 *RN*, 11 May 1851, p. 7.

Reynolds's Newspaper presented the reader with a relatively static physical presence. Save for one major change in layout in 1861, the paper altered little in the years of Reynolds's leadership. It remained familiar to its subscribers, presenting the same face year after year. A mixture of radical politics, practical advice and gossip, the newspaper strove to establish a personal relationship with its readers, giving them a forum for their interests and making them feel they had an advocate. The tone was authoritative without being haughty, pleading without being pathetic. David Vincent has it precisely right:

> *Reynolds's Newspaper* ... retained something of the tone of personal address upon which its predecessors had based their success. Although there were fewer meetings to report, the journalism preserved the direct, vigorous, demotic style of the open-air speech. The paper deliberately avoided the cadences of the establishment press, whilst at the same time losing no opportunity of criticising the class bias of its rivals. Even more so than the unstamped, it was explicitly an anti-newspaper newspaper, called into being by the shortcomings of the existing coverage of working-class affairs, and refusing to replicate the polite discourse of its corrupt opponents.[42]

Reynolds spoke to his readers on an intimate level, confirming their political beliefs, assuring them that in him and his newspaper they had a friend and advocate, and giving them a voice. He also entertained them, as he had done and would continue to do in his novels. Anne Humpherys has said that Reynolds was successful precisely because he did not try to resolve the many contradictory desires and impulses that existed within his readers.[43] He merely gave them what they wanted; the reason that he was able to do this, and do it almost instinctively, was that he had the same desires and impulses. He offered them himself, and they responded. As Elizabeth Long notes, group readings often form the basis for conversation and debate, and have for centuries.[44] For readers of *Reynolds's Newspaper*, that conversation centred on politics. The 'Tramp Socialist', a peripatetic radical who had first seen the *Newspaper* in 1850, described in 1906 the catalytic role it had played in the shop in which his father had worked:

> In those days few of advanced age among that class could read. Yet they were the keenest of politicians. Having the paper read daily kept them always abreast of the times. To secure one of their shop mates who could read would cost them what he could make – all work being done by piece.... If the services of a boy could be obtained, it would be quite a saving. So many days have I sat on a high, three-legged stool in the centre of that shop, shouting at the top of my young voice the Parliamentary speeches of those whose tongues have long been silent. It was only after the lapse of years that I realized the spirit of the hot debates that took place on the floor of that shop. Who can doubt that whatever of advanced thought is manifest among the workers of Dundee is the result of the efforts of those truly

---

42 David Vincent, *Literacy and Popular Culture: England 1750–1914* (Cambridge: Cambridge University Press, 1989), p. 253.

43 Humpherys, 'G.W.M. Reynolds', p. 89.

44 Long, 'Textual Interpretation as Collective Action', p. 196.

patriotic men, who regarded *Reynolds's* as their Holy Writ, and who were fully alive to the cant and hypocrisy by which they were surrounded.[45]

In its stubborn adherence to a mid-Victorian assessment of Britain's social structure, *Reynolds's Newspaper* remained true to George Reynolds's melodramatic bent. He had made his name and his fortune by writing melodramatic fiction, and saw melodramatic fact throughout English political society. This should not be surprising since, as has been noted before, popular political thought tends to be melodramatic in its expression. Peter Brooks has said that, in melodrama, '[t]he polarization of good and evil works toward revealing their presence and operation as real forces in the world. Their conflict suggests the need to recognize and confront evil, to combat and expel it, to purge the social order.'[46] Reynolds's reliance on melodrama to structure his and his newspaper's political argument proved to be in harmony with the assumptions of his readers, members of a radical reading public who could readily picture the day-to-day reality of their lives in a melodramatic manner. Reynolds and the *Newspaper* enabled them to see society clearly in a way that was, if not subtle and nuanced, at least real.

As Humpherys asserts, Reynolds did not express the 'two paradoxical elements in the popular mind: the desire for a better life defined predominantly by what the populace perceives as better in the lives of those "above" them and a contradictory tendency to want to destroy that very desired life because those that had it were seen as exploiting those that didn't'.[47] He did not want to destroy the desired lives of the elite, but rather peacefully to dismantle the system which kept the possibility of living those lives in the hands of an undeserving few. After that change had been made, the lives of those undeserving elite would be open to all, based on their individual efforts. His readers found that idea highly attractive.

The social system of England as Reynolds perceived it was both good and evil, reflecting the nature of the individual. Prefacing his work of fiction, *Master Timothy's Bookcase*, Reynolds tried to demonstrate that duality. The book 'endeavours', he wrote, 'to inculcate the doctrine, that good and evil are so intimately blended in all the creatures and affairs of this life, that those principles may be considered

---

45 *RN*, 29 April 1906. The Tramp Socialist's description of the reading aloud of *RN* as one might read 'Holy Writ' mirrors the role played by the psalms in monastic worship. As Kathleen Norris has noted, 'To say or sing the psalms aloud within a community is to recover religion as an oral tradition, restoring to our mouths words that have been snatched from our tongues and relegated to the page, words that have been privatized and effectively silenced. It counters our tendency to see individual experience as sufficient for formulating a vision of the world' (Kathleen Norris, *The Cloister Walk* [New York: Riverhead Books, 1996], p. 100). Interpretation of the text of *RN* was very much a collective action, in which the readers and listeners reinforced and refined their understanding of the world and the word.

46 Peter Brooks, *The Melodramatic Imagination* (1976; New York: Columbia University Press, 1985), p. 13. See also Anne Humpherys, 'Popular Narrative and Political Discourse in *Reynolds's Weekly Newspaper*', in Laurel Brake, Aled Jones and Lionel Madden (eds), *Investigating Victorian Journalism* (New York: St Martin's, 1990), p. 42.

47 Humpherys, 'G.W.M. Reynolds', p. 13.

inseparable'.[48] If good and evil – virtue and vice – existed in each individual, then they existed also in society. The benefits of civilization might be applauded, but the evils of society, which prevented the majority of the people from sharing in those benefits, had to be erased. The social system of England, creating as it did vast inequities of opportunity and wealth, and reinforced by an unnatural division of political power, had little if anything to recommend it. '[M]an', Reynolds wrote, 'is the creature of circumstances.'[49] He was also a creature of choice, but the choice of virtue, on which so much depended, was – for the majority – proscribed by circumstances. If the majority, the working classes, were to be saved from being forced to choose vice, the circumstances under which that choice was made – the social system – had to be changed. If Reynolds's actions in his personal life were not always consistent, his vision of a future republican society was both consistent and constant.

One of Reynolds's characters in *The Mysteries of London*, a poor boy who sneaks into Buckingham Palace to see the Queen, lies concealed under a couch in contemplation of the Prince Consort: 'Why', he thinks, 'are you so exalted, and I so abased? And yet your graceful person – your intelligent countenance – your handsome features seem to fit you for such an elevated position. Nevertheless, if I had your advantages of education ...'[50] The conclusion is unstated, but clear. As Reynolds saw it, the English social system would not allow any save the very few to gain those advantages of education with which a worthy person might earn an exalted position. This essential unfairness – the elevation of the undeserving and the degradation of the unfortunate – gave birth to the republicanism that was at the heart of his discourse. The essence of civilization, as he saw it, lay buried in the mire of English society. The aristocratic and monarchic elite that ran that society impeded the natural growth of a society based on republican egalitarianism. The solution to centuries of stagnation was not, he believed, violent revolution to create a classless society, but a peaceful and yet constant agitation to bring about fundamental change. He promoted evolution rather than revolution. Although Reynolds used the word 'class' to describe divisions within society, he also used 'the people' in a perhaps unconscious effort to show that society's divisions were based not solely on economics but on political and social power as well. This interpretation of political hegemony, that the power of society was exercised not only economically and physically, but also through the ideas that organized society, activated Reynolds's discourse. In response to the prevailing idea of 'respectable' society, Reynolds provided his own overarching idea of another type of respectability, in which all of 'the people' could act as the agents of reform. He described a language and idea that was a dramatic and active agent of social and political relations.[51] That language, that idea, provided an

---

48 G.W.M. Reynolds, *Master Timothy's Bookcase; or, The Magic Lantern of the World* (1841; London: James Gilbert, 1847), Preface, p. 2.

49 Reynolds, *Master Timothy's Bookcase*, Preface, p. 2.

50 G.W.M. Reynolds, *The Mysteries of London* (London: George Vickers, 1845), vol. 1, ch. 64, p. 199.

51 Cf. Mikhail Bakhtin, 'Discourse in the Novel', in M.M. Bakhtin, *The Dialogic Imagination: Four Essays*, ed. Michael Holquist, trans. Caryl Emerson and Michael Holquist (Austin: University of Texas Press, 1981), pp. 259–422.

alternative to the social and political history of the English people that was presented by the dominant elite. It was that 'New History of England', a history that *Reynolds's Newspaper* presented week after week, year after year, from which readers drew their republican energy, the 'wings of everlasting POWER'[52] that they could use to agitate for change. Reynolds's melodramatic language of reform without revolution, of republicanism and of English civilization was the common language of the mid-Victorian radical.

The society that Reynolds presented to his readers was a simple, unfair and moderately hopeful one. The working man who received all of his information of the world beyond his everyday experience from *Reynolds's Newspaper* saw a skewed but not inaccurate picture. This world he saw had an economic and political gulf that separated him from those who were 'worthy' of wealth. When Reynolds decried the aristocracy, he saw in them the rulers who denied him a political voice. When Reynolds called the mill owners 'slaveholders', he saw the men who were getting rich from his labour. When Reynolds castigated the 'shopocracy', he saw the local businessman who might have given him inferior goods for a high price, while not working as hard as he himself did. If his position was improving and he was able to find better lodgings and perhaps purchase for his family the new sewing machine the *Newspaper* had begun to advertise in 1873, then Reynolds reminded him that others had pulled further ahead.

If the reader was a soldier, he could read about the vast sums being paid to incompetent but well-connected officers, who ordered him to fight and die in what the *Newspaper* might tell him was a war for aristocratic or royal interests.[53] No wonder, he would think, that his officers tried to keep him from reading it. And he would wonder why he was being paid with little more than the Queen's shilling and the lash. Looking beyond the borders of his country, he would read about the monarchs of other nations, none of them good and some of them resolutely evil, such as the Tsar of Russia.[54] He would feel disgust at the manner in which they suppressed the natural democratic feelings of their subjects. He would cheer those heroes, such as Kossuth, Mazzini and Garibaldi, who fought for freedom. When rebellion did occur, he would often note that the *Newspaper* had predicted it.[55] When the people

---

52   The quotation is from Reynolds, 'Epilogue', in *Kenneth: A Romance of the Highlands* (London: John Dicks, [1852]), part 2, p. 144.

53   The army, Reynolds stated, 'belongs to a class – not to the nation' (*RN*, 11 October 1857, p. 8).

54   Not all foreign powers were treated so harshly, however. Reynolds seems to have been somewhat smitten by the Turks, probably because the Sultan had given shelter to Kossuth during his exile. See *RN*, 30 October 1853, p. 1.

55   In 1853, the first leader stated that most newspapers were astonished at the Chinese rebellion. There was no reason to be astonished, the leader reported, for what else could be expected, given the despotic nature of the Chinese government (*RN*, 21 August 1853, p. 8). The Sepoy mutiny was greeted with praise: 'We rejoice that the long-oppressed people of India have the spirit to rise against their tyrants. We rejoice that slavery has not utterly crushed their manhood' (*RN*, 2 August 1857, p. 1). Indian atrocities were deplored, but it was important to remember that English soldiers had also committed atrocities (*RN*, 23 August 1857, p. 1).

of France overthrew their king and elected a president, he would rejoice, although the *Newspaper* made sure to remind him that no Bonaparte could really be trusted. And when that president betrayed the French people by naming himself Emperor, he would nod over the front-page leader which rightly called it a crime, and would reflect that Reynolds was correct: the vote was not something to be cast lightly.[56]

He would look at the extent of the empire, the extent of which probably filled him with a quiet pride, and feel disconcerted when *Reynolds's Newspaper* pointed out that the political self-determination he sought for himself was being denied to the colonies.[57] When a former colony, the United States of America, proved to the world that a republic could work, he would feel admiration and envy. And when that country tore at itself in its civil war, he would feel the uneasiness that *Reynolds's Newspaper* projected, hoping that right would prevail. When the slaves were freed, he would rejoice. But through all the turmoil, he would focus on the news in England, for that was his home, his culture, where things were changing, albeit not fast enough. If, in 1867, he suddenly found himself allowed to vote, he might wonder why no men such as himself were standing for Parliament. *Reynolds's Newspaper* would remind him that a man with no outside income could not afford to be in Parliament, and that Parliament could alleviate the situation by paying its members, but that it refused to do so.

The reader might read the crime reports and be gratified to see that his 'betters' got into trouble, and he might find himself titillated and outraged at the aristocratic seduction of a housemaid, but then he would share *Reynolds's Newspaper*'s rage at their escape from the 'justice' inflicted on the lawbreakers in his neighbourhood. Through all of this, he would be angry, but he would not revolt, for Reynolds would assure him that victory would come, if only men such as himself continued to learn, to argue and to demonstrate. This was England, after all, and some day she would rid herself of the stranglehold of centuries of aristocratic rule and become what God intended: a republic.

In the meantime, though, he had to earn money to live.[58] But he would continue to read, to argue and to see injustice. While he made his living, supported his family and did not cause too much trouble, he would teach his children that the cause of justice was the cause of reform, and would read to them from *Reynolds's Newspaper*, which told the truth, and ensured him that his political beliefs were shared. Mid-Victorian England in the 'Age of Equipoise' was quietly agitated beneath its calm surface.

---

56 Napoleon III's downfall was the occasion of much rejoicing and hyperbole. The front-page leader's headline was simple: 'Exit Caesar' (*RN*, 18 September 1870), p. 1.

57 For example, in 1851 Gracchus called for British withdrawal from the colonies, so that the natives there might determine their own fates. In that way, British citizens would not have to pay in taxes or in blood to support an 'unnatural system' (*RN*, 20 July 1851, p. 7). Reynolds himself asserted that England governed India badly for the sake of a few thieves (*RN*, 12 June 1853, p. 1; 19 June 1853, p. 1).

58 The day-to-day necessity of earning a living can greatly inhibit revolutionary activity. See, generally, W.L. Burn, *The Age of Equipoise: A Study of the Mid-Victorian Generation* (New York: W.W. Norton, 1964), esp. p. 110.

Chapter 5

From Journalism and Fiction into Politics

Michael Diamond

Virulent personal attacks on royalty and aristocracy were a characteristic feature of *Reynolds's Newspaper*. These were written in extravagant language, attacking both the political and personal lives of their subjects and, typically, dwelling on their sexual depravity. An early signed front-page article, entitled 'The Crowned Miscreants and Harlots of the European Continent', besides listing the political crimes of Queen Maria Christina of Spain, described her as 'the bloated, gluttonous, depraved strumpet' and 'this lump of sensuality and grossness' who has had a bastard by a 'coarse-mannered, vulgar uneducated fellow'.[1] A few years later another front-page article, signed by Reynolds, was devoted to the marriage of Napoleon III of France, a figure who had incurred Reynolds's particular hatred for overturning the Second French Republic, and who was regularly excoriated throughout his reign. Reynolds describes the Emperor as a 'blood-stained murderer' and 'wholesale robber', one who is 'so loathsome and degraded' as to be unfit even for the company of the British aristocracy. Also, Reynolds alleges, he has been a frequenter of brothels. Although Reynolds cannot produce evidence against the morals of the Emperor's bride – he grudgingly admits that she may be pure – he claims that she has for some years been 'paraded by her mother in husband-hunting speculation in every great city of Europe' and that the mother has herself been the subject of scandal.[2]

In England, if Queen Victoria was spared on account of her exemplary family life, Reynolds remarks caustically that 'a monarch has only to abstain from the commission of open murder, gross and notorious adultery, or fornication' to be thought extraordinarily meritorious.[3] Prince Albert, however, was repeatedly attacked. *Reynolds's Newspaper* reacted in typical fashion to a proposal to erect a statue to him. This was 'one of the most nauseating, degrading and sickening specimens of grovelling self-abasement'.[4] Members of the aristocracy fared even worse. The Duke of Newcastle, Secretary for War at the time of the Crimean conflict, had a 'mental capacity amounting almost to the idiotic', for blind stupidity was 'the most remarkable of the hereditary characteristics of this noble family'.[5] An obituary of the Marquis of Londonderry states that there were 'few men in public life who evinced so little judgment'. He treated his Irish tenants like Russian serfs and 'seldom did a good action and never said a wise thing'. Among details of his

---

1 *RN*, 9 June 1850, p. 1.
2 *RN*, 11 December 1853, p. 1.
3 *RN*, 24 May 1857, p. 1.
4 *RN*, 13 November 1853, p. 1.
5 *RN*, 26 November 1854, p. 1.

personal life, 'the noise occasioned by his striking the wet-nurse of his infant child is not yet forgotten'.[6]

Reynolds even gave an innocuous announcement that the Duke of Cambridge, the Queen's cousin, had been elected Governor of Christ's Hospital a typical sexual innuendo, suggesting that the Duke's patronage would be distributed among 'the unrecognised bastards of the aristocracy, the children of their flunkeys, butlers and hangers-on'.[7] The ageing Duke of Wellington, long before his death, was celebrated as the personification of a glorious chapter in the nation's history. But his obituary in *Reynolds's Newspaper*, while it admits Wellington had been a good general, sees him as inferior to the great Napoleon, one of Reynolds's heroes. Even more damningly, 'as a politician the Duke's character had not a redeeming point.... The people of Great Britain have lost one of their sternest enemies – the Tories one of their staunchest friends'.[8] When Wellington's funeral was celebrated with all the pomp that was to be Churchill's in the next century, *Reynolds's Newspaper* treated it with scorn and contempt.

Reynolds of course knew that such attacks flew in the face of respectable opinion, and he relished the fact, as would his radical readers. But his vicious attacks on the rich and powerful were more than sensational journalism aimed at increasing the newspaper's circulation. They created a revisionist account of the events and personalities of the mid-nineteenth century, an alternative to the standard Fleet Street opinions. There is a consistent continuum between his journalistic attacks in *Reynolds's Newspaper* and the content of his fiction: both aim to provide a common radical account of English history. This view was foreshadowed in *Reynolds's Political Instructor*, the short-lived forerunner to *Reynolds's Newspaper*, in which Edwin Roberts offered a 'New History of England', examining the reign of each monarch from William the Conqueror to the present. Clearly with Reynolds's backing, Roberts argued that history as it has been previously taught was a tapestry of lies designed to conceal the fact that 'the lives of monarchs form the genealogy of crime'.[9] Reynolds himself repeated this claim in a signed article in *Reynolds's Newspaper*.[10] A new history was needed because deference to the past, and to royalty and aristocracy in particular, had marred all previous histories. Reynolds's historical novels and *The Mysteries of the Court of London* (1848–56), together with the historical references in *Reynolds's Political Instructor* and *Reynolds's Newspaper*, come near to forming such a work.

This shadowy history of England, told in violent language as a series of sensational events, begins in a discussion of the Norman Conquest, when the Conqueror's army chiefs are described as 'those rapacious adventurers and diabolic bloodhounds'. They committed 'satanic atrocities', were rewarded with grants of land and plundered the English people.[11] Having skipped the English Middle Ages, Reynolds describes

---

6   *RN*, 12 March 1854, p. 1.
7   *RN*, 26 March 1854, pp. 8–9.
8   *RN*, 9 September 1852, p. 1.
9   *RPI*, 10 November 1849, p. 5.
10   *RN*, 6 February 1853, p. 1.
11   *RN*, 2 October 1853, p. 8.

Henry VIII as 'the royal bluebeard'.[12] The immoral behaviour recounted in *The Necromancer* (1851–52) is mostly attributed to the supernatural being of the title, the King's double, who impersonates Henry in his amours.[13] However, Elizabeth I does not escape so lightly. Reynolds's novel *Mary Stuart, Queen of Scotland* (1859) is overwhelmingly concerned with Mary's persecution by her fellow countrymen, and only at the very end does she level the familiar accusation that 'the agents of Queen Elizabeth have, in her name, and at her instigation, hunted me to the block'.[14] But it is in the earlier novel *Canonbury House* (1857–58) that Reynolds enthusiastically assumes his role of historical revisionist. He claims that Elizabeth was never handsome or good-looking, despite 'the eulogies passed upon her alleged loveliness by the parasite poets and sycophant scribes of her own time and of subsequent periods'.[15] She spoke 'with a bitterness of tone and look which displayed all the natural rancour of her disposition, and gave the lie to those who proclaimed its magnanimity'.[16] Elizabeth is a 'cold-blooded, calculating yet capricious tyrant'[17] who is responsible for one innocent woman's being imprisoned for life in the Bastille and tries to make another mad by immuring her in an asylum. The two women are persecuted because they have learned Elizabeth's terrible secret – that she has given birth to an illegitimate daughter. Reynolds's Elizabeth is no Virgin Queen; she is yet another royal wanton unable to control her desires. The daughter's identity is revealed only at the end of the novel, although the alert modern reader may guess it sooner. This provides a link with the fictional method of *The Mysteries of the Court of London*. In both, the lusts of royalty and aristocracy constantly result in illegitimate children whose identity must be hidden, royal and aristocratic bastards who appear in different guises and enter into relationships with apparent strangers to whom they are later revealed as being blood relations.

Charles II was a favourite target in *Reynolds's Newspaper*. One suspects that his greatest crime for Reynolds, like that of Napoleon III, was to have destroyed a republic, but Reynolds gives most attention to his sex life. He is 'one of the most licentious, dissipated, and unprincipled scoundrels that ever disgraced the earth', 'a loathsome monster', allowed 'to foist all the bastard offspring of his filthy strumpets on the public purse'.[18] This does not prevent an advertisement for *The Rye House Plot* (1853–54), a novel set in his reign, from boasting that 'the reader is introduced to the superb Duchess of Cleveland, the beautiful Duchess of Portsmouth, and several other of the famous (and infamous) mistresses of the merry monarch'.[19] (Many advertisements for Reynolds's novels published in his newspaper are misleading: for

---

12 *RN*, 26 October 1851, p. 1.

13 See Chapter 11 in this volume by Louis James, 'Time, Politics and the Symbolic Imagination in Reynolds's Social Melodrama'.

14 G.W.M. Reynolds, *Mary Stuart, Queen of Scotland* (London: John Dicks, 1859), ch. 22, p. 103.

15 G.W.M. Reynolds, *Canonbury House, or The Queen's Prophecy* (London: John Dicks, 1858), ch. 1, p. 5.

16 Reynolds, *Canonbury House*, ch. 17, p. 48.

17 Reynolds, *Canonbury House*, ch. 65, p. 174.

18 *RN*, 13 July 1851, p. 1.

19 *RN*, 5 January 1857, p. 8.

example, the assertion that *Rosa Lambert* [1853–54] 'will contain nothing to shock even the most sensitive delicacy' is obviously untrue.[20]) Charles inevitably emerges badly from *The Rye House Plot*. He has seduced and then abandoned a young woman who has gone mad as a result. He has, it is true, sent her money, which never reached her, but her Puritan half-brother has more than a personal grudge against Charles. 'If he cast his eyes abroad, over the length and breadth of the land, he contemplated an amount of suffering, misery, exaction, and injustice which made him loathe the tyranny of the House of Stuart.'[21]

The King's brother, the Duke of York, is an even worse villain, and his role in the novel further reveals Reynolds's sensational use of his material. History relates that, during the reign of Charles II, the Earl of Essex was imprisoned in the Tower of London and found with his throat cut. The accepted explanation is that he committed suicide but that the enemies of the Duke of York, the future James II, put it around that the Duke had arranged to have him murdered. Reynolds not only accepts the Duke's guilt, he goes even further: he has the Duke personally cut the Earl's throat in one of the bloodiest scenes of violence in his whole oeuvre. In *The Massacre of Glencoe* (1852–53), published just before *The Rye House Plot*, James II has become King. When Roderick Macdonald, the Scottish hero, comes down to London to visit the court, the scene is a premonition of Reynolds's account of the Prince Regent's St James's Palace in *The Mysteries of the Court of London*: he tells the heroine he feels 'as if it were an atmosphere of sin and wickedness which I am breathing; the very air of this palace is laden with the oppressiveness of guilt'.[22] Like his brother, James II is depicted as both morally corrupt and tyrannical. In order to discredit the monarchy, Reynolds employs a plot common both in his work and in Victorian melodrama, substantiating the rumour that the King's only male heir has died in childhood and James has substituted another infant in order to ensure the male succession.

After such corruption, one would expect any substitute to the Stuarts to be welcomed. But although Reynolds writes that 'the country was for the most part well prepared to receive a liberator from the satanic tyrannies of King James',[23] this liberator, William III, fares no better at his hands. Contemporaneously with the publication of *The Massacre of Glencoe*, Reynolds was proclaiming in his newspaper that William III was 'a sovereign to be execrated and loathed as one of the scourges of the human race'.[24] In the novel, he is depicted as cold-blooded and heartless. Although the hero has twice saved his life, William treats him disgracefully. Even Reynolds could not depict this stolid King as a rapacious womanizer, but he blames him squarely for the Glencoe massacre, and his diatribe against the King's apologists offers an alternative history of England to that of the establishment:

---

20 *RN*, 6 November 1853, p. 8.

21 *The Rye House Plot, or Ruth, the Conspirator's Daughter* (London: John Dicks, 1854), ch. 104, p. 358.

22 G.W.M. Reynolds, *The Massacre of Glencoe* (London: John Dicks, 1853), part 2, ch. 66, p. 52.

23 Reynolds, *The Massacre of Glencoe*, part 2, ch. 75, p. 70.

24 *RN*, 5 September 1852, p. 1.

Vainly may the besotted, the bigoted or the ignorant apologise for William of Orange, seek to gloss over the share which he had in the Massacre of Glencoe.... No matter that he was the supporter of the Protestant faith and the opponent of Catholic tyranny; no matter that he delivered England from the sway of the detested Stuarts! ... He would have been a Musulman had it suited his purpose – he would have established, had the nation allowed him, as vile and persecuting a Protestant tyranny as was the Catholic one which he overturned.[25]

It was part of Reynolds's revisionism that he wanted to correct the pro-Protestant bias of previous historians. His special animus against Queen Elizabeth derives to some extent from his belief that, while full weight had been given to her sister Queen Mary in her persecution of Protestants, the Protestant Queen's persecution of Roman Catholics had been deliberately underplayed. Reynolds was no Catholic, but he believed in religious tolerance. During the anti-Catholic agitation stirred up by the Pope's appointment of Nicholas Wiseman as Cardinal and Archbishop of Westminster, Reynolds defended the Catholics in typically sensational language. Why should they not look up to the Pope, when the Protestants have looked up to 'such a vile profligate as Charles II, such a blood-stained miscreant as George III, and such a foul voluptuary as George IV?'[26]

By the Georgian period, Reynolds's political treatment of past history in his fictional novels was beginning to be elided with his journalism of the present. Reynolds's treatment of the 'foul voluptuary' George IV as the sex-obsessed villain of the first two series of *The Mysteries of the Court of London* needs little repeating here. One example, however, is Reynolds's description of the mysterious disappearance of Hannah Lightfoot, a young Quaker girl. In Reynolds's version, a blackmailer produces documentary proof that Hannah had been seduced and abandoned by the young George. At this point the mad King enters the bedroom where the Prince Regent is disporting with a mistress, and terrifies them with the ravings that reveal his guilt. What is more, it is revealed that Hannah and George have had a son, and because his true identity has had to be concealed, the son's half-sister, Princess Amelia, has unknowingly committed incest with him. While the whole House of Hanover is similarly vilified, many of Reynolds's most lurid sex scenes concern George III, revealing his particular detestation of that monarch. In *The Mysteries of the Court of London*, Reynolds yet again rails against the conventional history that he seeks to displace: 'It has hitherto been the custom and the fashion to speak of George the Third in terms of praise: historians for the most part denominate him a good King – and monarchy-worshipping panegyrists have endowed him with every possible virtue.' For Reynolds he is, on the contrary, 'so heartlessly tyrannical that he waged a sanguinary war against the brave Americans' and opposed the French Revolution.[27] It is worth noting that Reynolds was not much further removed from this historical period than Dickens was from the world of *Little Dorrit* (1855–57). Reynolds, like many of his contemporaries, had been born a subject of George III,

---

25   Reynolds, *The Massacre of Glencoe*, part 2, ch. 92, pp. 106–7.

26   *RN*, 23 February 1851, p. 1.

27   G.W.M. Reynolds, *The Mysteries of the Court of London* (London: John Dicks, 1849), vol. 1, ch. 82, p. 287.

and he was almost 16 when George IV died. Reynolds was bound to hate the enemy of the two great republics that were so dear to his heart, even if his political animus was channelled into attacks on the King's sexual depravity.

Reynolds spared George IV's daughter Charlotte, who died young, and she is used as an innocent figure, offsetting the perfidy of her relations. She felt that:

> she belonged to a family almost every member of which was steeped to the lips in vices, immoralities, and treacheries, if not stained with downright crime. It seemed to her, then, as if she were sprung from a doomed race – a race whose infamies had rendered it accursed in the sight of heaven, and whose punishment had to some extent – in the person of the lunatic King – commenced on earth.[28]

Even the Prince Regent is shocked by the bitter hatred of his mother, Queen Charlotte, for his wife Princes Caroline, although mother and son plot together to destroy the wife's reputation. Queen Charlotte is a figure of fiendish hatred against her daughter-in-law, her words hissing snake-like through lips that are white and quivering. He uses the 'good' Princess Caroline to attack the throne, in the way Princess Diana has been used in our own day. Likewise, the Prince Regent's sister, Princess Sophia, 'one of the frail and licentious daughters of George III',[29] is treated sympathetically, although she does have an illegitimate son who becomes a criminal.

In contrast, the Prince's younger brother, the Duke of Cumberland, is subjected to the full Reynolds treatment. In 1810 there had been a sensational scandal when one of the Duke's valets was found dead in his room with his throat cut and the Duke's shirt was covered in blood. Reynolds rejected the official explanation that the valet had attacked the Duke, and had then fled back to his own room, where he committed suicide. As in the case of the death of the Earl of Essex in the Tower, Reynolds took a sensational rumour and pushed it further. Although the incident is irrelevant to the plot of *The Mysteries of the Court of London*, Reynolds introduces it through a lady-in-waiting, who reveals not only that the Duke was the murderer, but also that he killed the valet because he had discovered he was committing incest with his sister, Princess Augusta. The wretched Duke of Cumberland himself lived long enough to have his death announced in *Reynolds's Newspaper*. The obituary described the Duke as 'a monster in human shape, a veritable fiend without a single redeeming quality'. Had he not been a prince, Reynolds declares, he would have perished on the gibbet: he summed up in his person 'perjury, adultery, seduction, incest and murder'.[30] Quite an obituary for an uncle of Queen Victoria!

In an advertisement in *Reynolds's Newspaper* for *The Mysteries of the Court of London*, Reynolds claimed his revelations were accurate. He announced that the second series 'will embrace, among other interesting matters, a full and fearless exposure of the particulars connected with the mysterious death of Sellis, the Duke of Cumberland's valet ... and a wide variety of occurrences in connection with the Court which history has purposely misrepresented, or which are as yet unknown

28 Reynolds, *MOCL* (1852), vol. 4, ch. 110, p. 2.
29 Reynolds, *MOCL* (1849), vol. 1, ch. 73, p. 258.
30 *RN*, 23 November 1851, p. 12.

to the public in general'.[31] Equally misleading is the assertion, in an advertisement for the reissue of the first series, that 'this extraordinary work gives the fullest and most fearless exposure of the Amours of the Family of George III and contains the most startling revelations in connection with the profligate and voluptuous career of George IV'.[32]

A cavalier treatment of historical facts when writing of the aristocracy was a feature common to both Reynolds's journalism and fiction. Yet in order to compare Reynolds's attack on the Hanoverians with others appearing in the nineteenth century,[33] we may consider another polemic, Charles Bradlaugh's *The Impeachment of the House of Brunswick* (1871). It was written by an author equally anti-Hanoverian, radical and republican, someone who would have been aware of Reynolds's work. It is sounder history, even if it is flawed by placing too much weight on the monarchy's influence on their times. But what we learn by such a comparison is that sounder is sometimes not necessarily more effective. Bradlaugh's history, with its ponderous prose, is of little interest to the twenty-first-century reader. Reynolds's melodramatic calumnies, however, for all their exaggeration and treatment of speculation as fact, and even though written with abandon for his popular audience and undoubtedly reflecting their own desires and views, still have a power of expression and the ability to rouse the reader to amazement, and sometimes amusement, a century and a half later.

---

31 *RN*, 10 November 1850, p. 13.
32 *RN*, 13 July 1851, p. 13.
33 Thackeray's lectures on 'The Four Georges' were given in 1855 and 1856 when Reynolds was in full flow, and published in 1860. Although they are much lighter in tone, Thackeray was still worried about his audience's response to his censure.

Chapter 6

'Some Little or Contemptible War upon her Hands': *Reynolds's Newspaper* and Empire

Antony Taylor

G.W.M. Reynolds is traditionally seen as a fragment of radical culture that persisted into the 1870s. Mediated through *Reynolds's Newspaper*, his ideas symbolize the overlap between the radical *demi-monde* of the 1840s and new styles within popular politics that predated and accompanied the rise of labour. As part of this re-evaluation, *Reynolds's Newspaper* has received timely analysis in recent work on the continuities within popular politics. Some central concerns of the paper under G.W.M. Reynolds's editorship, however, have been omitted from this wider reassessment. Analysis of Reynolds's attitudes to empire are notable for their absence. Yet for many contemporaries, the position of *Reynolds's Newspaper* on imperial issues was central, rather than peripheral, to its appeal. The question of the paper's core concern with empire, and its connections with G.W.M. Reynolds's broader political platform, deserves further scrutiny at a time when the topic of empire had been rediscovered in the historiography of Victorian Britain.

The columns of *Reynolds's Newspaper* teemed with imperial concerns. For Reynolds the empire was an emblem of the corruptions of crown and aristocracy. Gubernatorial sinecures, an imperial network of aristocratic administrators, Victoria's title of Empress of India and the aggressive foreign policy of 'Beaconsfieldism' demonstrated that many of the corruptions of British domestic politics were simply repeated on a world stage. Reynolds used the opportunities provided by royal titles and imperial wars to criticize lingering aristocratic and royal influences in the overseas possessions, where the empire assumed the characteristics of 'a gigantic system of outdoor relief for the aristocracy'.[1] Moreover, the colonial land issue reframed the Land Question and touched long-standing concerns about the dispossession of the English peasantry.

---

1 Bright used this term during a speech on British foreign policy in Birmingham in 1858; see A.J.P. Taylor, *The Trouble Makers: Dissent Over Foreign Policy 1792–1939* (London: Hamish Hamilton, 1957), p. 63.

Reynolds and Popular Radicalism

G.W.M. Reynolds occupies an ambivalent position within popular radicalism. A marginal figure during the Chartist period, prominent only in 1848, he nevertheless came to symbolize an unrepentant strand of popular politics that survived the collapse of the radical platform at mid-century.[2] Recalled by contemporaries in later years, he was sometimes imbued with all the characteristics of the internationalist generation of 1848, retrospectively rubbing shoulders with Kossuth, Mazzini, Garibaldi and Ledru Rollin, and remembered 'with the exception of Mr. Joseph Cowen' as 'the last English representative of this school'.[3] For many reformers of a later generation, *Reynolds's Newspaper* provided an introduction to the tenets of mid-Victorian radicalism. Its potent mix of scandal, disdain for hereditary position and enthusiasm for manhood suffrage came to typify the direction of radicalism at mid-century. Rohan McWilliam has pointed out that there is no firm evidence either way to indicate the continuing personal involvement of G.W.M. Reynolds in the production of the paper after the late 1850s.[4]

Nevertheless, drawing on the trademark style Reynolds had developed in his production of popular literature, the newspaper articulated contempt for the aristocratic and kingly leaders of society. In a circle that included his brother Edward Reynolds, the paper was central to the radical milieu of this period and to the ideas of 'a democratic old guard' who (as J. Morrison Davidson remarked) 'with myself were on duty long before there was talk of SDF, SF or ILP'.[5] Importing into the paper his skills as a writer of serial stories and penny shockers, Reynolds created an immediately recognizable brand that highlighted the injustices afflicting the poorer classes of society and charted their descent into poverty and immorality. His *Mysteries of London* examined the ways whereby '[t]he daughter of a peer is nursed through enjoyments and passes through an uninterrupted avenue of felicity from the cradle to the tomb; while the daughter of poverty opens her eyes at her birth upon destitution in all its most appalling shapes and at length sells her virtue for a loaf of bread'.[6]

Reynolds's Newspaper was not to everybody's taste. It outraged some. There is evidence of dislike for the paper from the nonconformist, respectable wing of

---

2   See, for the political significance of G.W.M. Reynolds in 1848, Ian Hargreaves, 'George W.M. Reynolds and "The Trafalgar Square Revolution": Radicalism, the Carnivalesque and Popular Culture in Mid-Victorian England', *Journal of Victorian Culture*, 7/1 (2002): 23–59.

3   E.B. Bax, 'Some Socialists in Britain', *Justice*, 20 April 1895, p. 4. Similar plaudits by political exiles feature in the radical press at the time of Reynolds's death; see *RN*, 22 June 1879, p. 1 and *The Englishman*, 28 June 1879, p. 205. It is rumoured that Reynolds ended his life as a respectable churchwarden: see E.S. Turner, *Boys Will Be Boys: The Story of Sweeney Todd et al.* (London: Michael Joseph, 1948; 1976 edn), p. 30.

4   Rohan McWilliam, 'The Mysteries of G.W.M. Reynolds: Radicalism and Melodrama in Victorian Britain', in Malcolm Chase and Ian Dyck (eds), *Living and Learning: Essays in Honour of J.F.C. Harrison* (Aldershot: Scolar, 1996), pp. 182–98.

5   J. Morrison Davidson, *Annals of Toil: Being Labour History Outlines, Roman and British* (London: William Reeves, 1899), pp. 333, 492.

6   Quoted in Turner, *Boys Will Be Boys*, p. 28.

radicalism. One staunch radical writing in the Fabian *Scout* echoed his father's verdict on the paper as 'a filthy rag'.[7] So immediately recognizable became the style of Reynolds's writing that real-life scandals prompted comparison with his more lurid and sensationalist descriptions. Commenting on the case of Mrs Ryve who, graphically alleging illegitimate descent from the Hanoverians, petitioned for recognition as the granddaughter of the Duke of Cumberland in 1866, the *National Reformer* was moved to comment that 'the report of the proceedings in Mrs Ryve's petition ... reads like a page from G.W.M. Reynolds's *Mysteries of the Court of London*'.[8] Despite its position at the interstices of respectable and unrespectable radicalism, the paper gained an extremely loyal following from the outset, circulating widely in London's radical clubs where Charles Booth remarked on its continuing presence in the 1880s and 1890s.[9]

Despite much research on the subject of *Reynolds's Newspaper*, and an increasing recognition of the contribution of this organ to the formation of mid-nineteenth-century radical opinion, recent explorations of the importance of *Reynolds's Newspaper* remain uneven.[10] Preoccupied with the domestic significance of the paper, and its role in promoting attacks on royalty or in shaping advanced liberal opinion, little attention has been devoted to the residual 'internationalism' that attracted Reynolds to discussion of the empire and its importance in expanding radicalism into an extra-European arena.[11] For G.W.M. Reynolds, empire was central to any discussion of corruption within government. In his eyes, the empire was a powerful 'outwork' of domestic corruption, in which the same forces that impeded liberty at home sought to expand their influence and increase their wealth, position and significance overseas.

Consideration of the empire in regard to the attitudes of the paper accords with recent debates about the centrality of empire within Victorian culture. Whereas once empire was seen purely as an opulent backdrop or a stage set for more important events, in recent years the broader framework of empire has been restored to centre stage, creating a greater appreciation of the currents of empire that fed back into the Victorian domestic environment.[12] Now seen as integral, rather than peripheral,

---

7   See the reminiscences of A.C. London in *The Scout: A Monthly Journal for Socialists*, 1 May 1896.

8   *National Reformer*, 10 June 1866, p. 362.

9   A. Fried and R. Elman (eds), *Charles Booth's London* (London: Hutchinson, 1969), pp. 296–7.

10   Imperial themes are barely mentioned in the two chief accounts: Virginia Berridge, 'Popular Sunday Papers and Mid-Victorian Society', in George Boyce, James Curran and Pauline Wingate (eds), *Newspaper History from the Seventeenth Century to the Present Day* (London: Constable, 1978), pp. 247–64; and Anne Humpherys, 'G.W.M. Reynolds, Popular Literature and Popular Politics', *Victorian Periodicals Review*, 16 (1983): 78–89.

11   For *RN* as a vector for republicanism see Antony Taylor, '*Reynolds's Newspaper*, Opposition to Monarchy and the Radical Anti-Jubilee: Britain's Anti-monarchist Tradition Reconsidered', *Historical Research*, 68/2 (1995): 318–37.

12   See, for examples, Catherine Hall, *Civilising Subjects: Metropole and Colony in the English Imagination, 1830–1867* (Cambridge: Cambridge University Press, 2002), ch. 1; Roger Hyam, *Empire and Sexuality: The British Experience* (Manchester: Manchester

the empire has been re-evaluated particularly in relation to radicalism. Shorn of its purely domestic and British concerns, radicalism is increasingly seen as a movement that posed questions about the balance of social forces existing both at home and in the colonies of settlement. As Miles Taylor and Peter Cain have demonstrated, the radical critique of empire had a long and vocal lineage.[13] By the early nineteenth century, the empire was no longer perceived as a benign institution that expressed the eternal verities of free trade, commerce and the free movements of peoples. Rooted in eighteenth-century debates about the revolt of the 13 American colonies, radicals detected a steady drift into militarism and conquest. For Richard Cobden's acolytes, empire imperilled free trade between countries and trading partners, precipitating damaging wars and endangering prosperity at home. In a platform linking Charles James Fox, William Molesworth, J.A. Roebuck, Edward Gibbon Wakefield and J.A. Hobson, the broader empire was now castigated both for exercising a detrimental effect on the colonists and amongst the administrators who experienced it at first hand, and for its lasting impact on the domestic politics of the United Kingdom.[14]

For many radicals, the new spirit pervading the empire was also partly a social phenomenon. Some critics saw the darker social aspects of the empire as imported directly into Britain. Radicals depicted the social groupings they opposed as monolithic, with strong financial networks that buttressed their position at home. The strongest criticisms of the social impact of empire emerged from the writings of Richard Cobden and the more militant Cobdenites who sought to extend the popular appeal of Cobden's ideas. From their point of view, defence of imperial concerns and dependency on a new financier caste created trade and banking interests with a vested interest in imperial expansion.[15] This outlook Peter Cain labels 'financial imperialism'.[16] For Cobden, empire held out the possibility for an expansion of corrupt aristocratic and financier influences. Equally, the great territorial, aristocratic families were able to reinforce their position by diversifying their investments into bonds and City investments reliant on overseas adventurism.

Here empire augmented the entrenched forces of aristocracy and their hirelings, allowing for the continuation of long-established notions of 'Old Corruption' revamped for the age of imperialism. Indeed, the new critiques of imperialism voiced by J.A. Hobson and other reformers bore many of the hallmarks of an older

---

University Press, 1990), chs 2, 4; and John M. Mackenzie, *Propaganda and Empire: The Manipulation of British Public Opinion, 1880–1960* (Manchester: Manchester University Press, 1987), chs 1–2.

13   See P.J. Cain, *Hobson and Imperialism: Radicalism, New Liberalism and Finance, 1887–1939* (Oxford: Oxford University Press, 2002), chs 1–3; Miles Taylor, '"Imperium et Libertas": Rethinking the Radical Critique of Imperialism during the Nineteenth Century', *Journal of Imperial and Commonwealth History*, 19/1 (1991): 1–23.

14   The most provocative summary of this position remains Taylor, *The Trouble Makers*, chs 2–4.

15   J.E. Thorold Rogers, 'British Finance: Its Present and Future', *Contemporary Review*, 34 (1879): 281–303.

16   P.J. Cain, 'British Radicalism, the South Africa Crisis and the Origins of the Theory of Financial Imperialism', in David Omissi and Andrew S. Thompson (eds), *The Impact of the South Africa War* (Basingstoke: Palgrave, 2002), pp. 173–93.

style in popular politics and traded in recognizable tropes familiar to a previous generation of radicals. This narrative built particularly on radical ideas articulated as early as the 1830s in John Wade's *Extraordinary Black Book*, where the role of the East India Company was seen as central in cementing and underpinning landed wealth at home.[17] As both Cain and Taylor argue, these notions provided a powerful criticism of empire and surfaced throughout the political community, encompassing middle-class radical attitudes and colouring the politics of more militant and plebeian Chartists and Owenites. It also featured strongly in the 1870s in opposition to Disraeli's foreign policy, and occurred as a critique of Gladstone's incursions into Egypt and of government policy at the time of the Second Boer War in 1899–1902.[18] Indeed, as Jonathan Schneer has demonstrated, there was an entrenched tradition of anti-militarism and popular plebeian radicalism in London in particular, where *Reynolds's Newspaper* found a ready audience in a strong radical constituency that argued for international peace and, exemplified by John Burns's candidature in Battersea, propounded a platform of opposition to empire in key elections like the 'Khaki election' of 1900.[19]

In recent years historians have also revisited popular perceptions of the imperial process. Debates about empire have now taken a cultural turn. Moving away from purely diplomatic and economic concerns, historians are reassessing empire in the light of contemporary debates about character, gender, 'Englishness' and the construction of British society. Against this background, themes such as migration, race and the 'imperial type' have re-emerged. The empire is now no longer simply a place in which exploitation or trade occurred, but rather has been re-evaluated as a managed space in which many of the characteristics and defining features of the mother country might be reinvented. As David Cannadine has argued, imperial bureaucrats, colonial administrators, explorers and military leaders took their cultural baggage with them to the dominions and sought to replicate many of the features of 'Mother England' against a broader colonial backdrop. Imitations of kingship, aristocracy, British domestic hierarchies and the parliamentary process became a marked feature of colonial society.[20] Where attempts were made to replicate or import a familiar domestic environment, they carried important implications for both the supporters and critics of empire. Radicals as well as conservatives were faced with the problem of understanding and unpicking structures that carried messages about home and abroad. Like supporters of empire, radicals who opposed imperial hierarchies tried to comprehend empire in terms of the politics and environment

---

17 John Wade (ed.), *The Extraordinary Black Book: An Exposition of Abuses in Church and State* (London: Effingham Wilson, 1832; repr., 1970), ch. 12.

18 C.C. Eldridge, *Disraeli and the Rise of a New Imperialism* (Cardiff: University of Wales Press, 1996), ch. 3.

19 Jonathan Schneer, *London 1900: The Imperial Metropolis* (New Haven, CT: Yale University Press, 1999), ch. 10; Alex Windscheffel, '"In Darkest Lambeth": Henry Morton Stanley and the Imperial Politics of London Unionism', in Matthew Cragoe and Antony Taylor (eds), *London Politics, 1760–1914* (London: Palgrave Macmillan, 2005), pp. 191–210.

20 See especially David Cannadine, *Ornamentalism: How the British Saw their Empire* (London: Allen Lane, 2001), chs 5–7; Mark Girouard, *The Return to Camelot: Chivalry and the English Gentleman* (New Haven, CT, and London: Yale University Press, 1981), ch. 14.

with which they were most familiar. For many radicals, empire was suffused with the spirit of the English caste system. Recent work in this area has demonstrated the ways in which colonial society in the white settler colonies became a replica of English society in the shires.[21] In this sense the empire was simply England, with all its social and political problems, writ large. Whereas this notion has been explored to reaffirm the aristocracy's view of its own imperial mission, the converse of this view, that the template provided by aristocracy carried messages for critics of imperial systems, has been surprisingly neglected. Despite a large literature that highlights particular episodes when anti-imperial critiques were deployed (e.g., Egypt in 1885, the First and Second Boer Wars[22]), there has been no systematic attempt to evaluate radical uses of 'Old Corruption' (or 'Old Iniquity' as *Reynolds's Newspaper* called it) to point up the deficiencies of the imperial system of government *per se*.[23]

Using *Reynolds's Newspaper*, this chapter seeks to reaffirm the radical commitment to understanding imperialism and highlights the important contribution made by the paper and other radical publications to shaping an anti-imperial vision rooted in a traditional critique of domestic government. Bernard Porter has recently questioned popular support and enthusiasm for empire. Citing a range of cultural and political evidence, he has dismissed the centrality of empire in Victorian society. Radical working men's newspapers, he suggests, evinced very little interest in overseas affairs, let alone imperial issues. In his narrative Porter includes one sparse section on Reynolds's writings in which he points up an apparent lack of interest in empire. Here Reynolds stands for a popular indifference to, rather than enthusiasm for, imperial issues.[24] Reynolds deserves better. This chapter, then, seeks to connect the ideas of G.W.M. Reynolds on empire with recent work on popular imperialism and its opponents. Repudiating Porter, this chapter aims to restore Reynolds's criticism of empire to centre stage and to understand the appeal of the paper he edited in terms of its obsessions with and enthusiasms for empire.

---

21   See, for example, John M. Mackenzie, *The Empire of Nature: Hunting, Conservation and British Imperialism* (Manchester: Manchester University Press, 1988), ch. 7.

22   See Donal Lowry, '"The Boers Were the Beginning of the End": The Wider Impact of the South Africa War', in Donal Lowry (ed.), *The South African War Reappraised* (Manchester: Manchester University Press, 2000), pp. 203–46; Richard Price, *An Imperial War and the British Working Class: Working-class Attitudes and Reaction to the Boer War* (London: Routledge and Kegan Paul, 1972), ch. 4; B. Porter, 'The Pro-Boers in Britain', in P. Warwick (ed.), *The South African War: An Anglo-Boer War, 1899–1902* (Harlow: Longman, 1980), pp. 239–57.

23   For 'Old Iniquity' see Catherine Hall, Keith McClelland and Jane Rendall, *Defining the Victorian Nation: Class, Race, Gender and the Reform Act of 1867* (Cambridge: Cambridge University Press, 2001), p. 93.

24   Bernard Porter, *The Absent-minded Imperialists: Empire, Society and Culture* (Oxford: Oxford University Press, 2004), pp. 126–7, 159–60.

Class and Empire

As in a British domestic setting, the concerns preoccupying *Reynolds's Newspaper* in the broader empire were aristocracy, land and monarchy. Aristocracy comprised the particular villains of the piece. Exposures of aristocracy were a common feature of the radical press. For G.W.M. Reynolds, the British aristocracy was tainted, bearing the historical stain of the Norman Conquest and carrying inherited predispositions towards tyranny that bent the British constitution to their will. *Reynolds's Newspaper* remarked: 'The Norman freebooters indeed elaborated a system of government so ingeniously compounded of violence and cunning, that to this day the mass of the people groan under it, while taught to believe they are in the enjoyment of a "glorious constitution" that is the envy and admiration of the whole world.'[25] Unpicking the history of aristocracy for most radicals meant revealing a history of avarice and self-interest. By the 1870s a substantial body of investigation by radicals like William Howitt, Howard Evans and Charles Bradlaugh had revealed the extent to which aristocracy retained its position within government, at court and in the army and navy. A feature in *Reynolds's Newspaper* commented: 'A few years ago very few of the people troubled themselves about the difference between pensions and perpetual pensions. Now they have lists of the dukes whose families have taken millions from the people in cash.'[26]

Imperial misdeeds retained a particular potency within the list of calumnies directed against the titled aristocracy. G.W.M. Reynolds's vision of aristocracy as rapacious and acquisitive that filled the pages of his popular penny novels was a notion that translated effectively into an imperial context. For *Reynolds's Newspaper* the currents fuelling extra-European expansion were similar to the forces operating to subdue liberty at home and were vigorously pursued in an act of naked class interest by the same closed caste.[27] Maintaining their power and position meant expanding their imperial interests. In the eyes of Reynolds and other radicals, the impulse here was towards fresh Norman Conquests in the wider world that would augment the wealth and station of Britain's traditional ruling elite and ensure that England 'is never without some little or contemptible war upon her hands'.[28] On this basis the history of empire and the history of Britain's aristocracy at home were inextricably intertwined.

From the early 1850s exposures of the imperial misdeeds of a transplanted British aristocracy littered the pages of *Reynolds's Newspaper*. Many of the images of aristocracy abroad propagated by the paper continued the overarching theme of conquest and expansion. *Reynolds's Newspaper* followed closely the line on the

---

25 *RN*, 27 January 1884, p. 3.

26 *RN*, 3 February 1884, p. 1. For the significance of contemporary compendiums of aristocratic wealth and landholding, see Antony Taylor, *'Lords of Misrule': Hostility to Aristocracy in Late Nineteenth- and Early Twentieth-century Britain* (Basingstoke: Palgrave Macmillan, 2004), ch. 2.

27 Hostility to aristocracy was a long-standing feature of Reynolds's publications. See the historical series 'The Aristocracy: Its Origin, Progress and Decay', in *RPI*, 17 November 1849, p. 14; 22 December 1849, p. 51; and 16 February 1850, p. 115.

28 *RN*, 12 November 1865, p. 3.

colonies expressed in John Wade's *Extraordinary Black Book* in the 1830s, that '[t]hese are a tremendous burthen [sic]on the resources of the Mother Country, chiefly to provide governorships, secretaryships, registrarships, agencies, and sinecures for aristocracy and their connexions'.[29] During periods of imperial misdeeds or at times of setbacks to the course of empire, the paper liked to remind its readers that the imperial domains were staffed by the offspring of the great hereditary families of the realm. Here it drew on historical memories of aristocratic freebooters and privateers like Warren Hastings, Lord Dalhousie and Lord William Bentinck.[30] *Reynolds's Newspaper* was particularly interested in Warren Hastings, believing that a reluctance to prosecute those who followed the same adventurism as he did demonstrated a steady decline in standards of probity within Parliament and the executive since the mid-eighteenth century.[31] For Reynolds, these society adventurers proliferated particularly in the wealthiest parts of the empire, where there was apparently most to gain. At times of unrest and rebellion, these were 'the real criminals – the common tyrants of both the British and Hindoos – the royal, aristocratic and commercial rulers and robbers of England and India'.[32]

In 1857, at the time of the Indian Rebellion, *Reynolds's Newspaper* returned to a vision of maladministration in India that drew on traditional concerns about the role of the East India Company at home, and apprehensions about the corruption and judicial despotism that seemingly characterized administration in the Indian subcontinent. These were recurrent themes within British radicalism, fostering Charles Bradlaugh's interest in India and his later role as an advocate of Indian interests.[33] For *Reynolds's Newspaper* there was no mistaking the source of the problems in India before the outbreak of the rebellion. In the columns by 'Gracchus' (for most of the nineteenth century written by G.W.M. Reynolds's brother, Edward) the characteristics of aristocracy became the metaphor for a broader misgovernment of the Indian empire:

> India hitherto has been the refuge where insolvent aristocrats retrieved their shattered fortunes; its armies have been officered by the pampered popinjays of London fashionable life; its treasures have been wasted upon indolent sinecurists and favoured pensioners; its people have been ground down by taxation, in order that the coffers of the India Company may be filled; in fact nepotism, imbecility, rapacity, and extortion have won a glorious

---

29   Wade (ed.), *The Extraordinary Black Book*, p. 379; see also 'John Hampden jr' (William Howitt), *The Aristocracy of England: A History for the People*, 2nd edn (London: Effingham Wilson, 1856), pp. 278–9.

30   See, on radical critiques of the Raj more generally, John R. McLane, *Indian Nationalism and the Early Congress* (Princeton, NJ: Princeton University Press, 1977), chs 1–2; Madhara Pannikar and an Englishman, *Indian Nationalism: Its Origins, History and Ideals* (London: Faith Press, 1920), p. 41.

31   *RN*, 11 January 1880, p. 3. For the connections between 'Old Corruption' and the Warren Hastings case, see Nicholas B. Dirks, *The Scandal of Empire: India and the Creation of Imperial Britain* (Cambridge, MA: Belknap Press, 2006), chs 2, 9.

32   *RN*, 2 August 1857, p. 9.

33   David Nash, 'Charles Bradlaugh, India and the Many Chameleon Destinations of Republicanism', in David Nash and Antony Taylor (eds), *Republicanism in Victorian Society* (Stroud: Sutton, 2000), pp. 106–24.

race and the blood and treasure of the glorious nation is now to be lavished, in order that the race may be continued to the benefit of a favoured few, and to the detriment of the suffering many.[34]

Here aristocracy provided a tainted well-spring for the habits of broader colonial administration. The paper's verdict on the consequences of the rebellion was a depressing one: 'Should the rebellion be suppressed, the same system which has provoked India to revolt will be continued – jobbery, corruption, torture and misrule will again flourish, until outraged humanity ultimately triumphs and Hindoostan becomes the possession of the Hindoo.'[35]

Where expansionism was prompted or proposed, aristocracy was generally depicted as the impetus behind it. In this, *Reynolds's Newspaper* located itself emphatically within the mainstream of radical politics. Against the background of Cecil Rhodes's annexation of Matabeleland and the 1896 Jameson Raid into the Transvaal, such objections to aristocratic expansionism became far shriller in the 1880s and 1890s. Depicted as thieves and robbers, distinguished only in their social class from the footpads of the street corner, aristocrats apparently pursued similar tactics on a much grander scale for the same goal of petty gain. In line with *Reynolds's Newspaper*'s view of imperial conquest, 'Owd Smeetom' (David Nicholl), Sheffield's eccentric radical and anarchist pamphleteer, inveighed against aristocratic misdeeds in Africa:

> Do you know what a charter is, 'ow'd lad'? Why it is a license to rob anyone weaker than yourself. Bill Sikes robs without a license on a dark night. They send 'im to a chokee with brown bread and skilly. The Hon. Cecil Rhodes and the Duke of Fife, and all the gang of aristocratic thieves and swindlers, with their hired lackeys of the press, rob with a license and that's the difference. Skilly for the Duke of Fife and Rhodes? No blooming fear. Champagne and turtle is more in their line. But they don't rob the rich like Bill Sikes, they rob the poor. Poor devils of niggers without a rag to their back. They stole their land, like they stole our land hundreds of years ago. And if the niggers object, they translate 'em to 'eaven with some dynamite or a maxim gun.[36]

Historical Perspectives

The new Normanism of empire haunted the pages of *Reynolds's Newspaper*. The subjugation of the Indian rebellion in particular was seen as employing techniques reminiscent of the Norman descent upon England. Moreover, for the paper, the Indian mutineers bore some similarity to the traditional heroes of British radicalism, notably William Tell.[37] Weighing the alleged atrocities by Indian princes and families sympathetic to the mutineers against the history of the English throne, it commented:

---

34 *RN*, 23 August 1857, p. 7.

35 *RN*, 4 October 1857, p. 7.

36 'Owd Smeetom', *Plague and Murder in Africa: Dynamite for Niggers* (Sheffield: David Nicholl, 1896), p. 2.

37 *RN*, 27 September 1857, p. 7. Colonial reformers and insurgents frequently compared themselves to the traditional heroes of British radicalism; see a long account of William Tell's

'The Queen of England owes her throne and the nobles their estates to crimes, little, if any, short of Nena Sahib and his fellow fiends in cruelty and horror ... We could fill a thousand volumes with the cruelties, the abominations, perpetuated by kings and queens of these kingdoms. Indeed, as we have observed, their whole power is based upon centuries of murder, rapine, pillage, torture and pollution.'[38]

In line with the emphasis placed by *Reynolds's Newspaper* on the continuing echoes of the Norman Conquest apparent in imperial expansionism, defeated races were frequently represented as subjugated Anglo-Saxons. Groups like the small proprietor class of ryots in India stood for a dispossessed peasantry everywhere 'robbed of their land and made subordinate to rack-renters (Zemindars)'.[39] This became a familiar trope in radical journalism from the middle years of the nineteenth century onwards. *Reynolds's Newspaper* invoked images from the *Anglo-Saxon Chronicles* of victims of the Norman aristocracy, quoting accounts of men hung upside down over fires, crushed by rocks and forced to endure adder-filled dungeons: 'The men were hung by their feet and by the thumbs, and then smoked with foul smoke. Knotted strings were put about their heads and writhed at until it went into their brain.' The paper saw the same impulses at work in the mass killing of Indian mutineers and the blowing of unfortunate prisoners from guns.[40] Nor were such images exclusively applied to the Indian subcontinent. Sympathizers often depicted the Maori in New Zealand as proxy Anglo-Saxons who shared the martial nature and island characteristics of the English.[41] For many radicals, the position taken by *Reynolds's Newspaper* on India in particular echoed romanticized visions of the community life of agrarian society on the Indian subcontinent. Indian village life was often portrayed as a surviving fragment of Aryan culture, similar in many ways to the lost rustic village communes of Anglo-Saxon England and, in the light of discoveries about the universalist nature of Aryan culture, apparently widely disseminated throughout Europe, bearing close ties of blood and kinship with similar societies.

For early enthusiasts of English village customs inspired by this line, the evidence from Indian precedents held out the potential to rediscover a feature 'which has now nearly everywhere been broken up into congeries of local observances, rural practices, peasant thoughts which lie loosely scattered up and down the country like the tesserae of some shattered mosaic pavement revealed only by the rude disturbance of the plough'.[42] For radicals, contemporaries could watch much the same story of

career in the New South Wales republican journal, *The Republican* (Sydney), 15 October 1887, p. 6.

38 *RN*, 27 September 1857, p. 1.

39 *RN*, 7 September 1856, p. 7. For contemporary concerns about the role of the ryots, see George Campbell, 'The Tenure of Land in India', in J.W. Probyn (ed.), *Systems of Land Tenure in Various Countries: A Series of Essays Published under the Sanction of the Cobden Club* (London: Cassell, Petter and Galpin, 1881 edn), pp. 213–89.

40 *RN*, 27 September 1857, p. 1.

41 J.O.C. Phillips, 'Musings in Maori Land: Or Was There a *Bulletin* School in New Zealand?', *Historical Studies*, 20/4 (1983): 520–35, and Tom Ballantyne, *Orientalism and Race: Arianism in the British Empire* (Palgrave: Basingstoke 2001), ch. 5.

42 George Laurence Gomme, *The Village Community with Special Reference to its Form and Survival in Britain* (in H.H. Ellis, *Contemporary Science Series*) (London: Walter Scott,

vengeance, economic dispossession and social dislocation that had afflicted their Saxon ancestors unfold on a broader imperial canvas in India, Afghanistan or the African colonies.[43]

Concerns about land use in the colonies echoed the images of a new Norman Conquest that dominated the contemporary radical press. Land theft occupied a central role within the history and memory of radical politics. Where land was monopolized or quite simply taken from indigenous inhabitants, it provoked comparison with the dispossession of the Anglo-Saxons by the power and authority of a transplanted Normanism. Most radicals saw landholding in the colonies and in Britain as co-joined. For *Reynolds's Newspaper*, the landowning aristocracy were themselves 'feudal Brahmins' exercising much the same spiritual and temporal power over their British tenants as their counterparts did over labourers on their estates in India.[44]

In common with other radicals, *Reynolds's Newspaper* was drawn particularly to the situation in India. Writing about the circumstances of the small proprietors there, the paper noted the implications for the great estate system at home of profitable investments raised on landed property overseas. Here the impact of aristocratic colonialism was twofold, with both British and imperial implications. The paper commented:

> An Englishman, we will say, has made a large fortune by the plunder of the ryots; from the same polluted source he derives a large annual income: he purchases an estate in this country for the maintenance of his family ... he does not depend on. As we have seen, he derives a yearly revenue from robbery in India: he is, in effect, quite independent of his English landed property; he can do with it as he pleases; he can convert it into a sheep walk, or a deer forest, or into a wilderness for still wilder and more unprofitable beasts for his own and his idle friends' barbarous amusements. The land thus thrown out of cultivation is so much abstracted from the nation's food. The bread of the people is diminished in quantity. And raised in price, and thus the British government of India is a double-barrelled infernal machine – one barrel destroys the Hindoo, the other the British labourer.[45]

For *Reynolds's Newspaper*, quasi-feudal landholding in the colonies added to the social and economic dislocation caused by the great estate system in Britain. Moreover, unrolling fresh conquests only added to the pace of dispossession for

---

1890), pp. 20–41. Later Indian nationalism, in part inspired by John Ruskin's ideas, drew strongly on notions of Indian village simplicity, opposed to the imported medieval institutions introduced by Europeans. For the role of this style of thinking in the ideas of Annie Besant, see Annie Besant, *England, India and Afghanistan* (Madras: Theosophical Publishing House, 1878), pp. 10–12, 30, 46; Besant, *India* (Madras: Theosophical Publishing House, 1913), pp. 9–42.

43 See for similarities between interpretations of English and Indian village life, J.W. Burrow, '"The Village Community" and the Uses of History in Late Nineteenth-century England', in Neil McKendrick (ed.), *Historical Perspectives: Studies in English Thought and Society* (London: Europa, 1974), pp. 255–84; Clive Dewey, 'Image of the Village Community: A Study in Anglo-Indian Ideology', *Modern Asian Studies*, 6 (1972): 291–338.

44 *RN*, 29 February 1880, p. 1.

45 *RN*, 7 September 1856, p. 7.

the English small proprietor class. Further land appropriations abroad seemingly increased the opportunities available to aristocratic interests. In New Zealand, the end of the Maori Wars in 1866 led to an influx of large landowners into North Island, squeezing out the small proprietors and causing the British republican C.C. Cattell to conclude that 'New Zealand is the colony of colonies where landed monopoly obtains to the greatest extent'.[46] Rooted in feudal precedence and the writings of Blackstone in his *Commentaries*, recently acquired land in the Australian colonies remained in the hands of the monarchy. Here the rights of the Crown took precedence, extinguishing all other claims and making Crown title the sole dispenser of ownership and possession. As Henry Reynolds has commented, '[t]he Norman kings it seemed cast very long shadows indeed, not only across the ages but over half the world as well'.[47] In the Australian colonies in particular, land taken by conquest was leased or redistributed to aspiring landowners in a manner that recalled the division of land amongst favourites by previous generations of monarchs. The parallels led radicals in Victoria to reprint the writings of Herbert Spencer on the origins of British landed titles and estates.[48]

Against this background, a vagabond peerage was seen as augmenting its fortunes by diversifying its assets into imperial wealth and exercising control over land on the new imperial frontiers. The class of large Australian landed proprietors, or 'squattocracy', seemingly served as an outlet for the fortunes of English migrant nobles or poorer younger sons. Sometimes depicted as an English aristocracy in exile, their immense landed wealth, interest in hunting and attempts to create a society season in Melbourne caused radicals both at home and in the colonies to draw comparisons with aristocratic life in the shires.[49] The term 'squattocracy' itself was a hybrid, evoking some of the long-established hostility to traditional aristocracies and symbolizing a visceral dislike for imported English manners and customs that echoed 'Old World Ways'.

Traditional images of Anglo-Saxon 'freeborn Englishmen' also migrated in opposition to the squatters. In the pages of William Lane's novel, *The Workingman's Paradise* (Sydney, 1892), all the bile of English emigrant Lane's dislike of the aristocracy and monopolistic landownership emerges in a speech in which his socialist character, Geisner, recalls: 'The free land days ... the free old German days when we were all barbarians and didn't know what a thief was, not only was

---

46   C.C. Cattell, 'The Lord and the State in New Zealand', *National Reformer*, 16 September 1888, p. 182.

47   Henry Reynolds, *The Law of the Land* (Ringwood, Victoria: Penguin, 1987), pp. 43–4.

48   *The Right to the Use of the Earth* (Melbourne: Land Reform League, 1870), pp. 6–7.

49   For the squatters in Victoria and New South Wales, see A.G.L. Shaw, *A History of the Port Phillip District: Victoria before Separation* (Carlton South: Meiyunyah, 1996; repr. Carlton: Melbourne University Press, 2003), ch. 6. For the squatters' interest in hunting, see Marion Hercock, 'A History of Hunting with Hounds in Western Australia', *Journal of the Royal Western Australian Historical Society*, 2/6 (2000): 695–712.

the land held in common, but the cattle also.'[50] Australian radical journals featured numerous complaints about titled ruffians in the Australian colonies terrorizing the small selectors and bearing the same names as the aristocratic families at home who were also busy clearing the poor off the land.[51]

For *Reynolds's Newspaper* there were too many such trace elements of aristocratic society in the white settler colonies. In contrast to some reformers in Australia and New Zealand, who saw possibilities for the rebirth of the freeborn Englishman on the margins of empire away from the traditional corruptions of Europe, the paper sought to deter emigration, stressing the continuities with, rather than departures from, traditional English social hierarchies evident in settler society.[52] In an editorial about emigration to Canada, it tried to dissuade potential migrants altogether, highlighting the inequities and injustices that created landless and dispossessed migrants in the rural districts: 'Why should these men love the British flag? ... What has England and England's boasted constitution done for those of her sons who toil the hardest of all her children? ... She has allowed them to be gradually robbed of their commons and their share of the soil in their own country, by heartless landowners and titled legislators.'[53]

For *Reynolds's Newspaper*, new titles, medieval social hierarchies and invented crypto-feudal traditions cemented the new societies created in the colonies. As David Cannadine points out, titles and imperial honours mimicked domestic hierarchies at home and provided inducements for local participation in imperial ceremonial.[54] British preferences for courting and using indigenous royal princes and traditional houses were roundly condemned by *Reynolds's Newspaper* on the grounds that they bred an indolent, parasitic class and encouraged the same vices and excesses that characterized royalty and aristocracy at home. Here it joined chorus with those radical voices that emphasized the willingness of the Raj in particular to work with

---

50 *The Workingman's Paradise: An Australian Novel by 'John Miller' (William Lane)*, ed. Michael Wilding (Sydney: Sydney University Press, 1980). Lane was much inspired by Owenite community models and the mythology surrounding the free Teutonic peoples of the German forests. He remarked: 'We Germanic peoples come into history as communists. From our communal villages we drew the strength which broke Rome down, the energy which even yet lets us live' (quoted by E.S. Wooster in *Communities of the Past and the Present* [Newllano, Louisiana: Llano Colonist, 1924], p. 50). It was these notions that led him to try to build the ideal community of 'New Australia' in Cosme, Paraguay. See, for a hostile account of this project, Stewart Grahame, *Where Socialism Failed: An Actual Experiment* (London: John Murray, 1912), chs 1–3.

51 See Peter Love, *Labour and the Money Power: Australian Labour Populism* (Carlton: Melbourne University Press, 1984), pp. 1–19.

52 For the Australian colonies and New Zealand as a 'New Arcadia' away from the corruptions of England, see John Eddy and Deryck Schreuder (eds), *The Rise of Colonial Nationalism* (Sydney: Allen and Unwin, 1988), chs 4, 5; Mark McKenna, *The Captive Republic: A History of Republicanism in Australia, 1788–1966* (Cambridge: Cambridge University Press, 1996), chs 5–6; Bruce Scates, *A New Australia: Citizenship, Radicalism and the First Republic* (Cambridge: Cambridge University Press, 1997), chs 3–4.

53 *RN*, 28 March 1875, p. 6.

54 Cannadine, *Ornamentalism*, ch. 7.

traditional princelings and royal families who fostered retrograde tendencies within government in the Indian subcontinent. It wrote of the situation in India in 1858:

> These princes are mostly shams or worse. They either cannot, or will not, protect the people of India from foreign robbers and oppressors. Indeed the native princes of India are the mere instruments of British rapacity. We use them as sponges, which suck the life-blood of Hindu industry; and then we – or rather our rulers for their own aggrandizement – squeeze these sponges dry. In this respect it is undeniable that the native princes of India are useful to the foreign masters of that country. And this, doubtless, is the reason why their right to representation is admitted; whilst the countless millions whose toil enriches the native tyrants and foreign conquerors of India have their rights ignored.[55]

For radicals, the creation of more titles and imperial honours threatened a further deterioration in this situation. Victorians like Edward Bulwer-Lytton devoted considerable energy to devising new systems of honours for the empire and suggested an imperial peerage for India.[56] Radicals saw the creation and manipulation of honours as illustrative of the bogus and invented nature of many traditional titles, both at home and in the imperial realms, and as a method for cementing further links with established landowning and royal hierarchies at home. In 1880 it rejoiced at the Canadian Federation's rejection of a planned royal governor-generalship, revelling in its antipathy to 'the new-fangled innovations royalty insists upon'.[57] Where imported honours proliferated, it was perceived as providing an impetus towards greater imperial integration and as a mask for more nakedly aggressive forms of imperial endeavour.

Amongst British radicals, the Royal Titles Bill of 1876 provoked particular alarm. The title of empress evoked comparisons with the Caesarist despotism of Napoleon III in France that was especially loathed and feared by reformers. *Reynolds's Newspaper* saw him as 'the most accomplished and bloodthirsty traitor of modern times'.[58] Under Louis Bonaparte imperial titles were associated with heavy-handed action against domestic dissent at home, suggested a dependency on the army and implied a brutal policy of conquest overseas. Imperial acts of war were themselves often compared to 'Bonapartism' in *Reynolds's Newspaper*. During the British invasion of the Indian kingdom of Oude in 1857, it invited its readers to imagine the position of the royal family and inhabitants of Oude by reference to an imagined parallel French invasion of Britain: 'Suppose that Louis Napoleon landed in England, with an immense army, conquered the country, marched to London, deposed Queen Victoria, and sent her a prisoner to France, there to live upon a paltry pension; would not the English people consider themselves justified in rising at the first convenient opportunity to restore their legitimate sovereign and expel the invader? This is now the aim and object of the people of Oude.'[59] Importing the title of empress for Victoria flouted the Revolution Settlement of 1688 and the conventions of the British monarchy,

---

55 *RN*, 18 April 1858, p. 1.
56 See Robert Blake, *Disraeli* (London: Eyre and Spottiswoode, 1966), pp. 562–3.
57 *RN*, 14 March 1880, p. 4.
58 *RN*, 27 September 1857, p. 7.
59 *RN*, 6 September 1857, p. 7.

and was suggestive of a steady slide into Bonapartism. 'It has an ugly sound to English ears,' wrote *Reynolds's Newspaper*; 'Roman Emperors were tyrants; Russian Emperors were the same; and the two Bonapartes who assumed this obnoxious title were determined despots.'[60] For *Reynolds's Newspaper* it transformed Victoria into a 'golden puppet' simply serving the needs of empire builders. Correspondents to the paper also reviled the title. One described it as 'a dirt-bespattered title [pinned] to an old lady's mantle'.[61] For the paper as a whole, the title of 'Brummagem empress' summed up the tawdry and self-serving nature of such baubles, expressive of Disraelian imperial ambitions and Victoria's interest in the precedent and status they conferred in relation to other European royalty.[62]

Such notions also touched a raw nerve in the white settler colonies. Emigré British radicals like George Black in New South Wales similarly complained about large numbers of imported dynastic scions in the colony, festooned with bogus imperial titles and honours. Closeness to Britain was measured in terms of the expanded numbers of such titles. More intimate ties of defence via imperial federation projects were condemned on this basis. Black wrote: 'Imperial Federation means that we shall be saddled with a lot of noble idlers, the Leiningens, the Battenburgs, the Queen's grandsons and others; the fat billets are nearly all occupied at home and the taxpayer's patience is nearly exhausted, it will be our turn for bloodletting'. The country, he averred, would swarm with 'distinguished sundowners' and illustrious 'Murrumbidgee whales' in the event of an alliance with Britain.[63] In the Australian colonies there were significant precedents for the creation of imaginary titles with real or conferred status. For some years the squatters had sought formal adornments that recognized their status as a de facto aristocracy. In 1853 William Charles Wentworth led a lively campaign for the establishment of a hereditary House of Lords as the Upper Chamber for the New South Wales legislature following Edward Bulwer-Lytton's suggestions for the creation of an Australian colonial peerage, featured in his novel *The Caxtons* in 1849.[64] Though greeted with some derision, this project reinforced the impression that dynastic ambition and aristocratic privateering remained common throughout New South Wales. Thereafter, the taint of snobbery and aristocratic pretension hung around Government House in Sydney and dogged the society and social events held there.[65] For most radicals, the systems of imperial

---

60 *RN*, 12 March 1876, p. 4. For the radical campaign against Disraeli's Royal Titles Bill, see Taylor, '*Reynolds's Newspaper*, Opposition to Monarchy and the Radical Anti-Jubilee', pp. 321–2.

61 *RN*, 13 February 1876, p. 2; 4 June 1876, p. 3.

62 *RN*, 19 March 1876, p. 1.

63 George Black, *Why I am a Republican* (Sydney: Sir Robert Bear, 1891), p. 18.

64 M. Clark (ed.), *Sources of Australian History* (Oxford: Oxford University Press, 1957), p. 312; C.N. Connolly, 'The Origins of the Nominated Upper House in New South Wales', *Historical Studies*, 20/1 (1982): 53–72; Ged Martin, *Bunyip Aristocracy: The New South Wales Constitution Debate of 1853 and Hereditary Institutions in the British Colonies* (London: Croom Helm, 1986), ch. 3.

65 See James Jupp, *The English in Australia* (Cambridge: Cambridge University Press, 2004), pp. 103–5; Penny Russell, 'The British Colonial Class and Comportment in Nineteenth-century Australia,' *Royal Historical Society Transactions*, 12 (2002): 431–53.

titles and honours were anyway largely co-joined, reinforcing ties with the mother country and frustrating calls for Home Rule in the dominions which correspondents in *Reynolds's Newspaper* declared to be articulated very loudly in the Australian colonies.

Antique titles, imperial monarchy, landownership, peripatetic governors subservient to the interests of the Colonial Office, old aristocratic connections and aspiring *nouveaux riches* families in the colonies fostered a view of the empire as a place of despotism and absolutist tendencies. *Reynolds's Newspaper*'s verdict on empire was that it was 'that hateful thing which has brought so much evil in the world'.[66] A common comparison for domestic and colonial radicals was with the tsarist domains. The Australian *Republican* journal edited by the radical poet Henry Lawson remarked:

> What the Czar of Russia now is, the English church and the aristocracy would make the sovereigns of our own empire if they were only powerful enough to do it. We can with readiness read the lesson. The evil of monarchy is none the less an evil because it has become somewhat modified. The germs of tyranny flow through its system and from time to time we must expect from it the epidemics of persecution which leaves liberty scarred and our hopes dolorous.[67]

Radical visions of risings in the colonies echoed the theme of mistreatment and persecution meted out to those who campaigned for their rights against this unjust system. Furthermore, harsh treatment of risings presaged the ways in which the British working class might be treated. For reformers the aggressions of empire fed back into the domestic environment. They provided a fantasy of violence in domestic confrontations. The Governor Eyre episode in Jamaica in particular fuelled radical fears about the potential for oppression dormant in the British state system.[68] There are distinctions to be drawn here between the treatment of the white settler domains and the colonies with predominantly black populations, regarded as too backward or dangerous for imperial Home Rule. In Jamaica fears of black majority rule during the 1840s led to the reimposition of control by the Colonial Office. Subsequently, a rising in Morant Bay in 1865 prompted savage reprisals by irregular macaroon militias led by General Hobbs and Crown forces. The riots, which evoked comparison with the Indian rebellion and the Haitian rebellion of the 1790s, resulted in the deaths of 436 black rioters and the flogging of 600 more, including women and children.[69] In Britain opinion divided between those who applauded the punitive actions of Governor Eyre against the rebels and those who were outraged by his actions.[70] For *Reynolds's Newspaper*, the draconian suppression of the rebellion demonstrated

---

66 *RN*, 19 March 1876, p. 1.

67 *The Republican* (Sydney), 4 July 1887, p. 2. For comparisons between the government of Poland under the tsars and the government of the empire under Queen Victoria, see *RN*, 25 February 1866, p. 1.

68 Hall, McClelland and Rendall, *Defining the Victorian Nation*, ch. 4.

69 Hall, McClelland and Rendall, *Defining the Victorian Nation*, p. 201.

70 Catherine Hall, *White, Male and Middle Class: Explorations in Feminism and History* (Cambridge: Cambridge University Press, 1992), pp. 255–95.

again the potential for despotism within the imperial system. It highlighted especially the double standards and hypocrisy of aristocrats who had sided with the North against the slaveholding South in the American Civil War and who now endorsed the actions of Eyre: 'Now, though, the Negroes are exposed to unparalleled tortures and indignities under the shield of a monarchy, these squint-eyed and spurious philanthropists will not utter one word in condemnation of Governor Eyre, lest by so doing they should help to bring disgrace and odium on the monarchic government and aristocratic absentees whose paid servant and authorised executioner he is.'[71] Again, fears of methods imported direct from the colonies to deal with domestic disturbances resurfaced. The paper alluded to Lord Elcho's observation: 'That in the event of a similar occurrence in this country, he hoped the example of the Jamaica macaroons would be followed by the English soldiers and volunteers [and this action would be] endorsed by the whole aristocracy. Many of our rulers, in fact, long for a Governor Eyre method of dealing with reformers and Hyde Park working-class meetings.'[72]

For radicals the precedent for the treatment of the rebellion was located deep in the political past and drew from the Whig constitutionalist tradition. *Reynolds's Newspaper* made allusion to the seventeenth-century Monmouth rising, drawing comparisons between events in Jamaica and the behaviour of Kirk's Lambs on the battlefield of Sedgemore in 1685, and the bloody oppression of dissidents by the Austrian General Haynau following the 1848 revolutions in Hungary.[73] The mobbing of General Haynau by Chartists during a visit to London in 1850 had established this revenge against Austrian repression as a staple of radical memory in Britain.[74] Moreover, the Jamaica massacres became integral to a long-standing narrative about Toryism that made a connection between the 'bloodthirstiness' of empire building and the 'lesson in blood' read to the English working poor by an earlier Tory government at Peterloo.[75] Writing in 1865, *Reynolds's Newspaper* warned working men: 'Let Englishmen think of these things, for although Irishmen and Negroes are the present victims, who knows [who] may be the next people exposed to the tender mercies of the Hobbs, the Eyres and the Wodehouses, who defend the authority of Queen Victoria.'[76]

Conclusion

Reynolds's Newspaper found a wide readership from the early years of its foundation. Many of its readers were preoccupied with its commentary on domestic affairs.

---

71   *RN*, 24 December 1865, p. 1.

72   *RN*, 5 August 1866, p. 4.

73   *RN*, 10 December 1865, p. 3.

74   Dorothy Thompson, *The Chartists: Popular Politics in the Industrial Revolution* (Hounslow: Temple Smith, 1984), p. 132.

75   *RN*, 10 September 1876, p. 4. Charles Bradlaugh also compared punitive governmental action against the Boers in 1880 to the events of Peterloo; see Charles Bradlaugh, *Toryism from 1770 to 1879* (London: C. Bradlaugh and A. Besant, 1880), p. 5.

76   *RN*, 26 November 1865, p. 1.

Fig. 6.1   Republican tendencies in the Australian colonies are expressed by this
             cartoon of Australia invited to join the 'republican dance of France
             and the U.S.' (*The Boomerang*, 6 July 1898).

For others, however, its exploration of imperial themes created a parallel vision, in
which governmental abuses at home overlapped with the pursuit of a flawed and
discredited foreign policy abroad in the wider empire. Many of its readers valued its
critique of empire. Its interest in imperial issues meant that *Reynolds's Newspaper*
found a wide circulation throughout the colonies. Letters from the white settler
dominions (the Cape colonies, Australia and New Zealand in particular) were a
regular feature of the paper.[77] In the Australian colonies in the 1880s its republican
stance chimed with a popular vein of anti-monarchist sentiment. Here it reached
such a wide audience that it inspired a number of imitators, notably English émigré
John Norton's derivative *The Truth*, popularly dubbed 'the Australian *Reynolds's*',
and J.F. Archibald's radical/nationalist *Bulletin*.[78] *The Truth* preserved the imperial

---

77   *RN*, 30 July 1899, p. 2.
78   See M. Cannon, *That Damned Democrat: John Norton, 1858–1916: An Australian
Populist* (Carlton: Melbourne University Press, 1981), pp. 3–10; *RN*, 30 July 1899, p. 2. For
the influence of *RN* on J.F. Archibald during a visit to Britain, see S. Lawson, *The Archibald
Paradox: A Strange Case of Authorship* (Ringwood, Victoria: Allen Lane, 1983), pp. 104–11;
McKenna, *The Captive Republic*, pp. 135, 172–3.

concerns of *Reynolds's Newspaper* intact and echoed much of its tone on foreign policy adventurism. It talked of a 'so-called "Imperial Policy"' marked by

> [a]ggression and insolence; oppression and massacre; eternal wars and rumours of wars; Indian mutinies with patriotic Sepoys tied to and blown from the cannon's mouth ... two China wars to force the cursed opium trade upon China ... a New Zealand War against the grossly-wronged and gallant Maories ... and a dozen other little wars of oppression against unoffending and comparatively defenceless Black races; and all for what? – the so-called interest of the British trader and the glory of the British flag. Bah![79]

Throughout its career, *Reynolds's Newspaper* maintained a consistent stance on empire: it disapproved. The line first taken by G.W.M. Reynolds persisted after his death and placed *Reynolds's Newspaper* firmly in the camp of anti-imperial causes, from the campaign against Gladstone's decision to annex Egypt in 1885 through to the pro-Boer platform of 1899–1902. It was especially visible in the agitation against the acquisition of Egypt in 1885 that was shot through with many traditional radical concerns and preoccupations. Decrying the war's impact on the prosperity and well-being of 'the working-classes of England', campaigners sought to mobilize the forces of a disparate radicalism and resurrected fears about 'the irresponsible waging of war with their lives and their money at the discretion of kings and aristocrats'.[80] For *Reynolds's Newspaper* colonial nationalists from the white settler colonies and beyond were to be honoured. Hindoo reformers were embraced. Afghan and Zulu tribesmen were roundly praised. The Boer irregular commandos in the First Boer War were 'sturdy republicans' preserving some of the virtues of Cromwell's Commonwealthmen and spearheading campaigns against the spread of imperial interests in South Africa.[81] Throughout its career, the paper always sought to maintain the integrity of subject peoples. Attempts to subdue the spirit of the Zulu by establishing agricultural land colonies were condemned for simply placing tribesmen into the hands of usurers and profitmongers.[82] The paper's verdict on empire in the year after G.W.M. Reynolds's death remained a typically robust one: 'How can we raise our voice against spoliation, robbery, cruelty, and wrong if practiced by some other powerful nation, when there is no authoritative voice that can say one word in justification of our doings in Africa and Asia?'[83]

79 *The Truth* (Sydney), 27 September 1896, p. 4.

80 See a speech by J.E. Thorold Rogers at St James's Hall, reported in the *National Reformer*, 12 April 1885, p. 293.

81 *RN*, 18 January 1880, pp. 1, 3; Antony Taylor, 'Medium and Messages: Republicanism's Traditions and Preoccupations', in Nash and Taylor (eds), *Republicanism in Victorian Society*, pp. 1–11.

82 *RN*, 23 January 1887, p. 1.

83 *RN*, 18 January 1880, p. 3.

Fig. 6.2   Gladstone, accompanied by death, ignores his previous protestations of peace and leads Britain into imperial adventurism in Egypt in 1885 (*The 1885 Gladstone Almanack*, London: Blackwood and Sons, 1886).

In his study of English manners, the honours system and social structures throughout the empire, David Cannadine highlights the importance of status and title in the broader imperial domains.[84] His reading demonstrates the existence of a project to 'Anglicize' the colonized and to work with structures that harmonized with the prevailing social conventions at 'home' or to directly import them from

---

84 Cannadine, *Ornamentalism*, chs 5, 7.

Britain. Similar depictions of empire occur in *Reynolds's Newspaper*. From a very different perspective to the conservative defenders of the empire cited by Cannadine, *Reynolds's Newspaper* sought to highlight the deficiencies in this model. In its view, rather than liberating themselves from the social constraints of traditional hierarchies and landed monopoly, the inhabitants of the empire felt themselves shackled by the same social forces that had kept progress in Britain in check for so many centuries. Indeed, empire breathed new life into a decrepit and tottering social system. Empire mattered to radicals in nineteenth-century Britain. It held up a mirror that reflected the injustices and inequities of 'home'. *Reynolds's Newspaper* expressed radical hostility to the tone of the imperial agendas and the status and hierarchy that were so central to imperialism itself. In so doing, the preoccupations of the paper demonstrate 'persistencies' within the radical platform with regard to empire and restore the radical plebeian position on anti-imperialism to recent debates about the role and significance of imperialism within popular politics.

PART III
The Urban *Mysteries*

Chapter 7

An Introduction to G.W.M. Reynolds's 'Encyclopedia of Tales'

Anne Humpherys

At the end of his mammoth eight volumes of *The Mysteries of the Court of London* in 1856, G.W.M. Reynolds added a postscript in which he noted that '[f]or *twelve* years, therefore, have I hebdomadally issued to the world a fragmentary portion of that which, as one vast whole, may be termed an Encyclopedia of Tales'.[1] By this label Reynolds called attention to one of the more distinctive elements of his 12-year project that included the four volumes (two series of two volumes each) of *The Mysteries of London* (1844–48) and the eight (four series of two volumes each) of *The Mysteries of the Court of London* (1848–56), with their dozens of different fictional plots and first-person histories, journalistic information, political diatribes and internal references and footnotes to current events. He did indeed include in this work, taken as a whole, examples of nearly every popular genre from gothic melodrama to sentimental romance, from journalistic leaders to scientific processes.[2]

Reynolds was undoubtedly using the term 'encyclopedia' in a loose way, simply drawing attention to the variety of material in his 12-volume work, but it is instructive nonetheless, even as is Pierce Egan's sense that London was 'a complete CYCLOPÆDIA'.[3] Both are trying to indicate the vastness of their subject and justify the nature of their modes of representation. Reynolds notes in several places the expansiveness of his project, and congratulates himself on his ability to keep it all together: 'As the subject grows upon us, our energies appear to take the

---

1   G.W.M. Reynolds, *The Mysteries of the Court of London* (London: John Dicks, 1856), vol. 8, Postscript, p. 412, emphasis in original.

2   In another place, I labelled this totalizing type of fiction an 'urban mysteries genre', which was marked by an identifiable method of plotting that gradually twisted together a number of disparate stories into one plot and at the same time wove all the different volumes into one thematic statement, a version of the conventional nineteenth-century representation of London as a city of contrasts particularly between the rich and poor, the palace and the slum. (A common adage for would-be writers in the period was in fact write character like Dickens and plot like Reynolds, a linkage that neither of the two would have appreciated.) See my article 'Generic Strands and Urban Twists: The Victorian Mysteries Novel', *Victorian Studies*, 34 (1991): 455–72.

3   See Chapter 9 in this volume by Stephen James Carver, 'The Wrongs and Crimes of the Poor: The Urban Underworld of *The Mysteries of London* in Context'.

colossal proportions adequate to the task of elaborating it: our imagination expands commensurately with the labour which it has to perform.'[4]

Beyond giving us an insight into Reynolds's ambitions and self-congratulation, what else might the label 'encyclopedic' tell us about the biggest bestseller of the nineteenth century by 'the most popular writer' of the century?[5] The term 'encyclopedic narrative' has its own history. In 1976, Edward Mendelsohn coined the phrase to describe an unrecognized literary genre made up of only seven works: Dante's *Commedia*, Rabelais's five books of Gargantua and Pantagruel, Cervantes's *Don Quixote*, Goethe's *Faust*, Melville's *Moby Dick*, Joyce's *Ulysses* and, Mendelsohn's main interest, Pynchon's *Gravity's Rainbow*.[6] Subsequently his definition has been applied to other works such as Umberto Eco's *Foucault's Pendulum*. Alan Clinton argues in fact that the label 'encyclopedic narrative' can be useful in thinking about many postmodern novels.[7]

But rather than moving forward in time with Mendelsohn's generic definition to see what it can tell us about postmodern literature, I would like to move backwards and, in a manner of speaking, sideways, that is, to see what can be learned by applying the term not to the great canonized works of the past or to literary postmodern fictions, but rather to a work of immense popularity in the nineteenth century which has no claim to great literature but which was widely imitated across the globe and influential in several places, particularly in India.[8] For despite what may seem presumptuous on my part in linking Reynolds's mammoth *Mysteries* series with Mendelsohn's seven great books, Reynolds's project does fulfil many of Mendelsohn's defining characteristics of the 'encyclopedic narrative', and thinking about Reynolds's achievement in these terms can throw some light on the reasons for the work's popularity and influence.

Few modern readers of Reynolds's *Mysteries*, even those familiar with more than the first series, think of the work as one long expanded text. Reynolds himself, however, apparently did, and this is a view supported by the work's publishing history. In his postscript to the last volume of *The Mysteries of the Court of London*, he describes his 'Encyclopedia of Tales' as 'comprising six hundred and twenty-four weekly Numbers'.[9]

---

4   Reynolds, *MOCL* (1849), vol. 1, ch. 94, p. 350.

5   *The Bookseller*, July 1879, p. 660.

6   Edward Mendelsohn, 'Encyclopedic Narrative: From Dante to Pynchon', *Modern Language Notes*, 91/6 (Comparative Literature): 1267–75. See also Edward Mendelsohn, 'Gravity's Encyclopedia', in George Levine and David Leverenz (eds), *Mindful Pleasures: Essays on Thomas Pynchon* (Boston: Little, Brown, 1976), pp. 161–95.

7   Alan Clinton, 'Conspiracy of Commodities: Postmodern Encyclopedic Narrative and Crowdedness', *rhizomes.05* (Fall 2002), www.rhizomes.net/issue5/clinton.html (accessed 30 December 2006).

8   See Priya Joshi, *In Another Country: Colonialism, Culture, and the English Novel in India* (New York: Columbia University Press, 2002), pp. 35–93, for a discussion of Reynolds's influence on the development of the Indian novel. See also Chapter 15 in this volume by Sucheta Bhattacharya, 'G.W.M. Reynolds: Rewritten in Nineteenth-century Bengal'

9   Reynolds, *MOCL* (1856), vol. 8, Postscript, p. 412.

The project began in 1844 when the first weekly number of *The Mysteries of London* was published in penny numbers by George Vickers;[10] these weekly numbers continued until 1848. The first series told the story of two brothers, Richard and Eugene Markham, who made a pact to see who would be most successful. Richard, the good brother, though he begins in poverty and unfair imprisonment, ultimately becomes the ruler of an Italian state and husband to a virtuous and influential woman. Eugene, the bad brother, goes from crime to crime and is finally murdered by his manservant. The novel also chronicles the deeds of the criminal Anthony (Tony) Tidkins, the Resurrection Man (because he is, among other things, a body snatcher).

Around the time Reynolds was finishing the second series, which carries over a few characters like Richard Markham as ruler of Castelcicaland and whose many plots are similar to those in the first series, he was in financial difficulties. He fell out with his publisher and did not write another series under the title *The Mysteries of London*. As noted in the Introduction to this book, Reynolds ultimately went into partnership with his assistant John Dicks, who succeeded in making Reynolds a rich man and who himself became one of the most important publishers of cheap books in the century. Vickers continued *The Mysteries of London* for a year with Thomas Miller and E.L. Blanchard as authors. Reynolds and Dicks also continued the series, but with a new title, *The Mysteries of the Court of London*,[11] designed to cash in on the popularity of the first series and which continued in four series of two volumes each from September 1848 to December 1855 or January 1956.

There were 102 weekly parts in the first and second series of *The Mysteries of London*, and close to that for all four series of *The Mysteries of the Court of London*. There were some 800 double-column pages in each series, some million and a half words (for a total of around nine million words for the whole 12 volumes). *The Mysteries of London* had 52 illustrations by George Stiff in each of its two series,

---

10 The immediate source was Eugène Sue's *Les Mystères de Paris* (1842–43). Other possible sources include Pierce Egan's *Life in London* (1821–22) and *Les Mystères de Londres* (1842–43) by another Frenchman, Paul Feval.

11 The title *The Mysteries of the Court of London* is clearly appropriate for the first two series of the continuation, which centre around the scandalous doings connected with the Prince Regent, who figures as a character. At the end of the second series the narrator says he does not intend to follow the Prince Regent's career when he became George IV. In his postscript Reynolds acknowledged this divergence and in the process defined what he saw as the unifying idea behind the whole:

> In respect to the Third and Fourth Series of 'THE MYSTERIES OF THE COURT OF LONDON,' it may be alleged by some that the title is to a certain degree a misnomer, inasmuch as the incidents which they contain bear slightly any reference to the British Court. But a Royal Court, in the proper acceptance of the term, is limited not to the circle of the sovereign alone: it includes the aristocracy – the satellites revolving about the central sun. In this sense, therefore, it will be seen that there is no actual misnomer in the titles of the Third and Fourth Series of 'THE MYSTERIES OF THE COURT OF LONDON'; but that they constitute fitting pendants and sequences to the First and Second series. (Reynolds, *MOCL* [1856], vol. 8, Postscript, p. 412)

while *The Mysteries of the Court of London* also contained 52 illustrations in each series. In the first series of this continuation the illustrator was Henry Anelay, in the second and third, W.H. Thwaits, who also illustrated the fourth with F. Gilbert. Each weekly number cost a penny, and each month the weekly numbers were bound together with a distinctive cover and sold for sixpence. When a series was finished it was almost immediately issued in a two-volume book form so that by 1848 there were three different forms of publication for each volume. The whole series was reissued over and over again in different formats, and through this seemingly endless reissue the *Mysteries* project reputedly sold over a million copies during the second half of the nineteenth century. It was imitated in the rest of Europe, in the United States and in Russia,[12] and popular in India both in English and Indian translations.

One element in Reynolds's *Mysteries* that was influential and which his imitators repeated was his unrelenting portrayal of the sensational in modern urban life. But the form of the *Mysteries*, that is, its effort at totalization through multiple tales – what I, following Reynolds, am calling 'encyclopedic' – had wide impact. It is the argument of this chapter that the work's 'encyclopedic' characteristics, coinciding with much of Mendelsohn's definition, are among the important elements of its popularity. Of course, Reynolds did not include 'everything' in his encyclopedia of tales. There is very little representation of middle-class home life or occupations, the great subject of the Victorian novel, nor is there any representation of the industrial workers of the north, the subject of the social fiction of the 1840s and 1850s by writers like Elizabeth Gaskell or Dickens, particularly in *Hard Times* (1854). Reynolds's encyclopedia of tales clearly excludes this expanded middle: his representation of the struggle for life in 'London' is between the upper and the lowest classes. As Stephen James Carver argues in Chapter 9 of this volume, the conflict is between the upper classes and the criminal class. The emphasis on the middle class in the canonized novels of the Victorian period, on the other hand, results in another kind of exclusion, an excluded bottom as it were. Reynolds is at pains to correct this absence in his *Mysteries* and to present an alternate social view to that of novelists like Dickens and Thackeray. This alternate view both constructed his working-class readers' sense of victimization and gave them a sense of vicarious empowerment, as Henry Mayhew discovered when

---

12   From America came *The Mysteries of New York* (1848) by E.Z.C. Judson and the anonymous *The Mysteries of Philadelphia* (1844); from Germany, *The Mysteries of Berlin* (1845). David S. Reynolds remarks that Sue's and Reynolds's mysteries 'prompted a whole string of American "city-mysteries" novels: Philip Pendant, *The Mysteries of Fitchberg* [n.d.]; Caroline Hargrave, *The Mysteries of Salem!* (1845); Henry Spofford, *The Mysteries of Worcester* (1846); Frank Hazelton, *The Mysteries of Troy* (1847); the anonymously published *Mysteries of Nashua* (1849); Ned Buntline, *The Mysteries and Miseries of New Orleans* (1851); and George Lippard, *The Quaker City* (1845)' (David S. Reynolds, *Beneath the American Renaissance* [New York: Knopf, 1988], p. 82). See also Michael Denning, *Mechanic Accents: Dime Novels and Working-class Culture in America* (London: Verso, 1987), pp. 85–6. E.F. Bleiler says that Reynolds's *Mysteries of London* 'was translated, immediately after British publication, into French, German, Italian and Spanish' and 'enjoyed a wide circulation (in German) in the Russian Empire, where it was officially banned' (Introduction to Reynolds's *Wagner the Wehr-Wolf* [New York: Dover, 1975], p. vii).

interviewing costermongers, because of the degree to which Reynolds berated the aristocracy.

To investigate this sense of empowerment further, we might turn to Mendelsohn's discussion of the encyclopedic narrative. He lists some 15 defining characteristics,[13] the first being the obvious one of an attempt at total inclusiveness. These works attempt to render the full range of knowledge and beliefs of a national culture, while identifying the ideological perspectives from which that culture shapes and interprets its knowledge.[14] In Mendelsohn's words, they are written by a 'writer whose work attends to the whole social and linguistic range of his nation, who makes use of all the literary styles and conventions known to his countrymen'.[15]

The effort of totalization, the effort to portray a national culture, the effort to represent the social and, if not linguistic, then generic range of his nation, is, without much of a stretch, a description of Reynolds's *Mysteries*. It is true that Reynolds has not taken 'his place as national poet or national classic',[16] that role being filled, according to Mendelsohn, by Shakespeare. But to Reynolds's contemporary readers, the work might indeed have been experienced as a 'national classic'. For whatever the limitations of his texts that come from oversimplification, Reynolds does project an epic view. Further, his texts contain clear and repeated ideological perspectives that were familiar to his readers, if an anathema to many middle-class readers, and outdated and reductive to his later readers. These are that power is held and abused by an oligarchy, which Reynolds identifies as the aristocracy and its stooges in the church, the law and the industrial and monied middle classes, and further that this oligarchy is selfish, hedonistic, irresponsible and arbitrary in its use of power, impoverishing and criminalizing the working and lower classes in general. There are hints, however, that there is a connection between crime and the social dislocation that came about through rapid industrialization and the reduction of all working relationships to what Thomas Carlyle called the 'cash nexus'.

Reynolds's articulation of this ideology comes both from his narrator's many rhetorical intrusions in the narrative and from the narrative's structure. His plots are primarily ordered by ideological binaries that were clichés even in his own time: high and low; honest and deviant; law-abiding and criminal; good and bad. The latter are repeatedly represented by siblings: Richard and Eugene in *The Mysteries of London*; in *The Mysteries of the Court of London* two sisters, Octavia, seduced by the Prince Regent in disguise, and Pauline, who resists an aristocrat and converts

---

13 Significant characteristics of the encyclopedic narrative as defined by Mendelsohn in his *Modern Language Notes* essay, in addition to the ones I discuss here, include the following: the texts 'occupy a special historical position in their cultures' and the writer 'attends to the whole social and linguistic range of his nation' ('Encyclopedic Narrative', pp. 1267–8); 'all include a full account of a technology or science' and 'offer an account of an art outside the realm of written fiction' ('Encyclopedic Narrative', pp. 1270–71). They 'attend to the complexities of statecraft' and are 'an encyclopedia of literary styles, ranging from the most primitive and anonymous levels of proverb-lore to the most esoteric heights of euphuism' ('Encyclopedic Narrative', p. 1271).

14 Mendelsohn, 'Gravity's Encyclopedia', p. 162.

15 Mendelsohn, 'Encyclopedic Narrative', p. 1268

16 Mendelsohn, 'Encyclopedic Narrative', p. 1268.

him into a do-gooder; in the second series two more sisters; and in the fourth series two more brothers. His structural principle is one of contrast: the night in the harem of the Marquis of Holmesford is followed by a heroic scene as Richard leaves to fight for freedom in Italy. A warm and friendly home in Clapton is contrasted with a scene in Bethlem Hospital; the first sight of a criminal's secret hideout is followed by a description of the secret lower chamber of the post office where mail is opened and tampered with.

From our perspective (and that of Karl Marx[17]) this ideology was old-fashioned when Reynolds wrote it, though there are hints of a more complex analysis. Richard C. Maxwell, for example, has argued that Eugene Markham, or Mortimer Greenwood as he calls himself, is a new kind of middle-class villain.[18] Further, the misdeeds in the second series of *The Mysteries of London* include economic crimes – forgery and various con jobs, though there are plenty of seductions and a murder or two – and in *The Mysteries of the Court of London* Reynolds returns to the 'Old Corruption' analysis.[19]

Reynolds's ideological intrusions would not have had the force they did, however, were the institutions they berate – the aristocracy, the government, the church, the legal system, education, the monied classes – not understood by the reader as representative of a whole system. Reynolds wrote his *Mysteries* during the same period that many others were struggling to find ways to describe what seemed to them a new and difficult world. John Stuart Mill called it an age of transition ('Signs of the Times' [1829]), and Thomas Carlyle argued that society was an organic body ('Characteristics' [1831]), a description that fits Reynolds's plotting connections (as well as those of Dickens in *Bleak House* [1852–53]). While Auguste Comte coined the term 'sociology' in 1837, Reynolds's 'encyclopedia of tales' actually attempts an analysis of what that discipline might investigate. Reynolds's portrayal of a modern urban centre where everyone is linked might be seen as too reliant on chance, coincidence and providence. But it could just as easily be viewed as a sociological insight into the interconnectedness of all elements of society, a modern social perspective adumbrating the paranoid postmodern encyclopedic view of Thomas Pynchon.

---

17 Marx was dismissive of Reynolds's involvement in Chartist politics and his self-proclaimed radical bent in his mass-market *Reynolds's Newspaper*. He thought him 'a rich and able speculator' whose espousal of the Chartist view 'shows this position must still be a "bearable" one' (quoted in Virginia Berridge, 'Popular Sunday Papers and Mid-Victorian Society', in George Boyce, James Curran and Pauline Wingate [eds], *Newspaper History from the Seventeenth Century to the Present Day* [London: Constable, 1978], p. 254).

18 Richard C. Maxwell, 'G.W.M. Reynolds, Dickens and the Mysteries of London', *Nineteenth-century Fiction*, 32 (1977): 192–3.

19 Ian Haywood argues that in *MOCL* 'the backdating of the story to the later eighteenth century meant that the "Old Corruption" discourse of melodramatic political analysis was entirely appropriate', and that this allowed Reynolds to 'construct an historical fantasy world: an unreformed society of extreme moral and political degradation which functioned as a "shadow" of the Victorian present' (*The Revolution in Popular Literature: Print, Politics, and the People, 1790–1860* [Cambridge: Cambridge University Press, 2004], p. 21

How did Reynolds achieve this view in the light of his reductive representations? Mendelsohn says of encyclopedic narratives that they are 'the products of an epoch in which the world's knowledge is larger than any one person can encompass, [and so] they necessarily make extensive use of synecdoche'.[20] Thus, not only does Reynolds make his plots and interpolated tales represent the whole of English society at mid-century through expansion and multiplication, but also his binary simplifications lose some of their reductiveness through repetition of character types and situations, as well as recurrent narrative comment. In this way, Reynolds's *Mysteries* are also generalized through synecdoche.

This literary process begins with the synecdoche in his titles. There are scenes in all the series that take place outside of London, and indeed one of the binaries he uses is city versus country. The titles of his works, *The Mysteries of London* and *The Mysteries of the Court of London*, use 'London' as a representation of the whole of the social order, even as the term 'mysteries' suggests its potential incomprehensibility.[21] Reynolds puts it this way: 'as London is the heart of this empire, the disease which prevails in the core is conveyed through every vein and artery over the entire national frame'.[22] The figure of 'London' works as a synecdoche for all of England at mid-century, not only because the plots usually begin in London and all the characters pass through the city even if they do not live there, but also because identifying 'London' as a name for all the events that happen in the 12-volume series reflects a cultural phenomenon that all experienced and some understood: the great nineteenth-century shift of power from the provincial landed aristocracy to the urban centres of finance and industry.

This process of synecdoche is related to the very element we might see as Reynolds's greatest weakness as analyst of nineteenth-century English society and culture: the melodramatic simplifications inherent in his binaries. The use of repetition here is crucial, for the many repetitions of generic scenes (cross-dressing for both men and women, underground dungeons, slum gathering places like the 'boozing kens' or the 'kitchin kins' in *The Mysteries of the Court of London*) and typical characters over many numbers, series and volumes have a cumulative effect that ultimately makes them appear to be representatives for the general forces governing the whole of the social order: individualism run rampant and unchecked by a corrupt legal system, and the absence of what we would call a safety net for the vulnerable; selfish sensuality that gives free rein to the debaucheries of the powerful; urbanization itself with its crowding that facilitates both individual anonymity and

---

20 Mendelsohn, 'Gravity's Encyclopedia', p. 162

21 Malcolm Gladwell makes the distinction between a 'puzzle', which can be solved by sufficient information, and a 'mystery', which no amount of information can decide absolutely, crediting the analysis to Gregory Treverton. The identity of Eugene Markham and Mortimer Greenwood is a puzzle that is solved when we have the information that shows they are the same person, but where the ultimate source of power is in 'London' remains a mystery that no amount of information will solve. See 'Open Secrets: Enron and the Perils of Full Disclosure', *New Yorker*, 8 January 2007, p. 44.

22 G.W.M. Reynolds, *The Mysteries of London* (London: George Vickers, 1845), vol. 1, ch. 58, p. 179.

the surveillance and chance encounters that make it impossible to hide. As Reynolds, ever expansive and self-congratulatory about his methods, says:

> In our former works ... we have introduced our readers to low dens of the same description as these ... but we do not consider that we are to be blamed on the score of repetition.... We purposely and with studied intent recall public attention again and again to the horrible abodes which poverty is compelled to seek, where vice lurks and where crime conceals itself. For we boldly and unhesitatingly charge to the account of our legislators and rulers the existence of those sinks of abomination.[23]

The scenes of the Marquis of Holmesford's private harem and the Prince Regent's various seductions, betrayals and machinations come to stand for the whole of aristocratic corruption; the dismal lodging of Bill Bolter in *The Mysteries of London* stands for the whole of the working classes' resulting destitution; and the arch criminals the Resurrection Man in *The Mysteries of London* and Joe the Magsman in *The Mysteries of the Court of London*, by working both for the corrupt aristocracy and for themselves, represent the wide-ranging results of the unholy alliance between the powerful and the criminal to abuse the innocent. The personal histories, written in recognizable popular genres of the fallen-woman and road-to-ruin plots, taken together, cumulatively stand in for all the forces that destroy the vulnerable in mid-century England.

But while the ideology and the necessary use of synecdoche in this encyclopedic narrative provide a centrifugal unifying element in Reynolds's texts, other elements have the opposite effect – a centripetal force that threatens to undermine the coherence. According to Mendelsohn, the encyclopedic narrative is also 'an encyclopedia of literary styles', 'an encyclopedia *of* narrative'.[24] While Reynolds's story lines can be wound together in a unifying structure through clever plotting and a heavy use of the forces of chance and coincidence made believable by the crowding of the modern city, the multiplying expansiveness of the encyclopedic form has the opposite effect. The proliferation of 'literary styles' – of genres of narrative and modes of representations – fragments the text and brings into question its totalizing narratological assertion of complete understandability.

As a result, Reynolds's texts are in a constant state of formal as well as thematic tension that is not dissimilar to the tensions that exist in actual encyclopedias, with their contrasting principles of accumulation and condensation reinforced by a rigid structure for entries and the discipline of alphabetization. Reynolds has his own methods for keeping his encyclopedic narrative from breaking the narrative apart. One is the repetition of tag phrases to indicate shifts from one plot or one genre to another: 'Before, however, we resume the thread of our narrative, we must pause for a few moments to describe Octavia and Pauline.'[25] Or there is the the opposite: 'We must now inform the reader of a circumstance which we did not choose to interrupt our narrative to relate before.'[26] Or even: 'Grieved as we are to leave the reader in

---

23 Reynolds, *MOCL* (1853), vol. 5, ch. 58, p. 283.
24 Mendelsohn, 'Gravity's Encyclopedia', pp. 163–4, emphasis in original.
25 Reynolds, *MOCL* (1849), vol. 1, ch. 2, p. 10.
26 Reynolds, *MOCL* (1850), vol. 2, ch. 46, p. 75.

a state of suspense relative to the issue of the adventure of Pauline Clarendon and the Prince of Wales, we must nevertheless break the thread of that episode for a short space and return to Covent Garden Theatre.'[27] There is also the unifying force of genre. The massive text is pulled together by one generic pattern, that of gothic melodrama, a combination of the horror of the gothic and the moral binaries of melodrama, which controls the potential chaos introduced by the multiplication of genres and plot. The many criminals who rob, kidnap and murder are major elements in the melodramatic gothic that Reynolds exploits in the *Mysteries*. Within that unifying master genre, however, Reynolds intersperses a number of other genres that expand the text in an encyclopedic manner.

For example, a dominant popular genre Reynolds inserts is that of the moralized but sensational lives of criminals that formed the immensely popular *Newgate Calendar*. In his *Robert Macaire in England* (1840), discussed by Rohan McWilliam in Chapter 2 of this volume, Reynolds had tried his hand at the literary novel version of the *Newgate Calendar*, written in the vein of Edward Bulwer-Lytton's *Eugene Aram* (1832), William Harrison Ainsworth's *Jack Sheppard* (1839) and Charles Dickens's *Oliver Twist* (1837–38). But in *The Mysteries of London* he goes back to the older form. In the *Newgate Calendar*, the criminal lives are conventionally told in the first person, and in Reynolds's *Mysteries of London* nearly every criminal gets to tell his life story, even the terrible Resurrection Man, who was once the good son of a smuggler but whose criminal career is due, according to him, to the 'overbearing conduct and atrocious tyranny of the more wealthy part of the community'.[28]

Reynolds's *Newgate Calendar* narratives frequently occur when several characters are sitting in a tavern or other gathering place waiting for a partner in crime or a victim to show up, and thus they are both integrated into the main gothic melodramatic plot and generically and thematically opposed to it. The purpose of the *Newgate Calendar* narrative was to detail the crimes of these famous criminals for both voyeuristic pleasure and exemplary warning. But the first-person narration of the criminal's life, his or her earlier innocent childhood and subsequent fall into crime – usually the result of false imprisonment or institutional abuse – creates sympathy for the criminal, which is why contemporaries criticized as immoral the Newgate novels that grew out of the popular *Calendar*. Reynolds's villains can be suddenly transformed into sympathetic victims whose life stories demonstrate how parental abuse and institutional neglect turn people to crime. Once the first-person narrative is finished, however, the character turns back into the villain and remains both unredeemed and unredeemable for the rest of the text until he is brought to a violent justice. (In the case of the Resurrection Man, he is murdered by his enemy Crankey Jem.) What keeps this potentially destabilizing genre shift from fragmenting the coherence of the text, however, is synecdoche as each interpolated tale is generalized. As one of the listeners to the Resurrection Man's autobiography declares, 'in nine cases out o' ten the laws themselves make men take to bad ways, and then punish them for acting under their influence'.[29]

---

27 Reynolds, *MOCL* (1850), vol. 2, ch. 41, p. 84.
28 Reynolds, *MOL* (1845), vol. 1, ch. 62, p. 191.
29 Reynolds, *MOL* (1846), vol. 2, ch. 192, p. 191.

At the same time, both the gothic melodrama and the *Newgate Calendar* 'autobiographies' are cheek by jowl in Reynolds's text with another popular genre that combines voyeurism and critique, that of the silver fork narrative, which strives to give an insider's view of the trivialities of the aristocracy, both its beauties and its comforts, and also its excesses and its misdeeds, for its middle-class readers. The silver fork genre was popular from the mid-1820s to the mid-1840s and was identified mainly with Benjamin Disraeli (*Vivian Gray* [1826]), Edward Bulwer-Lytton (*Pelham* [1828]) and the 'queen' of the silver fork novelists, Catherine Gore (*Women As They Are, Or the Manners of the Day* [1830], her first of many big hits). The silver fork characteristics of detailed description of the houses and dress of the aristocracy and the romance and seduction of their lives are prevalent in many of the plots in the eight volumes of *The Mysteries of the Court of London*. As one might expect, however, Reynolds favours the decadence and sexual encounters of the aristocracy in his version of this popular genre, and combines them with gothic melodrama and *Newgate Calendar* autobiographies in order to make his ideological point about the corrupt oligarchic power base's penetration of the entire society.

Thus, Reynolds's work integrates all the seemingly random and fragmented genres, lives, stories and fates into one comprehensible whole, an encyclopedia of genres unified by an insistent theme. An example in *The Mysteries of London* is the tale of a pot boy who sneaks into Buckingham Palace, ostensibly to steal the plate. But he becomes enamoured of the Queen and rather than thieving, he spies on her and Prince Albert. This part of the sequence mimics the silver fork novels in its fascination with the intimate details of the life of the aristocracy. Yet another genre is inserted into this sequence, a series of interpolated tales of assassination. The boy, inflamed by these tales, tries to kill Albert, introducing into the sequence a story taken from the newspapers. Finally, the narrator, in a long interruption, creates sympathy for the boy: 'when the poor creature who is goaded to desperation, *does* strike – can we wonder if, in the madness of his rage, he deals his blows indiscriminately, or against an innocent person?'[30] In the first series of *The Mysteries of the Court of London*, there are many similar interchanges as the Prince Regent goes about his seductions and depredations among all classes.

Reynolds also introduces the pursuit and escape genre made popular by *Jack Sheppard*, besides sentimental romance, and especially, in the last volume of the last series of *The Mysteries of the Court of London*, the oriental tale, which is set in the East and concerns itself with western myths about harems and particular types of violence. In Reynolds's version of this genre, much of the final action takes place in a fictional place, Inderbad in Hindostan, where the villain, the Burker, is killed by a giant snake; in the end Queen Indora marries an Englishman, 'to whose policy that kingdom owed the liberty of its institutions and the spirit of strict justice which animated the execution of its laws'.[31] In this imperial export of English values, this conclusion repeats that of the first series of *The Mysteries of London*, where the English hero marries a foreign bride and becomes the benevolent ruler of a fictional Italian state.

---

30 Reynolds, *MOL* (1846), vol. 2, ch. 210, p. 247.
31 Reynolds, *MOCL* (1856), vol. 8, ch. 163, p. 402.

These literary genres are not the only forms Reynolds introduces into his text. He also engages social realism in many of his descriptions and in pure informational journalism as if the news and novel had never been generically separated: in one place he gives a sort of map of London for 'those readers who are but indifferently acquainted with the topography of this large metropolis',[32] and in other places he includes a dictionary of criminal slang, samples of street ballads, quotations from newspapers and footnotes about current or historical events or sources for his claims. His descriptions of urban locations are like those in the many novels of urban realism.

Rohan McWilliam has called Reynolds a political 'sponge',[33] a metaphor that applies as well to his narrative techniques. But as with a sponge, though many different elements may be absorbed, what comes out when the sponge is squeezed is something other than the sum of its parts. In the case of the *Mysteries* that new thing is an encyclopedic narrative, one that is coterminous with the rise of sociological investigation (the *Mysteries of London* was published just before Henry Mayhew began his monumental survey of poverty in London, *London Labour and the London Poor* [1850–52]) and made possible by the many parliamentary reports on 'The Condition of England' published during the 1840s. Though Reynolds's *Mysteries* cannot claim the national significance that Mendelsohn says is essential in the 'true' encyclopedic narrative, its use of many of the techniques of that genre gave its contemporary readers the sense that here was something different, new and thus of national significance to them. All of this helps account for both the work's popularity among its working- and lower-class readers and the horror with which its middle-class readers rejected it.

Like most popular literature, Reynolds's *Mysteries*, after being continually in print for over half a century, fell into oblivion. Critics have for much of the twentieth century ignored it. The literary genres Reynolds used have fallen into disrepute and his social critique has not worn well. But the *Mysteries* are nonetheless essential to an understanding of nineteenth-century mid-century Britain. The encyclopedic nature of this major fictional work gave its readers the sense that they might be able, with the author's help, to understand how the world they were living in worked; how all parts of the fragmented and multitudinous 'London' fit together; how its people and its parts, its classes and its institutions, related to one another. It is not our view now, but in its day it was an encompassing and immensely popular perspective, and we cannot fully understand the Victorian period without taking account of it.

---

32 Reynolds, *MOCL* (1851), vol. 3, ch. 22, p. 78.

33 See Rohan McWilliam, 'The Mysteries of G.W.M. Reynolds: Radicalism and Melodrama in Victorian Britain', in Malcolm Chase and Ian Dyck (eds), *Living and Learning: Essays in Honour of J.F.C. Harrison* (Aldershot: Scolar, 1996), p. 184.

Chapter 8

Lost in Translation: The Relationship between Eugène Sue's *Les Mystères de Paris* and G.W.M. Reynolds's *The Mysteries of London*

Berry Chevasco

In the summer of 1842 France became gripped by a literary phenomenon the like of which hitherto had been unknown there and, to a large extent, anywhere else. From June 1842 until October 1843 French readers were spellbound by the serialization of a single work of fiction, *Les Mystères de Paris* by Eugène Sue. Although both the author and his novel are now largely forgotten, it would be difficult to overstate the sensation caused at the time by this *feuilleton*, as serialized fiction in France was then known. *Cabinets de lecture*, reading rooms where most of the reading public could hire newspapers and journals to read, were forced to ration the time allowed for the *Journal des Débats*, the Parisian newspaper whose circulation soared as a result of Sue's serial. The great literary commentator of the period, Charles Augustin Sainte-Beuve, wrote in July 1843 when *Les Mystères de Paris* had the nation in its tightest grasp:

> In the cafés, they fight over the *Débats* in the morning; they charge as much as *ten* sous for the time it takes to read the episode of Sue's story. When the author is late by one day beautiful society ladies and chambermaids are all in a state of turmoil ...[1]

That both society ladies and chambermaids were anxious to read the same work is significant. The appeal of *Les Mystères de Paris* across the social spectrum in France was one of the factors that set it apart from earlier fiction by Sue or indeed by any other French author. This breadth reflected one of the consequences of the profound social and economic changes that characterized the nineteenth century in France, indeed in Europe as a whole. Increasing industrialization, the growth of urban population, improved railway connections throughout the country and an increase in literacy brought on by educational reforms earlier in the century had revolutionized

---

1   Sainte-Beuve, 28 July 1843, *Chroniques Parisiennes* (Paris: Garnier Frères, 1930), p. 80. Original: 'Dans les cafés, on s'arrache les *Débats* le matin; on loue chaque numéro qui a le feuilleton de Sue jusqu'à dix sous pour le temps de le lire. Quand l'auteur retarde d'un jour les belles dames et les femmes de chambre sont en émoi ...' (Unless stated otherwise, all English translations are my own.)

the publishing market, particularly for fiction. Up until this change novels had been produced in the traditional three-volume format and had been effectively luxury items, exclusively available to the social elite. Responding to the economic and social shifts of the period, newspapers began to compete for a growing market of new readers and in the late 1830s serialized fiction, the *feuilleton*, became a powerful component in the subsequent circulation battle between periodicals.

The study of Eugène Sue has been so neglected of late that any examination of the impact of his fiction now must be accompanied by at least a brief introduction to his life and works. Sue was born in Paris in 1804 to an *haute bourgeoise* family of physicians. His father in fact was doctor to Napoleon and the baby Eugène's godmother was Josephine, soon to be empress. Sue's family were conservative scientists and had been so for generations. They were moneyed and respectable, if not actually aristocratic. Yet Sue rebelled from family tradition and turned first to painting and then to writing. He became part of the group of young writers in Paris, then as now the cultural centre of the country, who wrote partly because it was a fashionable pursuit for young men of a certain social set but which also included those who gained their livelihood as writers, such as Honoré de Balzac and Alexandre Dumas.

Sue's early romantic stories written in the 1830s gave rise to comparisons with the American James Fenimore Cooper's novels, which were much in vogue in France. One paper of the day called Sue the 'French Cooper'.[2] In Britain, critics acknowledged Sue's place amongst important contemporary French authors and even preferred him over his contemporaries.[3] Sue's subsequent novels focused on the vicissitudes of French high society and he briefly became the darling, the 'beau Sue' as he was then dubbed, of the social elite and the literati who frequented the aristocratic salons of Paris. Readership of his fiction remained confined to those few who could afford novels in book form and his renown at this point was equally limited to that sector of French, and also British, society. To a large extent Britain had paralleled France in this respect and novels had been and therefore remained luxury items. This was especially the case with French novels, which were seldom translated and thus could be read exclusively by the educated elite.

Then in 1842 Sue's career and reputation took on an entirely new character in both countries. The *Journal des Débats* approached Sue to write a *feuilleton* and he began to produce *Les Mystères de Paris*, a departure both from his own previous oeuvre and from the forms which fiction had taken generally in France. *Les Mystères de Paris* was innovative in both its format and its subject matter. Needless to say, the increase in literacy in France and Britain had been most notable amongst the poorer classes. These were the new readers who flooded the market and who eagerly welcomed the affordable serialized fiction. The appetite for this fiction on both sides of the Channel began to fuel the success of writers and newspapers. In Britain Dickens had profited considerably by using this format. Indeed, his well-documented success recalls that of Sue, although both authors have suffered very different fates in literary history. The apocryphal story of crowds waiting on the docks of America

---

2   'Plik et Plok', *Revue des Deux Mondes*, 4 (January 1830), p. 207.
3   'French Naval Romances', *Foreign Quarterly Review*, 21 (July 1838), pp. 423–4.

to receive the latest instalments detailing the death of Little Nell in the serialization of *The Old Curiosity Shop* is the only example comparable to the eventual response to Sue's *Les Mystères de Paris*.

Sue's serialization featured an unusual setting for the prevailing tastes of the time and a particularly sensitive topical subject matter, the lives of the urban poor. *Les Mystères de Paris*, as its title suggests, takes the French capital as its setting and explores the urban underworld of Paris's criminal and poor quarters, exposing the need for social reforms. Many of the novel's principal characters are destitute, struggling with poverty in scenes of gritty realism. Some are also murderers and prostitutes portrayed sympathetically rather than moralistically. *Les Mystères de Paris* exposes a dark, disturbing world of urban poverty, social injustice, criminality and corruption. Almost no other novel before, with the exception of Dickens's *Oliver Twist* (1837–38), had focused to such an extent on the grimmer realities of urban life. Sue's sympathy for the urban underworld and those living on society's margins certainly provoked a conservative reaction in France. However, his novel also inspired admiration from the growing factions of those concerned with social reform. The rise in the urban population, poor living conditions and cholera epidemics earlier in the century had highlighted the need for social and political change. The rumblings of political unrest had already begun to shake the foundations of the July Monarchy and the political climate that was ultimately to lead to the Revolution of 1848 was taking shape in the politically charged salons of Paris, where Sue's novel seemed to strike a chord.

Despite the story's sombre theme, however, its instalments unfold with Sue's characteristic romantic, elegant touch. Its protagonist, for example, is a darkly handsome Byronic prince who visits the city's slums in disguise to help the poor and to impose justice on wrongdoers. The bleak realism of the novel is lightened by this romance and the combination made the serial a huge popular and financial success. Sue's fame spread rapidly throughout all sectors of French society. His success became legendary and very quickly had an impact in other parts of the world. By 1844 six translated editions of *Les Mystères de Paris* were available in Britain alone and many others, as well as imitations, were produced throughout Europe and America in the same period.

In the spring of 1845 *Bentley's Miscellany* in Britain published an article titled 'Outlines of Mysteries' whose tone hints at the underlying concerns about contemporary popular fiction in general:

Mysteries, it appears, are no longer to remain so. Authors … start up and show to the world that at least to them there have never been such things as mysteries. The veil of France is torn from her by a Frenchman, who certainly pays no high compliment to his country, by exposing vices of the most hideous character, and which are certainly much better hidden both from the young and old. The moral to be drawn from melodramatic vice and virtue is very questionable. This mysterymania has crossed the Channel. Authors are manufacturing vices by the gross …[4]

---

4   Alfred Crowquill, 'Outlines of Mysteries', *Bentley's Miscellany*, 17 (May 1845), p. 529.

Bentley's does not feel any need to name the French author who has spawned this 'mysterymania'. Any contemporary reader would immediately recognize that the article alluded to Eugène Sue. Sue's career had become a byword for success in writing and anyone seeking to gain their livelihood or increase their fame and influence as a writer would not have been able to ignore the example of Sue's achievement. In terms of monetary gain alone, his accomplishment was indisputable. Dickens sought him out, for example, when he visited Paris a year later in 1846, and he was not alone is his interest.[5] Articulating some of the mainstream concerns of the time surrounding popular novels, Thackeray, for example, specifically targeted Sue for criticism, labelling him a 'literary merchant' and deploring his reputation as a humanitarian and a writer of talent.[6]

However, Dickens and Thackeray are not the authors condemned in the *Bentley's* article. Dubious translations and imitations of *Les Mystères de Paris* were numerous, as the article indicates, and these were being produced by a body of publishers who were already notorious as the sources of the cheap popular fiction causing disquiet amongst the mainstream in Britain. The appetite for fiction amongst the new readers of the poor and working classes in Britain had amounted to a 'literary revolution',[7] according to one later critic. Cheap fiction was flooding the market, much of it sensational, some of it pornographic, some of it subversive. This curious mixture arose in part because some of this fiction was produced from Holywell Street in London, a location as infamous for its radical tracts as for its pornographic material. The street itself and those operating there became synonymous with salacious publishing. Many of these sought to profit from the 'mysterymania' that *Bentley's* describes and produced their own versions of Sue's novel.

The *Bentley's* article refers only implicitly to the many authors 'manufacturing vice' in Britain, but it does single out one other work along with Sue's novel for specific censure. 'Outlines of Mysteries' ends by pointing directly at a novel by a British author who had already become the subject of mainstream hostility: 'we see "The Mysteries of Paris", "The Mysteries of London"; but who is really capable of lifting the veil and showing the dark reality?'[8] *Bentley's* readers would have known that this latter was the work of G.W.M. Reynolds, who had begun to serialize his novel in 1844. This early association of Sue with *The Mysteries of London* was enough to establish a widely held assumption in Britain of a direct link between Sue's novel and Reynolds's work. As Reynolds's serialization progressed, that assumption was strengthened by a series of press articles as well as less conspicuous but equally effective connections such as advertisements in most of the papers of the day promoting the two works together. These appeared regularly, sometimes

---

5   Charles Dickens to John Forster, 5 September 1847, in Graham Storey and K.J. Fielding (eds), *The Letters of Charles Dickens* (Oxford: Clarendon Press, 1981), vol. 5, p. 159.

6   'The Thieves' Literature of France', *Foreign Quarterly Review*, 31 (April 1843), pp. 231–49.

7   Margaret Dalziel, *Popular Fiction One Hundred Years Ago: An Unexplored Tract of Literary History* (London: Cohen and West, 1957), p. 2.

8   Crowquill, 'Outlines of Mysteries', p. 529.

confounding the two authors, often claiming that Sue's novel was 'Uniform with the Mysteries of London'.[9]

It was not an association that advanced Sue's reputation in Britain. His fiction quickly became labelled as irredeemably 'popular' and a sea change took place in the British reception of Sue. His novels remained widely read yet he lost the credibility of mainstream critics, who ceased to review his work except within the context of the prevailing controversies of the dangers of popular fiction. The perceived association between Reynolds and Sue intensified the developing prejudice in conservative circles already wary of Sue's nationality and inclination towards republicanism. The supposition that the two novels of urban 'mysteries' were somehow closely aligned was established and remained compelling enough that it persists today.

Yet Reynolds's novel is an altogether different sort of work from *Les Mystères de Paris*. Indeed, the two authors had nothing in common despite the public supposition that Sue had inspired Reynolds's novel. *Les Mystères de Paris* had led to financial and popular success for Sue, but also had linked his name with the most powerful political figures of the time.[10] Sue remained a respected figure throughout this period despite some of the controversy surrounding his novels, even achieving elected office as a *député* briefly in 1850. Throughout most of the 1840s his works were still enjoyed, indeed celebrated, by the fashionable and powerful as well as by the poor and working classes in France.

However, Reynolds had a very different role in British society. Although originally moneyed and middle-class, Reynolds did not align himself with the gentlemanly classes. Rather than choosing to follow in his family's tradition and become a naval officer, Reynolds became a writer and journalist. He lived in France where a number of his ventures failed, and when back in Britain he attempted to repeat the successes of authors like Dickens by close copies or plagiarisms of their well-known works. This inspired contempt and resentment from mainstream writers in general and from Dickens in particular. Dickens dismissed Reynolds as one whose name 'with which no lady's, and no gentleman's, should be associated'.[11]

Before writing *The Mysteries of London*, Reynolds had also frequently appeared in the bankruptcy courts in London, which further sullied his reputation with the respectable middle classes. His cases were heard regularly from 1836 to 1840, as attested by one of his critics later.[12] With each case Reynolds had been freed from liability to his creditors and allowed to continue to earn his living as a writer, legally unfettered but morally suspect in the eyes of disapproving commentators.

Eventually Reynolds came to embody the fears and distaste that certain types of popular fiction and its producers elicited in the literary and journalistic establishment. This hostile opinion was compounded by the enormous success of *The Mysteries of London* among readers. This work was followed later in the period by the serialization

9   *Family Herald*, 2 (October 1844), p. 425.
10 Sainte-Beuve, *Chroniques Parisiennes*, 6 November 1843, p. 132.
11 Charles Dickens to W.C. Macready, 30 August 1849, in *The Letters of Charles Dickens*, vol. 5, p. 603.
12 Thomas Clark, *A Letter addressed to G.W.M. Reynolds reviewing his conduct as a professed Chartist* (London: Thomas Clark, 1850), p. 10.

of *The Mysteries of the Court of London*, which continued to appear until 1856. The huge circulation of Reynolds's novel, which even at the beginning of its serialization was estimated to have been between 30,000 and 40,000 and which was reported to have expanded still further, brought 'national celebrity', actually notoriety, to the author.[13] Reynolds's radical sympathies were apparent from the initial stages of *The Mysteries of London*, which openly criticized the social elite with particularly revolutionary rhetoric. After the serialization had been running for some years, one bookseller described the novel to Thackeray as a great success with readers because 'it lashes the aristocracy!'[14]

Like their respective authors, *Les Mystères de Paris* and *The Mysteries of London* in fact share very little in common. Certain superficial features do seem to form a bond between the works. Gothic motif and melodramatic stagecraft abound in both. Both are complicated narratives set in the urban slums of the two great metropolitan centres of Paris and London. Both range beyond that world to contrasting scenes of pomp and privilege. Similar intrigues, disguise, secret documents, murderous plots, stock villains and heroines and wicked criminals with slang nicknames as central characters – La Chouette and Le Maître d'école in Sue's novel, the Resurrection Man, the Cracksman and the Buffer in *The Mysteries of London* – all feature in both works. The novels also focus on detailed portraits of the life of the urban poor and attempt to excite an emotional response for their plight. However, these apparent similarities obscure the essential dissimilarities. Any connection between *Les Mystères de Paris* and *The Mysteries of London* is at best 'problematic', as acknowledged by one modern commentator.[15] A number of distinctions emerge with any careful reading. Language, style and tone all vary enormously between the two works; more importantly, however, the two carry fundamentally opposing views.

Although Sue and Reynolds both became involved in populist politics on the strength of the political messages in their fiction, the purport and the tone of those messages are wholly different in their fiction. Sue's novel exposes the horrors of the lives of the Parisian poor in order to rouse the active sympathy of those in power and to encourage humanitarian reform. His pleas to the more comfortable reader punctuate the novel and his calls for reforms, even when detailed and demanding, are never incompatible with an essentially paternalist view of society. Sue's fundamental premise in *Les Mystères de Paris* is that the ruling classes are essentially well meaning and humane. Social injustice and the deprivations of poverty exist because those in power are largely ignorant of the urgency of the problems suffered by other parts of society. Once they are made aware of the distress and desperation of the poor, Sue felt that his rich readers could not fail to respond to improve society. To do so was essentially their duty, both morally and socially, and to that end he argues his case with the combination of passion and intellectual clarity peculiar to French thought.

13 Trefor Thomas, 'Introduction', in G.W.M. Reynolds, *The Mysteries of London*, ed. Trefor Thomas (Keele: Keele University Press, 1996), pp. vii–x.

14 William Makepeace Thackeray, *Christmas Books, Rebecca and Rowena*, in George Saintsbury (ed.), *The Oxford Thackeray* (London: Henry Frowde, [n.d.]), p. 624.

15 Richard Maxwell, *The Mysteries of Paris and London* (Charlottesville: University of Virginia Press, 1992), p. 337.

The destitute but honourable jewel maker, Morel, whose portrait is central to Sue's political and humanitarian message, outlines the fundamental vision of the novel in a conversation with his long-suffering wife:

> Oh! those rich, they are so hard! [she says] – No harder than others, Madeleine. But they don't know, you see, what it is to be miserable. They are born happy, they live happy, they die happy: for what reason would you want them to think of us? ... they do not know [what it is to be miserable].[16]

The implication is that once the rich know of the social wrongs they can put right, they will do so without hesitation. Sue presents a number of examples in his narrative that prove his point. Prince Rodolphe, the philanthropic protagonist whose acts of benevolence and righting of wrongs form the core of the narrative, provides the reader with just such a conspicuous example of a privileged, indeed, in his case, royal, figure who acts for the good of those less fortunate. Rodolphe surrounds himself with a company of like-minded aristocrats who support his efforts. His attendant and helper, Sir Murph, is an English nobleman who implements many of Rodolphe's generous schemes. In the opening stages of the story, Rodolphe initiates his future wife, the Marquise d'Harville, in the joys of active charity and so transforms her frivolous life to one of rewarding purpose.

Sue's other portraits of the rich and the aristocracy are also, for the most part, sympathetic. These characters can suffer as well as the poor, as in the case of the distressed and ill Marquis d'Harville and the proud Comte de Saint-Remy. This latter has a son who wickedly dissipates his inheritance and sullies his father's noble name. After his portrait of the depraved young aristocrat, Sue laments the state of the many rich young men who, for lack of guidance and direction, squander their fortunes and are consequently denied useful and rewarding lives:

> ... through a lack of instruction the rich too fatally have their suffering, their vices, their crimes.
>
> Nothing is more frequent or more distressing than these mad, sterile extravagances which we have just described, and which always lead to ruin, discredit, baseness or infamy. It is a deplorable spectacle ... disastrous ... as if one saw a flourishing field of wheat uselessly ravaged by a herd of wild beasts. Without doubt inheritance and property are and should be inviolate, sacred.... Acquired or transmitted wealth must shine magnificently in the eyes of the poor and suffering classes. For a long time hence there will be those dreadful disproportions which exist between the millionaire Saint-Remy and the worker Morel. However, as much as those inevitable conditions are sacred, protected by the law, those who possess so much must use it as morally as those who possess only probity, resignation, courage and passion for their work.
>
> In the eyes of reason, human rights and even in the interest of society, of course, a large fortune should be an hereditary deposit, confided to prudent, firm, skilful, generous

---

16 Eugène Sue, *Les Mystères de Paris* (Paris: Charles Gosselin, first published 1844; this edition, 1963), p. 293. Original: 'Oh! Ces riches, c'est si durs! ... – Pas plus durs que d'autres, Madeleine. Mais ils ne savent pas, vois-tu, ce que c'est que la misère. Ça naît heureux, ça vit heureux, ça meurt heureux: à propos de quoi veux-tu que ça pense à nous? ... ils ne savent pas.'

hands who, charged at the same time to increase as well as to bestow that fortune, would know how to strengthen, enliven, benefit all those who have the good fortune to find themselves within their splendid salutary circle ...

How many young people ... masters at twenty years of age of considerable wealth, waste it madly in idleness, boredom and vice, because they do not know how better to employ their riches, both for themselves and for others![17]

The passage ends with Sue equating the evils faced by these young privileged members of society with those faced by the poor: 'The rich man is thrown into society's midst with his wealth just as is the poor man with his poverty.'[18] The author pleads for a closer understanding and cooperation between rich and poor,

> an honest, intelligent, equitable association which assures the well-being of the worker without undermining the fortune of the rich ... and which, by establishing ties of affection and gratitude between these two classes, would safeguard the tranquillity of the state forever.[19]

Social reforms are urged ardently in the novel, but these are reforms which would unite rather than divide social groups and reinforce rather than threaten the stability of society. Both in his paternalism and in his reasoned plea for sympathy and reform, Sue in fact bears much more resemblance to Dickens, especially in his later novels, than to Reynolds, a resemblance recognized by at least two distinguished critics on both sides of the Channel, George Eliot and Joseph Milsand, but generally disregarded in Britain then and now.

---

17 Sue, *Les Mystères de Paris*, pp. 577–8. Original: '... faute d'enseignements, les classes riches ont aussi fatalement leurs misères, leurs vices, leurs crimes. Rien de plus fréquent et de plus affligeant que ces prodigalités insensées, stériles, que nous venons de peindre, et qui toujours entraînent ruine, déconsidération, bassesse ou infamie. C'est un spectacle déplorable ... funeste ... autant voir un florissant champ de blé inutilement ravagé par une horde de bêtes fauves. Sans doute l'héritage, la propriété sont et doivent être inviolables, sacrés.... La richesse acquise ou tranmise doit pouvoir impunément et magnifiquement resplendir aux yeux des classes pauvres et souffrantes. Longtemps encore il doit y avoir de ces disproportions effrayantes entre le millionaire Saint-Remy et l'artisan Morel. Mais, par cela même que ces disproportions inévitables sont consacrées, protégées par la loi, ceux qui possèdent tant de biens doivent en user moralement comme ceux qui ne possèdent que de probité, résignation, courage et ardeur du travail. Aux yeux de la raison, du droit humain, et même de l'intérêt social bien entendu, une grande fortune serait un dépôt héréditaire, confié à des mains prudentes, fermes, habiles, généreuses, qui, chargées à la fois de faire fructifier et de dispenser cette fortune, sauraient fertiliser, vivifier, améliorer tous ceux qui auraient le bonheur de se trouver dans son rayonnement splendide et salutaire ... Que de jeunes gens ... maîtres à vingt ans d'un patrimoine considérable, le dissipent follement dans l'oisiveté, dans l'ennui, dans le vice, faute de savoir employer mieux ces biens et pour eux et pour autrui!'

18 Sue, *Les Mystères de Paris*, pp. 577–8. Original: 'le riche est jeté au milieu de la société avec sa richesse, comme le pauvre avec sa pauvreté.'

19 Sue, *Les Mystères de Paris*, pp. 577–8. Original: 'une association honnête, intelligente, équitable, qui assure le bien-être de l'artisan sans nuire à la fortune du riche ... et qui, établissant entre ces deux classes des liens d'affection, de reconnaissance, sauvegarderait à jamais la tranquillité de l'État.'

In *The Mysteries of London* the political message is utterly at odds with that of Sue. The wealthy and the aristocracy are deemed to be 'enemies of the people' and the author's tone is designed to excite resentment amongst the novel's poorer readers. In his prologue, Reynolds sets forth the premise upon which his novel will be written. The passage becomes formulaic and it appears regularly throughout the serialization, reiterating the novel's emotive revolutionary message:

> There are but two words known in the moral alphabet of this great city; for all the virtues are summed up in the one, and all vices in the other: and those words are
> WEALTH | POVERTY.
> Crime is abundant in this city: the lazarhouse, the prison, the brothel, and the dark alley, are rife with all kinds of enormity; in the same way as the palace, the mansion, the clubhouse, the parliament, and the parsonage, are each and all characterised by their different degrees and shades of vice. But wherefore specify crime and vice by their real names, since in this city of which we speak they are absorbed in the multi-significant words – WEALTH and POVERTY? … Crimes borrow their comparative shade of enormity from the people who perpetuate them: thus it is that the wealthy may commit all social offenses with impunity; while the poor are cast into dungeons and coerced with chains, for only following at a humble distance in the pathway of their lordly precedents.[20]

Sue also acknowledged that vice and crime were present in all classes, but he did so in order to further understanding and sympathy between disparate social groups. Here the sentiments encourage discord and hostility among the working classes towards the more fortunate groups in the social hierarchy. The rhetoric is, in short, seditious. Reynolds's narrative reflects this and thus is full of unscrupulous, wicked aristocrats, both male and female, who, unlike Sue's aristocratic characters, are only too knowledgeable about the world. The rich characters in *The Mysteries of London* are, for the most part, self-interested, scheming and immoral rather than simply ignorant and idle.

Reynolds goes even further than criticism of the aristocracy in *The Mysteries of London*, however, and attacks the monarchy in his novel. For the middle and ruling classes of Britain, the stability of the crown was a great source of pride and security in a changing world. According to a general British view, France had rid herself of a crowned head in the Revolution and her history since had reflected nothing but disorder. By attacking the monarch, Reynolds is threatening the very foundations of Victorian society. Indeed, he denounces all the components of the social establishment, including the church. Sue expressed anti-clerical sentiments in a later novel, *Le Juif Errant*, which was serialized at the same time as *The Mysteries of London*, but in *Les Mystères de Paris* the church is not a target for criticism. The only cleric is a benevolent ally in Rodolphe's plan of redemption for the young prostitute Fleur de Marie. Sue reveres rank and royalty in his novel and makes much, for example, of Prince Rodolphe's exalted status. *The Mysteries of London*, on the other hand, condemns rank, royalty and the church equally. In one of the many

---

20 G.W.M. Reynolds, *The Mysteries of London* (London: George Vickers, 1845), vol. 1, ch. 1, pp. 1–2.

passages describing London's slums, Reynolds indulges in some of the revolutionary rhetoric characteristic of the novel as a whole:

> Is it not dreadful to think that we have a sovereign and a royal family on whom the country lavishes money by the hundreds of thousands – whose merest whims cost sums that would feed and clothe from year to year the inhabitants of such a place as Lock's Fields; – that we also have an hereditary aristocracy and innumerable sleek and comfortable dignitaries of the church, who devour the fruits of the earth and throw the parings and the peelings contemptuously to the poor; – in a word, that we have an oligarchy feasting upon the fatted calf, and flinging the offal to the patient, enduring, toiling, oppressed millions; – is it not dreadful, we ask, to think how much those millions do for Royalty, Aristocracy, Church, and Landed Interest, and how little – how miserably little, Royalty, Aristocracy, Church, and Landed Interest do for *them* in return?[21]

The slum concerned in this passage is called Lock's Fields and is the setting for another key example of the important distinctions between *The Mysteries of London* and Sue's novel. In describing the poor homes of the slum dwellers, Reynolds follows much of the pattern adopted by Sue in *Les Mystères de Paris* and emphasizes the damp, dark, cold conditions in which the poor are forced to live. However, Reynolds chooses to spell out one of the evils of these dreadful, crowded conditions that Sue had studiously failed to mention in his descriptions of poverty: the likelihood of incest. Reynolds's bald statement defies an especially sensitive social taboo and could only have been meant to shock:

> In that densely populated neighbourhood that we are describing, hundreds of families each live and sleep in one room.... The wealthy classes of society are far too ready to reproach the miserable poor for things which are really misfortunes and not faults. The habit of whole families sleeping together in one room destroys all sense of shame in the daughters: and what guardian then remains for their virtue? But, alas! A horrible – an odious crime often results from the poverty which thus huddles brothers and sisters, aunts and nephews, all together in one narrow room – the crime of incest![22]

Both the frankness of the language and the voyeuristic dwelling on details of forbidden sexuality are characteristic of Reynolds's treatment of sex throughout his novel and are in complete contrast to Sue, whose descriptions of sex and sexuality are restrained. Although parts of *Les Mystères de Paris* are titillating, such as the flirtation between Rodolphe and La Rigolette, reference to sex almost always remains oblique. There is little to shock the reader. Sue's characters remain fully clothed and personal decency is highly regarded in the novel. Only one character is seen partly unclothed. Towards the end of the novel, the dress of a poor woman, La Louve, slips down from her shoulder when she braves the River Seine to save the drowning Fleur de Marie. However, the image is not meant to be sexually alluring. It serves instead to emphasize the raw courage of La Louve's rescue and links her character with the French emblem of the Revolution, Marianne, thus ennobling and endearing Sue's character still further.

---

21 Reynolds, *MOL* (1847), vol. 3, ch. 9, p. 27.
22 Reynolds, *MOL* (1845), vol. 1, ch. 17, p. 43.

Only one passage in *Les Mystères de Paris* presents sexuality more directly. In a highly suggestive passage, the notorious Ferrand is finally undone by his lust for the beautiful, cunning Cecily. Although the details of her seductive mastery of this evil character are particularly unabashed, the sexuality of the scene is not gratuitous. Ferrand's downfall not only demonstrates the evil corruption of lust, but also provides the culmination of many of Rodolphe's schemes of benevolence and retribution. Cecily herself remains fully clothed throughout the episode and then escapes from her victim without any physical contact. He eventually goes mad and both this scene and his obsession for the girl are more reminiscent of a Faustian fable than of pornography.

The Mysteries of London, however, abounds in scenes of explicit sexuality which do border on the pornographic. Many of the female characters are deliberately disrobed and sexual activity is openly described. Reynolds's handling of sex in *The Mysteries of London* is wholly unlike the indirect approach typical of 'respectable' Victorian fiction and would certainly have invited censure. A passage describing the secret lust of one character, the Reverend Reginald Tracy, who, like Ferrand in Sue's novel, is a base hypocrite and maintains outward probity, will serve as an example:

> Reginald stepped into the recess formed by the door of one of the bedchambers in that spacious mansion; and scarcely had he concealed himself there when he saw Ellen, with the child in her arms, pass across the landing at the end of the passage, and enter a room on the other side.... She wore a loose dressing-gown of snowy whiteness.... When the rector beheld her descend in that bewitching *negligee* [*sic*], – her hair unconfined, and floating at will – her small, round, polished ankles glancing between the white drapery and the little slippers, – and the child, with merely a thick shawl thrown about it, in her arms, – and when he observed a bath in that chamber which she entered, he immediately comprehended her intention.... His greedy eyes were applied to the key-hole; and his licentious glance plunged into the depth of that sacred privacy.... Reginald watched her proceedings with the most ardent curiosity: the very luxury of the unhallowed enjoyment which he experienced caused an oppression at his chest; his heart beat quickly; his brain seemed to throb with violence.... The fires of gross sensuality raged madly in his breast. Ellen's preparations were now completed ... she was partly turned towards the door; and all the treasures of her bosom were revealed to the ardent gaze of the rector.... His desires were now inflamed to that pitch when they almost become ungovernable.... And now the drapery had fallen from her shoulders, and the whole of her voluptuous form, naked to the waist, was exposed to his view. How he envied ... the innocent babe which the fond mother pressed to that bosom – swelling, warm, and glowing![23]

The character of Ellen Monroe further illustrates important differences between *The Mysteries of London* and Sue's novel. Ellen is one of the central female figures of Reynolds's novel. At the beginning of the narrative, she is a young, pure-minded girl who is gradually driven by poverty and hardship to pose as a nude model for artists, and from there to prostitution. Her character develops into that of an immoral, self-interested schemer who loses all moral sense:

---

23   Reynolds, *MOL* (1846), vol. 2, ch. 146, pp. 26–7.

In sooth, it was a pity that one of the brightest ornaments of female loveliness should have been lowered by circumstances from the pedestal of virtue and modesty which she would have so eminently adorned.[24]

Sue's beautiful sinner, Fleur de Marie, had also been forced to turn to prostitution to survive in the harsh world of the Parisian slums; however, her experiences did not taint her soul. Fleur de Marie remains paradoxically pure in heart and is revered as such throughout the novel. The apparent contradiction of a moral, saintly but fallen woman so commonplace in Catholic culture is incompatible with the Protestant conception of women. Reynolds splits the figure in two and presents the counterpart to the wicked Ellen Monroe in a paragon of feminine virtue, the spotless Isabella, who, when she finally marries one of the central figures of the novel, Richard Markham, does so with 'a halo of innocence about her ... an air of purest chastity'.[25] *Les Mystères de Paris* ends with Fleur de Marie's tragic death in which she too, despite her sordid past, is surrounded by an aura of pious purity. Such complexity and contradiction were unrealizable in *The Mysteries of London*. Indeed, the saintly Fleur de Marie figure is ultimately emblematic, lending a quality of jeremiad to *Les Mystères de Paris* that is wholly alien to the British novel.

The Mysteries of London is, in fact, radically different from *Les Mystères de Paris* in every important respect. All links between the two novels are altogether superficial. Nevertheless, the two works were closely associated by the British press in the 1840s, just as Sue's novel was gaining general attention in that country. Since Reynolds represented the worst of conservative fears concerning the role of popular fiction, the association could only have helped to stigmatize *Les Mystères de Paris* and therefore Sue's fiction generally in Britain. Sue's work thus became affiliated with the worst kind of popular fiction during a period of particular sensitivity to its power and effect.

That a deepening of prejudice against French fiction should be the result of an association with Reynolds was ironic. In 1839 Reynolds himself had presented a reasoned, balanced argument against just such prejudice in his *Modern Literature of France*. The substance of his discussion and his tone are virtually unrecognizable as those of the author of *The Mysteries of London*. Indeed, much of the work could have been written by a judicious, dispassionate commentator today:

Prejudice, which a celebrated political writer very happily denominated 'the spider of the mind', has done much to depreciate the value of foreign systems and institutions in the minds of the English. Hence is it that we daily hear even men of most liberal opinions expressing sentiments anything but impartial and just in reference to the French. This is more to be regretted, inasmuch as it is only by comparison, emulation, and research, that we can perfect or improve any system of laws, morals, literature, science or arts. But when we find the leading journals and periodicals of the English press still leaguing together against the French, with all the bitterness and hate which characterized the sentiments of the nation in those times when Napoleon rolled his war-chariot from the gates of Madrid to the palace of the Kremlin, ... we feel our regret at such injustice commingled with

---

24 Reynolds, *MOL* (1845), vol. 1, ch. 119, p. 367.
25 Reynolds, *MOL* (1846), vol. 2, ch. 223, p. 285.

a sentiment of pity, or indeed of contempt, for the narrow-mindedness of our fellow countrymen.[26]

It was not, however, for these considered views that Reynolds was known in the 1840s or for which he has been remembered, for the most part, since. The success and notoriety of *The Mysteries of London* overshadowed his other works and probably also overshadowed the early reception of Sue's *Les Mystères de Paris*. Both Sue and Reynolds became classified as 'popular', preventing then and now any recognition of their important role in British and French literary history. Most modern critics have forgotten that both in their own respective ways were among the few first to portray the dark and mysterious world of urban life that is now such an accepted vision in modern fiction and culture.

---

26 G.W.M. Reynolds, *The Modern Literature of France*, 2nd edn (London: George Henderson, 1841), vol. 1, pp. i–ii.

Chapter 9

The Wrongs and Crimes of the Poor: The Urban Underworld of *The Mysteries of London* in Context

Stephen James Carver

In his literary memoir of 1852, *Lions: Living and Dead*, John Ross Dix attributed the prodigious popularity of *The Mysteries of London* to the fact that the penny serial 'ministered to the depraved appetites of the lower classes',[1] while 'murders, seductions, robberies, horrors of all sorts, spiced with the abuse of the upper orders, formed the staple of the story'.[2] Dix did acknowledge some skill on the part of the author, Mr G.W.M. Reynolds, who wrote 'like a steam engine',[3] but concluded that 'as a writer his works will not perpetuate his name, for none of them have a vitality sufficient to reserve them from the rubbish of the cheap and nasty school of literature'.[4] This final prophecy has largely been fulfilled. Reynolds doesn't even make it into Malcolm Elwin's *Victorian Wallflowers*.[5] Critically, Reynolds has always resided in an underworld of sorts, but, given the *mise-en-scène* of *The Mysteries of London*, 'a labyrinth of dwellings whose very aspect appeared to speak of hideous poverty and fearful crime', where else could he be?[6]

The nineteenth-century London underworld, that subterranean social space intimately connected with urban poverty and crime, has been usefully defined by Kellow Chesney as the realm of 'certain classes of people whose very manner of living seemed a challenge to ordered society and the tissue of laws, moralities and taboos holding it together'.[7] In 1832 (a year after Reynolds sets the opening of *The Mysteries of London*), *Fraser's Magazine* warned of a new and dangerous urban underclass, 'a distinct body of thieves, whose life and business it is to follow up a

1   John Ross Dix, *Lions: Living and Dead, or Personal Recollections of the Great and the Gifted* (London: Tweedie, 1852), p. 284.

2   Dix, *Lions*, p. 284.

3   Dix, *Lions*, p. 282.

4   Dix, *Lions*, p. 288.

5   Malcolm Elwin, *Victorian Wallflowers* (London: Jonathan Cape, 1934). Elwin's 'unjustly neglected writers' are: John Wilson ('Christopher North'); William Maginn; R.H. Barham ('Ingoldsby'); W.H. Ainsworth; John Forster; Wilkie Collins; Ellen Price (Mrs Henry Wood); R.D. Blackmore; and Marie Louise de la Ramée ('Ouida').

6   G.W.M. Reynolds, *The Mysteries of London* (London: George Vickers, 1845), vol. 1, ch. 1, p. 4.

7   Kellow Chesney, *The Victorian Underworld* (London: Penguin, 1991), p. 32.

determined warfare against the constituted authorities, by living in idleness and on plunder'.[8] This 'criminal club' or 'underworld' was ruthless, organized, and in many ways paralleled the society in whose shadow it dwelt, with its own black economy, apprentices, craftsmen and leaders.

Reynolds stages almost half of *The Mysteries of London* in this criminal underworld, contributing to a body of writing that attempts to represent and define this growing urban underclass. Such underworld writing can be fact or fiction, or both; it can originate from within, for example James Hardy Vaux's *Memoirs of a Transport* (1819), or from those merely visiting. The latter group can be tourists, such as Pierce Egan, writers of romance like Ainsworth and Bulwer-Lytton, serious novelists, most notably Dickens, or social investigators from home and abroad, such as Henry Mayhew and Flora Tristan. *The Mysteries of London*, however, includes aspects of all these writers' approaches to the urban Other. Reynolds's epic serial – much more than merely the copy of Eugene Sue's *Les Mystères de Paris* (1843) often supposed[9] – reads more like Tristan's *London Journal* at its most polemical, with a Newgate plot by Ainsworth and Bulwer-Lytton and additional dialogue by Pierce Egan. It is political gothic, a radical melodrama and a penny blood that cites official statistics, anticipating both the autobiographical statements of Mayhew's street folk and Dickens at his darkest and most Manichaean.

In his guide, *Life in London* (1821–22), Pierce Egan set down many of the narrative rules for future writers in the underworld, including Reynolds. Egan presented the city as a vast cultural text, its delights available to anybody willing to decipher its secrets: 'The Metropolis is a complete CYCLOPÆDIA'.[10] Like Reynolds, Egan defined by contrasts: 'EXTREMES in every point of view, are daily to be met with'.[11] And like Reynolds, Egan was not overly concerned with the honest poor. His underworld was largely the realm of thieves, drunks, whores and bare-knuckle fighters, a glamorous demographic and no mistake. Although Egan's exploration of the underworld offered a new language of representation, this was not accompanied by social commentary. His was a Regency innocence, not yet the Victorian experience that Reynolds would bring.

In decoding the dark side of London, Egan made much use of the Enigma Code of the underworld, flash slang, which, once cracked, allowed the traveller full access. Considering himself something of a social explorer (he is more of a dandy on safari), Egan claimed linguistic authenticity, using 'the [strong] language of real life' himself because his intention was to report, without embellishment, 'living manners as they rise'[12] in an audio/visual reading of London as topographical epistemology.

---

8   *Fraser's Magazine*, 5 (1832), pp. 521–2.

9   See Chapter 8 in this volume by Berry Chevasco, 'Lost in Translation: The Relationship between Eugène Sue's *Les Mystères de Paris* and G.W.M. Reynolds's *The Mysteries of London*'.

10   Pierce Egan, *Life in London; or The Day and Night Scenes of Jerry Hawthorne, Esq. and his elegant friend Corinthian Tom in their Rambles and Sprees through the Metropolis* (1821–22; London: John Camden Hotten, 1869), p. 50.

11   Egan, *Life in London*, p. 50.

12   Egan, *Life in London*, pp. 110–11.

'Literary' flash stuck, becoming a staple of underworld representation. Ainsworth used it liberally ('Jigger closed! We'll be upon the bandogs before they can shake their trotters!'[13]); Thackeray sent it up mercilessly ('Nuffle your clod, and beladle your glumbanions'[14]); and Dickens rejected it as part of the unrealistic criminal romance, not the 'miserable reality' of the underworld. 'I endeavoured, while I painted it in all its fallen and degraded aspects', wrote Dickens of the Saffron Hill of *Oliver Twist*, 'to banish from the lips of the lowest character I introduced, any expression that could possibly offend.'[15]

Eliminated from literature after the Newgate controversy of 1839 – a moral panic concerning the pernicious effects of criminal romance on the lower classes – flash continued to be a verbal signifier of supposedly authentic underworld dialogue in the pages of popular paraliterature, as well as on the streets (it can often be heard in Mayhew). In the opening chapter of Sue's *Mysteries of Paris*, Rodolphe gains access to the underworld by first besting Chourineur with his fists, then pattering flash 'like a family man',[16] while all Reynolds's criminal characters speak flash fluently, though whether the dialogue of Reynolds's underworld is a matter of realism or romance is one of the many mysteries of *The Mysteries of London*.

When the costermongers talk to Henry Mayhew about their taste in reading in *London Labour and the London Poor*, their enthusiasm for Reynolds offers a contemporary insight into his location within the Newgate/gothic tradition:

> What they love best to listen to – and, indeed, what they are most eager for – are Reynolds's periodicals, especially the 'Mysteries of the Court'. 'They've got tired of Lloyd's blood-stained stories', said one man, who was in the habit of reading to them, 'and I'm satisfied that, of all London, Reynolds is the most popular man among them. They stuck to him in Trafalgar-square, and would again. They all say he's 'a trump', and Feargus O'Connor's another trump with them.[17]

The Mysteries of the Court of London was published by Reynolds and John Dicks between 1848 and 1856 after a dispute with his original publishers (George Vickers and George Stiff) led to Reynolds abandoning *The Mysteries of London*. Reynolds's sequel lacks the political edge of the original, concerned as it is with intrigues in the court of George IV. Politics is present, but diluted through the archaic setting. It is a sexy serial, but there are no more polemical Prologues.

Henry Mayhew's 'The Literature of Costermongers' concludes with this observation:

---

13 W.H. Ainsworth, *Jack Sheppard* (1839), in *Collected Works* (London: George Routledge and Sons, 1880), p. 23.

14 W.M. Thackeray, *Vanity Fair* (1848; London: Collins, 1949), p. 59.

15 Dickens, Preface to the third edition, *Oliver Twist; or, The Parish Boy's Progress* (1841; Oxford: Clarendon Press, 1966), p. lxiv.

16 Eugène Sue, *The Mysteries of Paris*, trans. anon. (1843; New York: M.A. Donohue, 1900), vol. 1, p. 5.

17 Henry Mayhew, *London Labour and the London Poor*, vol. 1 (1851; London: Frank Cass and Co., 1967), p. 25.

The tales of robbery and bloodshed, of heroic, eloquent, and gentlemanly highwaymen, or of gipsies turning out to be nobles, now interest the costermongers but little, although they found great delight in such stories a few years back. Works relating to Courts, potentates, or 'harristocrats', are the most relished by these rude people.[18]

'Sermons or tracts', by the way, 'gives them the 'orrors.'[19] They're not, apparently, reading Dickens either.

Reynolds is very much the successor of Edward Lloyd's penny bloods, as well as an inheritor and refiner of the earlier magazine, *Tales of Terror*. Compare, for example, the sensational sensations of the condemned Bill Bolter's death-dream in *The Mysteries of London* with stories like Ainsworth's 'Half-hangit' (1822) and Henry Thompson's 'Le Revenant' (1827). Like Signora Psyche Zenobia, Reynolds knew how to write a *Blackwood's* story, while bringing the codes and devices of the by now rather tired literary gothic to the streets of England. The medieval, European and Catholic settings of the eighteenth-century gothic were exchanged for the dark urban labyrinths of nineteenth-century London.

But these were not Reynolds's only obvious influences. He also followed in the more recent wake of the middle-class Newgate novelists, writers of criminal romances briefly in vogue in the 1830s and named after the infamous London gaol. Mayhew's 'gentlemanly highwaymen' refer to Bulwer-Lytton's *Paul Clifford* (1830) and to Ainsworth's *Rookwood* (1834) and *Jack Sheppard* (1839), as well as to their popular imitations. But the likes of Dick Turpin and Jack Sheppard have passed from the popular imagination, having been replaced by the more tangible figures of Feargus O'Connor and G.W.M. Reynolds as the working class finds a political voice in Chartism. They also liked the pictures.

Ainsworth's contribution to the gothic had been essentially to shift it to the English city with *Rookwood*, although he kept it well in the past, combining Eganesque linguistic and subcultural codes with the gothic through the legend of Dick Turpin. *Rookwood* followed *Paul Clifford*, but Bulwer-Lytton had resisted the gothic underworld in favour of a marriage of romance and radicalism, his highwayman paraphrasing Godwin from the dock in order to critique the Bloody Code and the plight of the poor: 'I come into the world friendless and poor – I find a body of laws hostile to the friendless and to the poor! To those laws hostile to me, then, I acknowledge hostility in my turn. Between us are the conditions of war.' Clifford also states that he was unjustly imprisoned as a youth, and that while inside he was subject to the 'corruption of example'.[20] A similar argument is offered by Reynolds's underworld characters. Politics is where Reynolds and Bulwer-Lytton meet, but never plot. If Reynolds, and indeed Sue, were influenced by a criminal romance, it was mainly by Ainsworth's *Jack Sheppard*, which anticipates the underworlds of both Sue and Reynolds, linguistically, melodramatically and, above all, gothically.

While the fashion for Newgate novels was on the wane in literary fiction (Ainsworth never wrote another, nor did his reputation recover, Victorian critics

---

18   Mayhew, *London Labour and the London Poor*, vol. 1, p. 27.

19   Mayhew, *London Labour and the London Poor*, vol. 1, p. 27.

20   Edward Bulwer-Lytton, *Paul Clifford* (1830; London: George Routledge and Sons, 1863), p. 200.

often dismissing him alongside the Regency, and therefore equally deviant, Egan), it lived on in the new marketplace. Reynolds takes from Ainsworth exactly the features that had made him both popular and such an easy target for moral outrage: the flash, the sex and the violence.

Reynolds's unorthodox treatment of fallen women also mirrors Ainsworth. In the *Mysteries of London*, Ellen Monroe, admittedly a middle-class woman impoverished by circumstance (one of Eugene's dirty deals) rather than born into squalor, successfully negotiates both city and text with her illegitimate child, even as unrepentant, sexually powerful prostitutes Edgeworth Bess and Poll Maggot are the only underworld characters left standing at the conclusion of *Jack Sheppard*. La Goualeuse, it will be remembered, does not survive *The Mysteries of Paris*, despite her noble origins. But Reynolds raises the stakes even higher than this, and completely politicizes the underworld.

In the 'city of fearful contrasts', Reynolds's London, '[t]he most unbounded wealth is the neighbour of the most hideous poverty; the most gorgeous pomp is placed in strong relief by the most deplorable squalor; the most seducing luxury is only separated by a narrow wall from the most appalling misery'.[21] This is, of course, the recognizable duality present in all urban writing, but with the additional language of class war. In the Prologue to *The Mysteries of London*, the city is socially, topographically, morally and textually doubled:

> There are but two words known in the moral alphabet of this great city; for all virtues are summed up in the one, and all vices in the other: and those words are

WEALTH | POVERTY.[22]

In the opening of *The Mysteries of London*, it is not *poverty* that occupies the author's attention but *crime*, and crime in relation to politics. What is contrary about Reynolds in the underworld is the relationship between portrayal and politics. As the Prologue has equated poverty with virtue and wealth with vice, 'The Old House in Smithfield' of the opening chapters hardly sets up the moral fable, the Condition of England Question, that the Prologue has suggested. An apparently upper-class youth gets lost in a 'horrible neighbourhood', takes shelter from a storm in a spooky but apparently empty house, lightning illuminating an ominous trap door in the floor, reminding him (and us) of 'fearful tales of midnight murders'.[23] A brace of flash-slinging villains then arrive, boozing and planning a robbery. We have entered the 'labyrinth of narrow and dirty streets' for the first time, and the space is immediately gothic (a stormy night, the old dark house) and menacing.[24] The locals may be 'dressed like operatives of the most humble class',[25] but they are far from honest labourers. By page 7 they've tossed the young man through the trap door. This is a

---

21 Reynolds, *MOL* (1845), vol. 1, ch. 1, p. 1.
22 Reynolds, *MOL* (1845), vol. 1, ch. 1, p. 1.
23 Reynolds, *MOL* (1845), vol. 1, ch. 1, p. 2
24 Reynolds, *MOL* (1845), vol. 1, ch. 1, p. 3.
25 Reynolds, *MOL* (1845), vol. 1, ch. 1, p. 4.

sensational hook, but hardly the expected social critique. The doubling of the text therefore is not so much between rich and poor as between plot and Prologue.

Identity is similarly doubled: pretty much every central character has at least one alter ego, then often doubled again – gender is unstable from the first chapter – and, as a policeman tells Richard, '[i]f I arrested all impostors, half London would be in prison'.[26] Trefor Thomas sees such things as a 'self-conscious mockery of Gothic motifs'.[27] Is this satire or sadism? Probably both, another textual doubling. As always, the text is as ambivalent as the identity of its characters, and of its author. As another policeman tells Richard, who has just escaped from the Resurrection Man and his 'Mummy' and is trying to explain the horrors of their Spitalfields slaughterhouse, '[t]his is London, you know – and it is impossible that the things you have described could be committed in so populous a city'.[28] We get the gallows humour. The Resurrection Man's house contains something arguably worse than the gallows, his own 'infernal invention' for concealing murder (even death goes in disguise) where victims are strung up like beef in a meat locker and drowned, head first, in a bowl of water. The exhumed corpse is allowed to ripen a bit, so that it 'might not appear too fresh to the surgeon to whom it was sold!'[29] There is also an accompanying illustration. When the police storm the gaff, the Resurrection Man detonates the place (he has a precautionary habit of mining his hideouts), spraying Bird-cage Walk with blackened body parts. In *The Mysteries of London*, Reynolds has escalated the violence already present in Ainsworth's underworld, and out-gothicked the gothic.

As Reynolds's labyrinthine multi-plot unfolds, this over-the-top underworld continues, invariably depicted as criminal rather than simply poor. In the parallel narrative, the wealthy, from the mercantile to the aristocratic, are, as promised, thoroughly dissolute. Only in the manner of their crimes and punishments do the social classes differ. When the young man from the Old House in Smithfield is later revealed to be Eliza Sydney, and the thugs from Smithfield return to rob the villa where she is staying, George Montague (the protean Eugene) fights them off, but then tries to take advantage of the terrified and vulnerable woman. Only by defending her honour with a dagger concealed beneath a pillow does Eliza avoid being raped. The contrast between wealth and poverty in this context is no contrast at all. Scenes alternate between high and low society, both being as bad as each other.

Sightings of the honest poor are rare. After Richard Markham is collared at the 'hell' (gambling house), he observes how the genuinely underprivileged (in one of their few appearances in the text) are treated at the Station House. A beggar is obviously a 'rogue and a vagabond', who'll therefore automatically get 'three months on the stepper' (treadmill), while a street-seller is nicked for obstructing the way and creating a nuisance – he'll go to prison, his family to the workhouse.[30] Because of

26 Reynolds, *MOL* (1846), vol. 2, ch. 1, p. 4.
27 Trefor Thomas, 'Introduction', in G.W.M. Reynolds, *The Mysteries of London*, ed. Trefor Thomas (Keele: Keele University Press, 1996), p. xvii.
28 Reynolds, *MOL* (1845), vol. 1, ch. 45, p. 130.
29 Reynolds, *MOL* (1845), vol. 1, ch. 43, p. 124.
30 Reynolds, *MOL* (1845), vol. 1, ch. 14, p. 36.

his 'standing in society', no charges are initially brought against Markham.[31] But these are minor injustices in the overall scheme of the narrative, and such ordinary unfortunates are peripheral at best. Reynolds cannot help but be constantly drawn towards the dramatic possibilities of the criminal underworld.

The opening scenes in Smithfield are pure Newgate. Dick Flairer and Bill Bolter are well down with the flash patter: brother thieves are 'blades', alcohol is 'lush' and 'bingo', and houses, whether hideouts or targets, are always 'cribs'. This sets the standard for the underworld slang of *The Mysteries of London*, which even includes flash songs – such as 'The Thieves' Alphabet' in chapter 23 – *à la Rookwood*. Even their names are flash – to bolt, to do a runner, remains a common slang term, but originally meant an escaped convict, or wanted man, which is Bolter's destiny in the plot, while to flair was to pick a pocket like lightning. What is most significant, however, is the 'Old House' itself, the history of which is discussed by the gang:

> 'I say, Bill, this old house has seen some jolly games, han't it?'
> 'I should think it had too. It was Jonathan Wild's favourite crib; and he was no fool at keeping things dark.'
> 'No, surely. I dare say the well-staircase in the next room there, that's covered over with the trap-door, has had many a dead body flung down it into the Fleet.'[32]

This recalls Jonathan Wild's murder of Sir Rowland Trenchard, whom he chucks down a well in *Jack Sheppard*.

Reynolds also makes use of an even more contemporary source of local legend. In the same month that *The Mysteries of London* commenced publication, October 1844, the *Journal of the London City Mission Society* had published a first-hand account of the area around Chick Lane (where Reynolds places the Old House) by Andrew Provan, including the history of such local 'thieves' houses'. Thomas Beames cites this in his chapter on Saffron Hill and Clerkenwell in *The Rookeries of London* (1850):

> In the thieves' house were dark closets, trap-doors, sliding panels, and other means of escape. In shop No. 3, were two trap-doors in the floor, one for the concealment of property, the other to provide means of escape to those who were hard run; a wooden door was cleverly let into the floor, of which, to all appearance, it formed part; through this, the thief, who was in danger of being captured, escaped; as immediately beneath was a cellar, about three feet square, from this there was an outlet to the Fleet Ditch, a plank was thrown across this, and the thief was soon in Black Boy Alley, – out of reach of his pursuers ... In one corner was a den or cellar concealed by a wall besmeared with soot and dirt, to prevent detection.[33]

---

31 Reynolds, *MOL* (1845), vol. 1, ch. 14, p. 36.
32 Reynolds, *MOL* (1845), vol. 1, ch. 2, p. 5.
33 Thomas Beames, *The Rookeries of London: Past, Present, and Prospective*, 2nd edn (London: Thomas Bosworth, 1852), p. 57.

Beames, following Provan, in a wonderful flourish of romance and realism, states that '[a]mong the inhabitants have been at different times, Jonathan Wild, Jack Sheppard, Jerry Abershaw, and Richard Turpin'.[34]

By the time of *The Mysteries of London*, however, these buildings had gone, demolished when New Street was opened between Farringdon Street and Clerkenwell. Bill and Dick comment on these future (to them) plans, but 'don't we know other cribs as good as this – and just under the very nose of the authorities too?'[35] They also suggest the place might be haunted, Bolter boasting that he wouldn't be frightened, even if 'every one wot has been tumbled down these holes into the Fleet, was to startup, and –'[36] but the image remains incomplete, as Eliza then makes him jump and he refuses to be left in the dark while his mate investigates. Such is the quintessential underworld space of *The Mysteries of London*: traditionally gothic, a *locus suspectus* in the most *Otrantoesque* sense of secret passages and trap doors, while also a symbol of underworld organization, slightly out of date, yet bizarrely accurate. Bolter's fantasy also leaves us with the perfect underworld metaphor of the sewer overflowing in a kind of undead return of the repressed.

Bolter and Flairer represent the overture of *The Mysteries of London*. They introduce the underworld themes of crime, anti-language and violence, and they are the first to invade the bourgeois surface (Mr Stephens's villa), returning to once more threaten Eliza Sydney, although driven back by the much more dangerous Montague. These characters have a little more stage time after the Station House episode, as the action shifts to 'a den of horrors' in the heart of Smithfield and Saffron Hill, continuing the textual/topographic contrast of wealthy scene/location then underworld. The language of the introduction is initially that of the social investigator: 'There were then but few cesspools; and scarcely any of those which did exist possessed any drains.... As if nothing should be wanting to render that district as filthy and unhealthy as possible, water is scarce.'[37] The description, however, becomes increasingly lurid:

> A short time ago, an infant belonging to a poor widow, who occupied a back room on the ground-floor of one of these hovels, died, and was laid upon the sacking of the bed while the mother went out to make arrangements for its interment. During her absence a pig entered the room from the yard, and feasted upon the dead child's face!
>
> In that densely populated neighbourhood that we are describing hundreds of families each live and sleep in one room. When a member of one of these families happens to die, the corpse is kept in the close room where the rest still continue to live and sleep. Poverty frequently compels the unhappy relatives to keep the body for days – aye, and weeks. Rapid decomposition takes place;– animal life generates quickly; and in four-and-twenty hours myriads of loathsome animalculae are seen crawling about.[38]

---

34 Beames, *The Rookeries of London*, p. 59.
35 Reynolds, *MOL* (1845), vol. 1, ch. 2, p. 5.
36 Reynolds, *MOL* (1845), vol. 1, ch. 2, p. 5.
37 Reynolds, *MOL* (1845), vol. 1, ch. 17, p. 43.
38 Reynolds, *MOL* (1845), vol. 1, ch. 17, p. 43.

The moral tone is here increasingly fractured by sensationalism, anticipating the 'terrible discovery' stories that were a staple of the *Illustrated Police News* a generation later. The effect is ambivalent, destabilizing – is this hardcore realism, or another gothic frame? Although he continues, '[t]he wealthy classes of society are far too ready to reproach the miserable poor for things which are really misfortunes and not faults',[39] Reynolds is actually setting a scene for a violent crime that is, as Himmelfarb puts it, 'so gratuitously sadistic that even the most sympathetic reader would have trouble attributing it to any "misfortunes" of poverty'.[40]

In a gothic inversion of family, the ragged children of Bill and Polly Bolter are returning home from a day's begging, to be beaten mercilessly by their mother for having made so little. The parents dine (well, they are far from destitute), and Polly raises the possibility of blinding their daughter because '[t]here's nothin' like a blind child to excite compassion'.[41] The son, meanwhile, will soon be able to help his father burgle, being small enough (like Oliver Twist) to 'shove through a window'.[42] Bolter goes down to the boozing ken, then returns home, gets into a fight with Polly and beats her to death in a dark pastiche of the death of Nancy in *Oliver Twist*, her head striking the corner of a table so that '[h]er left eye came in contact with the angle of the board, and was literally crushed in its socket'.[43] Bolter bolts, and ends up hiding out in the dungeon of the Old House in Chick Lane. Dick Flairer brings him supplies. When the police arrive, he assumes, quite wrongly, that his friend has sold him out and stabs him to death. (It was actually the Resurrection Man. There is none of the honour among thieves that Ainsworth introduced.) In a characteristic doubling of narrative, he is sentenced to death at the same time that Markham is being tried for forgery.

Bolter's execution is fascinating in its intertextual contrariness. There are echoes of 'A Visit to Newgate' from Dickens's *Sketches by Boz* (later recycled and refined as 'Fagin's Last Night Alive'), as the bells of St Sepulchre's toll and the clock counts down. There is also a quasi-religious nightmare of death by hanging and the descent into hell reminiscent of a late Georgian Tale of Terror, and even a dash of the eleventh plate of Hogarth's *Industry and Idleness*, 'The Idol 'Prentice Executed at Tyburn', as the ghoulish crowds gather for the 'grand national spectacle' and the local pubs 'drove a roaring trade throughout the day'.[44] Finally, there is a polemic against capital punishment:

> But the Law is vindictive, cowardly, mean, and ignorant. It is *vindictive* because its punishments are more severe than the offences, and because its officers descend to any dirtiness in order to obtain conviction. It is *cowardly*, because it cuts off from the world, with a rope or an axe, those men whose dispositions it fears to undertake to curb. It is *mean*, because it is all in favour of the wealthy, and reserves its thunders for the poor

---

39 Reynolds, *MOL* (1845), vol. 1, ch. 17, p. 43.
40 Gertrude Himmelfarb, *The Idea of Poverty: England in the Early Industrial Age* (London: Faber and Faber, 1984), p. 439.
41 Reynolds, *MOL* (1845), vol. 1, ch. 17, p. 45.
42 Reynolds, *MOL* (1845), vol. 1, ch. 17, p. 45.
43 Reynolds, *MOL* (1845), vol. 1, ch. 19, p. 51.
44 Reynolds, *MOL* (1845), vol. 1, ch. 36, p. 102.

and obscure who have no powerful interest to protect them; and because itself originates nearly half the crimes which it punishes. And it is *ignorant*, because it erects the gibbet where it should rear the cross.[45]

This both recalls and raises the abolitionist language of Dickens in *Barnaby Rudge*, where 'this last dreadful and repulsive penalty ... never turned a man inclined to evil, and has hardened thousands who were half inclined to good'.[46] Himmelfarb reads this as Reynolds seeking to 'legitimize the outlaw by illegitimizing the law', suggesting that the author here outdistances all of his reform-minded, even radical, contemporaries by not sympathizing with the dangerous classes but giving them 'the same moral status as the rest of society'.[47] Reynolds does sensationalize, true, but not sentimentalize.

Building upon this foundation, Reynolds then politicizes his narrative in an even more specifically class-conscious way, anticipating the first-person statements of Mayhew's subjects by giving underworld characters an opportunity to tell their own stories. As noted, this had been tried before by Bulwer-Lytton, but what Reynolds offers is a radical critique that was lacking in all the Newgate novels of the 1830s, as well as in Dickens's response to the criminal romance, *Oliver Twist*, where his acclaimed realism is as much melodrama as realistic and offers no serious call for reform (Oliver is of noble, or at least middle-class, birth, and the charity of both Brownlow and the Maylies is Christian rather than political).

The most striking example of this technique can be seen in 'The Resurrection Man's History', where the prosaically named Tony Tidkins takes over the narrative and tells his story to the locals of the Dark House boozing ken in Brick Lane, Reynolds here revealing a hidden narrative, the personal biography of a criminal.

Tidkins's father was arrested for petty smuggling, and his son watches his family destroyed while the local baronet, who controlled a vast contraband machine of which Tidkins Senior was a very small cog, was helped upon conviction by all the local gentry, eventually coming into a large inheritance which wipes his slate clean. 'I began to comprehend', muses Tidkins, 'that birth and station made an immense difference in the views that the world adopted of men's actions.'[48] His father's conviction makes it impossible for him, damned by association, to find honest employment. Tidkins finally cracks when the baronet horse-whips him for not opening a gate. He fights back, and is rewarded with two years for assault. Upon his release, now a hardened criminal, he calmly goes to the home of the justice who passed sentence and torches it, killing his only daughter, before burning down the baronet's castle: 'And the upper classes wonder that there are so many incendiary fires: my only surprise is, that there are so few!'[49]

There are similar accounts from the Buffer, the Whipper-in and his (prostitute) wife, Cranky Jem and the Rattlesnake (the Screech-Owl to Tidkins's Schoolmaster). Origins differ, but the moral in each case is pretty much the same. In the chapter that

45 Reynolds, *MOL* (1845), vol. 1, ch. 36, p. 101.
46 Charles Dickens, *Barnaby Rudge* (1841; London: Odhams, 1897), p. 383.
47 Himmelfarb, *The Idea of Poverty*, p. 444.
48 Reynolds, *MOL* (1845), vol. 1, ch. 62, p. 192.
49 Reynolds, *MOL* (1845), vol. 1, ch. 62, p. 195.

picks up and develops the Resurrection Man's history with other autobiographies, 'The Wrongs and Crimes of the Poor', Tidkins summarizes: 'Here we are, in this room, upwards of twenty thieves and prostitutes: I'll be bound to say that the laws and the state of society made eight of them what they are.'[50]

The Resurrection Man is the principal underworld villain of the serial, stalking Richard Markham and robbing, killing and exhuming his way through the text, impossible to destroy until the finale. He is finally killed by his own double, Cranky Jem, once a partner until Tidkins inevitably betrayed him. The Resurrection Man, blinded by his own powder, dies entombed alive by Jem in the manner of Ainsworth's arch-villain Alan Rookwood. Yet the Resurrection Man is also at times a revolutionary (and a much more interesting one than Richard in Castelcicala), with a proactive terrorist agenda apparent in his non-profit-making acts of retribution against his class enemies. Reynolds's message regarding the arsonist's revenge is unambiguous: the justice had it coming; let a complacent and corrupt establishment beware. 'Crime, oppression, and injustice prosper for a time; but, with nations as with individuals, the day of retribution must come.'[51]

The Resurrection Man even violates Buckingham Palace with the intention of stealing the plate[52] – the Palace no more to him than another crib to crack – initiating the Henry Holford story arc where voyeurism culminates in an assassination attempt on Prince Albert in an audacious, allegorically charged reworking of two real events from 1840.[53] Reynolds's symbolism would be obvious to the point of clumsiness if not for the sheer nerve of presenting Victoria as a character in his textual labyrinth, just another 'harristocrat', ignorant of the conditions in which the majority of her subjects exist. If the 'wrongs and crimes of the poor' suggest that the underworld villains are more socially sinned against than sinning, then the Resurrection Man is the definitive 'Nemesis of Neglect',[54] a super-criminal of supernaturally horrific dimension, created by a hopeless underclass upbringing for which the middle and upper classes take no responsibility. His anachronistic profession, in this context, is telling – as Marx wrote, '[w]hat the bourgeoisie therefore produces, above all, are their own grave-diggers'.[55]

Yet Reynolds's politics have always been questioned. Dickens, appalled at the Trafalgar Square demonstrations of 6 March 1848, separated Reynolds from the 'genuine working men who are Chartists', with whom he sympathized, and considered him an 'amateur' and 'a name with which no lady's, and no gentleman's,

---

50 Reynolds, *MOL* (1845), vol. 1, ch. 65, p. 202.

51 Reynolds, *MOL* (1845), vol. 1, ch. 186, p. 415.

52 When Holford does not return from the Palace, Tidkins breaks in himself to find the loot (Reynolds, *MOL* [1845], vol. 1, ch. 60, p. 187).

53 This episode was based upon the pot-boy Edward Oxford taking a shot at the royal couple on Constitution Hill, and Edmund Jones breaking into the Palace, where, said he, 'I sat upon the throne, saw the Queen and heard the Princess Royal squall'. Quoted from Stanley Weintraub, *Victoria* (London: John Murray, 1996), p. 151.

54 The figure of crime as cultural response envisioned by *Punch* during the 'Jack the Ripper' murders. See *Punch*, 29 September 1888.

55 Karl Marx, *The Revolutions of 1848: Political Writings*, vol. 1, ed. David Fernbach (London: Penguin, 1973), p. 79.

should be associated'.[56] Political allies never quite trusted Reynolds either. Also referring to the Trafalgar Square incident, where Reynolds had spontaneously taken the chair of a leaderless meeting, the radical engraver James Linton dismissed him as 'the tin kettle at the mad mob's tail',[57] while W.E. Adams said of him later that 'it was rather as a charlatan and a trader than as a genuine politician that G.W.M. was generally regarded by the rank and file of Chartism'.[58]

Admittedly much less vituperatively, this trend has continued in more recent attempts to reconcile the politics and plot of *The Mysteries of London*. Margaret Dalziel saw a contradiction between Reynolds's republican rhetoric and his rich, noble heroes, who represented 'the pleasure of imaginative participation in the life of a wholly undemocratic society'.[59]

In the seminal *Fiction for the Working Man*, Louis James acknowledges that *The Mysteries of London* 'shows a social conscience lacking in almost all other popular fiction at this time', but that Reynolds's abilities 'fell to the lure of sensation and easy popularity'. Ultimately, for James then:

> His radicalism serves a dramatic rather than a genuinely social purpose, and is finally subject to the conventions of romance.... The lower classes are made up of thugs, resurrection men, fences, prostitutes, or starving paupers. The best of the working classes as they really existed – the courageous artisan overcoming his difficulties by hard work and determination – is never shown. Reynolds's social criticism is overbalanced by his sensationalism.[60]

This position requires much of Reynolds as a popular author, although James is right concerning the absence of the decent working classes in the text. James's reading is endorsed by Richard Maxwell: 'To what end does Reynolds's unveiling of secrets proceed, besides the exploitative one? Not revolution: revolutions happen in Italy, where Richard makes his illustrious career. Reform seems equally distant.'[61] But as a costermonger (representative of Reynolds's working-class audience) tells Mayhew, '[l]ove and murder suits us best, sir ... *Macbeth* would be better liked, if it was only the witches and the fighting'.[62]

---

56   Charles Dickens to W.C. Macready, 30 August 1849, in Graham Storey and K.J. Fielding (eds), *The Letters of Charles Dickens* (Oxford: Clarendon Press, 1981), vol. 5, p. 603.

57   William James Linton, *James Watson: A Memoir* (Manchester: Heywood and Sons, 1880), p. 65.

58   W.E. Adams, *Memoirs of a Social Atom* (London: Hutchinson and Co., 1903), p. 245.

59   Margaret Dalziel, *Popular Fiction One Hundred Years Ago: An Unexpected Tract of Literary History* (London: Cohen and West, 1957), p. 141.

60   Louis James, *Fiction for the Working Man, 1830–1850: A Study of the Literature Produced for the Working Classes in Early Victorian Urban England*, 2nd edn (London: Penguin, 1973), p. 197.

61   Richard Maxwell, *The Mysteries of Paris and London* (Charlottesville: University Press of Virginia, 1992), p. 166.

62   Mayhew, *London Labour and the London Poor*, vol. 1, p. 15.

Gertrude Himmelfarb offers an alternative reading: 'Neither the conventions of the genre [gothic] nor the desire for popularity required him to express the views he did.'[63] This is a good point. Himmelfarb also challenges the demands critics make of Reynolds. 'They are asking of him', she writes, 'the kind of "social novel" that no radical of the time, not even Ernest Jones, ever wrote.'[64] Her conclusion, however, fails to convince:

> If Reynolds created no such heroes among the poor, it was not necessarily, as his critics suppose, because he was insufficiently resolute and radical to withstand the temptations of sensationalism. It may have been because his radicalism was of an entirely different order and because his idea of poverty was nihilistic rather than compassionate or heroic.... If there was any social message to be drawn from *The Mysteries of London*, it was that violence and depravity, licentiousness and criminality, were the only forms of existence, and potentially the only means of redemption, available to the poor.[65]

The problem is that any reading of *The Mysteries of London* is either reductive or ambivalent, ultimately falling, like Reynolds's Prologues, into the language of paradox. As Whittingham says to Mr MacChizzle, 'I'm bewildered in a labyrinth of mazes, sir'.[66]

It is best to embrace the contradictions. As Anne Humpherys has convincingly argued,

> Reynolds' political understanding was more complicated than he has been given credit for by later critics.... Reynolds' politics as well as his editorial stance and the contents of his fiction reflected the inclusiveness of popular culture. His contradictions were the contradictions of the audience he was writing for ... unless we take into account these contradictions in the popular mind, unless we are able to exercise our own negative capabilities as literary historians, we will not be able to understand fully either popular literature or popular politics.[67]

To quote some wisdom from Ainsworth: 'the truth is, to write for the mob, you must not write too weak. The newspaper level is the true line to take.'[68] And Reynolds took it.

The underworld of *The Mysteries of London* is not nihilistic, at least not in the way Himmelfarb uses the term, neither are the politics of its representation simply a pose calculated to exploit the new mass market. Reynolds intends the London underworld to be a reflection of the early Victorian city. From the Prologue, every social space has its shadow: 'Crime is abundant in this city: the lazarhouse, the prison, the brothel, and the dark alley, are rife with all kinds of enormity; in the same

63 Himmelfarb, *The Idea of Poverty*, p. 450.
64 Himmelfarb, *The Idea of Poverty*, p. 450.
65 Himmelfarb, *The Idea of Poverty*, p. 451.
66 Reynolds, *MOL* (1845), vol. 1, ch. 46, p. 134.
67 Anne Humpherys, 'G.W.M. Reynolds, Popular Literature and Popular Politics', *Victorian Periodicals Review*, 16 (1983): 87–8.
68 Ainsworth to James Crossley, 7 April 1838, Crossley Papers (Archives Section, Local Studies Unit), Central Library, Manchester.

way as the palace, the mansion, the clubhouse, the parliament, and the parsonage, are each and all characterised by their different degrees and shades of vice.'[69] If there is epistemological confusion, it is a cultural response to the city itself. When Reynolds commenced the serialization of *The Mysteries of London* in 1844, the population of London was approximately two million. By the completion of the second series in 1848 (the end of the original title published by Vickers), it had grown to two and a half million – at a rate of growth of 146 per cent from the beginning of the nineteenth century.[70]

As Humpherys has argued, such a social upheaval was crucial to the development of the mysteries novel:

> The mysteries novel could not come into being until the modern city itself was visible, until the effects of rapid expansion and change were evident in the disappearance of the old and construction of the new, until the unavoidable and startling differences between classes of people and places that resulted from rapid growth were a commonplace, and, most importantly, until the institutional structures which were to manage growth and control its results were a recognised part of urban life.[71]

'Mysteries', she continues, refers linguistically to the fragmented and hence incoherent experience of the modern city as well as the resulting feelings of disconnectedness.[72] In *The Mysteries of London*, this disorientation is topographical, moral and textual. As W.E. Adams concluded, Reynolds (whose urban vision anticipates the postmodern) was, indeed, 'before his time'.[73]

Such a demeanour of strangeness suggests, ultimately, a new form of urban gothic – not in the traditional sense of bourgeois cultural anxiety, but a political gothic, aimed at the same audience it is, in part, dramatizing and seeking to energize. As Thomas Beames wrote a few years later: 'Yet who were they whom the vast array of the 10th of April were in arms to resist. Were they not the inhabitants of our Rookeries? Did not each poor quarter of the town pour forth its multitudes to swell the great gatherings on Kennington Common? And ... so the Rookeries of London were the nuclei of the disaffected.'[74]

Reynolds was also at Kennington Common on 10 April 1848 – the year of European revolution, and the conclusion of *The Mysteries of London* – taking the chair in O'Connor's absence. Greeted by prolonged cheering, he spoke, reported the *Illustrated London News*, 'at considerable length', under a banner that read: 'The voice of the people is the voice of God.'[75] Had he not been blinded, entombed and dead, the Resurrection Man would have loved that.

---

69   Reynolds, *MOL* (1845), vol. 1, ch. 1, p. 1.

70   Eric J. Evans, *The Forging of the Modern State: Early Industrial Britain* (London: Longman, 1983).

71   Anne Humpherys, 'Generic Strands and Urban Twists: The Victorian Mysteries Novel', *Victorian Studies*, 34 (1991): 456.

72   Humpherys, 'Generic Strands and Urban Twists', p. 456.

73   Adams, *Memoirs of a Social Atom*, p. 244.

74   Beames, *The Rookeries of London*, pp. 255–6.

75   *Illustrated London News*, 15 April 1848.

Chapter 10

Reynolds's *Mysteries* and Popular Culture

Juliet John

I would rather have the affectionate regard of my fellow men, than I would have heaps and mines of gold. But the two things do not seem to me incompatible.[1]

So Dickens addressed his rapt audience while speaking in America in 1842. At that time, Dickens could not perhaps have imagined that G.W.M. Reynolds, the plagiaristic author of *Pickwick Abroad; or the Tour in France* (1837–38), would soon be thought of by some as 'the most popular writer of our time'.[2] Reynolds and Dickens were unusual in the extent to which they made 'heaps and mines of gold' from literature that was popular in the sense that it both sold in vast quantities and claimed to speak for 'the people' – a capacious phrase which included particularly, for both authors, the dispossessed, the marginalized and the oppressed. A touchstone of debate in modern cultural theory is the idea of a tension between the goals of commercial culture and those of a genuinely 'popular' culture consonant with the values and interests of the people, and of a more equal society.[3] Whereas Dickens has

---

1   Charles Dickens, 1 February 1842, in K.J. Fielding (ed.), *The Speeches of Charles Dickens: A Complete Edition* (Oxford: Clarendon Press, 1960), p. 21.

2   *The Bookseller*, 3 July 1879, p. 660.

3   Perhaps the most well-known statements of this position come from the Frankfurt School Marxist theorist Theodor W. Adorno, *The Culture Industry: Selected Essays on Mass Culture* (London: Routledge, 1991); the high cultural Dwight MacDonald, 'A Theory of Mass Culture', in Bernard Rosenberg and David Manning White (eds), *Mass Culture: The Popular Arts in America* (Glencoe, IL: Free Press, 1957), pp. 59–73; and the writings of Michel Foucault. Cultural studies has in obvious respects moved away from such blanket pessimism about popular culture in a capitalist context, exploring, for example, the multiplicity of cultures submerged beneath the term 'mass culture'; utilizing Gramsci's concept of hegemony and Bourdieu's notions of cultural capital and ideological status apparatus to refine binary models; exploring the ideas of Stuart Hall and the Birmingham School on cultural agency; and celebrating the power of the popular at the end of the critical spectrum. However, there is a sense in which, despite postmodern interventions, the question of the relationship between capital and agency or political consciousness still haunts the study of mass culture. As Simon Frith puts it: 'academic approaches to popular culture still derive from the mass cultural critiques of the 1930s and 1940s, particularly from the Marxist critique of contemporary popular culture in terms of the production and circulation of commodities', even if a keynote of latter investigation has been 'to accept the Frankfurt reading of cultural production and to look for the redeeming features of commodity culture in the act of consumption' ('The Good, the Bad, and the Indifferent: Defending Popular Culture from the Populists', in John

been praised for his ability 'to negotiate and frequently to transcend the boundaries between popular and radical culture in a way that virtually no other mid-nineteenth-century writer was able to do', Reynolds has never quite been able to throw off Dickens's sideswipe that he was one of the 'Bastards of the Mountain, draggled fringe on the Red Cap, Panders to the basest passions of the lowest natures', or Marx's verdict that he was a 'scoundrel', a 'rich and able speculator'.[4] Even at the height of his popularity, Reynolds could not assume that his sales figures were an index of the 'affectionate regard' of his 'fellow men'. Indeed, from his day to ours, the regard of fellow writers and political sympathizers in particular has been as suspicious as it has been affectionate.

Distrust of Reynolds has arisen from the suspicion that the people were less important to him as people than they were as consumers – or that his political radicalism was less important to him than his commercialism, and indeed that it functioned to mask his commercialism. Although Reynolds was more active in his support for aggressive radical movements like Chartism than Dickens ever was, it is Dickens who has been most valued, in the words of Sally Ledger, as:

> a cultural bridge between, on the one hand, an older, eighteenth-century political conception of the People: and, on the other hand, a distinctly mid-nineteenth-century, modern conception of a mass-market 'populace' that had been created by the rise of the commercial newspaper press.[5]

Indeed, Ledger credits Dickens with the ability 'to transcend the boundaries between popular and radical culture in a way that virtually no other mid-nineteenth-century writer was able to do', 'to transcend the high/low culture divide', and in 'moving between these two conceptions of the People (a political entity) and the (mass-market) populace (a commercial entity)', with the ability 'to politicize the latter to an extent unrivalled in the second half of the nineteenth century'.[6] Ledger's

---

Storey [ed.], *Cultural Theory and Popular Culture: A Reader*, 2nd edn [London: Prentice Hall, 1998], p. 571). Among other cultural theorists seeking to mute the uncritical celebration of commercial mass culture is the film theorist Paul Willemen, who argues that populists are employing 'a principled refusal to countenance the possibility that vast sections of the population have come to derive pleasure from conservative orientated media discourses' (Review of John Hill's *Sex, Class and Realism: British Cinema, 1956–1963*, in *Framework*, 34 [1987]: 35).

4   Sally Ledger, 'From Queen Caroline to Lady Dedlock: Dickens and the Popular Radical Imagination', *Victorian Literature and Culture* (2004): 576; Dickens, 'Preliminary Word', *Household Words*, vol. 1 (30 March 1850), p. 1; Karl Marx to Ferdinand Lassalles, 28 April 1862, in Saul K. Padover (ed.), *The Letters of Karl Marx* (Englewood Cliffs, NJ: Prentice Hall, 1979), p. 465; Marx to Friedrich Engels, 8 October 1858, quoted in Virginia Berridge, 'Popular Sunday Papers and Mid-Victorian Society', in George Boyce, James Curran and Pauline Wingate (eds), *Newspaper History from the Seventeenth Century to the Present Day* (London: Constable, 1978), p. 254. Dickens's description of Reynolds invokes the context of French revolutionary politics, 'the Mountain' being the radical wing of the Jacobins, and the 'Red Cap' the symbol of the *sans culottes*.

5   Ledger, 'From Queen Caroline to Lady Dedlock', p. 576.
6   Ledger, 'From Queen Caroline to Lady Dedlock', p. 578.

historical specificity in the last respect perhaps gestures to Reynolds's prominence in the first half of the century, *Reynolds's Miscellany* (1846–69) especially combining sales figures that Dickens's journalism would never rival with overtly politicized material such as his series of 'Letters to the Industrious Classes'.[7] There are voices less celebratory than those of Ledger and of Dickens himself about his ability to be culturally inclusive, politically radical and commercially successful: Anne Lohrli, for example, has accused Dickens of a kind of 'dishonesty' and superficiality in the style of *Household Words*; Helen Small has questioned whether the audiences at Dickens's public readings were actually as inclusive of the lower classes as the Dickens publicity machine suggested, and has argued that the Readings worked to depoliticize their audiences:

> Dickens's Readings represent an attempt to redefine the experience of culture in such a way that it is seen to express the potential irrelevance of class to fundamental sympathies and sensibilities.[8]

Though Dickens too has his doubters, however, the reputation for 'dishonesty', particularly in politics, has stuck more firmly to Reynolds than to Dickens. There are good reasons for this, of course: Anne Humpherys has pointed to 'that frustrating blend of calculation and politics that marks his works', for example, and to his 'contradictory mixture of social conformism and political radicalism'.[9] But these criticisms could equally be made of Dickens. Distinctive to Reynolds (as opposed to Dickens) are accusations of impurity – both of sexual impurity and of indiscriminate, irresponsible borrowings from 'street literature' in order to appeal to the widest and lowest tastes for commercial gain.

Anne Humpherys has argued convincingly that there is a kind of 'negative capability' in Reynolds's apparent inconsistencies and ideological shape-shifting.[10] Another way of putting this is that Reynolds exhibits, perhaps more than Dickens, a Bakhtinian 'dialogism' in his incorporation of so many extra-literary discourses: he flaunts his hybridity. There is arguably a kind of honesty in this. From one perspective, then, Dickens was right to call Reynolds a 'Bastard', but Reynolds is open about his 'bastardy'. More importantly, despite Reynolds's ironically 'thoroughbred' status as a low and/or mass cultural author, his work is sophisticated and open about the

---

7   *RM*, 13 January–14 May 1847.

8   Anne Lohrli, 'Introduction', in Lohrli (comp.), *Household Words: A Weekly Journal, 1850–1859, Conducted by Charles Dickens: Table of Contents, Lists of Contributors and Their Contributions, based on The Household Words Office Book in The Morris L. Parrish Collection of Victorian Novelists, Princeton University* (Toronto: University of Toronto Press, 1973), p. x; Helen Small, 'A Pulse of 124: Charles Dickens and a Pathology of the Mid-Victorian Reading Public', in James Raven, Helen Small and Naomi Tadmor (eds), *The Practice and Representation of Reading in England* (Cambridge: Cambridge University Press, 1996), p. 275.

9   Anne Humpherys, 'G.W.M. Reynolds, Popular Literature and Popular Politics', *Victorian Periodicals Review*, 16 (1983): 86, 87.

10   Humpherys, 'G.W.M. Reynolds', pp. 83–8.

inevitability of cultural fluidity in this 'first age of mass culture'.[11] Reynolds's heyday was, of course, an age before mass culture had become a byword for an Adorno-esque 'culture industry', seen to function as a capitalist instrument of political control or an opiate for the masses.[12] Reynolds is acknowledged to be an important figure in the history and politics of nineteenth-century popular culture. What this chapter wishes to stress, with particular reference to *The Mysteries of London* (1844–48), is not simply Reynolds's place in popular culture but the prominence of popular culture as an object of analysis in the work of Reynolds. Reynolds's analysis of 'popular culture' is as wide-ranging and elastic as the term itself: in *The Mysteries of London*, working-class culture (including literacy and education), 'mass' commercial culture, the mass commodification of modern urban life, the democratization of culture and the relationship between radical politics and cultural formations are all subject to analytical scrutiny.

It is indeed possible to argue that one of the reasons that Reynolds has been seen, in the words of W.E. Adams, 'rather as a charlatan and a trader than as a genuine politician' is very much to do with both his commercial success and the openness of his work about the importance of money in both politics and cultural formations.[13] Dickens's Boston trumpeting of his desire for popularity and money[14] is atypical of Dickens, who publicly tended to follow the convention of literary Romanticism in depicting culture (even popular culture) as offering individual growth (even transcendence) through escape from the material and the social worlds. Reynolds, by contrast, holds up the idea of culture as commerce for view. Perhaps the most overt and fascinating passage in *The Mysteries of London* respecting cultural mobility and/or hybridity comes when Reynolds proffers a topographical anatomy of the relationship between literature and the streets. The description of Holywell Street and Paternoster Row offers a literal way in to the subject of street literature and its cultural and economic place in nineteenth-century London:

> HOLYWELL STREET was once noted only as a mart for second-hand clothing, and booksellers' shops dealing in indecent prints and volumes. The reputation it thus acquired was not a very creditable one.
>
> Time has, however, included Holywell Street in the clauses of its Reform Bill. Several highly respectable booksellers and publishers have located themselves in the place that once deserved no better denomination than 'Rag Fair'. The unprincipled vendors of demoralising books and pictures have, with few exceptions, migrated into Wych Street or Drury Lane; and even the two or three that pertinaciously cling to their old temples of infamy in Holywell Street, seem to be aware of the incursions of respectability into that once notorious thoroughfare, and cease to outrage decency by the display of obscenities in their windows.
>
> The reputation of Holywell Street has now ceased to be a by-word: it is respectable: and, as a mart for the sale of literary wares, threatens to rival Paternoster Row.

---

11   'Introduction', in Laurel Brake, Bill Bell and David Finkelstein (eds), *Nineteenth-century Media and the Construction of Identities* (Houndmills: Palgrave, 2000), p. 7.

12   See n. 3 above.

13   W.E. Adams, *Memoirs of a Social Atom* (1903; repr. New York: A.M. Kelley, 1968), p. 235.

14   See epigraph.

It is curious to observe that, while butchers, tailors, linen-drapers, tallow-manufacturers, and toy-vendors, are gradually dislodging the booksellers of Paternoster Row, and thus changing the once exclusive nature of this famous street into one of general features, the booksellers on the other hand, are gradually ousting the old-clothes dealers of Holywell Street.

As the progress of the American colonist towards the far-west drives before it the aboriginal inhabitants, so do the inroads of the bibliophiles menace the Israelites of Holywell Street with total extinction.

Paternoster Row and Holywell Street are both losing their primitive features: the former is becoming a mart of miscellaneous trades; the latter is rising into a bazaar of booksellers.[15]

While the colonial metaphor immediately attracts the modern critical eye, what Reynolds is describing is not simply the high cultural appropriation of low (or even counter-) cultural space. What he is describing is a process of cultural traffic or migration in which no person, group or place acts as a centre of power. The city becomes 'a mart for the sale of literary wares' and a 'mart of miscellaneous trades'. Economic forces shape cultural appetites and vice versa. Power resides in market forces generated in the context of a burgeoning democracy (and vice versa) and undermining the purity of high and low cultural spaces. If anything, the losers in the city as 'mart' are at the extreme ends of the cultural spectrum – the 'indecent' and the 'exclusive'. In this description, market forces operate to undermine the extremes of high and low alike, working to create the middle ground(s), which will itself be subject to change and relocation. Ironically, whereas Dickens's posthumous reputation has benefited from the move to the cultural middle ground in an era of capitalism and democracy, it is Reynolds on the 'draggled fringe' who has suffered in the long term.

In the description of Holywell Street and Paternoster Row, culture is subject to the forces of commerce, just as commerce is subject to cultural agency. The text as a whole is clear about the idea of mass culture as a form of capital, not simply for cultural producers but for cultural consumers. In simple terms, like Dickens, Reynolds believed in 'The Amusements of the People',[16] idealistically as a means of entertainment, education and politicization, and more hard-headedly (in the case of literacy) as a form of social and economic currency. It is noteworthy how many of the autobiographical interpolations from working-class or underclass characters in *The Mysteries of London* contain accounts of some education, and how often the speakers attach value to education and cultural experience; in the lives of such characters, moreover, education is often curtailed with negative consequences. The Resurrection Man, for example, is barred from the Sunday school and church he has been attending because his father was found to be a smuggler and bodysnatcher,

15 G.W.M. Reynolds, *The Mysteries of London* (London: George Vickers, 1845), vol. 1, ch. 103, pp. 318–19 [p. 157]. Page references in square brackets are cross-references to G.W.M. Reynolds, *The Mysteries of London*, ed. Trefor Thomas (Keele: Keele University Press, 1996).

16 This is the title of Dickens's best-known (two-part) essay on popular culture, published in *Household Words*, vol. 1 (30 March 1850), pp. 13–15; vol. 1 (13 April 1850), pp. 57–60.

the parson telling him that he was 'calculated to pollute honest and good boys'.[17] This withdrawal of education politicizes as well as marginalizes him and sets him 'a-thinking about the state of society'.[18] Later he commits arson as an act of revenge on the aristocracy (whose crimes have been overlooked by society), and afterwards 'composed a song upon the subject', commenting with some self-consciousness:

> You may laugh at the idea of me becoming a poet; but you know well enough that I received some trifle of education – that I was not a fool by nature – and that in early life I was fond of reading.[19]

'The Incendiary's Song' celebrates the power of 'the Lucifer match' in 'the hand of the desperate poor'. Violence has become the most effective means to cultural expression even in a character who has the capacity to write poetry; tellingly, it is violence rather than poetry which gains the most attention from those who exclude 'the voice of the people'.

The Rattlesnake attends for a period a school

> founded for the purpose of furnishing education to the children of pit-men who were prudent enough and well disposed enough to pay a small stipend for that purpose, that stipend being fixed at a very low rate, as the deficiency in the amount required to maintain the establishment was supplied by voluntary contribution.[20]

In her case, however, the fees are paid by a generous gentleman whose house she has robbed, but he is so moved by her life story and plight that he supports her. Education is, as so often, however, left to random benevolence. Crankey Jem's father is a 'popular minister'/hypocrite;[21] Jem's tale is what Trefor Thomas calls 'an unusual addition to the popular literature of transportation'.[22] Jem is criminalized for not being able to give 'a satisfactory account of himself' when he is *starving – houseless – friendless – pennyless*[23] in the course of a narrative in which he is indeed able to give a satisfactory account of himself. Some convicts of his acquaintance keep 'slang journals during the passage' of their transportation, and 'read them once a-week to the rest'.[24] Jem obliges the reader with a sample and a translation of the typical fare from these journals in the language of the criminal underworld. Jem, however, who has a 'smattering of education', does not employ slang as the main language of his autobiographical interpolation. Jem's choice to reject slang as the language of his narrative, like his refusal to take part in cannibalism even at the prospect of his own death, acts as a sign of his potential to contribute usefully to mainstream, 'civilized' society. He is an underclass tragic hero in the Romantic mode: nicknamed 'Crankey' because his 'fits of deep despondency and remorse' make him seem 'not right in

17 Reynolds, *MOL* (1845), vol. 1, ch. 62, p. 192 [p. 108].
18 Reynolds, *MOL* (1845), vol. 1, ch. 62, p. 192 [p. 108].
19 Reynolds, *MOL* (1845), vol. 1, ch. 62, p. 196 [pp. 116–17].
20 Reynolds, *MOL* (1845), vol. 1, ch. 116, p. 360 [p. 185].
21 Reynolds, *MOL* (1846), vol. 2, ch. 191, p. 177 [p. 261].
22 Reynolds, *MOL*, ed. Thomas, p. 259.
23 Reynolds, *MOL* (1846), vol. 2, ch. 191, p. 178 [p. 262].
24 Reynolds, *MOL* (1846), vol. 2, ch. 191, p. 179 [p. 264].

the head'[25] to his criminal companions, his tragedy is his stunted potential. Jem is originally criminalized simply for being an orphaned 'vagabond'; he is a 'vagabond' because the chapel school in which he has been educated until the age of 15 rejects him when he is orphaned. Thus, in Jem's case, the legitimate provider of education and salvation generates the kind of criminal narrative which so worried the legal and cultural establishment in the nineteenth century.[26]

In a memorable passage in *The Mysteries of London* denouncing the 'oligarchy' which 'has cramped the privileges and monopolised the rights of a mighty nation', Reynolds juxtaposes a denunciation of the Poor Laws, the Game Laws and the Corn Laws with a celebration of 'the march of intellect':

> Although our legislators – trembling at what they affect to sneer at under the denomination of 'the march of intellect' – obstinately refuse to imitate enlightened France by instituting a system of national education, – nevertheless, the millions of this country are now instructing themselves!
>
> Honour to the English mechanic – honour to the English operative: each alike seeks to taste the tree of learning, 'whose root is bitter, but whose fruits are sweet!'
>
> Thank God, no despotism – no tyranny can arrest the progress of that mighty intellectual movement which is not perceptible amongst the industrious millions of these realms.
>
> And how excellent are the principles of that self-instruction which now tends to elevate the moral condition of the country. It is not confined within the narrow limits which churchmen would impose: it embraces the sciences – the arts – all subjects of practical utility, – its aim being to model the mind on the solid basis of Common Sense.
>
> …
>
> There breathes not a finer specimen of the human race than a really enlightened and liberal-minded Englishman. But if *he* be deserving of admiration and applause, who has received from the lips of a paid preceptor – how much more worthy of praise and respect is *the self-instructed mechanic!*[27]

The juxtaposition is carefully structured, as throughout the serial Reynolds appears to posit culture and education as key weapons in the fight against social inequality. Indeed, culture and education are as important as potential agents of change in the social critique of *The Mysteries of London* as money or class consciousness.

The critical debate about Reynolds's stance in relation to class politics is well established, Patrick Joyce most memorably positioning Reynolds as 'a crucially important bridge between the old radicalism and the new'.[28] 'Old radicalism' involved the idea of an opposition between 'the people' and a powerful, corrupt aristocracy, whilst 'new radicalism' involved a newer, class-based vision of inequality and politicized opposition. Reynolds's sense of the role of culture, and particularly

---

25 Reynolds, *MOL* (1846), vol. 2, ch. 191, p. 178 [p. 262].

26 See 'Introduction', in Juliet John (ed.), *Cult Criminals: The Newgate Novels*, 6 vols (London: Routledge, 1998), vol. 1, for a summary of anxieties over so-called 'Newgate' novels in the nineteenth century.

27 Reynolds, *MOL* (1846), vol. 2, ch. 185, p. 156 [p. 249].

28 Patrick Joyce, *Visions of the People: Industrial England and the Question of Class, 1848–1914* (Cambridge: Cambridge University Press, 1991), p. 66.

popular culture, as an instrument of political change has received less attention in relation to his career than the more familiar categories of money and class. Despite this, for Reynolds, progress was a matter of culture as well as of politics and money. While the relationship between Reynolds's career and his politics is staple critical fare, his attitudes to popular culture have seemed less important or discernible through the larger contours of his cultural practices. However, the figuring of popular culture in Reynolds's writings can cast a great deal of light on the position of Reynolds in popular culture, and indeed on the seemingly conflicted relationship between his politics and his commercial populism.

In *The Mysteries of London*, for example, Reynolds appears to consciously position the diverse and expanding Victorian culture industry as a site where the interests of radicalism(s) and commercialism converge. Perhaps the most obvious site of enquiry in this respect, however, is found not in the career of a 'self-instructed mechanic' but in that of Ellen Monroe. Ellen is the daughter of a middle-class gentleman who falls on hard times, and as a result she takes up a career as a model, initially for a statuary, then for a painter, a sculptor and eventually a photographer (in what Trefor Thomas claims is 'the earliest fictional record of the new technology called the daguerreotype'[29]). Ellen is seduced by one of the text's rogues, George Montague, and forced to support herself and her child. Within the restricted choices that are available to her, Ellen decides to leave the sweatshop conditions of life for seamstresses and make her living in various fields of the burgeoning cultural industries. She works as a (fraudulent) subject for a so-called professor of mesmerism, and also as a ballet dancer. As Ellen herself puts it, 'I sold myself in detail'.[30] Perhaps her most memorable role comes when she decides to disguise herself as a man, purchasing male clothing from Holywell Street (the new home of so many booksellers) in the pretence that she is going to a 'masquerade'[31] (and secretly arming herself with a pistol).

Ellen is not working class by background but finds herself trapped on what a Marxist might call the working-class side of the cash nexus. Her career involves her in the production of what would traditionally be thought of as 'high' art (for example, painting and sculpture), as well as in a variety of 'popular' entertainments (like mesmerism and theatre). Her work as a photographer's model means that she is subject to the technology that was to facilitate the mass dissemination of visual culture; though Ellen, like most of her contemporaries, would not have been aware of the future cultural impact of photography, there is textual evidence to suggest that Reynolds had some sense of the possibilities and problems that might attend this new art form. What Ellen's career highlights more generally, however, is that blurring of any notional line between 'high' and 'low' culture in Reynolds's cultural vision; both are shown to be increasingly subject to the forces of commercialism and mass dissemination. It demonstrates, moreover, the potential of the cultural industries and cultural entrepreneurship to counteract entrenched inequalities of class and gender.

---

29 Reynolds, *MOL*, ed. Thomas, p. 73.
30 Reynolds, *MOL* (1845), vol. 1, ch. 70, p. 218 [p. 129].
31 Reynolds, *MOL* (1845), vol. 1, ch. 104, p. 319 [p. 158].

Ellen Monroe's story is a double narrative: it charts the possibilities and problems that attend the democratization of culture. On the one hand, there are suggestions throughout that her career in the cultural industries is degrading her purity. When she works as a model, for example, she starts by being paid to show her face, and is gradually forced to reveal more and more of her body. The mysterious old hag who introduces her to the world of cultural industry is figured as a kind of inverted fairy godmother; the implication throughout is that she will be revealed as more pimp than saviour, leading Ellen down a slippery slope to a life in prostitution. When 'she disposed of her whole body to the photographer', for example, Reynolds seems to feel obliged to insert a paragraph of conventional moral condemnation:

> A tainted soul now resided in a pure body. Every remaining sentiment of decency and delicacy was crushed – obliterated – destroyed by this last service. Pure souls have frequently resulted in tainted bodies: witness Lucretia after the outrage perpetrated upon her:– but here was essentially a foul soul in a chaste and virgin form.

This paragraph is out of keeping with the majority of the narrative, however. Indeed, the very next paragraph blames her nudity on 'dire necessity' and the 'old hag' who was scheming 'to model the young maiden to her purposes':

> For it was with ulterior views that the designing harridan had introduced the poor girl to that career which, without being actually criminal, led step by step towards criminality.[32]

What is interesting and innovative about Ellen's story, however, is that the inevitable does not happen. Ellen is in fact able to earn a living in various cultural pursuits which require her to display herself, without falling into the career of prostitution that was often associated in the public consciousness with careers like acting, which involved the public display (to varying degrees) of the female body.[33] She takes what she needs from the cultural marketplace, but is intelligent and principled enough to avoid becoming part of the Victorian sex industry. Thus, the idea that the 'old hag' controls her is a conventional cover story: the reality is that Ellen becomes an entrepreneurial agent in the cultural marketplace. Even when she agrees to model nude for the photographer, the text clearly states that she did so for money:

> She drew a veil over her countenance, and was about to retire in disgust and indignation, when the Frenchman, who was examining a plate as he spoke, and therefore did not observe the effect his words had produced upon her, mentioned the price he proposed to pay her. Now the artist paid better than the statuary; the sculptor better than the artist; and the photographer better than the sculptor. She therefore hesitated no longer; but entered the service of the man of science.[34]

---

32 Reynolds, *MOL* (1845), vol. 1, ch. 56, p. 175 [p. 89].

33 See Tracy C. Davis, 'Actresses and Prostitutes in Victorian London', *Theatre Research International*, 13 (1988): 221–34.

34 Reynolds, *MOL* (1845), vol. 1, ch. 56, p. 175 [p. 89].

The idea that commercial culture corrupts thus shadows Ellen's narrative, but only faintly: the overwhelming image, in Ellen's case, is of culture as a burgeoning industry offering multiple possibilities, economic, social and aesthetic, for 'the people' as agents and/or consumers. Moreover, the vision of Victorian cultural formations suggested by Ellen's career is complex and sophisticated. It is notable, for example, that Ellen is not exploited by her employers in the industry, and any sexual threat to her comes from a licentious clergyman rather than a cultural entrepreneur. Indeed, those who pay her, even for her face and body, treat the relationship as a business contract; she is viewed by them as an aesthetic rather than a sexual object. Her womanhood is professionally necessary for the image created, but otherwise it is of little interest. In society in general, however, this is not the case, so from one perspective, the burgeoning cultural industries offer her more autonomy than she is generally afforded. When working for the artist, for example, her virtue 'was not tempted':

> The artist saw not before him a lovely creature of warm flesh and blood; he beheld nothing but a beautiful and symmetrical statue which served as an original for his heathen divinities and pastoral heroines. And in this light did he treat her.
> He paid her handsomely ...[35]

If Reynolds is careful to stress the economic rather than sexual nature of Ellen's business dealings, however, he is also keen to reveal that 'high' culture is no less grounded in market conditions than the popular cultural industries in which Ellen is involved. Indeed, Ellen's career clearly emphasizes that cultural 'impurity' or hybridity is characteristic of all cultural products, not simply of those that appeal to the mass market. It is striking, for example, that Ellen's face and figure are mainly used to create 'classical subjects' and iconic images of the 'proper feminine' such as Madonnas, goddesses, queens and 'pastoral heroines'[36] – images on which Victorian moral, social and cultural formations were grounded. It is also true, however, that her image is used to model 'opera dancers, and actresses in theatrical clubs', and that it is disseminated in commercial contexts such as 'insurance offices' as well as in 'catholic chapels'.[37] The implication is that no art is 'pure' and untainted by market conditions. Indeed, in an ironic reversal, Reynolds implies that Ellen has at least as much worth and purity as some of the subjects and consumers of the art purchased by high society. The artist, for example, 'was a portrait-painter as well as a delineator of classical subjects' and:

> When he was employed to paint the likeness of some vain and conceited West End daughter of the aristocracy, it was Ellen's hand – or Ellen's hair – or Ellen's eyes – or Ellen's bust – or some feature or peculiar beauty of the young maiden, in which the fashionable lady somewhat resembled her, that figured upon the canvas.[38]

---

35 Reynolds, *MOL* (1845), vol. 1, ch. 56, p. 174 [p. 87].
36 Reynolds, *MOL* (1845), vol. 1, ch. 56, p. 174 [pp. 86–7].
37 Reynolds, *MOL* (1845), vol. 1, ch. 56, p. 173 [p. 86].
38 Reynolds, *MOL* (1845), vol. 1, ch. 56, p. 174 [p. 88].

Ellen eventually loses her job with the artist because he manages to pass off Ellen's image as that of 'a marchioness of forty-six', who promotes him as 'the greatest of English painters' so successfully that he wins the commission to paint 'the physiognomy of the Czar'.[39]

The substitution of Ellen for high cultural subjects and high society ladies undermines conventional associations between art and authenticity. The idea that Ellen is used as the model for multiple copies of the Madonna, for example, likewise emphasizes the idea of culture as creating 'products' rather than unique works. Moreover, Reynolds is acutely aware not only of the workings of the cultural marketplace but also of the implications of what Walter Benjamin has famously called 'The Work of Art in the Age of Mechanical Reproduction' (1936).[40] However, while Benjamin is upbeat in his assessment of the democratic possibilities of 'mechanical reproduction' in art and the diminution of the importance of ideas such as those of the 'aura' and the 'original', Reynolds blends optimism with hard-headed realism. It is perhaps no accident, for example, that Ellen is obliged to show most of her body to the photographer. Her transition from working as a model for a statuary to a sculptor to a painter to a photographer in some ways approximates the progress of modern art: her image becomes more easily disseminated, and (in her eyes at least) more abject as her story progresses. It is telling, for example, that in *The Mysteries of London*, the nude photographs of Ellen that could be most easily circulated are not disseminated as widely as the more fully dressed reproductions of the painter and other artists: they are instead 'preserved, in all attitudes, and on many plates, in the private cabinet of a photographer at one of the metropolitan Galleries of Practical Science'.[41]

Reynolds's implication is that the cultural marketplace functions as a shifting continuum so that if so-called high art is intertwined with commercial art, then the logic of the market necessitates that commercial and high art are intertwined with pornography. The democratizing of art in the nineteenth century identified by Benjamin necessarily involves, for Reynolds, its exposure to the power of the lowest common denominator. Thus, though it is true that Reynolds's texts pander to soft porn tastes, it is also correct that he subjects those tastes to economic and political scrutiny. In *The Mysteries of London*, for example, it is not just the Resurrection Man who trades in bodies: artists do likewise. What is problematic in the case of the latter, however, is that while the bodies represented are mainly female, the creating eye is often male. But while Reynolds is not above the temptation to sexualize the female body to attract certain readers, as has been mentioned, he also consciously exposes the economic and power relations that create and sustain the market for female flesh. Perhaps the most obvious example in this respect comes in his treatment of the Marquis of Holmesford, a character like Thackeray's Lord Steyne, said to be based on the notorious voluptuary, the Marquis of Hertford. The Marquis tells Greenwood: 'Wine and women, my dear Greenwood … are the only earthly enjoyments worth

---

39 Reynolds, *MOL* (1845), vol. 1, ch. 56, p. 174 [p. 88].

40 In *Illuminations*, ed. Hannah Arendt, trans. Harry Zohn (London: Fontana, 1973), pp. 211–44.

41 Reynolds, *MOL* (1845), vol. 1, ch. 56, p. 175 [p. 89].

living for. I hope to die, with my head pillowed on the naked-heaving bosoms of beauty, and with a glass of sparkling champagne in my hand.'[42] The Marquis keeps 'a harem' around him for his pleasure, 'a bevy of lovely creatures', one of whom he bought at a 'Slave-Market' in Constantinople;[43] 'when I make love to her', he claims, 'she swears by the Prophet Mahommed that she is happy here'.[44] In this case, the Marquis does indeed die as he has always wished, his head in the bosom of one of his sex slaves. The hideousness of the Marquis both physically and morally – especially in 'the absence of his false teeth'[45] – is made apparent to the readers. More importantly, the women in his harem are sympathetically presented. He pays them all for services rendered before he dies, and their delight at payment reveals their straightforwardly mercenary motives. However, it is the rich, powerful man who is judged. Kathleen, the Irish girl who provides his deathbed and gains 'a ring of immense value'[46] in return, is described without irony as having a 'kind and generous heart'.[47] She is pitied above all for having to endure his touch: 'The Irish girl shuddered in spite of herself – shuddered involuntarily as she felt the cheek of the Marquis grow cold and clammy against her bosom.'[48] The fact that the Marquis does indeed die the death of his dreams, however, suggests a hard-headed economic realism on Reynolds's part: money and status allow the Marquis to live and die as he wishes. Contrary to the spirit of fairy tale or moral allegory so often invoked by Dickens, vice is not punished.

This is not to argue that Reynolds is a socialist feminist, but that he is clearly conscious of the economic and political dynamics that underpin the market for pornography and prostitution. *The Mysteries of London* both exposes and exploits these dynamics, and it is perhaps because of this kind of double perspective that Reynolds has been labelled a 'bastard' and a 'scoundrel'. Dickens could also be seen to be guilty of exploiting the very abuses he was proposing to reform. He argued that what he called the 'attraction of repulsion', for example, was 'as much a law of our moral nature, as gravitation is in the structure of the visible world'.[49] Indeed, his interest in, and fictional focus on, dead bodies, crime and public hanging would no doubt have made him envy the surreal 'Museum of Crime' in *The Mysteries of London*.[50] Whereas Reynolds's representation of popular cultural activities is typically non-judgemental, moreover, Dickens can both champion and patronize the cultural pursuits of 'the people': a comparison of Reynolds's representation of 'the free market of the New Cut'[51] with those of Dickens (in 'The Amusements of the

---

42   Reynolds, *MOL* (1846), vol. 2, ch. 172, p. 97 [p. 238].
43   Reynolds, *MOL* (1846), vol. 2, ch. 172, pp. 98–9 [pp. 239–41].
44   Reynolds, *MOL* (1846), vol. 2, ch. 172, p. 99 [p. 241].
45   Reynolds, *MOL* (1846), vol. 2, ch. 252, p. 401 [p. 298].
46   Reynolds, *MOL* (1846), vol. 2, ch. 252, p. 402 [p. 298].
47   Reynolds, *MOL* (1846), vol. 2, ch. 252, p. 402 [p. 302].
48   Reynolds, *MOL* (1846), vol. 2, ch. 252, p. 402 [p. 302].
49   Letter on capital punishment, *Daily News*, 28 February 1846.
50   Reynolds, *MOL* (1846), vol. 2, ch. 138, pp. 4–7 [pp. 201–6].
51   Reynolds, *MOL* (1846), vol. 2, ch. 186, pp. 158–9 [pp. 250–52].

People' and 'Two Views of a Cheap Theatre') is instructive.[52] Whereas Reynolds relishes the carnivalesque lack of order and control over the '[p]enny peep-shows, … itinerant quacks …, stalls covered with odd numbers of cheap periodicals', and so on,[53] Dickens's main purpose in representing the New Cut is to explore ways in which 'The Amusements of the People' can be improved.

It is no doubt partly because of his impulse not only to reach but also to improve 'the people' that Dickens censors his use and representation of the burgeoning mass market for culture. In this respect, sex provides a litmus test for a key difference between the two authors. The relative absence of sex in Dickens's work suggests not simply that Reynolds was more degraded than Dickens, but that Reynolds was more open in his analysis of the 'free market' for popular entertainment, and perhaps more accepting of the notion of the free market. It is this acceptance of market forces in the cultural sphere that has seemed to sit oddly with Reynolds's political radicalism, though it is open to question whether Dickens's typical sublimation or translation of political or economic discourse into moral or humanist discourse is any more 'honest' or consistent with a politics of 'the people'.

The key to the distrust that has consistently attached itself to Reynolds lies in attitudes past and present to money, and to the relationship between culture, commerce and politics. Reynolds nailed his political colours publicly to the 'radical' mast, and he made money from so doing. There can be an assumption in today's post-Marxian theoretical climate that a political radicalism that purports to empower the working class should be anti-capitalist. Though Reynolds attacks a capitalist like Greenwood and his associates in *The Mysteries of London*, his most urgent and consistent protest is related to the injustice of the class system, which is seen as the major source of the extremes of wealth and poverty. When he literally enumerates monetary inequalities, for example, the root cause of these inequalities is clearly related to classist hierarchy, and not the other way around:

> The lowest step in the ladder is occupied by that class which is the most numerous, the most useful, and which ought to be the most influential.
> The average annual incomes of the individuals of each class are as follows:–

The Sovereign	£500,000.
The member of the Aristocracy	£30,000.
The Priest	£7,500.
The member of the middle classes	£300.
The member of the industrious classes	£20.[54]

Indeed, in the representation of the cultural sphere in *The Mysteries of London*, there is a sense in which entrepreneurship and the 'free market' are seen as positive, modern weapons against the class system.

---

52   [The Uncommercial Traveller], 'Two Views of a Cheap Theatre', *All the Year Round*, vol. 2 (25 February 1860), excerpted in Michael Slater and John Drew (eds), *'The Uncommercial Traveller' and Other Papers*, The Dent Uniform Edition of Dickens' Journalism, 4 vols (London: Dent, 2000), vol. 4, pp. 52–62.
53   Reynolds, *MOL* (1846), vol. 2, ch. 186, p. 159 [p. 251].
54   Reynolds, *MOL* (1845), vol. 1, ch. 58, p. 179 [p. 93].

Reynolds would not then necessarily have seen his radicalism and his cultural entrepreneurship as mutually exclusive, and in this he was not necessarily deluded. As John Drew has convincingly argued, the heyday of Dickens and Reynolds 'significantly predated the conglomeration and commercialization of the late Victorian "massocratic" press'.[55] Though during the mid-century control of the popular press did shift, under the influence of press industrialization, from the working class to wealthy businessmen, 'there was an important transitional stage during which the dominant force in print media was exerted by a number of hard-working radical editors and publishers who *themselves* became (if they were lucky) wealthy businessmen'.[56] Reynolds was one of these radicals made good. But the making of money from popular radical culture was not necessarily, at a time before cultural production became subject to 'the demotivating consumerism of state-sponsored capitalism', an act of gross hypocrisy.[57]

Reynolds was not, in other words, operating in an Adorno-esque global culture industry that made money from imposing false consciousness on cultural consumers. Historical context can only be invoked so far, however, to defend his political integrity. As we have recounted, some of the most damning judgements on Reynolds have come from contemporaries. The focus for Marx and Adams is on his money and his morals (or lack of them) and there is a suggested link between the two: for Marx, for example, he was a 'scoundrel' as well as a 'rich and able speculator'; for Adams, he was seen 'rather as a charlatan and a trader than as a genuine politician'. It is interesting that out of the three commentators, Dickens objects least to Reynolds's commercialism: for Dickens, Reynolds is one of the 'Bastards of the Mountain, draggled fringe on the Red Cap, Panders to the basest passions of the lowest natures'. His objection is that Reynolds does not offer something higher and better to 'the lowest natures'; even his radical politics are bastardized and 'draggled'.[58]

Dickens perhaps most closely hits the spot. It is difficult not to imagine Reynolds smiling at the accusation that he was a 'rich and able speculator' and 'a charlatan and trader' rather than a 'genuine politician'. In *The Mysteries of London*, as throughout his career, Reynolds is open about his vision of the cultural marketplace as 'a mart for the sale of literary wares'. The cultural 'bazaar', for Reynolds, exchanges products and capital like any other market, and 'the people' should access and exploit its possibilities in a society where they are denied so many kinds of capital. No political writer, for Reynolds, could operate in a 'genuine' place that is not a 'bazaar of booksellers'. Dickens's objection is not principally to the idea of culture as commerce but to Reynolds's ready willingness to accept the tastes of the market and to pander to the rule of the lowest common denominator.

Whereas in today's critical climate, then, we have a tendency to associate 'dishonesty' in popular writers with an attempt to subject consumers to covert ideological control, Reynolds's political inconsistencies and his surrender to the

---

55   John Drew, *Dickens the Journalist* (Basingstoke: Palgrave, 2003), p. 187.
56   Drew, *Dickens the Journalist*, p. 187.
57   Drew, *Dickens the Journalist*, p. 187.
58   See n. 4 above for an explanation of the political connotations of Dickens's well-known description of Reynolds.

tastes of the cultural 'mart' suggest a forfeiting of control. It can be argued that there is a certain honesty, or 'negative capability', in this, but this honesty, to contemporaries at least, was as amoral as it was moral. At a time when cultural paternalism was routinely seen as responsible rather than oppressive, Reynolds's radical rants, his discursive porousness and his vision of culture as commerce seemed to militate against notions of responsibility and respectability. If he was indeed one of the 'Bastards of the Mountain', however, he was also a self-conscious analyst of his own cultural hybridity and that of the new mass cultural marketplace. Reynolds threatened Victorian culture not principally with anarchy but with the spectre of its own impurity.

PART IV
Popular Culture

Chapter 11

Time, Politics and the Symbolic Imagination in Reynolds's Social Melodrama

Louis James

In his essay on the gothic elements in *The Mysteries of London*, Daniel S. Burt compared reading Reynolds's serial to the experience of sitting in a mid-Victorian working-class theatre:

> Like the stage melodrama that is in part thrilling adventure and part morality play, Reynolds's fiction is also a kind of all-purpose entertainment: a guided tour through brothels, lady's boudoirs, elegant drawing rooms, and gin shops, in which the reader can get his full penny worth of practical advice, sentiment and terror that combines the tabloid and the tract.[1]

Reynolds himself seems to have been more interested in the social realities of theatre life as he portrayed them in *Ellen Percy, or The Memoir of an Actress* (1855–57) than in theatrical practice itself. It is significant that while all Dickens's early novels were immediately transferred to the stage, there are virtually no dramatizations of Reynolds's fiction.[2] Burt, who notes that Reynolds's inclusive fiction was hardly fitted to the enclosed theatre, suggests one reason for this. He aptly quotes Reynolds's own punning comment on *The Mysteries of London*: 'Shakespeare said, "All the world is a *stage*"; we say, "All the world is an *Omnibus*."'[3] But there are other ways in which Reynolds's fiction, if on the page rather than behind footlights, was rooted in nineteenth-century melodramatic practice. For the 'respectable' Victorian reader, Reynolds was a writer who abandoned standards of taste and morality to exploit the lowest predilections of his readership. If his periodicals featured serious educational articles, he published these alongside luridly sensational fiction; his novels contained

---

1   Daniel S. Burt, 'A Victorian Gothic: G.W.M. Reynolds's *The Mysteries of London*', in Daniel L. Gerould (ed.), *Melodrama* (New York: New York Literary Forum, 1980), p. 153.

2   Only two examples have survived: *Mary Price; or the Adventures of a Serving Girl* (Royal Queens' Theatre, 1850) is only remotely related to Reynolds's novel. However, *The Catacombs of Paris* (undated holograph), based on a tale in part 14 of *Pickwick Abroad* (in the Pettingell Collection, University of Kent, Pett. Mss. C 21. Spec. Coll.), is attributed to Reynolds, and although the handwriting is inconclusive, its dramatic qualities indicate Reynolds might have been the author.

3   Burt, 'A Victorian Gothic', p. 141; G.W.M. Reynolds, *The Mysteries of London* (London: George Vickers, 1845), vol. 1, ch. 44, p. 102.

documentary passages as objective as those of Henry Mayhew, but these were embedded in narratives of melodramatic excess. Yet such contradictions are central to what John G. Cawelti has termed the literature of 'social melodrama'.[4]

Social Melodrama

Cawelti used the term social melodrama in his pioneering study of popular culture to describe a genre that 'synthesizes the archetypes of melodrama with a carefully and elaborately developed social setting'; it exploits the emotional and moral appeal of the stage form, while at the same time drawing on 'the interest inherent in a detailed, intimate and realistic analysis of major social or historical phenomena'.[5] To understand a genre that was to become a staple of modern bestsellers and television 'soaps', Cawelti traces the genre back to its origins in the European upheavals surrounding the French Revolution of 1789. Melodrama marked the death of the earlier tragic vision, and the birth of a new consciousness in which the human rights of individuals were pitted against the oppression of societies corrupted by inequalities of inheritance, class and wealth. It emerged out of a period in which the old religious bases of morality were being challenged, and yet when social changes were foregrounding moral issues as never before. Peter Brooks has noted:

> the French Revolution and its aftermath ... is the epistemological moment which [melodrama] illustrates and to which it contributes: the moment that symbolically, and really, marks the final liquidation of the traditional Sacred and its representative institutions (Church and Monarch), the shattering of the myth of Christendom, the dissolution of an organic and hierarchically cohesive society, and the invalidation of the literary forms – tragedy, comedy of manners – that depended on such a society.[6]

If the new consciousness challenged church and state, it elevated human emotions over intellectual values that had been acquired by privileged education and were determined by class. In the Romantic movement it privileged the working of the heart over that of the intellect. It was embodied in the first play specifically classified as a '*melodrame*': Rousseau's *Pygmalion* (1772). This was a monologue in which mime and music intensified the emotions until, at the play's climax, the artist's passion turned the stone statue into Galatea's sacramental flesh. René Charles Guilbert de Pixérécourt (1773–1844) realized the demotic potential of the form, writing and producing an estimated 120 melodramas between 1797 and 1838 to entertain and morally educate the post-revolutionary Parisian masses, those 'who could not read'.[7] His plays were intense and spectacular, drawing on traditional folk

---

4   See John G. Cawelti, *Adventure, Mystery, and Romance* (Chicago: University of Chicago Press, 1976), pp. 260–95.

5   Cawelti, *Adventure, Mystery, and Romance*, p. 261.

6   Peter Brooks, *The Melodramatic Imagination* (New Haven, CT, and London: Yale University Press, 1976), p. 15.

7   On Pixérécourt and the origins of melodrama, see the articles by J. Paul Marcaux, Gabrielle Hyslop and Bruce A. McConnachie in James Redmond (ed.), *Themes in Drama, 14: Melodrama* (Cambridge: Cambridge University Press, 1992), pp. 47–104.

theatre to choreograph moral issues within highly complex plots. They were great entertainment. But they also involved actors and audience in a shared, passionate experience, based on the universal emotions of terror, love, wonder and delight. After Pixérécourt's *Coelina; ou L'Enfant de Mystère*, adapted by Thomas Holcroft as *A Tale of Mystery*, thrilled audiences at Covent Garden in 1802, the form came to dominate the popular stage in Britain.

Pixérécourt demonstrated that the form could be infinitely flexible, and his melodramas ranged from gothic romance to dog drama, from Robinson Crusoe (in a play little indebted to Defoe) to contemporary historical scandal. The simplified morality of melodrama melded seamlessly with the social conflicts of a turbulent era, transforming the struggle between 'Evil' and 'Good' into that between 'Oppressor' and 'Oppressed', between the 'Rich' and the 'Poor'. Religion became what Peter Brooks has called the 'moral occult ... the domain of operative spiritual values which is both indicated within and masked by the surface of reality.... It is the repository of the fragmentary and desacralized remnants of sacred myth.'[8] Melodrama, at once a set of formal conventions and a way of understanding life, came to embody a symbolic consciousness of social reality. Ellen Rosenman elsewhere in this volume cites what Cornelius Castoriadis has termed the 'social imaginary', signifying, as Rosenman puts it, 'a realm of dream, fantasy and desire that underlies and produces the social doctrines, practices and institutions that imperfectly embody it'.[9] The revelation that the hero or heroine is an illegitimate child of the aristocracy could signify for the disenfranchised reader a belief in the human equality of all social groups. Similarly, the labyrinthine plots of melodrama, with their extraordinary coincidences and marvellous resolutions, reflected the invisible working of providence, while the many disguises and startling revelations of identity embodied the fragmented consciousness of modern urban life. But they also gave reassurance. Priya Joshi has written that for readers of Reynolds in India as in Britain:

> the coincidence and interconnectedness that Reynolds's characters constantly encountered as they traversed the mazelike urban environment of London in the Mysteries series (or the equally alienating geography of France, Scotland, or Constantinople in some of the other novels), underscored the essential, albeit paradoxical, *community* of a world that, despite its enormity, was small enough for characters, treasures, reunions, and murderers to meet and remeet over and over again, as in a village square.[10]

For Indian readers, she noted, the complexity of Reynolds's plots resonated with readings and performances of the *Mahabharata* and the *Ramayana*.

Douglas Jerrold's *Black-Ey'd Susan; or, All in the Downs* (Royal Surrey Theatre, London, 1829), a melodrama that was to become the most popular play of the

---

8 Brooks, *The Melodramatic Imagination*, p. 5.

9 See Chapter 13 in this volume by Ellen Bayuk Rosenman, 'The Virtue of Illegitimacy: Inheritance and Belonging in *The Dark Woman* and *Mary Price*'; Cornelius Castoriadis, *The Imaginary Institution of Society*, trans. Kathleen Blamey (Cambridge, MA: Polity, 1987).

10 Priya Joshi, *In Another Country: Colonialism, Culture, and the English Novel in India* (New York: Columbia University Press, 2002), p. 88. Joshi writes of Reynolds being esteemed as a 'classic' writer in India, pp. 74–92.

era, illustrates the domestication of melodrama. The play is set in Deal, a town Jerrold knew well from childhood, and the stage sets depicted the streets of the Kent Channel port in the aftermath of the Napoleonic Wars in realistic detail. The virginal heroine of Pixérécourt has now become a young wife, Susan, whose sailor husband, William, is serving abroad with the British navy. The villains are those who might have threatened any unprotected girl of limited means in this situation – her predatory landlord, an unscrupulous smuggler, and Crosstree, a drunken sea captain. William returns just in time to save Susan from rape by Crosstree, only to recognize the assailant as his own captain. Naval law requires William to hang for striking a superior officer. The story would have been topical at a time when campaigners were protesting against the injustices of military discipline.[11]

But, in the way of social melodrama, Jerrold moves seamlessly from the mundane to the marvellous. Stylized in presentation, the main characters acquire emblematic significance. Susan is Wordsworth's rural innocent, William, a representative of the valiant sailors who saved England from Napoleon and were establishing the British Empire. He is the victim of both an unjust legal system and the metaphysical evil[12] embodied in Doggrass, the villain who has concealed secret information that William had been discharged from the navy for bravery at the moment he struck Crosstree. Doggrass is so eager to see William's execution that he falls overboard and drowns. But as a cannon is fired, his body rises from the water with the document of release.[13] William is saved, and leads a rousing chorus of 'Rule Britannia'.

Cawelti has noted that

> social melodrama is concerned not only with the affirmation of traditional conceptions of morality but with integrating and harmonizing what might be called the conventional wisdom with new currents of value and attitude. This gives the social melodrama a unique importance for the period of its creation.[14]

Jerrold's play wavers between a radical attack on an unjust legal system and a conservative belief that, unaided by human action, Good will prevail, although the plot finally comes down on the side of providence.[15] It is here that we see the fundamental difference between most popular melodrama and Reynolds's distinctive take on the genre. Reynolds never wavers. Victims in his social melodramas are never rescued by fate, and any benign outcome is dependent on instinctive human goodness

---

11   Reynolds's novel *The Soldier's Wife* (1852–53) was banned as subversive by the English military authorities.

12   Herman Melville used Jerrold's play as a source for *Billy Budd, Sailor*, posthumously printed in 1924.

13   This practice is referred to in Mark Twain's *Huckleberry Finn* (1884), ch. 8, when Huck hears firing as he escapes downriver: 'You see they was firing cannon over the wave, trying to make my carcass coming up.' If the practice were based on the belief that the drowned, hearing the cannon, think it is the Day of Judgement when 'the sea shall give up its dead' (Revelation 20:13), the ending would have been doubly melodramatic.

14   Cawelti, *Adventure, Mystery, and Romance*, p. 267.

15   In *Mutiny at the Nore* (Royal Coburg Theatre, 1830), Jerrold attempted to reverse this perspective, and the curtain goes down as Parker is hanged – the play was not a popular success.

triumphant over corrupt individuals in a mercenary society. As Ian Haywood has well observed, Reynolds's plots do not reveal an immanent providence but, on the contrary, act 'to demystify the action, and to remind the reader that all plots are socially and politically generated'.[16]

Reynolds and Melodrama

Reynolds came to discover the potential of social melodrama in writing *The Mysteries of London*. In the fictional form, the closed structure of stage melodrama plots opened up into a sequence of thrilling crises, driven on by the dynamic of the reader's constantly deferred expectation. Reynolds was not the first popular novelist in England to exploit the modality, which had been notably pioneered by Dickens. As Stephen Carver has argued elsewhere in this volume,[17] Reynolds's immediate inspiration was Dickens's *Oliver Twist* (1837–38) and Harrison Ainsworth's *Jack Sheppard* (1839); another source was Ainsworth's *Old St Paul's* (1841), which had dramatized the London underworld as a setting for sensational adventure: George Vickers, the later publisher of Reynolds's *Mysteries*, titled a penny issue plagiarism of Ainsworth's novel *The Mysteries of Old St Paul's* (1841). Still closer in time, in 1843 James Malcolm Rymer launched *Lloyd's Penny Weekly Miscellany* with his serial *Ada the Betrayed*, a sensational urban tale that broke with convention by featuring a resourceful, brave and physically active heroine who dressed as a man to survive the perils of the London underworld. Although it was to be a very different work, in October 1844 Reynolds began his own penny weekly serial, *The Mysteries of London*, with a young woman in the dangerous city underworld disguised as a male.

While the *Mysteries* are the best known, they are not Reynolds's only novels in the mode. Less familiar are his fictional 'memoirs', a sequence of long penny issue novels written in the first person, each of which takes a particular social and occupational perspective on English society. *Mary Price* (1851–52) explored the life of a servant girl; *Rosa Lambert* (1853–54), a high-class courtesan; *Joseph Wilmot* (1853–55), life in service; while *Ellen Percy* (1855–57) presented life in and around the theatre. As these are discussed in Graham Law's chapter elsewhere in this volume,[18] I will here examine still another group, some 20 novels that Reynolds first wrote to appear in the *London Journal* and *Reynolds's Miscellany*. Although they later reappeared in volume form, they bear the marks of their first provenance. Composed in short instalments, they required constant crises to keep their readers coming back for more, and used sensational subjects to compete each week with the attractions of news and improving information. Sensitive to current tastes and events that can change the direction of the narrative while it is in progress, as we will see,

---

16 Ian Haywood, 'Reynolds and the Radicalisation of Victorian Serial Fiction', *Media History*, 4/2 (1998): 125.

17 See Chapter 9 in this volume by Stephen James Carver, 'The Wrongs and Crimes of the Poor: The Urban Underworld of *The Mysteries of London* in Context'.

18 See Chapter 12 in this volume by Graham Law, 'Reynolds's "Memoirs" Series and "The Literature of the Kitchen"'.

they are particularly revealing of the way Reynolds exploited the modality of social melodrama.

Their relationship to contemporary events and issues, however, may be veiled, for social melodrama requires a certain distancing from immediate actuality. Reynolds's uncharacteristically short and sharply focused novel, *The Seamstress, or The White Slave of England*, has been seen as an example of Reynolds's use of fiction as campaigning journalism. Reynolds does indeed give a detailed account of the costs, wages and profits of the exploitative fashion industry, and traces its organization from buyers down to the workers themselves. But the novel appeared in *Reynolds's Miscellany* from 23 March to 10 August 1850, some years after December 1843 when Thomas Hood had made the scandal of the seamstresses' plight a popular cause in *Punch* with 'The Song of the Shirt', and almost a decade after R.D. Granger's 1841 parliamentary report to the Children's Employment Commission first revealed the dressmakers' plight.[19] It was stale as news. But freed from the need to campaign, Reynolds set about developing the melodramatic possibilities of the situation. He isolates two 'white slaves', opposites in morals and sensibility. The virtuous Virginia lives in a back attic on Tavistock Street, while the feckless Julia Bartlett lives (both physically and morally) in a room below. 'The contrast between the two young females was assuredly great,' comments Reynolds. 'The one was the personification of a luxurious sensuousness: the other was the impersonation of the tenderest sensibilities.'[20] Virginia's (at this point unknown) aristocratic blood is hinted at by her 'princess and the pea' sensitivity to her wasted talents:

> 'Three-and-sixpence!' the words struck like a panic into the heart of Virginia – for the poor girl had calculated upon at least double that sum as recompense not so much for the time as for the skill employed in carrying out the special artistic design of the fashionable milliner who had originally cut out the dress.[21]

If we expected a Cinderella story, Reynolds sets about disabusing us by locating her situation firmly within political economy, setting her in the larger web of financial and sexual exploitation that equally affects the fashionable world of Lady Belmont and her aristocratic relations threatened with bankruptcy, and Virginia Mordaunt, her illegitimate seamstress daughter. The spiders in the centre are the lawyer Collinson and Mr Soloman the moneylender, an unholy alliance of the legal and financial systems that provokes Reynolds into biblical eloquence:

> Upon ancient Egypt did God in his wrath send the plagues of darkness, locusts, and murrain; but over modern Europe has Satan diffused a far more awful pestilence of competition.

19　For the serial and its background see Rohan McWilliam, 'The Melodramatic Seamstress: Interpreting a Victorian Penny Dreadful', in Beth Harris (ed.), *Famine and Fashion: Needlewomen in the Nineteenth Century* (Aldershot: Ashgate, 2005), pp. 99–114.

20　G.W.M. Reynolds, *The Seamstress* (London: John Dicks, [1857?]), ch. 12, p. 36. All my references are to Dicks's reissue of Reynolds's novels in single volumes, with the exception of *Wagner the Wehr-Wolf,* which refers to the facsimile edited by E.F. Bleiler (New York: Dover, 1975).

21　Reynolds, *The Seamstress*, ch. 2, p. 8.

And [it is] this accursed system which makes the emporium of Messrs. Aaron and Sons flourish for the benefit of its proprietors...[22]

There is no final reconciliation to reveal the immanence of ultimate Good. Virginia is recognized by and reconciled to her aristocratic mother, signalling, as Ellen Rosenman's thesis suggests, her equality as a human being, and her admirer and potential husband the Marquis of Arden visits her. But she then dies, enfeebled by her sufferings, and this is followed by a violent climax of duelling, suicide and brain fever that kills off all the other main protagonists in the story. If the sensational ending may seem at odds with the social realism of other elements in the book, it reflects the modality of social melodrama, a genre that Reynolds takes still further when he extends the form into the gothic and the oriental.

Social Melodrama as a Gothic Mode

Reynolds's *Faust*, his first major contribution to the *London Journal* (4 October 1845 to 18 July 1846) when he became editor, was written to compete with the success of Edward Lloyd's penny bloods. These in 1844 had included James Malcolm Rymer's *The Black Monk* and T.P. Prest's *Vileroy; or the Horrors of Zindorf Castle*. Reynolds's novel, with its menacing atmosphere, dark dungeons and secret passage, owes much to such lurid works – he entitled chapter 2 of *Faust*, perhaps unthinkingly, 'The Mysteries of Linsdorf Castle'. Reynolds had learned the dramatic appeal of the breathless staccato of Lloyd's serials, which was indebted to the style of the 'penny-a-line' reporters who were paid by the column inches, not by content. But with its pauses and apostrophes, it would have had the ring of popular theatre for its unsophisticated audience:

> Then [Faust] had shut his eyes, even in the midnight darkness of the dungeon, as if he could thus draw a veil over his maddening thoughts.
> But still those thoughts haunted him in a thousand ghastly and appalling shapes, till he became afraid of the obscurity of his cell – hence his longing for the presence of the sun.
> But what was the youth's crime?
> He had loved – and still loved – a noble lady – dearly, madly, loved her.
> O Theresa! Thine image seemed to smile at times amidst the gloom of his imprisonment, as the star from the midst of the thunder-clouds cheers the ocean-tossed mariner.
> Yes – thee he loved as fervently and well as ever man could love and thy young heart beat with reciprocal tenderness for him.
> But he was poor – a humble student; and Theresa was the only daughter and heiress of the Lord of Rosenthal.[23]

---

22 Reynolds, *The Seamstress*, ch. 27, p. 77.
23 Reynolds, *Faust*, 'Prologue', p. 5.

Fig. 11.1   '"'Tis she! 'Tis she!" articulated the enraptured Faust.' Illustrator
               Henry Anelay. Frontispiece to G.W.M. Reynolds's *Faust* (1846),
               referring to the 'Prologue', p. 7.

Faust is about to be executed for his amorous presumption, but is rescued by
Satan, who releases him in exchange for his soul, and who then bargains that of
Faust's first-born son as the price of his marriage to the virtuous (and wealthy)
Theresa. There is little love in the matter: their marriage is hardly consummated when
Faust falls for the wiles of Ida von Czernin, 'a woman of iron nerves and desperate
purpose', and unhappily married. When Theresa bears Faust a son, Maximilian,
Faust, having pledged his son to Satan, simultaneously drugs Theresa and the wife
of a neighbouring archduke, both being in childbirth, enabling him to exchange his
infant son Maximilian for the archduke's daughter, Adela.[24] The scene then turns to
Rome in the year 1497, with its papal intrigues and rioting mobs. Here Faust becomes
enamoured of a mysterious veiled lady. Ida dresses as a man and tries to murder her,
but her rival kills Ida first with a jet of poison from her ring.[25] The veiled lady is
revealed to be none other than Lucrezia Borgia lusting after Faust, although even
Faust 'recoils with horror from such a fiend in the shape of an angel'.[26] Meanwhile
Faust's (still unacknowledged) son, Maximilian, who is pledged to Satan, falls in
love with his adopted Adela. Faust's artist companion Otto Pianalla, who was Ida's
erstwhile brother but is as virtuous as his sister was evil, averts tragedy. When Faust
tells him of the impending crisis, Otto makes the perilous ascent up an ice-bound
Mount Ararat to find Noah's stranded Ark, from which he cuts the one charm that
can free Maximilian from Satan, a sliver of its 'sacred gopher-wood'. This talisman

---

24 Reynolds, *Faust*, ch. 22, p. 46.
25 Reynolds, *Faust*, ch. 46, p. 90.
26 Reynolds, *Faust*, ch. 59, p. 117.

delivers Maximilian from his curse, enabling him to marry Adela.[27] Frustrated in her lust for Faust, Lucrezia turns her affections to Otto, offering him a choice between her bed or an agonizing death in her 'iron coffin', possibly a Poe-inspired torture room with contracting walls.[28] In the event the Duke of Ferrara liberates Otto, his chastity intact, while Satan drags Faust down Vesuvius to Hell.

It may be hard to see from this summary the basic social reality demanded by social melodrama. But Reynolds is at some pains to site Faust's fantastic exploits in actual time and space. There is a continual reference to dates: the novel opens with the sentence, 'It was the commencement of August 1493', and Faust meets his final fate on 31 July 1517. The action is constantly cross-referenced to actual historical events, sometimes with explanatory footnotes. Since the story is set before the invention of watches, hours and minutes are measured by 'clepsydrae', early water clocks that root fantasy in a time without modern timekeeping. Reynolds was clearly pleased with this device, and introduces clepsydrae into subsequent gothic romances.[29] A tireless educationist, Reynolds uses his bizarre story to draw his readers into learning about the life of early Renaissance Italy, just as the serial itself attracted them to read the serious articles in the adjacent columns of the *London Journal*.

Reynolds's great disagreement with the main Chartist movement was his view, expressed in as early as 1836 and never withdrawn, that 'Universal Suffrage in the hands of the people, before they are educated, is as dangerous as a razor in the hand of an infant'.[30] For Reynolds 'knowledge is power'[31] because it brings an understanding of the social consequences of action, and so demystifies 'good' and 'evil'. Reynolds stripped the traditional Faust legend of its religious connotations. Faust sells his soul not out of spiritual ambition but to save his neck, and to gain a rich, aristocratic bride. Reynolds insists his story carries a practical moral for the reader, and at one point adds a footnote to warn anyone carried away by the narrative's excitement 'that the real object and aim of his tale [should be] thoroughly understood. This is ... to show the evil consequences of vice and the beauty of virtue.'[32] Even the wonders with which Satan entertains Faust have their social aspects. Satan satisfies Faust's desire for spectacle with a massive eruption of Vesuvius, but this kills thousands; his ambition to create an event so immense that it will 'paralyse the usual proceedings of society' leads Satan to invent the plague of the Black Death.[33] Evil comes from love of money. In the Julian Alps, Otto Pianalla meditates on 'the principles of human misery! That constant strife for gold – that warring by day and intrigue by

---

27 Reynolds, *Faust*, ch. 94, p. 174.

28 Reynolds, *Faust*, ch. 42, pp. 170–72.

29 Reynolds, *Faust*, ch. 25, p. 54. See also *The Coral Island*, p. 110; *The Bronze Statue*, pp. 120, 122.

30 G.W.M. Reynolds, *A Sequel to Don Juan* (London: Paget and Co., 1843), Canto 1, v. lxxxvii, p. 35. The Chartist Thomas Clark quoted this against Reynolds in his hostile 'open letter' (Thomas Clark, *A Letter addressed to G.W.M. Reynolds reviewing his conduct as a professed Chartist* [London: Thomas Clark, 1850]).

31 The phrase 'knowledge itself is power', translated from Bacon's *Religious Meditations: Of Heresies*, became the rallying cry of British radicals in the 1830s.

32 Reynolds, *Faust*, ch. 56, p. 107.

33 Reynolds, *Faust*, ch. 86, pp. 158–60.

night to obtain the dross whose spells are so potent, whose magic is so prolific.'[34] Satan provides a framework for the story, but the real black magic is Faust's lust for money, and the power and sexual gratification it brings. Faust is contrasted with Otto, with his love of art, delight in the beauties of nature and selfless love of others. When Faust himself does nothing to save his own son, Otto risks his life to save the soul of Maximilian.

Faust shows Reynolds attempting a new kind of social melodrama, and its success helped set the *London Journal* on its way to become the most popular penny journal of the period. However, he must have known that the story's appeal lay not in the good characters but in the evil, in particular Ida and the demonic Lucrezia. *Wagner the Wehr-Wolf* (1846–47), which marked Reynolds's break with Vickers to set up his own *Reynolds's Miscellany*, is an experiment with the form that radically *reverses* the conventional values of melodrama. Satan gives Wagner, once the servant of Faust, eternal life in his service in exchange for suffering a monthly change into a werewolf. Wagner's metamorphoses are paralleled by the story's moral transformations. Nisida, Wagner's fearsome lover, inverts the melodramatic characteristics of male and female:

> Terrible was she in the decision of her masculine – oh more than masculine character; for beneath that glorious beauty with which she was arrayed, beat a heart that scarcely knew compunction – or that, at all events would hesitate at nothing calculated to advance her interests or projects.[35]

She loves Wagner 'madly … after the fashion of her own strange and sensual heart' with 'voluptuous and sensual desires even to an extreme'.[36] Yet her caring passions are murderous. Her greatest love is for her brother Francisco: it is 'a holy sentiment, and a gloriously redeeming trait in the character of this wondrous woman of a mind so darkly terrible'.[37] But believing a curse will destroy Francisco if he marries, she ruthlessly eliminates any woman to whom he is attracted. Later, in a romantic episode reminiscent of the Haidée episode in Canto 2 in Byron's *Don Juan*, she and Wagner find happiness on an idyllic desert island. '[T]hey would wander on the sands, to the musical murmur of the rippling sea, – their arms clasping each other's necks – their eyes exchanging glances of fondness – hers of ardent passion, his of more melting tenderness.'[38] But the island is the haunt of a giant (Freudian?) anaconda snake, which nearly strangles Nisida to death, and Wagner's monthly vulpine rampages rupture the idyllic peace. The story runs the full gamut of gothic sensations. Murderous banditti ply their trade, while the horrors of the Spanish Inquisition move the narrative into soft pornography when Nisida immures the innocent Flora, who has the misfortune to be Francisco's lover, in a convent of semi-clad, self-flagellating Carmelite nuns, a scene

---

34 Reynolds, *Faust*, ch. 32, p. 63.
35 Reynolds, *Wagner*, ch. 29, p. 50.
36 Reynolds, *Wagner*, ch. 29, p. 50.
37 Reynolds, *Wagner*, ch. 29, p. 50.
38 Reynolds, *Wagner*, ch. 54, p. 94; compare Byron, *Don Juan*, Canto 2, beginning with verse clxxxiv, 'And thus they wandered forth, and hand in hand …'.

vividly illustrated in the accompanying woodcut.[39] Reynolds completes his reversal of conventions by denying Wagner or Nisida just retribution at the end. Wagner is saved from damnation by a mysterious 'Christian Rosicrucian', and dies peacefully with Nisida, leaving Flora and Francisco to their happy married future. Absurd in its plot, excessive in its emotions and extravagant in its spectacular descriptions, the work nevertheless remains one of Reynolds's most enjoyable creations.

But the novel is exceptional in Reynolds's oeuvre. A romantic title, *The Coral Island, or The Hereditary Curse*,[40] belies a gnomic work written, Reynolds claimed, in response to a house guest's challenge to compose, with nothing far-fetched, 'a mystery so well veiled and maintained that I should be unable to see through it'.[41] Set largely in fourteenth-century Naples, it is a parable given social significance, when it first appeared in *Reynolds's Miscellany*, by a contemporary popular uprising in Italy. In the novel Queen Joanna, aided by Adrian Tiepolo, the city's physician general, conducts a reign of corruption and terror in Naples. They are opposed by the reformers Julian, Marquis of d'Altamura, and his presumed son Valentino, supported by a populist movement led by the chieftain Burina. Interpolated into this saga, a series of apparently unconnected episodes traces the progress of 'the Old Man of the Coral Island' from the Pacific back to his homeland, Italy.

Fig. 11.2   'The Old Man followed the reptile with his eyes.' Illustrator Frederick Gilbert. Woodcut for 'The Third Interlogue', G.W.M. Reynolds, *The Coral Island* (1849).]

---

39 Reynolds, *Wagner*, ch. 49, pp. 32ff.
40 *RM*, 15 July 1848–31 March 1849.
41 'Notice to Our Readers', *Weekly Magazine*, 1 July 1848, p. 222.

The two stories come together when the triumph of Italian reform coincides with the Old Man's return. A violent storm precipitates him into the sea, from which he is rescued by the leading reformers. He reveals that he is Ludovico d'Altamar, a previous ruler of Naples, who went into penitential exile to purge himself and his city from the legacy of an ancestral curse. This originated in the robbery and murder of an ancient Jew, a crime that left the ruling house burdened with guilt and also, because the victim was diseased and infectious, with the leprosy that now affects Naples' heir-apparent, Valentino. The curious plot identifies financial rapacity as social disease, and the Old Man's personal odyssey to a simple life in the Pacific becomes a private quest for cleansing, one that parallels the social struggle of the Italian reformers. On the Eden-like Coral Island the Wanderer discovers a herbal remedy for his leprosy, which he carries back to cure Valentino and, through him, the kingdom of Naples.

The role of the combined forces of church and state in bringing down the Italian radicals at the time *The Coral Island* was concluding its run in *Reynolds's Miscellany* may have contributed to the savage tone of the novel that followed it, *The Bronze Statue, or The Virgin's Kiss*.[42] This is set in Austria, whose revolution had also failed in 1848, back in the time of the Reformation. The noble John Zitzka is leading a popular revolt against the aristocracy and the Inquisition, a combination that had defeated the Italian reformers. Social melodrama requires that fiction is rooted, however improbably, in an actual context, and Reynolds takes pains to assure his readers that the Inquisition is not just a bugbear of gothic romance, but historical fact. While a translation of Paul Feval's *Mysteries of the Inquisition* was running anonymously in the *London Journal*, the editor (presumably Reynolds) in 'Notices to Correspondents'[43] poured scorn on gothic representations of the Inquisition, declaring that Maturin in writing *Melmoth the Wanderer* 'evidently knew nothing at all about this tremendous tribunal'. Instead he directed readers to the historical facts as laid out in 'Llorente's "Critical History in the Spanish Inquisition"'.[44] However, Reynolds takes liberties greater than Maturin's. The Inquisition is embodied in the bronze statue of the title, a large and beautiful effigy of the Virgin Mary. This opens to reveal a spike-filled interior within which, in 'the Virgin's kiss', the Inquisition's victims are slowly and agonizingly skewered before finally being dropped into an elaborate system of revolving knives below. A brilliant image suggestive of the savagery within religious idolatry, the 'statue' can hardly sustain a full-length novel, and the political and religious setting opens out into a curiously hybrid narrative.

---

42 *RM*, 31 March 1849–31 March 1850.

43 *LJ*, vol. 1, no. 19 (28 June 1845), p. 288.

44 An actual work by Juan Antonio Llorente, translated into English by John Lilburn in 1823.

Fig. 11.3   'Into the interior of the bronze statue was the wretched Carthusian precipitated.' Illustrator Henry Anelay. Woodcut for G.W.M. Reynolds, *The Bronze Statue* (1850), ch. 95.

The novel includes a romance centred on a gothic pile with its secret passages, dungeons and torture chamber, and chapter 3 is actually called 'The Mysteries of Altendorf Castle'. Then a moral allegory reminiscent of Spenser's *Faery Queen* tells how the noble knight Sir Ernest de Colmar combats the forces of evil, aided by Angela, a mysterious and heroic 'forest maiden' wearing full armour. A dark-complexioned beauty, Satanias (Daughter of Satan), and a radiant Gloria ('daughter of Glory') compete for Sir Ernest, and are finally revealed as the same maiden tempting him under two guises with the delights of passion and of chastity. Sir Ernest rejects the two-faced temptress and defeats his enemies, physical and spiritual. Finally he is revealed as Albert, emperor of Germany; Angela is identified as the daughter of the triumphant John Zitzka, and they marry. The Inquisition is exposed and its Monks in their turn perish horribly with the 'Virgin's kiss'.

Reynolds's hatred of the established church led him to take up a story seized on by Protestants at the Reformation as anti-Catholic propaganda. According to the legend, the reign of a ninth-century pope reputedly came to an abrupt end when 'Pope John' gave birth to a child and was revealed as 'Joan', and she was lynched for her presumption by the outraged faithful. Reynolds correctly sets his story *Pope Joan, or The Female Pontiff*[45] in Dark Ages Spain at a time when it was divided between the Christian Asturias to the north and the Muslim kingdom to the south. He offers a broadly accurate account of Spain in the ninth century, illustrated by a half-page

---

45 *RM*, 10 August 1850–25 January 1851.

map. Reynolds takes a political viewpoint, portraying the Muslim culture as superior to the Christian: the 'arts and sciences and all kinds of elegant accomplishments were both patronised and practiced to a far greater extent in the dominions of the [Moorish] King of Cordova than in those of the King of Asturias'.[46]

But then Reynolds got into difficulties. The subject drew him to the legend of the hundred Christian virgins paid annually to Cordova after the battle of Zamora. In 1881 Gounoud was to make this the sensational subject of his opera, but in mid-century Britain, as articles in *Reynolds's Newspaper* show,[47] Reynolds's sympathies with oriental culture were intensified by his sympathy for the beleaguered Turkish Empire in the Crimea, and his pro-Muslim stance limited his treatment of the episode. He improbably represents the 'tribute' of virgins as a diplomatic transaction between the two communities conducted with courteous chivalry by the Muslims in the cause of peace. At this point Reynolds appears to lose interest in his story. As his readers would have neither known nor cared about the Roman Catholic Church in the ninth century, Reynolds throws away any attempt at historical accuracy, introducing the sixteenth-century Spanish Inquisition into the story and reducing his narrative into a conventional gothic adventure. Pope Joan becomes more like a boyish Joan of Arc as she eludes the persecution of the Inquisition, aided by her companion Berthhold, a reneged abbot. Reynolds gives little attention to her election as pope, and the culmination of the legend is perfunctorily crammed into the last chapters. As she is a heroine, Reynolds is even denied the éclat of exposing her giving birth, and she is murdered by the superstitious mob with her chastity intact. After the literary failure of *Pope Joan*, Reynolds transferred his efforts in historical fiction onto the safer ground of more familiar territory.

Historical Melodrama

The novels of Sir Walter Scott, with their partly fictional characters meticulously set in historical contexts, contributed an important element to social melodrama and created a novel genre that allowed Reynolds scope for the rewriting of British history from a radical perspective, as examined by Michael Diamond elsewhere in the volume.[48] *The Necromancer*[49] combines the gothic and historical modes, and indeed, in the eponymous main character, the gothic physically invades the Renaissance period. Lord Danvers, born in 1351, on 31 June 1382 enters into a pact with Satan, by which he would enjoy 150 more years of youth and wealthy living. But during that time he had to entrap the souls of six virgin women for Satan, or he himself would be damned to eternity. The main story is set in Gothic Carisbrook Castle on the Isle of Wight, and in Grantham Villa beside Greenwich, at a time, 1510, when London is bustling with the excitement of the young Henry VIII's recent accession to the throne. Musadora, a heroine as beautiful as she is spirited, is set up by her

---

46   Reynolds, *Pope Joan*, ch. 19, pp. 22–3.

47   For example, 'Sympathy and Succour for the Turks', *RN*, 16 October 1853, p. 1.

48   See Chapter 5 in this volume by Michael Diamond, 'From Journalism and Fiction into Politics'.

49   *RM*, 27 December 1851–31 July 1852.

father and uncle to attract the attention of Henry and so gain them an entry into the royal court. But Musadora also catches the eye of Danvers who, unknown to her, is looking for the sixth virgin whose love would enable him to finally escape Satan's clutches. Having the power to change shape at will, he transforms his body into the double of Henry VIII and wins Musadora with a fake wedding. Before he can finally claim her, however, the real king bursts in, astounded to find himself confronted by his own apparition. Musadora's 'husband' transforms back into Danvers, while she drops senseless on the floor. 'A thunderbolt falling on her head, would have been mercy at that moment.'[50]

The novel draws to a close on the night of 31 May 1532, when, in the 'more than Egyptian darkness' of Carisbrook Castle hall, Danvers is about to cheat fate by entrapping Marian, a young virgin, in the last moments before he is to meet his doom. Unfortunately for him, however, a Lord Gerald St Louis, while travelling on Mount Lebanon, had encountered an anchorite who told him of Danvers's evil history, and in a vision he sees Danvers 'in search for a sixth and last virgin victim!'[51] Hurrying to England, St Louis meets up with Musadora, and, armed with a crucifix, they burst in on Danvers just before the stroke of midnight. Musadora reveals to Danvers[52] that Marian is their own daughter, a child conceived during his brief metamorphosis as Henry VIII but kept unaware of her parentage until now. (If we count the fact that Danvers fathered her while in the body of the king, Marian is a threefold child of mystery, a high tally even for Reynolds.) Frustrated by Musadora and her crucifix, Danvers is saved from incest. But at the hour of midnight he crumbles into a withered old man before, with 'a sound as of huge and mighty wings sweeping through the heavy black atmosphere', he disappears into Satan's realm, screaming 'in tones of wildest agony'.[53] Radiance filling the sky as the souls of his five released victims stream up to Heaven completes the novel's spectacular climax.

But tastes were moving away from the traditional gothic, and Reynolds turned towards the greater historical realism of Sir Walter Scott, writing *Kenneth, a Romance of the Highlands*.[54] The novel may also indicate Reynolds's increasing concern for his female readership, for it is written in a gentler tone, with greater attention to the romantic feelings of his heroine, Evelina, daughter of the Earl of Glenelg. The story is set in the picturesque scenery of sixteenth-century Scotland, and although there are the mandatory gothic castles, with banditti replaced by plundering clansmen, there is a marked absence of the torture and violence of previous serials. Even the Catholic monk Father Ignatius is considered a just man by his limited religious lights, in line with Reynolds's dislike of a purely Protestant reading of British history. Throughout the story, Kenneth, a noble foundling, combats the treacherous McAlpine clan, who are allied to English forces intent on ruling by subversion. Kenneth is finally revealed as Edgar Marquis of Allandale, whose parents the McAlpines have murdered. He claims back his lands, and with them gains the beautiful Evelina.

---

50 Reynolds, *Necromancer*, ch. 37, p. 121.
51 Reynolds, *Necromancer*, ch. 54, p. 174.
52 Reynolds, *Necromancer*, ch. 59, p. 184.
53 Reynolds, *Necromancer*, ch. 59, p. 185.
54 *RM*, 25 January–27 December 1851.

Reynolds's support for the Scottish highlanders against the perfidious English also directs the plot of *The Massacre of Glencoe*,[55] set in the later seventeenth century. The mysterious Count de Helder tours the country, ostensibly to work against Dutch influence, but is finally revealed as the skulking, disguised William of Orange himself, a heartless schemer whom Reynolds reveals as mainly responsible for the massacre. The noble Roderick Macdonald provides the melodrama, surviving the malicious schemes of his brother Allan and the beautiful Ida Campbell, who once loved Roderick but whose frustrated love has turned her into a murderous fiend. Roderick survives the massacre, marries his true love Ellen Glenfawn and becomes laird of the Macdonalds.

Fig. 11.4   'The Merchant opened a Gate, through which the Queen at once passed.' Illustrator E.H. Corbould. Frontispiece to G.W.M. Reynolds, *Canonbury House, or The Queen's Prophecy* (1858).

The Rye House Plot, or Ruth, the Conspirator's Daughter[56] moves to England in the same period. Popular historical works including William Harrison Ainsworth's *Windsor Castle* (1843) and J.F. Smith's *Stanfield Hall* (1849–50) had strengthened the historical foundations of melodramatic plots in popular fiction by tying the action to an actual location. In his account of the Rumbold family, Reynolds reconstructs life in Rye House in Hoddesdon, Sussex, which he recreates with woodcuts and maps. The story links history with politics, providing Reynolds with a chance to pillory Charles II, whom he particularly loathed.[57] He reveals that the novel's young hero, Lawrence Lee, was the illegitimate child of the monarch himself, conceived

55   *RM*, 31 July 1852–18 June 1853.
56   *RM*, 18 June 1853–19 August 1854.
57   For Reynolds's attitudes to royalty here and in *Canonbury House*, see Chapter 5 in this volume by Michael Diamond.

when, as a young prince, Charles raped Henrietta (Harriet), Rumbold's wife. In harrying Lawrence, Charles has been persecuting his own son. Finally Lawrence, his wife Ruth, Harriet and a band of others opposed to Charles flee England for America. There Lawrence becomes elected Chief Minister of the new, class-free republic of Oliphanta.

Reynolds is making the radical point that in persecuting its domestic enemies, British royalty was attacking its own kith and kin. This view is central to *Canonbury House, or The Queen's Prophecy*.[58] This is set at the time of Elizabeth I, a Queen portrayed as never beautiful, and now, six years from her death, crabbed and loveless. Through her life she has mercilessly persecuted the Spencers of Canonbury House, together with their friends and allies, in an attempt to silence those who there witnessed her, in her youth, secretly giving birth to a baby daughter. Unknown to her, the child has survived. But when finally Elizabeth kneels to acknowledge the child, her long-lost daughter dies, destroyed by her mother's unknowing persecution. Despite its historical absurdities, which include Sir Walter Raleigh riding into a tournament in full armour to defend his honour against claims that he had been a pirate, the vengeful character of the decaying Queen makes the novel one of Reynolds's more readable historical ventures. It was followed by *Mary Stuart, Queen of Scotland*,[59] a story that recounts Mary's doomed relationship with Darnley with broad historical accuracy, and all is the duller for it.

The Oriental and the Crimean War

A Byronic interest in the oriental had engaged Reynolds as early as *Wagner*, which included adventures in the Crusades set in the Middle East. Following the social melodrama formula, he foregrounded historical context, and in one episode, when describing the Siege of Rhodes, a footnote apologizes for the 'slight anachronism' of placing it in July 1521 rather than spring of 1522, 'to suit the plot of our tale'.[60] In *Pope Joan*, Reynolds had championed the Muslim culture and society as more civilized than that of the Christian Crusaders. But by mid-century, war clouds over the Crimea were giving a region of Byronic romance a darker cast. In late 1854 the British and French forces landed in the Crimea and took up positions for the siege of Sevastopol. Public interest grew intense, prompting Astley's Amphitheatre to mount J.H. Stocqueler's *The Battle of the Alma* on 25 October 1854, just under a month after the actual battle of 20 September. To exploit this interest, Reynolds commenced *Omar, a Tale of the Crimean War* on 6 January 1855. With Crimean events featuring day by day in the London press, Reynolds had little option but to follow the known facts. This did not, however, limit his use of the setting for melodramatic ends. The title refers to the hero Theodore Lottos, a Croatian who had joined the Muslim army in protest against the Austrian oppression of his homeland, and who rose to become the Omar Pasha of the title.

58 *RM*, 11 July 1857–1 May 1858.

59 *RM*, 14 May–24 December 1859.

60 Reynolds, *Wagner*, ch. 47, p. 82.

Melodramatic interest is provided by Catherine Volmar, who, disguised as a Zoave, nurses her sweetheart, the wounded English officer Captain Sidney Hazlewood, and by Edgar Osbourne, loved by a Circassian princess. Yet by the end of 1855, scandals of misadministration mired the war, and as patriotic enthusiasm turned to disillusionment, Reynolds evidently found his story losing its appeal. The final instalments show hasty disengagement, and the story comes to an inconsequential end on 5 January 1856, recording the fall of Sevastopol, but published before peace was declared with the Treaty of Paris three months later. The Crimean conflict gives a contemporary touch to Reynolds's *The Loves of the Harem, a Romance of Constantinople*, a novel which ran alongside *Omar* in weekly parts during 1855, for a young Greek hero sees off a Russian warship by frightening its captain with (fabricated) threats of a Turkish submarine. But the most sensational of Reynolds's titles is relatively lacking in sensational revelations, and the narrative turns into a pretext for Khalil, a Turk, to recount seven tales with an oriental setting.

Leila, or The Star of Mingrelia,[61] Reynolds's last 'oriental' novel, shows a full return to the form of social melodrama. Set in and around the time of the Crimean War, it combines an actual setting with theatrical plots. At times it also looks forward to the 'lost world' adventures of Haggard and Buchan. Mingrelia is a remote province in the Georgian Caucasus, hiding the secret Vale of Gulistan, '*a paradise hemmed in by a circular chasm of heights inaccessible from without or within*',[62] except through a secret tunnel under the mountains. The valley also conceals a treasure cavern. Leila and her cousin Aladyn, later christened Danial, are the country's Princess and Prince in waiting. But – bringing the story into actuality – Mingrelia is trapped between the Turkish presence centred in Constantinople and the 'iron hand' of an expansionist Russia. Within the community itself, Leila is harassed by bandits under Kiri Karaman, and by Tunar, the treacherous employee of the patriotic merchant Mansour. Pretending friendship, Myrrha, the wife of Karaman, betrays Leila into captivity. Myrrha is then bitten by a deadly snake. The community 'wise-woman' brings Myrrha back to life in a ceremony of purification, aided magnanimously by Leila, who forgives Myrrha her treachery. Shortly afterwards Leila is drugged and sold to Turkish slave traders: taken to Constantinople, she is selected for the Sultan's harem.

But before harm can befall her, a compatriot slave, Klodissa, gives her a potent drug, and, taken out of the city as dead, Leila awakes and escapes with her saviour back to Mingrelia. In a subplot, Dorval, a French count, who had come to Mingrelia in search of its secret valley, has been arrested by the Turks as a Russian spy and imprisoned in the remote Garanrog Castle. Over the years he has assembled materials to make a hot-air balloon on a disused turret. When Tunar becomes a fellow-prisoner, Dorval completes his construction and both fly from the castle, landing in the Vale of Gulistan. In a complicated narrative, Tunar discovers the secret caverns but loses his way, and, surrounded by untold riches, dies of starvation. Dorval saves the life of Klodissa, who has been wounded by bandits. Perhaps as Reynolds's gesture towards the beneficent role of the French allies in the Crimean War, Klodissa rewards Dorval

---

61 *RM*, 5 January–5 July 1856.
62 Reynolds, *Leila*, ch. 36, p. 112.

with treasure from the cave, and he escapes in his balloon back to Paris. There, ensconced in a mansion on the Champs Elysées, he refuses to reveal the location of the Georgian El Dorado.

The story is vigorously anti-colonial. Mingrelia survives the upheavals of the Crimean War and, through Danial's skilful diplomacy, wins a secret article in the Treaty of Paris by which it achieves independence from Turkey. Leila and Danial marry and rule over their restored kingdom. Contemporary events in the Middle East made this more significant than the conventional happy ending, for it celebrated local communities returning to traditional ways after the war. In the manner of social melodrama, it also fused actuality with moral issues. Leila is Reynolds's first (and only) Christian heroine, the devotee of an ancient cult free from western influence. Her salvation from the Sultan's harem is associated with spiritual rebirth: she awakes from apparent death to a 'new life – to an existence that God grant may henceforth be a happy one!'[63] With her radiant goodness she becomes an emblem of reconciliation. Under her influence, the bandits abandon 'their ways of intrigue and iniquity'[64] and help create the country's hopeful future. In a final melodramatic twist, Klodissa is revealed to be none other than Myrrha, the bandit's wife. Converted by her near-death experience and Leila's forgiveness, she has disguised herself and atoned for her betrayal by rescuing Leila, who, thinking back, reflects that she had 'a vague misty idea that she was not altogether unknown to me'.[65] Unusually for melodrama, both its main protagonists are women.

The benign tone of the novel reflects changes in Reynolds's own life. As described in the Introduction to this volume, in 1854 he had moved with his family from London to the Kent coast of his childhood. Living in Gothic House, Herne Bay, Reynolds put his energies into social activities, becoming a stalwart member of the community's Improvement Committee and helping to draw up the house-numbered street plan which gave the town a practical identity. In 1856 he bought the spacious Belmore Hall on the town's outskirts. According to William Watson's *A Visitor's Guide to Herne Bay* (1855; published by Reynolds's own London office), this was 'a superb mansion in the midst of a spacious garden.... The hothouses and conservatories are fitted up on a costly plan and produce splendid grapes.'[66] Now financially secure, Reynolds no longer had to write furiously for a living and, like the ageing Candide, could cultivate his garden. The idyll was sadly ended in 1858 by the death of his beloved Susannah and his retreat back to London.

But the previous decade had been extraordinarily productive. Reynolds's penny issue serials have received most critical attention. However, the lesser-known magazine serials examined here, if often uneven, padded out and overloaded with secondary narratives, contradict the image of Reynolds as a repetitive literary hack. They show restless invention and ingenuity, a skill in plotting and in the manipulation of concealed identities that makes him the true forerunner of the sensation novelists

---

63 Reynolds, *Leila*, ch. 25, p. 79.
64 Reynolds, *Leila*, ch. 54, p. 162.
65 Reynolds, *Leila*, ch. 54, p. 164.
66 Harold Gough, 'G.W.M. Reynolds at Herne Bay', *Bygone Kent*, 6/5 (May 1985): 279. I am grateful to Mrs Monica North for bringing this article to my attention.

of the 1860s.[67] There is the use of crude but resonant images, as in *The Bronze Statue* where he embodies the delusions of ritualistic religion in the terrible 'iron maiden' Virgin; or when in *The Coral Island* he links a financial crime with leprosy and, with pre-Marxist insight, shows its cure found through a return to pastoral simplicity. Reynolds possessed a 'politically baptized' imagination. In his prose melodramas even outlandish plots, situations and characters can serve to dramatize his political convictions and invest social issues with the energy of popular theatre.

---

67 The influence of Reynolds on Mrs Braddon's novels is well discussed by Jennifer Carnell in her introduction to *The Black Band, or the Mysteries of Midnight* ([1861–62], rpt. Hastings: Sensation Press, 1992). See also Chapter 12 in this volume by Graham Law.

Chapter 12

Reynolds's 'Memoirs' Series and 'The Literature of the Kitchen'

Graham Law

Towards the end of 1851, announcements of yet another new story by the proprietor began to appear in Reynolds's periodicals.[1] *Mary Price, or The Memoirs of a Servant-Maid* was around the twenty-fifth novel to appear under Reynolds's signature since *The Youthful Impostor* was issued in three volumes in Paris in 1835, and already it represented at least his twelfth serial tale since teaming up with publisher John Dicks in 1848.[2] In more than one respect, however, *Mary Price* constituted a new departure. The novel was to be narrated in the first person and have a domestic setting in contemporary England, a combination of features that had no precedent in the author's oeuvre. The bulk of Reynolds's previous novels had been historical or gothic romances, while the minority with modern settings, like the early Pickwickian comedies, *The Mysteries of London* begun in 1844 in imitation of Sue, or the recent social protest novel *The Seamstress, or The White Slave of England* (1850), had all employed an omniscient narrator and tended to avoid scenes of family life. To emphasize this formal innovation, the advertisements for *Mary Price* included a lengthy explication of the rationale of the new work:

> To dissect the social body in the minutest manner – to penetrate beneath the surface of every-day life – to draw aside the veil from the domestic hearth, and look deep into the modes of existence practiced by families of all grades – and thus to lay bare the mysteries of English society, – such is a faint shadowing forth of the author's design in his New Tale. In carrying out this aim he has adopted a machinery which has appeared to him the best suited for the purpose – namely, the autobiography of a Servant-Maid, whose experience, observations, and adventures in the various families which she successively enters, form the basis of the work.[3]

Further, since the mid-1840s all of Reynolds's instalment novels had run for rather less than a year in one or other of the new penny literary miscellanies[4] – with the admittedly monstrous exception of *The Mysteries of London* itself, which effectively

---

1   Similar announcements are found in both *RN* and *RM*.

2   Though often hazy on dates of initial fascicle publication, the most comprehensive bibliography remains that in Reynolds's *Wagner the Wehr-Wolf*, ed. E.F. Bleiler (New York: Dover, 1975), pp. 153–60.

3   *RM*, 15 November 1851, p. 272.

4   In March 1845 Reynolds became the founding editor of George Vickers's *LJ*, where a handful of his stories appeared before he left to start *RM* in November 1846.

appeared over an unbroken sequence of 12 years, independently in penny numbers or monthly parts making up six biannual series.[5] Contrary to the rule, *Mary Price* was to be published not in *Reynolds's Miscellany* but in fascicles, starting in early November 1851 and reaching a conclusion two years later in a total of 104 weekly numbers. Moreover, the novel was only the first of four autobiographical narratives of everyday life published in numbers in overlapping sequence during the 1850s. The sequels were *Joseph Wilmot, or The Memoirs of a Man Servant* and *Ellen Percy, or The Memoir of an Actress*, both of which ran for two years from July 1853 and 1855 respectively, plus *Rosa Lambert, or The Memoirs of an Unfortunate Woman*, which appeared over a single year from November 1853.[6] Though the 'Memoirs' sequence is little more than half of the length of *The Mysteries of London* in its entirety, it nevertheless amounts to just short of 3,000 pages in the original fascicle format, with its compact print in double columns, or something over three million words.

Reynolds's 'autobiographical' sequence seems to have reached an exceptionally wide readership, both when originally issued and in later Victorian decades. The initial popularity of the series is indeed indicated by the fact that it continued for so long. Advertisements often recommended the subsequent narratives as 'companions' to *Mary Price*, which, it was claimed, had reached readers 'by hundreds of thousands'.[7] On the completion of the initial serial run, the works became immediately available in annual cloth-bound volumes priced at 6s, 6d each, and thereafter remained on sale as part of an expanding uniform edition of Reynolds's major fiction.[8] From the early 1860s, taking advantage of the abolition of the substantial paper tax, all four narratives were reissued in serial form at half the original price, with two numbers a week for just a penny. From the early 1870s, each was included in the series of 'Dicks's English Novels' as small-format sixpenny volumes in paper covers, still in double columns but in even smaller print and with only a handful of the original illustrations: *Rosa Lambert* appeared first as volumes 118–19 (out of an eventual total of 243), while the other three followed in their original sequence, each occupying four volumes. The entire 'Memoirs' sequence thus became available to readers for a total of seven shillings, only a fraction more than the cost of a single volume in

---

5   In thus conflating Reynolds's *MOL* (1844–48) and *MOCL* (1848–56) into a single sequence, I follow the author himself in the Postscript to the latter work: 'For *twelve* years, therefore, have I hebdomadally issued to the world a fragmentary portion of that which, as one vast whole, may be termed an Encyclopedia of Tales' (G.W.M. Reynolds, *The Mysteries of the Court of London* [London: John Dicks, 1856], vol. 8, Postscript, p. 412, emphasis in original). The reason for the change of title was that the initial publisher, George Vickers, continued to use the original, recruiting Thomas Miller and E.L. Blanchard to write a third series (1848–50).

6   I overlook here Reynolds's *The Young Duchess*, published by Dicks in 52 weekly parts from June 1857. Though announced as 'A Sequel to Ellen Percy' and subtitled 'Memoirs of a Woman of Quality', it is not written in the first person and has little structurally in common with the other four.

7   E.g., in *RM*, 20 January 1855, p. 415.

8   Citations from the 'Memoirs' sequence by volume and page numbers refer to these bound original editions; chapter numbers have been added to facilitate cross-reference to subsequent formats.

the original format. The same plates were still being used in the 1880s, when the complete series was reissued in coloured wrappers with the legend 'People's Edition', and thus remained available into the twentieth century.

While the whole sequence followed the same basic pattern, with much recycling of plot tropes and character types both within and between the four narratives, there remain many signs of variation and development that suggest that the 'Memoir' format is used to explore as well as repeat. Among other reasons, Reynolds's domestic sequence of the mid-1850s is of interest because it prefigures many of the characteristics of the 'sensation' novels that became fashionable among the middle-class subscribers to literary magazines and circulating libraries from the early 1860s. This can be seen most clearly in the unsettling combination of commonplace domestic settings and illicit or outlandish events, found alike in the sensation fiction of Wilkie Collins, Mary Braddon, Ellen Wood and Charles Reade, to name only the best-known practitioners; such a conjunction was indeed foreshadowed in the promise to 'draw aside the veil from the domestic hearth, and ... lay bare the mysteries of English society' of the original announcement of *Mary Price*. Contemporary critics were quick to trace the source of sensationalism's blatant transgression of social and sexual proprieties to narrative aimed at a proletarian audience. One outraged commentator suggested that Braddon had succeeded in 'making the literature of the kitchen the favourite reading of the Drawing-room',[9] while a review of Collins's *Armadale* saw 'Sensational Mania' as a 'virus ... spreading in all directions, from the penny journal to the shilling magazine, and from the shilling magazine to the thirty shillings volume'.[10] Similarly, among the quantities of critical ink dispensed over the last couple of decades in accounting for the Victorian sensation boom, there has often been acknowledgement of the form's antecedents in the working-class 'bloods'.[11] But in neither era has there been much inclination to come to cases: in the relevant literature, both Victorian and contemporary, I have not been able to come up with a single reference specifically to the relevance of Reynolds's 'Memoirs' series to the emergence of sensation narrative.[12] The purpose of the present chapter is thus to try to remedy this deficiency. I focus in particular on three emergent features shared by Reynolds's seminal domestic autobiographies and the major sensation novels of the

9   [W. Fraser Rae], 'Sensation Novelists: Miss Braddon', *North British Review*, 43/3 (September 1865): 198.

10   [J.R. Wise], 'Belles Lettres', *Westminster Review*, n.s., 30/3 (July 1866): 270.

11   Typical examples can be found in Winifred Hughes, *The Maniac in the Cellar* (Princeton, NJ: Princeton University Press, 1980), pp. 41–2; Ann Cvetovich, *Mixed Feelings* (New Brunswick, NJ: Rutgers University Press, 1992), pp. 14–17; and Deborah Wynne, *The Sensation Novel and the Victorian Family Magazine* (New York: Palgrave, 2001), pp. 9–10.

12   Though their extensive readership, formal features and timing render them of special relevance to the emergence of sensation fiction, I do not, of course, wish to imply that Reynolds's 'Memoirs' are the sole or earliest exemplars of domestic fiction for the proletariat; for a wider perspective, see Louis James's discussion of 'The Paradox of the Domestic Story', in *Fiction for the Working Man, 1830–1850: A Study of the Literature Produced for the Working Classes in Early Victorian Urban England* (London: Oxford University Press, 1963), pp. 97–113.

following decade: 'the presence of the present', in Richard Altick's phrase; the mixing of realism and melodrama; and the ambiguous representation of sexual impropriety.

The Presence of the Present

As Altick has demonstrated, Victorian fiction was preoccupied with 'topicalities', that is, the sites, incidents and issues focused on in the news media of the day.[13] The tendency was especially remarkable in novels first published in serial form, where the reader typically encountered fictional narrative alongside reports, commentary or advertisements concerning current events. In the 1860s traditionalists found egregious instances of this trend in sensation fiction, where the adjective pointed not only to the effect of the narrative on the nerves of the reader, but also its sources in the contemporary mass media. In a scathing critique of the sensation boom in the *Quarterly Review*, for example, the Rev. H.L. Mansel used the term 'Newspaper Novel' to indicate that salacious material was flooding into light middle-class reading from the popular Sunday crime-and-scandal journals,[14] obviously including the radical *Reynolds's Newspaper*. Among Reynolds's extensive output of serial fiction, this breaching of the traditional barriers between literature and journalism is most clearly visible just after the mid-century in the sequence of 'autobiographical' narratives beginning with *Mary Price*.

To begin with, the 'Memoirs' are extraordinarily specific concerning their settings in terms of both location and chronology. Though all four narratives cover a good deal of ground, each begins with the childhood memories of the eponymous hero-narrator, celebrating her or his place of birth in some detail – in the cases of Mary Price, Joseph Wilmot, Ellen Percy and Rosa Lambert, respectively, the market town of Ashford in Kent, the outskirts of Leicester, the centre of Leeds and a rural parish in Cheshire – and returns with considerable frequency to the home territory during the long and circuitous course of the story. At the same time, each regularly specifies the year and season, month or even date of outstanding events. It is thus straightforward to ascertain that *Mary Price* and *Joseph Wilmot* commence respectively in 1826 and 1836, both concluding around 1850, that *Ellen Percy* occupies 1832–45, while *Rosa Lambert* opens as late as the summer of 1840 and closes with her death on 28 July 1852, a few months after the sequence as a whole began to be published. Clearly there is here some concerted Cobbett-like attempt to cover the social condition of England during the author's lifetime.

With an appeal to readers similar to that used in the 'Notices to Correspondents' featured in the back-pages of *Reynolds's Miscellany*, a slightly later and expanded version of the announcement of the appearance of *Mary Price* also revealed the intention that the sequence should incorporate the personal experiences of its subscribers:

---

13   Richard D. Altick, *The Presence of the Present* (Columbus, OH: Ohio State University Press, 1991), p. 2.

14   [H.L. Mansel], 'Sensation Novels', *Quarterly Review*, 113/2 (April 1863): 499.

... it is Mr. Reynolds's object, by his new tale, to *shame* those families which are now despotic towards their servants into a more humane and Christian-like behaviour. *Servants who have special grievances to complain of, would do well to send the particulars to Mr. Reynolds, who will render the information available in the working out of his story.*[15]

While this soliciting of reader contributions does not seem to have been repeated for the later novels, such a call must have provoked many subscribers to engage with the unfolding fictional narrative with more than half an eye to contemporary events as reported in the radical weekly papers.

Perhaps more obviously and consistently, though, the 'presence of the present' is flagged by intrusions of the author's personal preoccupations into the pseudo-autobiographical 'Memoirs'. It is obviously no accident that, at the beginning of the sequence, East Kent was chosen as Mary Price's home ground, since this was familiar territory to the young Reynolds, who was born in Sandwich and educated at the grammar school in Ashford. Moreover, in his maturity the author returned to the area, residing from 1854 to 1858 at the seaside resort of Herne Bay, where subscribers to *Reynolds's Miscellany* were instructed to send correspondence. It is also remarkable how frequently the later memoirs return to this familiar home ground. Though quite a number of scenes in *Ellen Percy* take place in and around the ports of Dover and Ramsgate, this tendency is especially noticeable in *Rosa Lambert*. When in search of a new 'protector', the fallen heroine of that novel typically heads for the West End theatres or the flamboyant Sussex resorts of Brighton and Hastings, but retreats to the safer havens of the north Kent coast when she needs to hide a relationship from the eyes of the world, or to the rural protection of Sittingbourne when it is necessary to conceal the birth of an illegitimate child. Thus it is especially traumatic when, towards the end of the narrative, seemingly secure in Ramsgate in the summer of 1849, the heroine records the outbreak of cholera in the area followed by violent storms off the north Kent coast, one of which causes the death by shipwreck of her latest lover, both the killer disease and the inclement weather being phenomena attested in the press of the day.[16]

The wider peregrinations of the memoirists also frequently allow the author to ride current hobby horses, typically of an overtly political nature but occasionally blatantly commercial. For example, while trying to pursue her eloping sister, Mary Price ends up over the Scottish border, where she manages 'to introduce a brief but faithful description of Gretna-Green, borrowed from a popular novel bearing the same title'.[17] To prevent misunderstandings, an editorial note confirms that the cited

---

15 *RM*, 22 November 1851, p. 288, italics in original.

16 The topicality of the references is clearly flagged: 'the reader will bear in mind that I am now writing of the month of August, 1849' (*Rosa Lambert*, ch. 51, p. 375). On the cholera outbreak, see Christopher Collins, 'Cholera and Typhoid Fever in Kent', Kent Archaeological Society, www.kentarchaeology.ac/authors/004.pdf (accessed 9 October 2006). On the weather, compare the coverage in the local press during the early autumn of 1849: for example, the *Kentish Gazette* (11 September 1849, p. 3) reported recent severe electrical storms and torrential rain on the east Kent coast, resulting in damage to shipping, while the *Canterbury Journal* (13 October 1849, p. 3) referred generally to 'the late tempestuous weather'.

17 Reynolds, *Mary Price*, ch. 108, p. 127.

passage derives from the 1848 serial novel by Mrs G.W.M. Reynolds, still available in a bound volume from John Dicks at 5s, 6d.

It is in *Joseph Wilmot*, though, that the protagonist travels most extensively, thus allowing the author the greatest freedom to air his views as an international socialist. Out of service and forced to wander penniless through the Lancashire mill towns, Joseph finds himself compelled to speak at length of 'how the factory slaves (for such indeed they are in every sense of the term) are plundered, scorned, insulted, and oppressed by their bloated intolerant masters'.[18] Most of the second volume of the novel is given over to the manservant's adventures on the continent. In Paris he witnesses the corruption of the government of Louis-Philippe and sympathizes with the revolutionaries, while in Milan he learns of the tyranny of the Austrian oppressors and the valour of the Italian patriots. Earlier, in Florence, witnessing the execution of an enemy, Joseph nevertheless declares himself a resolute opponent of the barbarous practice of capital punishment, arguing in a lengthy digression that 'man impiously usurps the authority of the Almighty when he assumes a control over the life of a fellow creature', thus engaging in a debate then ongoing in the London press.[19] Back in London, in scenes that prefigure those in a number of sensation novels, notably Charles Reade's *Hard Cash* (1863), Joseph experiences at first hand the cruelty and injustice resulting from the inadequate regulation of private lunatic asylums.[20]

Perhaps the most interesting example of the author's abrupt intrusion of 'the presence of the present' is the continuation of his political battle of words with Charles Dickens through the medium of the 'Memoirs' series. In his private correspondence, Dickens had quickly shown his disdain for 'amateur' (i.e., bourgeois) Chartists in general and Reynolds in particular, following the latter's chairing of the outlawed meeting in Trafalgar Square on 6 March 1848.[21] Though from its beginnings in March 1850 Dickens's miscellany *Household Words*, together with the monthly news supplement *Household Narrative*, had made no secret of its antipathy to the Charter, Reynolds was not personally attacked until the *Household Narrative* editorial of April 1851. There it was noted that 'the first name affixed to this Chartist programme is that of a person notorious for his attempts to degrade the working men of England by circulating among them books of a debasing tendency'.[22] Since John Dicks's establishment was then situated off the Strand at 7 Wellington Street North, only a step from the offices of *Household Words* at number 16, it is likely that the two authors crossed paths occasionally. Prior to the editorial attack Dickens had been treated generously as a friend of the people in the columns of *Reynolds's Newspaper*;

---

18 Reynolds, *Joseph Wilmot*, vol. 1, ch. 50, pp. 267–8.

19 Reynolds, *Joseph Wilmot*, vol. 2, ch. 101, p. 120. Similar outcries against the 'barbarian and brutal' institution of capital punishment are found in *Mary Price*, vol. 1, ch. 70, pp. 343–4 and vol. 2, ch. 130, pp. 242–3. Throughout the 1840s and 1850s, the topic was discussed regularly in *The Times*, for example, so that a leader of 12 July 1850 referred to the 'annual controversy on capital punishment'.

20 Again there was a long-standing debate on the subject in *The Times*, with editorials on the subject on 5 January 1849, 28 July 1858 and 19 August 1858.

21 See N.C. Peyrouton, 'Dickens and the Chartists', *The Dickensian*, 60, 2/3 (Spring/ Autumn 1864): 78–88, 152–61; here pp. 84–8.

22 Peyrouton, 'Dickens and the Chartists', pp. 155–6.

thereafter there followed a series of *ad hominem* ripostes from the issue for 8 June 1851, with its long diatribe on 'Charles Dickens and the Democratic Movement', beginning: 'That lickspittle hanger-on to the skirts of Aristocracy's role ...'.[23] Not all were confined to the columns of *Reynolds's Newspaper*: on more than one occasion the abuse was recycled in fictional form in the 'Memoirs'. A striking example occurs in *Mary Price*, where the effete aristocrats of Harlesdon Park fête

> a great literary character ... Mr Charles Wiggins, who from having been a penny-a-liner on the *Morning Chronicle*, had by dishing up all kinds of absurdities which he called "humour", and throwing into the hodge-podge a dash of maudlin sentimentalism ... managed to establish his renown as a popular author ...[24]

Despite the superficial anachronism – according to the declared time scheme of the novel the scene takes place in the late 1820s when Dickens was still in his teens – few readers can have missed 'the presence of the present' in this sudden intrusion of the topics of the day into Reynolds's fictional world.[25]

The Mixing of Realism and Melodrama

In the 'Memoirs' series, as in the sensation novels of the 1860s, the counterpulls of realism and romance are articulated most overtly in the tensions between commonplace domestic settings and outrageous or uncanny events. Thus, in the opening chapters of *Mary Price*, for example, the calm contentment of the humble cottage of the Price family, with the husband represented as an industrious journeyman carpenter and the wife a painstaking housekeeper and mother, is abruptly disturbed by the appearance of a mysterious nobleman at the window, leading breathlessly to the apparent violent deaths of both the heroine's parents. As this example might suggest, in the 'Memoirs' novels the security of the customary is more often found in simple, rural settings, while the intrusion of unnatural horror is most typically associated with aristocratic urbanity. While this pattern is a familiar one from much earlier modes of popular literature, and clearly reflects the rather outmoded nature of Reynolds's radicalism, more consistently figuring power as land rather than capital, we should nevertheless note that it is also one that is retained in a number of the seminal sensation novels, including both Wilkie Collins's *The Woman in White* (1859–60) and Ellen Woods's *East Lynne* (1861).

In addition, tensions between realism and romance are emphasized by the double structure of the 'Memoirs' narratives. First, each of the four novels exhibits an episodic framework shaped by how the hero-narrators make a living as subordinates. Both Mary and Joseph earn their keep as resident domestic servants, and the sequence of households that employ them over the course of the narrative, with the faults and foibles of their various masters and mistresses, lends the works a picaresque quality.

---

23 Peyrouton, 'Dickens and the Chartists', pp. 157–8.
24 Reynolds, *Mary Price*, vol. 1, ch. 67, p. 364.
25 There is a similar attack on 'Mr Charles Diggins' in *Joseph Wilmot*, vol. 1, ch. 67, p. 364.

Indeed, this is given a formal status in *Mary Price* in the sequence of chapter headings from 'IV My First Place' to 'CXV My Twelfth Place'. Yet something similar is true of Ellen and Rosa, who are subject to the whims and wills of a lengthy series of theatre managers and 'protectors', in the careers as play actress and 'kept mistress' that circumstances respectively force upon them. In each case the course followed is less a linear progress than a circular maze, with a good deal of backtracking and returning to old haunts, so that mentors from previous phases of the story constantly reappear and interact with current ones. In the process, the narrator is able to offer a panoramic view of the social hierarchy, and the reader is encouraged to compare tyrannies or kindnesses, distinguishing between the greater and lesser good or evil. At the same time, the episodic structure facilitates the intercalation of stories by others met along the way, together with the insertion of correspondence, diary entries and other personal documents that re-establish connections with places and people left behind. Cumulatively, this gives the narrative an authenticated, documentary quality that in some respects prefigures the technique explored by Collins in *The Woman in White*, most notably where the narrative transmitted by Walter Hartright is 'told by more than one pen, as the story of an offence against the laws is told in Court by more than one witness'.[26] In sum, this episodic patterning clearly represents the pull of realism in the 'Memoirs' sequence.

Yet each novel has an alternative principle of organization that simultaneously reflects the powerful attraction of the melodramatic. It is true that, in all the 'Memoirs', many of the independent episodes and intercalated stories rely heavily on the mechanisms of mystery and suspense for their narrative interest, and employ gothic trappings familiar from *The Mysteries of London*. This is unsurprising given Reynolds's prolific output and the common pressures of weekly serialization. Further, though, with the significant exception of the shorter novel, *Rosa Lambert,* to which I shall return, each of the 'Memoirs' shares an overarching plot founded in romantic comedy that exists in tension with the episodic rhythm of the picaresque. Each of the three full-length narratives slowly but inexorably moves the long-suffering narrator-protagonist from impoverished beginnings, through a gradual clarification of a core mystery concerning their family identity, towards a long-awaited happy ending in marriage with a lover encountered early in the narrative, a union which raises them to a position of, or confirms their status as, a titled landowner.

The pattern is best exemplified in *Ellen Percy*, where the tensions between the picaresque rhythm and romantic plot stand out most starkly and immediately. Faintly echoing Dickens's recent performance in *Hard Times* (1854), Reynolds's novel opens in the great northern industrial city of Leeds,

> in one of those low quarters which almost exclusively swarm with the poorest members of the manufacturing population – in the midst of a labyrinth of narrow filthy streets, interspersed with huge dingy factories – and beneath an atmosphere almost everlastingly blackened by the smoke vomited forth from the giant chimneys that overlooked the whole maze of habitations.[27]

---

26 Wilkie Collins, *The Woman in White*, ed. Harvey Peter Sucksmith (London: Oxford University Press, 1975), p. 1.
27 Reynolds, 'The Old House at Leeds', *Ellen Percy,* vol. 1, ch. 1, p. 2.

Though the house where the young protagonist lives is 'the gloomiest' in this grim landscape, we quickly learn that the darkness is not due to the apparent cause: Ellen Percy is not one of the benighted factory girls but rather the grandchild of a miserly moneylender. Over the course of the narrative the old house acquires more gothic features as it emerges that her father did not die in her infancy but was transported as a forger, and that her poverty is the result of her grandfather being poisoned, and her inheritance stolen, by a villainous employee. In discovering her own antecedents and recovering her inheritance, Ellen also establishes the lost right of her cousin and childhood sweetheart Henry Wakefield to a country seat, so that the couple end the novel not only happily united but also with the titles of Earl and Countess of Carshalton.

In *Rosa Lambert*, however, the overarching structure is one of romantic tragedy that creates rather less tension with the demands of realism. Here, there is no discovery of a lost family fortune: Rosa remains to the end what she was at the beginning, the unfortunate daughter of a financially impoverished and morally deficient clergyman. The final reversal of fortune leads not to wealth and contentment but to the sudden loss of health, beauty and the chance of social salvation, and a rapid descent into prostitution and consumption, while the denouement offers the narrator no fairytale fantasy to compensate for the trials and injustices suffered along the way. During another terrible storm at Ramsgate, Rosa Lambert experiences a nightmare vision of a future that is both her own and that of the many women who share her situation:

> I beheld with appalled imagination the countless thousands upon thousands of unfortunate women dragging themselves through all degrees, varieties, and grades of loathsome misery in the great metropolis of this so-called *civilised* country. And again I shuddered to the deepest confines of my being, as I thought that if I lived long enough, I too must be as one of those, sinking lower and lower …[28]

The sole, deferred consolation allowed at the end of this novel, following the heroine's contrition and confession, is the Christian hope of peace and union beyond the grave. Early in the narrative Rosa encounters the humble young clergyman, Arthur Brydges, and through the ups and downs of her professional sexual career continues to regard him as her one true but unconsummated love. Social disapproval and her own moral compunction repeatedly prevent her from accepting his sacrificial acts of forgiveness and offers of marriage, so that their relationship can be figured as that of Mary Magdalene and Christ. In this novel, Reynolds thus stakes out some of the ground that will be explored in many later sensational novels with a social mission, notably Wilkie Collins's *The New Magdalen* (1873) and *The Fallen Leaves* (1879).

Reynolds's Ambiguous Depiction of Sexual Impropriety

Judging from the way it was marketed, with the 'Memoirs' sequence Reynolds was attempting to tone down the salacious reputation that had adhered to his tales throughout the 1840s, and to orient his new work towards a female readership

---

28 Reynolds, *Rosa Lambert*, ch. 51, p. 378.

understood to be more careful of the proprieties. This may well have been in part the result of pressure from Reynolds's business and domestic partners. His publisher John Dicks must have been aware of the economic advantages now being enjoyed in the marketplace by those penny journals targeting a domestic audience, like the *Family Herald*,[29] as opposed to the more daring fare still offered by *Reynolds's Miscellany* itself, while his wife Susannah was indeed already helping to nudge the *Miscellany* in this new direction by contributing both the occasional romantic tale and a regular culinary column. Be that as it may, Reynolds's intentions in this respect are amply witnessed by internal evidence from the opening novel in the sequence, where with Mary Price the author succeeds for the first time in portraying a heroine of strong will but virginal purity.

The saga of Mary's triumphant resistance to the lengthy assaults on her virtue by the vicious Sir Aubrey Clavering owes much to Samuel Richardson's *Pamela* (1740), though her tormentor, despite his sudden reform at the end of the narrative, is not the man she eventually marries. The moral scheme of the novel in this regard is plain to see. Just as Mary has two brothers who repeat the pattern of the popular parable of the good and bad apprentices, so she has two sisters, one of whom pursues the virtuous course pioneered by the heroine while the other goes down the primrose path. Sarah Price does not marry in Gretna Green but serves instead as the kept mistress of a series of degenerate aristocrats. In the process, she experiences little in the way of authorial sympathy, and is conveniently removed by a fittingly painful and contrite death. The advertisements for the completed novel in volume form could thus guarantee that it 'would constitute an elegant present from a parent to a daughter, or from a gentleman to a young lady'.[30] Further, the unsullied virtue of Mary was cited in advertisements to allay doubts about the propriety of the ensuing narratives: *Joseph Wilmot* was promised to have 'the same high moral purpose in view', while subscribers to *Rosa Lambert* were reassured that 'the same readers who ... regarded "Mary Price" as a welcome guest at their homes and firesides, may, in all confidence, bestow their patronage on this work'.[31]

The narratives themselves, however, tell a rather different story. The young Joseph Wilmot has rather more in common with Fielding's Joseph Andrews than Richardson's Pamela, and is often embarrassed by the amorous advances of fellow domestics or frustrated mistresses. At one stage, through a confusion with her debauched twin sister Violet, he abandons his beloved and virtuous Annabel as a fallen woman, and accidentally fathers a child on the besotted Lady Calanthe Dundas. Nevertheless, Joseph undergoes little in the way of penance before his eventual marriage and social elevation. If such inconsistencies can be explained away as the male author's unthinking acceptance of the sexual double standard, the same cannot apply to the last two works in the series. Though Ellen Percy herself survives the novel with her virtue

---

29   The Manchester publisher Alexander Heywood noted that the *Family Herald* 'addresses itself to the fairer sex in a great measure, and to that perhaps may be attributed its very large circulation'; see *Report from the Select Committee on Newspaper Stamps*, House of Commons Papers, 17: 558 (1851), no. 2502.

30   *RM*, 13 August 1853, p. 48.

31   *RM*, 20 January 1855, p. 415.

intact, the experiences of her intimate friends, Juliet Norman and Mary Glentworth, starkly illustrate the extreme vulnerability of the subordinate female, when both lose their reputation through no fault of their own – the former is the victim of a mock marriage ceremony while the latter proves to be the illegitimate daughter of the kept mistress of an aristocrat.

It is in *Rosa Lambert*, though, that the presentation of sexual impropriety is most complex and disturbing. The opening scenes of these 'memoirs of an unfortunate woman' are especially shocking.[32] The novel begins with what seems an idyllic moment of romance, with the pretty daughter of a poor parish priest courted by the rich and handsome son of the local squire as she strolls placidly through the woods. Yet when she gladly responds to his wooing, she is appalled to discover that marriage is not his intention, and runs home distraught only to find her family in turmoil as the accumulation of debt finally threatens to submerge the household. With no other remedy apparent, each member in turn succumbs to dishonesty, a process culminating in the chapter headed 'The Four Guilty Ones', where Rosa's return with the most substantial contribution provokes a horrified response. She defends herself:

> 'Do not all cry out at me ... Have you not all, one after the other, tried your own resources? You, father, plundered the farmer of the tithe-money – you, mother committed a fraud on your sister – you, Cyril, robbed a carriage on the high-way – and what was left for me to do but sell my virtue?'[33]

Although physical force is used to obtain Rosa's sexual favours on several occasions over her subsequent career, this first fall under financial constraint is presented as the worst violation, while the vicious youth who buys her honour is represented as the blackest villain.

But this initial sense of moral outrage at Rosa's misfortune is not maintained consistently throughout the novel. Her second experience of male villainy seems to convince her of the necessity of female resignation: 'I was doomed to become the victim of man's perfidiousness ... it was a fate against which it were vain to struggle.'[34] Later Rosa often treats her own forced dishonour as culpable, so that she refuses to return home because of the shame this would bring on her family ('How could I – lost and degraded as I was – seek the paternal home?'),[35] or feels compelled to refuse an offer of marriage from a humble but kindly protector ('I was no longer worthy: villainy had forced me aside from the path of constancy which I had resolved to pursue').[36] This last after she has once again been raped, this time by her cousin, John Haverstock, so that he can win 1,000 guineas in a wager with an aristocratic friend who soon repeats the feat. A little later, though, she comes to regard such ubiquitous male perfidy as justification for female aggression ('Let me buckle on a kindred armour to wage a kindred warfare. Let me too be selfish and egotistical; let

---

32   It is significant that when *Rosa Lambert* was reissued as a serial in the early 1860s, the subtitle was changed to 'The Memoirs of a Clergyman's Daughter'.

33   Reynolds, *Rosa Lambert*, ch. 4, p. 21.

34   Reynolds, *Rosa Lambert*, ch. 5, p. 28.

35   Reynolds, *Rosa Lambert*, ch. 15, p. 117.

36   Reynolds, *Rosa Lambert*, ch. 29, p. 229.

me think only of myself').[37] Thus, Rosa begins to experience satisfaction from the way that her mature beauty seems to guarantee an uninterrupted sequence of ever wealthier and more elevated protectors, and on more than one occasion takes pleasure in deceiving her official patron by giving herself to a younger lover. But such periods of confidence are often succeeded by moments of contrition, where she confesses that 'I was no longer frail through imperious necessity – I was depraved through sheer wantonness'.[38] And, as we have already seen, the novel ends in Rosa's social destitution but spiritual rehabilitation.

In the course of this moral switchback ride, the gender roles assigned by mid-Victorian bourgeois convention, with the code of chivalry that often metaphorically underpins them, come under severe pressure. This is reinforced by the way in which the narrative so often explores the theme of cross-dressing and gender confusion. When Rosa is brutally raped by her cousin, for example, he gains access to her chamber by dressing himself in the clothes of her intimate friend, his own sister Joanna, who 'bears a striking resemblance' to her 'effeminate' brother.[39] In a more comic vein, when Rosa takes revenge on a jealous protector, she dons a false moustache and military uniform to mercilessly horsewhip him in the guise of a fictional brother in the dragoons. All this is indeed heralded in the opening pages of the novel, where the perfidious squire's son is also represented as extraordinarily effeminate. The lengthy passage in question concludes: 'if he had chosen to dress himself up in female apparel, he might easily have passed for one of the sex. His lips were of the richest red – somewhat pouting – and forming a mouth such as might be envied by any lovely girl.'[40] Here, Reynolds's lurid imaginings, as he performs his own female impersonation in the role of the unfortunate woman, offers a precedent for those notorious scenes in Braddon's seminal sensational works of the early 1860s, where flaxen-curled Lucy Audley stuffs a surplus husband down a well, or statuesque, black-eyed Aurora Floyd flogs a cringing groom for mistreating her dog.

If, finally, Reynolds's sexual radicalism in his contributions to 'the literature of the kitchen' in the 1850s is distinctly circumscribed, then so is that of the sensationalists of the following decade. What both clearly share is a doubt about how far to go that seems to have been governed by commercial uncertainties as well as by ideological waverings. In the end what most separates him from Collins, Braddon, Wood or Reade is the sheer scale of Reynolds's narrative imaginings. The seemingly endless series of penny parts in the 'Memoirs' sequence fulfilled the function of soap opera for a mid-Victorian popular audience in ways that the middle-class literary miscellanies in which the sensation novels appeared never quite did. It is this also that renders *Mary Price* and its successors so inaccessible to later generations. Today they are only available at best in major research libraries or to intrepid collectors, and it is equally difficult to imagine persuading a publisher to reprint or a group of college students to read them in their monstrous entirety.

---

37 Reynolds, *Rosa Lambert*, ch. 33, p. 247.
38 Reynolds, *Rosa Lambert*, ch. 35, p. 271.
39 Reynolds, *Rosa Lambert*, ch. 28, p. 217.
40 Reynolds, *Rosa Lambert*, ch. 1, p. 3.

Chapter 13

The Virtue of Illegitimacy: Inheritance and Belonging in *The Dark Woman* and *Mary Price*

Ellen Bayuk Rosenman

The recent surge of interest in working-class writing has alerted scholars to some of its distinctive features, especially the close interrelation between fiction and politics. Melodrama infused political writing with a keen, Manichaean sense of right and wrong, powerlessness and power, distributed along class lines, while Chartist fiction vividly depicted the plight of workers through the frustration, despair and resistance of its characters. As Ian Haywood writes, 'the supposed barrier between the fictional and the political was highly permeable'[1] in working-class publications. As a Chartist activist, journalist and novelist, G.W.M. Reynolds traversed this barrier professionally and pioneered forms of politically relevant literature, interpolating polemics throughout his sprawling sensational novels. His phenomenally popular *Mysteries of London* (1844–48) reported annual statistics on poverty, for instance, while *The Seamstress* (1850) analysed the system of middlemen that depressed the wages of seamstresses through the speeches of a starving seamstress turned well-heeled prostitute with an impressive grasp of political economy. In these instances, permeability is achieved in the manifest content of the text, through direct reference to economic exploitation.

Less visible but equally important is the fantasy content of popular fiction – the sensational rhetoric and improbable plots that have generally been exempted from serious analysis, whether literary or political. But these features also have political meaning, though it is less easy to locate. It emerges from what Cornelius Castoriadis calls the 'social imaginary', a realm of dream, fantasy and desire that underlies and produces the social doctrines, practices and institutions that imperfectly embody

---

1   Ian Haywood, *The Revolution in Popular Literature: Print, Politics, and the People, 1790–1860* (Cambridge: Cambridge University Press, 2004), p. 172. See also Anne Humpherys, 'Popular Narrative and Political Discourse in *Reynolds's Weekly Newspaper*', in Laurel Brake and Aled Jones (eds), *Investigating Victorian Journalism* (New York: St Martin's, 1990); Rohan McWilliam, 'The Mysteries of G.W.M. Reynolds: Radicalism and Melodrama in Victorian Britain', in Malcolm Chase and Ian Dyck (eds), *Living and Learning: Essays in Honour of J.F.C. Harrison* (Aldershot: Scolar, 1996), pp. 182–98; Martha Vicinus, *The Industrial Muse: A Study of Nineteenth-century British Working-class Fiction* (New York: Barnes and Noble, 1974).

it. Surfacing from this realm, 'imaginary significations' make manifest the social imaginary, giving form to its inchoate, unspecified desires:

> Every society ... has attempted to give an answer to a few fundamental questions: Who are we as a collectivity? What are we for one another? Where and in what are we? What do we want; what do we desire; what are we lacking? ... The role of imaginary significations is to provide an answer to these questions, an answer that, obviously, neither 'reality' nor 'rationality' can provide.[2]

Reality and rationality cannot provide answers because these questions are not 'referential':[3] they are not posed explicitly and do not address the actual conditions of society. Instead, they extend the horizon of possibility, gesturing towards ideals rather than concrete political platforms or existing social structures. Working-class fiction and politics share the same social imaginary, a mythology of Englishness in which a forgotten but foundational past guarantees all English people full membership in the social body, a fantasied condition that defines political and economic exclusion as a scandalous injustice. Imaginary significations materialize this condition, furnishing it with a logic and a history.

In politics, the rhetoric of natural rights, along with the recurring symbols of the land and the hereditary aristocracy, performs this function. In G.W.M. Reynolds's *Mary Price*[4] and Malcolm J. Errym's *The Dark Woman*[5] imaginary signification takes the form of the same improbable but symbolically significant plot: that of aristocratic illegitimacy. In both novels, an impoverished character, revealed to be a member of a noble family through an illicit liaison, takes her or his rightful place within the family and society. As remote as this story might seem from the material realities of working-class readers, it nevertheless enacts the desire for social belonging. The idea of the social imaginary and its imaginary significations explains why, first, these novels fashion themselves from such particular – and particularly unlikely – materials, and second, why, in spite of their implausibility, they are politically relevant. Far from being 'escapist literature of the simplest sort',[6] in the words of Peter Haining's anthology of penny dreadfuls, these novels body forth the idealist underpinnings of popular politics, organizing utopian aspirations into compelling and accessible fantasies.

Although these novels are largely forgotten now, they would probably have been widely read in their day. Reynolds, one of the period's most popular novelists,

---

2   Cornelius Castoriadis, *The Imaginary Institution of Society*, trans. Kathleen Blamey (Cambridge, MA: MIT Press, 1987), pp. 146–7.

3   Castoriadis, *The Imaginary Institution of Society*, p. 147.

4   G.W.M. Reynolds, *Mary Price, or The Memoirs of a Servant-Maid*, 2 vols (London: John Dicks, 1852, 1853).

5   Malcolm J. Errym [James Malcolm Rymer], *The Dark Woman; or, the Days of the Prince Regent*, 2 vols (London: John Dicks, 1861). Rymer also published as Malcolm J. Merry. In this chapter I refer to him as 'Errym' because that is the name he used as the author of *The Dark Woman* and as a contributor to *RM* (see note 8).

6   Peter Haining, *The Penny Dreadful; or, Strange, Horrid & Sensational Tales!* (London: Victor Gollancz, 1976), jacket copy.

made *Mary Price* available in weekly penny issues, then in monthly and volume format. Errym was a bestselling novelist in his own right, jokingly called 'Ada' by his fellow-writers because of the runaway success of his penny dreadful *Ada the Betrayed* (1843).[7] He worked exclusively for *Reynolds's Miscellany* for several years, including the period when he wrote *The Dark Woman*, and so would have been immersed in Reynolds's radical politics, narrative practices and sensational style.[8] In other words, I see both novels as participating in a popular convention that, because of Reynolds's immense reach as an activist, journalist and novelist, must be reckoned with in any consideration of working-class reading.

Class and Narrative Conventions

Before I turn to *The Dark Woman* and *Mary Price*, I want to lay out some of the more familiar conventions of canonical novels that they revise so strikingly. These popular novels are easily disregarded because their fantasies depart in so many ways from those of the middle class, which has conditioned our sense of both Victorian culture and of plausible or persuasive narrative conventions. One reason working-class fiction seems so unrealistic is that it shows little interest in the middle-class characters who, one way or another, are assumed to dominate 'the nineteenth-century novel'.[9] The social imaginary of the middle class, obsessed with the urban working-class poor as the dark Other of bourgeois propriety, was largely irrelevant to these popular novels – not only for the obvious reason that they were not interested in 'othering' the working class but also because the middle class was not useful for their symbolic redistribution of power.[10] These novels did not reverse the gaze to 'other' the middle class, in which they have little psychic investment.[11] In contrast, the

---

7   George Augustus Sala, *London Up to Date*, 2nd edn (London: A. and C. Black, 1894), pp. 287–8.

8   Shortly before the publication of *The Dark Woman*, *RN* reported a party in Reynolds's honour attended by 'Mr. Errym', who is praised as one of the paper's 'principal contributors' (7 July 1861, p. 9).

9   From Ian Watt's early formulation to Michael McKeon's more complicated model of class formation to Dhor Wahrman's observation that the middle class controlled the means of *textual* if not political representation, the middle class has been considered a defining, though not exclusive, focus of Victorian fiction. See Ian Watt, *The Rise of the Novel: Studies in Defoe, Richardson, and Fielding* (Berkeley: University of California Press, 1957); Michael McKeon, *The Origins of the English Novel, 1600–1740* (Baltimore: Johns Hopkins University Press, 1987); Dhor Wahrman, *Imagining the Middle Class: The Political Representation of Class in Britain, c.1780–1840* (Cambridge: Cambridge University Press, 1995).

10   For what is still the most forceful articulation of this binary, see Peter Stallybrass and Allon White, *The Politics and Poetics of Transgression* (Ithaca, NY: Cornell University Press, 1986), pp. 123–48.

11   In *RN*, Reynolds mapped a different binary in which the middle class was absorbed into the aristocracy as a kind of copycat oppressor rather than a new economic force, employing a series of phrases that yoke old and new exploiters together: 'The Birth Aristocracy and the Money Aristocracy' (7 September 1851, p. 1), 'the joint aristocracies of birth and money' (12 October 1851, p. 8), 'the Birth Aristocracy and the Moneyocracy' (2 November 1851, p. 8).

aristocracy provides a rich symbol for the thematics of appropriation and belonging because it was imagined to enjoy an unshakeable social legitimacy. Through the laws and customs of inheritance, an aristocratic family line had, at least in theory, an inalienable identity and position: while its fortunes might rise or fall, only the end of the bloodline could eradicate its entitlements. Paradoxically, the exclusionary inherited privilege that so enraged Reynolds as a political thinker provided fertile imaginative material for redrawing the boundaries of society in fiction.

The treatment of illegitimacy undergoes a similar and even more dramatic revision amounting to a complete reversal. Because of its investment in female virtue, family boundaries and the transmission of property, canonical fiction presents illegitimacy as a ticking time bomb, waiting to explode apparently stable identities and relationships. While it does not always take the same form or produce the same consequences, illegitimacy is nearly always profoundly disruptive: a signifier of scandal and sexual transgression, a stigma – justified or not – on an apparently respectable member of society, a psychic wound, a dangerous secret. In Wilkie Collins's *Woman in White* (1859–60), it is suggestively linked to Anne Catherick's mental instability and Percival Glyde's malevolence; in Collins's *No Name* (1862) it exiles the Varnstone sisters from their beloved home. In Dickens's *Bleak House* (1852–53) it brutally undermines Esther's sense of self-worth as she labours under the stigma of bastardy. Women who bear these children, such as Lady Dedlock of *Bleak House* and Mrs Transome of George Eliot's *Felix Holt* (1866), are paralysed by remorse and the fear of discovery. As Jenny Bourne Taylor asserts, illegitimacy 'became the center of clashing concepts of shame, guilt, and responsibility, the social construction of otherness and the meaning of social inheritance'.[12]

A quick glance at the complicated plot of *Felix Holt*, which offers the most direct contrast to the novels I discuss, suggests the dark implications of the illegitimacy plot in canonical fiction. When Harold Transome returns to England from a shadowy past abroad and decides to run for Parliament, he asserts himself in a world he barely knows. Treating people and customs with casual disdain, he antagonizes Jerrym, a powerful local lawyer who has protected the family estate in his absence. At the height of their conflict, Jerrym thunders, '*I am your father*',[13] knowing that this revelation will dishonour and disinherit Harold and expose his mother's infidelity. Harold's illegitimacy only confirms his tenuous attachment to his family and the community. With his mysterious foreign past and high-handed ignorance, he has always *seemed* illegitimate. Although he eventually reclaims the estate, this announcement strips him of his sense of entitlement. Family bonds are destroyed; parent–child relations are sites of shame, dishonesty and aggression.

The status of the estate itself further challenges family relationships. Generations past, it came into the possession of Harold's family – actually named Durfey – when

---

12   Jenny Bourne Taylor, 'Nobody's Secret: Illegitimate Inheritance and the Uncertainties of Memory', *Nineteenth-century Contexts*, 21 (2000): 574. Anthony Trollope's *Dr Thorne* (1858) is a rare departure from this pattern, featuring an illegitimate heroine who is never stigmatized by her community. I thank Deborah Morse for this reference.

13   George Eliot, *Felix Holt, the Radical*, ed. Peter Coveney (Harmondsworth: Penguin, 1972), p. 581, italics in original.

a profligate son angered his father by selling his rights to the highest bidder. Adopting the Transome name to mask the contingency of their ownership, Harold's family retains the estate through Jerrym's unscrupulous manipulations despite a superior claim. When Harold's parentage is revealed, illegitimacy opens a chasm between generations, underscoring the fact that there is nothing natural about the passage of the estate from one hand to another. Although Peter Coveney complains that 'there is nothing being said *through* [this] complexity',[14] its mind-bending convolutions are exactly the point, for they insist on the arbitrary, unstable nature of patrilineal inheritance and its assumption of a secure bloodline. Here inheritance is subject to individual caprice, while family boundaries can be redrawn by a sharp lawyer for the right price. Figuring female transgression, male hubris and the fragility of generational ties, Harold's illegitimacy not only signifies the unworthiness of the Durfey-Transome family, it also exposes the system of inheritance as arbitrary, unjust and itself illegitimate.

In *The Dark Woman* and *Mary Price*, the discovery of illegitimacy is, surprisingly, a good thing, enabling worthy characters to ascend socially without leaving their working-class identities and virtues behind. These popular novels create 'a slippage, a shift in meaning in which available symbols are invested with other significations than their "normal" or canonical signification',[15] in Castoriadis's words, as they foreground the aristocracy and reverse the meaning of illegitimacy in canonical novels described above. Anchored in aristocratic bloodlines, the new-found status of popular protagonists signifies a durable, inalienable social membership immune to the vagaries of fortune or individual will. Further, these characters deserve, enjoy and maintain their new status, in contrast to canonical novels in which class ascension seldom brings happiness, and new social identities are generally represented as both fraudulent and insecure, a dangerous form of 'passing'.[16] But in *The Dark Woman* and *Mary Price*, the honesty and humility bred by a modest upbringing rejuvenate corrupt aristocratic families, infusing them with a much-needed moral tone. Breaking the log jam of fixed social structures, illegitimacy inserts new characters into chains of inheritance, granting them 'bodies that matter',[17] to adapt a familiar phrase. While

---

14 Eliot, *Felix Holt*, p. 629.

15 Castoriadis, *The Imaginary Institution of Society*, p. 127. Note also Castoriadis's claim that '[e]very symbolism is built on the ruins of earlier symbolic edifices and uses their materials' (p. 121). While the traditional symbolism of the aristocracy cannot be said to be in ruins, Reynolds and Errym rework both its traditional significance as a site of privilege and its meaning within radical politics – the 'Old Corruption' that gorges itself on the nation's resources. The familiarity of the aristocracy as a symbol as well as a group of actual individuals and families is surely part of the power of these novels to speak to their readers.

16 Consider Pip's estrangement at the end of *Great Expectations* (1860–61) and the careers of such schemers as Lady Audley, Becky Sharpe, Lizzie Eustace and Ferdinand Lopez. There are obvious exceptions to this generalization, such as Jane Eyre in *Jane Eyre* (1847) and Lucy Morris in *The Eustace Diamonds* (1873), but for these characters social mobility certifies a legitimacy they already possess by virtue of birth – in spite of their relative poverty, they are both gentlewomen.

17 Judith Butler, *Bodies That Matter: On the Discursive Limits of 'Sex'* (New York: Routledge, 1993).

common law called the bastard *filius nullius*, 'the son of no one' with no claim to inheritance or the family name, the protagonists of *The Dark Woman* and *Mary Price* achieve both in what the novels present as a fitting redistribution of privilege.

The Plot of Aristocratic Illegitimacy

The central plot of *The Dark Woman* hinges on the claim of Linda Mowbray that her son Allan Fearon is the legitimate child of the Prince Regent and therefore heir to the English throne (among her many identities, Linda leads a band of criminals under the alias 'The Dark Woman'). Beginning the novel in near poverty, in love with an equally virtuous and equally impoverished seamstress, Allan shows no interest in social advancement. Indeed, believing himself to be an orphan, he has no inkling of his relationship to either Linda or the Prince Regent. Even when his mother finds him, he refuses to accept any of her considerable resources because he cannot be sure they really belong to her and thus to him: 'I know not from whence these riches have come to you, but for the present I would fain be poor Allan Fearon, with nothing to depend on but these two hands, and this willing mind, for subsistence, than I would share the wealth the source of which I know not.'[18] His fears are well grounded, for Linda has amassed her wealth through her illegal activities as 'The Dark Woman'. A model of personal virtue, Allan clearly outshines the legitimate members of the royal family, especially the Prince Regent's notorious daughter Charlotte. The Dark Woman asks the Prince Regent rhetorically:

> Who and what is this daughter that you so madly prefer to the son providence has preserved for you? Dare you compare them? What is he? Is he not all that is noble – all that is great – all that a prince should be? ... And the daughter? What is she? ... A thing of wild impulses and willful caprices – a creature who even now finds it difficult to fill up the circle of her attendants, from the natural dislike of those who are modest, honourable, truthful, and gentle, to endure Princess Charlotte ...[19]

In the end, although Linda's marriage certificate proves a forgery, as illicit as her fortune, and 'the laws, civil and ecclesiastical'[20] cannot acknowledge him as a legitimate son, his lack of legal status does not erase the blood tie between Allan and the Prince Regent. 'The Regent is my father by *nature*',[21] Allan declares, and his father agrees. Linda and the Prince Regent fight their battle over succession with documents, but these are flimsy, ineffectual tokens that can be forged, misdated, falsely authenticated with stolen seals and destroyed. Blood is the thing itself, the ultimate determinant of identity, whose authority these papers vainly try to usurp. While this tie is not enough to place him within the royal succession, it does qualify him to become a member of the royal family and grants him access to his father's wealth, which he regards as rightfully his, unlike his mother's. It would be 'a false

18 Errym, *The Dark Woman*, vol. 1, ch. 92, p. 354.
19 Errym, *The Dark Woman*, vol. 1, ch. 110, p. 416.
20 Errym, *The Dark Woman*, vol. 2, ch. 146, p. 117.
21 Errym, *The Dark Woman*, vol. 2, ch. 146, p. 117.

and poor pride',[22] he decides, to refuse what is, after all, family money. The royal bloodline confers other benefits as well: the Prince Regent renames him Allan Fitz-George to signify their relationship, appoints him an officer of the Guards, declares him 'a prince of blood royal',[23] and grants him the title of Earl. Allan is no social impostor who has learned to mimic upper-class manners but whose 'real' lower-class identity always lurks below the surface. Genetically coded for his new rank, he can rest secure in his Earldom.

Reynolds's *Mary Price* rests on the same improbable fantasy of noble illegitimacy. Though the titular heroine is not herself illegitimate, her mother is the cast-off child of an illicit union involving the wealthy Clavering family. Like Allan, Mary is characterized by her worthy conduct and indifference to material temptations. Just as Allan refuses his mother's fortune, Mary rejects an employer's gift of fine clothing, preferring to remain a servant-girl rather than ape the elegance of a lady. And, as in *The Dark Woman*, personal virtue is a necessary but insufficient condition for social mobility. The noble Sir Quentin is prevented from proposing to Mary because his parents require him to marry within his class, that is, to find a wife who possesses both an aristocratic lineage and £30,000. When Mary inherits the requisite fortune from a wealthy friend, Quentin's older brother still refuses to sanction the marriage: 'Who made her a lady?' he asks rhetorically.[24] Quentin declares, 'Her own merits', but despite her faultless character, Mary's worth must be certified by blood.[25] This, too, the novel eventually provides, when the villainous Sir Aubrey Clavering, who has tormented her throughout the novel, inherits the family estate and reveals on his deathbed that Mary is actually his cousin through the illicit liaison of their shared grandmother. He announces: 'The blood of the Claverings rolls in your veins, Mary Price; and therefore I have willed unto you – and for many reasons, to *you* alone – the Hall and the domain of my ancestors.'[26] Sir Aubrey insists that she publicly declare her membership to the family by taking the name of Clavering, as Allan was rechristened Fitz-George, and that she take on sole possession of the estate: 'in case of marriage, I was to have my own property settled upon myself; and the meaning of these injunctions was explained by the desire of the testator to ensure me a firm position in wealth and prosperity against the vicissitudes and casualties of life.'[27] Through her eight employers, numerous relocations, threats, kidnappings, hair's-breadth escapes, Mary has seen her share of the 'vicissitudes and casualties of life', but Sir Aubrey's conditions should give us pause. Mary is about to marry her true love, the only character in the 700-page novel honourable enough to deserve her. Why does she need protection from such a paragon of a husband?

In point of fact, this is a prudent move, since when Eustace conceives the wild scheme of actually working for a living – 'Suppose, Mary – that I obtain [the £30,000]

---

22 Errym, *The Dark Woman*, vol. 2, ch. 146, p. 117.
23 Errym, *The Dark Woman*, vol. 2, ch. 246, p. 354.
24 Reynolds, *Mary Price*, vol. 2, ch. 146, p. 328.
25 Reynolds, *Mary Price*, vol. 2, ch. 146, p. 328.
26 Reynolds, *Mary Price*, vol. 2, ch. 159, p. 346, italics in original.
27 Reynolds, *Mary Price*, vol. 2, ch. 159, p. 348.

– suppose I acquire it by dint of honest industry'[28] – he is quickly embroiled in an unscrupulous speculation, loses all his money and is sent to debtors' prison, from which Mary eventually rescues him with her first inheritance. But the answer goes deeper than her patrician lover's ignorance of sharp business practices. Ironically, her depraved cousin proves a better guarantee of stability than her exemplary husband because family inheritance is given to her absolutely and permanently. In contrast to *Felix Holt*, inheritance is presented as fixing the inheritor in a secure social position and family identity. As in *The Dark Woman*, when Allan says, 'The Regent is my father by *nature*', that same magic word signifies the inalienability of blood relations. When his snobbish brother threatens to disavow their relationship if he marries Mary, Eustace declares: 'But who gives you the power, Ferdinand.... You are my brother – and you cannot unmake yourself from what *nature* has made you.'[29] Likewise, nature grafts Mary firmly to a family and a social place of her own, independent of marriage.

In their use of aristocratic inheritance to establish identity and prosperity, these works run counter to the dominant trend Ruth Perry identifies in realist novels: the increasing importance of conjugal over consanguine relations, of the chosen and constructed family over the family of origin. In these popular novels, however, personal attachments cannot be secured until consanguine relationships are uncovered and certified. Perry notes that an early eighteenth-century shift in inheritance practices consolidated the boundaries of the nuclear family; its 'psychological effect', she notes, was 'to reinforce loyalty to families constructed by marriage and undermine "investment" [in both economic and emotional sense] in those families one had been born into'.[30] Perry traces the reverberations of this shift in the literary dominance of the marriage plot. In these popular novels, however, families of origin retain a central place, offering more relevant symbolic patterns for the fantasy of belonging.

The Politics of Fiction: Natural Rights and the Land

Rewarding its humble protagonists with aristocratic status, the plot of noble illegitimacy might seem to represent, at best, a crude wishful thinking, and at worst, bad faith, especially for Reynolds, whose unrelenting attack on the aristocracy secured his popularity with working-class readers. As a political fable, however, this plot resonates strongly with Chartist ideas in circulation around the novels. The imaginary construction of a foundational, inclusive British nation underlies popular politics and fiction, linking them through shared fantasies of entitlement and restitution.

---

28 Reynolds, *Mary Price*, vol. 2, ch. 127, p. 227.

29 Reynolds, *Mary Price*, vol. 2, ch. 147, p. 330, my italics.

30 Ruth Perry, *Novel Relations: The Transformation of Kinship in English Literature and Culture, 1748–1818* (Cambridge: Cambridge University Press, 2004), p. 215. This pattern structures the resolution of *Felix Holt*, in which Esther, the true inheritor of the Transome estate, gives it up to Harold so that she can marry the novel's working-class hero and remain close to her humble adoptive father.

At the heart of this political message is the idea of 'natural right', one of the most potent and widely used rhetorics of popular protest. This rhetoric claimed that all members of society were entitled to political representation and economic security but that the rapaciousness of the upper classes had unjustly excluded the poor – just as Mary Price and Allan Fearon are exiled from the privileges that should be theirs by birth. The idea of natural rights insisted that the people did not claim any new or unjustified power but sought only their birthrights as Englishmen. As E.P. Thompson writes, Chartists demanded that 'the community ... succor the needy and the helpless, not out of charity, but as of right'.[31] When Allan rejects his mother's riches but embraces his father's privilege, when Mary refuses her employer's gift of clothing but accepts the Clavering estate, these novels make just such a distinction between charity and rights. They insist upon the deserved inclusion of their protagonists as a literal matter of birthright.

Above all, these fantasies were concentrated in the figure of the land, stolen from its legitimate heirs, the people. Radical politics asserted a historical origin to this theft, tracing it to the Norman invasion, when foreigners seized English land to reward their allies and secure their control of the country.[32] In these arguments, land took on several meanings. It was source and symbol of the nation's abundant resources, illicitly appropriated by generations of wealthy noblemen for their own private use through the acts of enclosure and the game laws. It was also a trope for the nation itself, which should have belonged to all its people. Perverting 'the land' into private property, the aristocracy then erected property qualifications for suffrage that disenfranchised most of the population. In this form, land signified the people's confiscated rights to their own nation. The land, then, was a potent, multi-layered symbol within the rhetoric of natural rights, which in turn emerged from the social imaginary that posited a unified, egalitarian pre-Norman England.

Reynolds drew extensively on these interlocking ideas of the land in *Reynolds's Newspaper*.[33] Consistently throughout the 1850s and 1860s, he attributes injustice and

---

31 E.P. Thompson, *The Making of the English Working Class* (1963; New York: Vintage, 1966), p. 760.

32 For an elaboration of this idea, see Anne Janowitz, 'The Case of Romantic Chartism: Rethinking Class', in Wai Chee Dimock and Michael T. Gilmore (eds), *Literary Studies and Social Formations* (New York: Columbia University Press, 1994), p. 252; Michael Shirley, 'On Wings of Everlasting Power: G.W.M. Reynolds and *Reynolds's Newspaper*, 1848–76' (PhD thesis, University of Illinois, 1996), pp. 63–4. The fact that, even in the allegedly indigenous, pre-Norman Britain, land was still transferred through inheritance suggests the extent to which this argument, though based in history, was also imaginary, and also suggests why the plot device of inheritance is so important in these popular novels. It is a problematic that must be worked out.

33 Although some critics have found Reynolds's obsession with land and the aristocracy outdated, revisionist scholarship has pointed to his continuing relevance in the second half of the century, especially considering the aristocracy's ongoing political if not economic dominance (see McWilliam, 'The Mysteries of G.W.M. Reynolds', and Shirley, 'On Wings of Everlasting Power'; also Margot Finn, *After Chartism: Class and Nation in English Radical Politics, 1848–1874* [Cambridge: Cambridge University Press, 2003]). Even in terms of economics, the factory system was not yet a hegemonic institution; it 'had not achieved the

poverty to the privatization of the land: 'in the exhaustless bounty of nature might be found not merely sufficiency but likewise a superfluity, for every dweller on British soil; and yet the land is still either locked up in the possession of the monopolists, or else left waste and unprofitable', he declares.[34] The idea that possession of land was the 'heritage and birthright' of the people was a continuing theme in *Reynolds's Newspaper*.[35] The day the first instalment of *Mary Price* appeared, *Reynolds's Newspaper* called the inherited lands, wealth and privilege of the aristocracy 'stolen goods' that were 'robbed'[36] from the people and then turned into 'heir-looms',[37] confined in exclusionary chains of inheritance. Proffering some small redress to this injustice, *Reynolds's Newspaper* ran frequent advertisements for the Freehold Society, which promised to help readers regain both the actual property and the political enfranchisement that should have been theirs all along: 'By a mere saving of twopence per day, a working-man may place himself upon the same footing in the event of an election as the proudest aristocrat in the country.'[38]

Journalist and activist Julian Harney echoes this claim. Serving with Reynolds on the executive commission of the National Charter Association from 1849 to 1851, Harney was also a fellow editor whose newspapers, *Democratic Review* and *Red Republican*, were advertised by Reynolds as useful resources for his readers. In his demand for the redistribution of wealth, Harney implicitly clarifies the plot of aristocratic illegitimacy:

> The feudal aristocracy being doomed to expire, care should be taken that no new aristocracy be allowed to take their place. With that view, THE LAND MUST BE MADE NATIONAL PROPERTY.... THE LAND BELONGS TO ALL, and the natural right of all is superior to the falsely asserted rights of conquest or purchase.[39]

In the era of the aristocracy's decline, the land should revert to its rightful owners, the people of England. While the Freehold Society proposed a small-scale, practical step towards redistributing land, *The Dark Woman* and *Mary Price* offer a fantastic imaginative fulfilment of Harney's demand, refashioning this hoped-for restitution in their implausible plots. The aristocracy willingly grants its privilege to working-class protagonists by recognizing their 'natural right' to inherit land, wealth and social standing through their shared bloodline, just as journalist-activists like Reynolds and

---

dominance in mid-Victorian imaginations that we might expect in part because [it] had not achieved that dominance in production.... [I]n 1850, less than half of British textile workers were employed in factories.' See Elaine Freedgood, *Factory Production in Nineteenth-century Britain* (New York: Oxford, 2003), p. 2. Remember too that London, home of Reynolds's papers and much of his audience, was a heterogeneous metropolitan centre and not a factory town like Manchester or Birmingham.

34 'Conditions and Prospects of the Country', *RN*, 12 October 1851, p. 1.

35 'Freedom's Boast and Slavery's Reality', *RN*, 21 September 1851, p. 1.

36 'Shall the Extension of the Suffrage be Partial or Universal?' *RN*, 2 November 1851, p. 8.

37 'Murderous Result of Vile Game Laws', *RN*, 2 November 1851, p. 14.

38 *RN*, 5 October 1851, p. 14.

39 Julian Harney, 'The Charter and Something More!' *Democratic Review of British and Foreign Politics, History, and Literature* (February 1850), p. 351.

Harney insisted on the restoration of unjustly confiscated 'heir-looms' – the land and political participation that ought to have been the rightful property of all.

Reynolds's treatment of the game laws, like his condensation of inherited privilege into the metaphor of the 'heir-loom', operates as a hinge between the concrete novelistic detail and fantasies of belonging, suggesting in miniature the method of these novels. Symbolizing and re-enacting aristocratic theft, game laws appear frequently in Reynolds's journalism. During the serialization of *Mary Price*, *Reynolds's Newspaper* launched a series of protests against their existence and enforcement. The figure of the poacher became a kind of activist, exercising his legitimate right to partake of nature's plenty, unlike 'the pampered aristocrat who fattens upon pensions granted to his harlot ancestry, or estates acquired by the political prostitution of himself or his forefathers'.[40] It is no accident, then, that one of Mary's most celebrated actions is to testify on behalf of an alleged poacher who is attacked by Clavering's evil gamekeeper – a deed famous enough to acquire its own name, 'The Derby Incident'. Throughout the novel, Mary is regularly hailed as the heroine of the trial by miscellaneous characters. Although her testimony does not seem particularly heroic, its prominence lies in its symbolic meaning, as a protest against the appropriation of land. Her inheritance not only rewards her as a deserving person but also appropriates and democratizes aristocratic privilege, delivering the Clavering estate to someone with no interest in policing the geographical boundaries of her new-found status.[41]

Within this political context, the illegitimacy that functions as a stigma in common law and canonical fiction takes on a positive meaning. First, it registers the protagonists' distance from the depravity of aristocrats in their strong characters, nurtured in their respectable working-class homes, as we saw in the contrast between Allan Fearon and Princess Charlotte, and in their divestiture of aristocratic prerogatives such as game laws. Second, paradoxically, it represents the legitimacy of their claim to inclusion, an entitlement signified by blood ties. Through illegitimacy, these novels can both dis-identify with the abuses of 'Old Corruption' and loosen the boundaries of its privileges. (Contrast this double attitude with the simpler fantasy of the foundling plot, in which the discovery of *legitimate* noble birth erases the protagonist's humble origins, implying that only pure noble blood can produce gentility and encouraging straightforward identification with the higher social order.[42]) These novels emplot the rhetoric of natural rights in their narrative conventions to enact its underlying desires.

---

40   'Poaching No Crime', *RN*, 2 November 1851, p. 6. This issue, published almost simultaneously with the first instalment of *Mary Price*, contained another attack, 'Murderous Result of Vile Game Laws' (p. 14). Such articles continued into the next decade; see 'A Sharp-sighted Gamekeeper', about a gamekeeper who testified to the identity of an alleged poacher although he was standing over five hundred yards away (5 January 1862, p. 6). Thus, while *The Dark Woman* does not include any incidents of poaching, the issue continued to surface in its general context as a reminder of illicit aristocratic possession of land.

41   It must be said that *Mary Price* also has limits as a version of Chartist politics. 'Universal' suffrage actually meant universal *male* suffrage.

42   For a discussion of the contrast between bastards and foundlings in the eighteenth century, see Lisa Zunshine, *Bastards and Foundlings: Illegitimacy in Eighteenth-century*

Contextual elements encouraged readers to see these novels as more than escapist fantasies. Produced in a context saturated with arguments about the injustice of class relations in which fiction and political commentary overlapped, these novels took on another layer of significance within what Margot Finn calls 'the ... infrastructure of late Chartism' – the network of publishers, activists and authors engaged in radicalizing the masses through fiction as well as polemic.[43] Emerging from this network, intertextual references pointed readers back and forth from politics to entertainment. They constitute one of the most important signifying resources of popular fiction. Reynolds's publications stood at the centre of this network. *Mary Price* was advertised extensively in both *Reynolds's Miscellany* and *Reynolds's Newspaper*, which ran an excerpt in the 2 November 1851 issue to pique readers' interest. *Reynolds's Miscellany* and *Reynolds's Newspaper* also advertised *The Dark Woman* when it first appeared.[44] Harney, who insisted that the land should revert to the people, promoted Reynolds's journalism in his own publications, a favour that Reynolds returned.[45] Since many members of the working class did their reading in public institutions such as coffee houses, mechanics institutes, working-class libraries, factories and workshops that carried an array of printed material, these intertextual relationships were close at hand.[46] Furthermore, readers would likely have known how to use this context to read fiction as a kind of political allegory. *Pilgrim's Progress* was a favourite of working-class readers, a fact that Chartist writers exploited in works such as Thomas Doubleday's *The Political Pilgrim's Progress*, in which the Radical and his family leave the City of Plunder and enter the City of Reform.[47] While Reynolds and Errym did not simply translate the Chartist platform into fiction as Doubleday did, these reading practices could infuse an unrealistic popular novel with political resonance.

At the same time, readers were encouraged to read *Mary Price*, at least, as a novel with genuine purchase on reality with subplots they would recognize as lived experience. Reynolds promoted it as a well-documented account of a servant's life as well as an exciting tale. Specific links told readers that the novel functioned as an exposé of domestic service, the largest form of employment in mid-century England.[48] *Reynolds's Newspaper* carried articles detailing the abuses suffered by servant girls

---

England (Columbus, OH: Ohio State University Press, 2005).

43   Finn, *After Chartism*, p. 116.

44   *RM*, 10 August 1861, p. 12; *RN*, 25 August 1861, p. 8.

45   Finn, *After Chartism*, pp. 115–16.

46   Richard Altick, *The English Common Reader: A Social History of the Mass Reading Public, 1800–1900*, 2nd edn (1957; Columbus, OH: Ohio State University Press, 1998), p. 342; Patricia Anderson, *The Printed Image and the Transformation of Popular Culture, 1790–1860* (Oxford: Clarendon Press, 1991), p. 146.

47   For a discussion of the popularity of *Pilgrim's Progress* among working-class readers, see Jonathan Rose, *The Intellectual Life of the British Working Classes* (New Haven, CT: Yale University Press, 2001), esp. pp. 93–8. Ian Haywood has reprinted Doubleday's allegory in Ian Haywood (ed.), *Chartist Fiction: Thomas Doubleday, The Political Pilgrim's Progress, Thomas Martin Wheeler, Sunshine and Shadow* (Aldershot: Ashgate, 1999), pp. 17–63.

48   Bruce Robbins, *The Servant's Hand: English Fiction from Below* (Durham, NC: Duke University Press, 1993), p. xi.

not long before the publication of *Mary Price*.[49] While Reynolds did not adapt specific incidents from these articles to his fiction (and the abuses described were probably horrific enough to destroy the reader's pleasure), he did signal his intention to provide a realistic story in his advertisements, which suggest an expanding sense of the novel's social relevance. Early notices define the novel as a class commentary on the plight of female servants – 'the tyrannies, caprices, and cruelties which they too frequently endure'. Subsequent advertisements in both *Reynolds's Newspaper* and *Reynolds's Miscellany* include this invitation to readers: 'it is Mr. Reynolds's object, by his new tale, to *shame* those families which are now despotic towards their servants into a more humane and Christian-like behaviour. *Servants who have special grievances to complain of, would do well to send the particulars to Mr. Reynolds, who will render the information available in the working out of his story.*'[50] Partway through the novel's serialization, he assured readers: 'Even before it [*Mary Price*] was published, and simply from the hint given to domestic servants in the advertisements, we received an immense number of letters from persons of that class, setting forth their grievances.'[51] Although I have no proof, this claim, along with the fact that Reynolds inserted his initial invitation after several segments of the novel had already been published, leads me to think that the first number prompted such letters, and that he saw the opportunity to draw readers further into the tale. It is impossible to know whether readers actually accepted this invitation or, if they did, whether Reynolds included their testimony in the novel. Certain sections could easily have been drawn from insider information: the description of one of Mary's employers forcing her to participate in his scheme to adulterate the groceries he sells, for instance, or the servants' shrewd reversal of exploitation by selling the cast-off clothing their employers condescendingly bestow on them, turning charity into economic enterprise.

But what may be more significant than the particular content is the kind of reception the advertisements and these incidents imply. Depictions of a servant's tribulations coexist with the improbable story of Mary's rise in status; the painful wrongs she endures are healed across the conventional divide between realism and the fantasy of aristocratic illegitimacy. As I have argued elsewhere, Reynolds's fiction operates according to a 'heterogeneous aesthetic'[52] in which different generic conventions exist side by side, with no attempt to achieve coherence. Jonathan Rose

---

49 'Alleged Brutality to a Servant Girl,' *RN*, 31 August 1851, p. 10; 'Ill Treatment of a Servant Girl,' *RN*, 5 October 1851, p. 13.

50 The original advertisement appeared in *RM*, 7 November 1851, p. 256, announcing the publication of *Mary Price* in weekly penny and monthly sixpenny parts. The advertisements asking servants to report their experience began in *RM* on 7 February 1852, p. 48, and continued through 20 March 1852, p. 144; the final advertisement for the novel appears in *RM* on 8 January 1853, p. 384. *RN* ran its first advertisement on 2 November 1851, p. 2, whetting readers' appetites with an excerpt depicting Mary's mistreatment at the hands of a harsh mistress: 'Oh! it was so easy for Mrs. Twisden to trample on *me*!' (italics in original). It added the invitation for readers to submit their own experiences on 16 November 1852, p. 8.

51 *RM*, 6 December 1851, p. 319.

52 Ellen Rosenman, *Unauthorized Pleasures: Accounts of Victorian Erotic Experience* (Ithaca, NY: Cornell University Press, 2003), p. 121.

makes a similar point about working-class readers for whom the 'frames' for fiction and non-fiction were flexible and 'interchangeable'[53] rather than mutually exclusive. It is possible that readers moved without dissonance from Mary's realistic deprivation to the fantasied restitution of aristocratic inheritance, tracing thematic continuities between the two in spite of what seems to us like a jarring shift in register. Encouraged to identify with Mary through first-person narration and through appeals to their own experience, readers could process the novel as the pseudo-autobiography of a realistic double while also absorbing its motivating desires.

The Dark Woman and *Mary Price* remind us that fantasy is not necessarily an escape from politics. It can function as a powerful form of address to a mass public and, even more significantly, can generate the symbolic investments that shape a movement's agenda. These novels also expand our sense of 'Victorian literature' as a large and variegated terrain, sharpening our understanding of the traditional canon by defamiliarizing its conventions. In the case of illegitimacy, the identification with social stigmatization has been made so consistently that this meaning seems natural, almost denotative. But its divergent treatment in *Mary Price* and *The Dark Woman* posits other definitions of respectability, other kinship values, and other structures of belonging. Emerging from a different social imaginary than that of their middle-class counterparts, these novels develop their own signifying resources, representing an alternative literary history. Following Fredric Jameson, Rob Breton recently characterized the *deus ex machina* device in Chartist fiction as an 'ideologeme', 'the smallest intelligible unit of the essentially antagonistic collective discourses of class';[54] illegitimacy, I would argue, has the same status. In making this claim, I am also urging a consideration of popular fiction as a distinctive body of literature with its own tropes, conventions and contexts that we are only beginning to understand.

---

53 Rose, *The Intellectual Life of the British Working Classes*, p. 106.
54 Rob Breton, 'Ghosts in the Machine: Plotting in Chartist and Working-class Fiction,' *Victorian Studies*, 47 (2005): 558.

Chapter 14

The Mysteries of Reading: Text and Illustration in the Fiction of G.W.M. Reynolds

Brian Maidment

As successive editions of the *Cambridge Bibliography of English Literature* have noted, 'the bibliography of Reynolds is extremely obscure'[1] and 'the publication dates of Reynolds's fiction are difficult to determine' with the various titles 'issued and re-issued in volume form by various publishers for decades',[2] usually after serialized first publication in magazines. The difficulties posed by such levels of unknowing are discussed elsewhere in this volume, but the fecundity, obscurity and popularity of Reynolds's work causes particular problems for even a brief general discussion of the illustrations which invariably accompanied, and on some occasions even structured, the texts. This chapter depends on many years of acquaintance with a good range of Reynolds's texts in various editions, and on some attempt to survey the periodical ur-texts of the novels. Yet only relatively little of Reynolds's output can be viewed in public collections in a range of editions. Additionally, survival of his work has largely depended on either the binding up of part issues into volume format or on hardback reissues. Many scholarly libraries have been reluctant to give shelf space to such apparently trivial and lowbrow ephemeral fiction, sharing the views of the anonymous author of *James Bright the Shopman* that 'cheap shilling novels ... issue from the press like fumes from the mouth of hell' and destroy 'all relish from anything less hurtful than themselves'.[3]

But if the 'lowness' and social obloquy heaped on Reynolds's work have caused his publications to survive in a haphazard way, the appearance of those volumes that do still exist creates further interpretative complexity related to the difficulties of reading off the social and intellectual level of the implied reader or likely purchaser of those kinds of serial fiction using the particular formats employed by Reynolds and his publishers. On the whole the volumes of Reynolds I have seen, even the 'cheap' Dicks reprints, look relatively sophisticated and even 'genteel' to modern eyes, with their double-columned pages held within discrete double rules, and with wood-engraved vignette illustrations, often highly finished and tonally complex,

1   *The New Cambridge Bibliography of English Literature*, ed. George Watson, 2nd edn (Cambridge: Cambridge University Press, 1969), vol. 3, p. 960.

2   *The Cambridge Bibliography of English Literature*, ed. Joanne Shattock, 3rd edn (Cambridge: Cambridge University Press, 1999), vol. 4, p. 1389.

3   Anon, *James Bright the Shopman* (London: John Henry Parker, n.d.), p. 37.

forming an immediately familiar first page to each of the serial parts. Thus the rhythm of serial publication, as well as its visual pleasures, was maintained even in the volume format of Reynolds's work, a rhythm largely denied in the volume reprints of writers like Dickens, Thackeray and Trollope,[4] who tended to use separate page illustrations to invoke an older, more stringent kind of gentility and thus established a subordinate role for illustration against the primacy of the text.

In the light of this kind of bibliographical complexity and interest in the formats of serial publication, this chapter seeks to offer, in addition to a brief discussion of Reynolds's extended and varied sequence of artist collaborators, some speculations about what might be called the 'reading experience' of Reynolds's texts, suggesting how his books both self-consciously acknowledge the visual elements of the text and yet, frequently, frustrate the reader by failing to maintain any kind of useful balance between the verbal demands of the text and the visual experience contained within it. In particular, the focus will be on *The Days of Hogarth; or The Mysteries of Old London* (first published in volume form in 1847–48 between Reynolds's two extended 'Mysteries' sequences), a novel conceived and worked through in an extremely complex relationship with its visual sources.

Reynolds's Illustrated Texts

Anything beyond a superficial reading of Reynolds's work begins to suggest a number of assumptions about the nature and purpose of illustration, not just in these particular fictions but also as part of wider Victorian reading practices. Almost all of Reynolds's novels were illustrated regardless of their cost or intended readership. Most of his works used serialized part issue publication as a mechanism for the display of a weekly title-page wood-engraved vignette, a practice drawn from the formats of magazine publication where the lead serialized fiction would advertise its presence graphically every week. This method of re-publication is hardly surprising given Reynolds's access to, and widespread use of, periodicals that he edited as the place of first publication of his fiction.[5] Given Reynolds's reputation as a 'popular' author, a subsequent assumption might be that the centrality of illustration to his work was largely driven by commercial rather than aesthetic motives, and thus primarily formed a means through which readers might be attracted to buying his work. Such attraction might derive from both aesthetic pleasures and the recognition of a 'brand' format of the kind used so successfully by Dickens and Thackeray in their weekly or monthly serializations.

But beyond the commercial imperatives that insisted on illustration, we must consider some more difficult issues to do with the ways illustrations are read and consumed. How were Reynolds's illustrations read or consumed alongside the

---

4   For a general overview of the relationship between Victorian fiction and its illustrators see John R. Harvey, *Victorian Novelists and Their Illustrators* (London: Sidgwick and Jackson, 1970). Of Reynolds's works, Harvey discusses *Pickwick Abroad* on pp. 15–16 and *The Days of Hogarth* on pp. 49–50, which he describes as 'a remarkable prose imitation' of Hogarth.

5   See Andrew King, *The London Journal 1845–1883: Periodicals, Production and Gender* (Aldershot: Ashgate, 2004).

texts? Did the illustrations provide a titillating introduction to each part issue aimed primarily at drawing in the reader to the purchase of the text? Or did they form some kind of 'alternative' narrative for the reader too lazy or adequately literate to tackle the serried double columns of printed texts? Were the illustrations ever detached from the text to form separate narratives or decorative effects in the form of scrapbooks or other autonomous forms of textuality? Or were the illustrations rather intended to be read closely and attentively alongside the text as a form of commentary on, or even interpretation of, the accompanying fiction? In this context, the distinction John Buchanan-Brown makes between 'embellishment' and 'illustration' in his study of early Victorian book illustration loses much of its force. Buchanan-Brown, asserting that 'both words are good period words', acknowledges that the strict sense of 'illustrations' is 'pictorial aids to the understanding of the text' but that his interest is in 'the decorative adjuncts of letterpress'.[6] Yet both these definitions offer images of a vastly subordinate and inferior status to that of the text, a view reiterated by Harvey, who remarks of *The Days of Hogarth* that 'the narrative is so contrived that these [i.e., the wood engravings] seem merely illustrations to Reynolds's prose'.[7] One issue discussed in this chapter is how far Reynolds's ostentatiously illustrated fiction, often assumed to be addressed to relatively unsophisticated readers, asserts visuality as a form of understanding and pleasure on a par with reading, especially given the invocation of visual intertexts in novels like *Pickwick Abroad* (1837–38), *Master Timothy's Bookcase* (1841) and in *The Days of Hogarth*.

Such issues to do with the relative autonomy of text and illustration are complicated by a second obvious characteristic of Reynolds's serial fiction – his widespread reliance on wood engraving as his chosen medium for illustrating his books and periodicals. Given the origins of Reynolds's texts as serials in periodicals, the choice must have been a simple one as only wood engraving allowed the long print runs and the integration between the typeset page and illustration that had become the sine qua non of mass-circulation magazines, but volume re-publication presented a broader range of possibilities. Reynolds did, of course, especially early in his career, use the kind of etched and engraved separate page engravings that Dickens sustained in almost all his serialized fiction, perhaps in the expectation that the single-plate full-page illustration would offer respectability, or even gentility, to his texts despite their wide circulation amongst all classes of readers. Reynolds's novels in this idiom, such as *Master Timothy's Bookcase* or *Pickwick Abroad*, fall somewhere between commercial and aesthetic homage to and subversive pastiche of the successful fictional formats of W. Harrison Ainsworth or Dickens himself. In using conventional artists like Crowquill, Phillips and Bonner for *Pickwick Abroad*, Reynolds acknowledged the importance of sustaining a picaresque and grotesque caricature idiom on into the early Victorian period.

---

6   John Buchanan-Brown, *Early Victorian Illustrated Books – Britain, France and Germany 1820–1860* (London and Newcastle: British Library, 2005), p. 10.

7   Harvey, *Victorian Novelists and Their Illustrators*, p. 49.

Fig. 14.1   'The Sutherland Arms', steel engraving by John Phillips[?], from
                 Reynolds, *Pickwick Abroad* (1837–38), p. 586.

Fig. 14.2   'A Night at Beauvais', steel engraving by John Phillips[?], from Reynolds, *Pickwick Abroad* (1837–38), p. 612.

In a tavern interior from an early edition of *Pickwick Abroad* (Figure 14.1), the central figure is depicted in tropes drawn from both late eighteenth-century caricature and from theatrical illustration of the same period. The dramatized body language combines with the slight enlargement of heads and hands in ways characteristic of caricature. The clothes deliberately exaggerate and render grotesque the body shape of the central character, with his neck seeming to be swallowed up in his cravat. Figure 14.2, another plate from *Pickwick Abroad* by Crowquill that reworked a favourite Regency song book comic moment – the sleeper interrupted by an unexpected incursion – might almost be a free-standing image from *Sketches by Seymour* or any other of the 1830s caricaturist's sketch books. It is an image that again focuses attention on the grotesque human body, with Pickwick's rotund belly resembling a globe with the pattern of his stretched waistcoat forming lines of latitude. These plates are extremely important because they suggest that Reynolds and his publisher Willoughby, in this one instance at least, were unwilling to pursue the course followed by Dickens in *Pickwick Papers*, where he abandoned the backward-looking Regency caricature idiom of the designs Seymour and Buss etched for the early numbers of Pickwick (and of course that of several artists like Onwhyn and Sibson[8] who provided extra illustrations outside the text) and embraced the more anodyne and whimsical visions of 'Phiz' (Hablôt K. Browne).[9] Additionally, in combining the etched full-page plates of Crowquill and Phillips with Bonner's vignettes, dropped into the printed page in *Pickwick Abroad*, Reynolds evoked not so much Dickens, whose experiments with vignette illustration had both begun and brusquely ended with *Master Humphrey's Clock*, as the Regency writer Pierce Egan, Sr, whose *Life in London* (1821–22) had comprehensively combined full-page illustrations, drawn and etched by the Cruikshank brothers in an unmistakeably Regency idiom, with a range of wood-engraved vignettes held within the printed page.

If the *Pickwick Abroad* illustrations sought to evoke the success of Dickens's novel without losing a commitment to a visual idiom drawn from Regency comic discourses, *Master Timothy's Bookcase* (Figure 14.3), whose frontispiece formed part of a series of full-page anonymous engravings held in ruled frames, abandoned caricature and the comic altogether in pursuit of something closer to George Cruikshank's etchings for Harrison Ainsworth's novels, such as the part-issued *The Tower of London* (1840), which was being circulated in serial form at exactly the same time. Both *Pickwick Abroad* and *Master Timothy's Bookcase*, then, used illustration largely as a form of intertextual reference, reproducing the idiom and format of illustrious and 'respectable' contemporary fiction in an effort to assert, in however ironic a way, the comparable merits and pleasures of Reynolds's works.

---

8   See J. Grego (ed.), *Pictorial Pickwickiana* (London, 2 vols, 1899), vol. 1, pp. 231–463.

9   For the early history of Dickens's illustrations see Grego, *Pictorial Pickwickiana*, vol. 1; Graham Everitt, *English Caricaturists and Graphic Humourists of the Nineteenth Century* (London: Swan Sonnenschein, 1886), pp. 230–34; Jane R. Cohen, *Charles Dickens and His Original Illustrators* (Columbus, OH: Ohio State University Press, 1980); Robert L. Patten, *Charles Dickens and His Publishers* (Oxford: Clarendon Press, 1978).

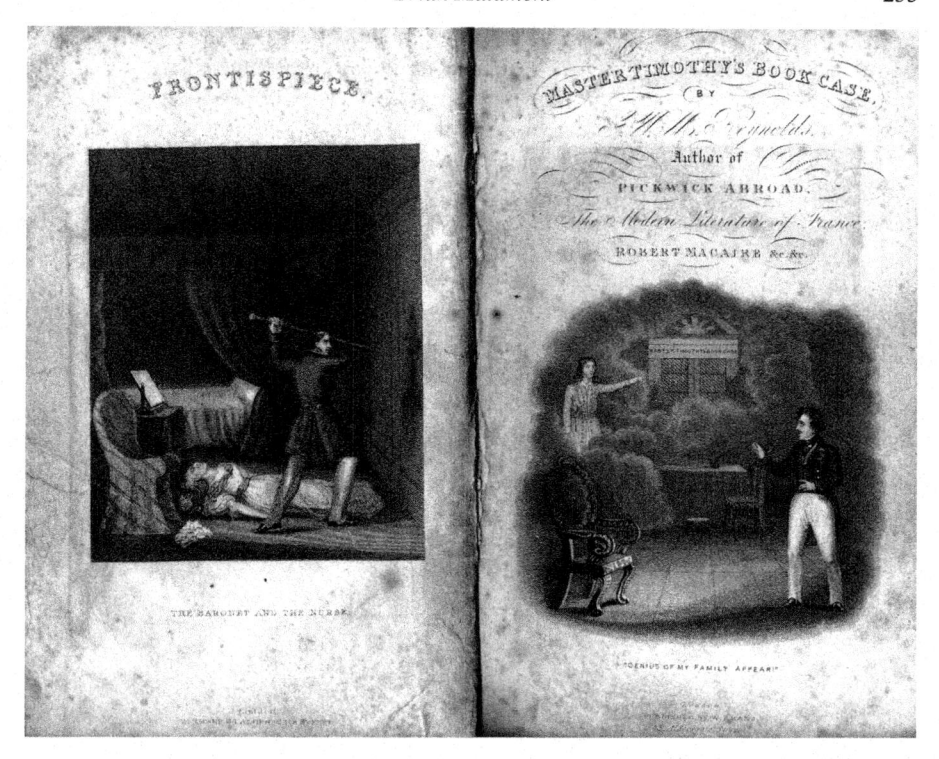

Fig. 14.3   Frontispiece and title-page, steel engraving, artist unknown, to *Master Timothy's Bookcase* (1841).

But, overwhelmingly, Reynolds's work was dependent on wood engraving for its visual impact, and his use of this reprographic mode leads to considerable difficulties about discriminating the cultural levels implied by the use of this medium. Clearly distinguished from, on the one hand, the single-plate engraved tradition and, on the other, the wood-cut vernacular, derived more from broadsides or theatrical prints than from caricature, of Edward Lloyd's penny issue novels by T.P. Prest and James Malcolm Rymer, the illustrations for Reynolds's novels exploited the new-found 'middle-browness' of wood engraving. Relatively sophisticated in tone, drawing on a vocabulary of theatrical gestures, still in touch with the caricature tradition but also well aware of the new purposeful use of wood engraving as a form of social reportage, both emblematic and, increasingly, naturalistic, wood engraving proved an extremely flexible and versatile medium for illustration. The attached sequence of images from the first volume of *The Mysteries of London* (1845) suggests something of this variety. Figure 14.4 combines a lively depiction of urban squalor, taking place under an emblematic miasma that only half conceals the dome of St Paul's Cathedral, with bravura theatricality. Figure 14.5 is essentially a dialogue between the grotesque and the urban picturesque, reducing low-life figures to simply outlined stereotypes in the manner of contemporary illustrations to urban sketches published in the London weekly magazines. Figure 14.6 combines the industrial sublime with a highly developed sense of pathos. All three illustrations, on quite a large scale for wood engravings, play off the blurred edge of the wood-engraved vignette block against the ruled linear framework of the text. Such a variety of generic allusions, pulling in caricature, reportage, the theatre, the gothic and melodrama, and emblematic richness suggests the levels of expressiveness that such apparently simple illustrations might aspire to. How, and to what extent, these allusive and generically complicated images were integrated into the reading experience of the text nonetheless is extremely difficult to decide.

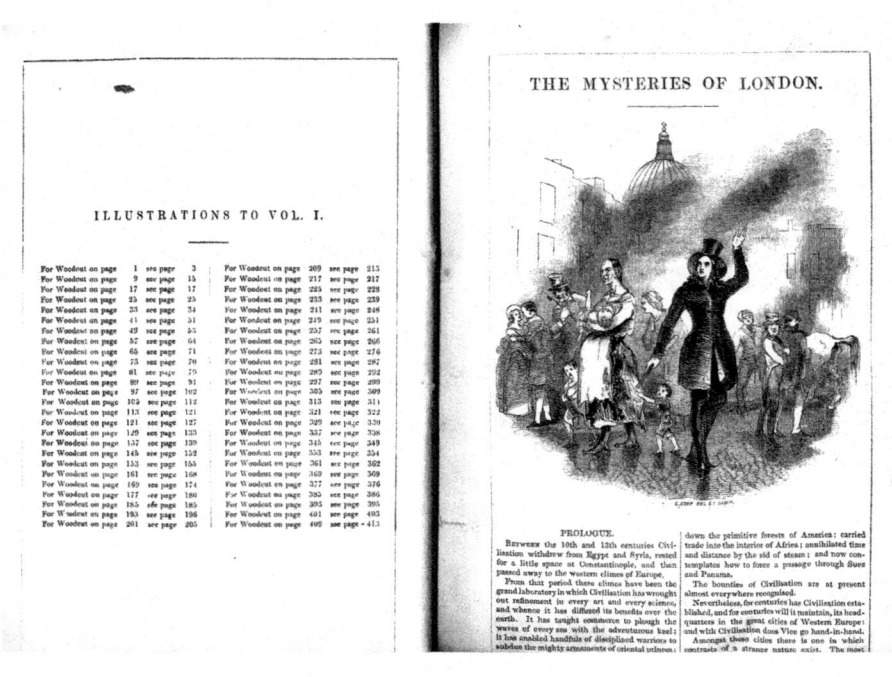

Fig. 14.4   Untitled wood engraving drawn and engraved by George Stiff, from G.W.M. Reynolds, *The Mysteries of London*, vol. 1 (1845), p. 1.

At first sight it might seem that the illustrators who were commissioned to illustrate Reynolds's work were readily available, reliable and reasonably well-known jobbing artists drawn from the large new pool of London-based artist/engravers that represented the second, post-Bewick wave of commercial wood engravers. Many of his artists did not sign their work and were not given credit on title-pages or contents lists. Other volumes, like *Mary Price* (1851–52), made the name of the artist, in this case Frederick Gilbert, part of the book's sales pitch: the title-page to volume 2 of the Dicks edition insists that the novel is 'beautifully illustrated by F. Gilbert'.[10] Such artists as were named at all are largely forgotten now, and were often not especially well regarded even by contemporaries such as Henry Vizetelly,

---

10   For Gilbert see: Rodney K. Engen, *Dictionary of Wood Engravers* (Cambridge: Chadwyck Healey, 1985), p. 98; Simon Houfe, *The Dictionary of British Book Illustrators*

whose *Glances Back Through Seventy Years* (1893) offered many harsh judgements on Victorian artist-engravers, judgements which have become the commonplaces of later reference books.[11] Certainly, several of Reynolds's artists had drawn and engraved widely in the 1840s for such pillars of the trade as the *Illustrated London News* and *Punch*. A few were specialist engravers who had built their trade through engraving the work of better-known artists. George Bonner, who drew and engraved the vignette wood engravings for *Pickwick Abroad*, for example, was the nephew of the celebrated Thomas Branston and an apprentice of yet another key figure in the evolution of the trade, John Henry Vizetelly.[12] When he set up his own business, which became quite a considerable one, Henry Vizetelly and W.J. Linton were among his apprentices, although both in later writings rather ungenerously described his work as uninspired.[13] Bonner spent much of his working life in the 1830s and 1840s engraving vignettes for comic publications after drawings by better-known artists like George Cruikshank and Robert Seymour. John Marshall, who drew the frontispiece for Reynolds's *The Drunkard's Progress* (1840), had similarly engraved illustrations for the Cruikshanks, notably their often-reprinted *Universal Songster*.[14] The illustrator of Reynolds's most characteristic book, *The Mysteries of London*, was the elusive but extremely substantial figure of George Stiff, linked closely to Reynolds as the proprietor and publisher of the *London Journal*.[15] Men like Marshall, Bonner and Stiff, largely overlooked today, nonetheless represented the new-found competence and reliability characteristic of the wood-engraving trade, and would have been obvious choices for an author or publisher on the lookout for adequate and prompt illustrative work.

But in fact Reynolds's most considerable and frequently used artists – Frederick Gilbert, John Gilbert, Henry Anelay, E.H. Corbould, George Stiff, Alfred Crowquill and John Phillips – represented an interesting cross-section of contemporary illustrators rather than a convenient gathering of jobbing wood-engraving specialists. Henry Anelay, for example, the illustrator of *Wagner the Wehr-Wolf* (1846–47), *The Seamstress* (1850), *Robert Macaire in England* (1840) and, most substantially, the first volumes of *The Mysteries of the Court of London* (1848–53), worked prolifically for a range of mass-circulation periodicals, beginning almost inevitably with the *Penny Magazine* and the *Illustrated London News* in the 1840s, and moving on to two of T.J. Smithies's graphically inventive temperance periodicals the *British Workman* (1845–1921) and the *Band of Hope Review* (1851–58).[16] In these two temperance periodicals, where Smithies deliberately gave his artists some degree

---

and Caricaturists 1800–1914, rev. edn (Woodbridge: Antique Collectors Club, 1978), p. 315.

11 Henry Vizetelly, *Glances Back Through Seventy Years*, 2 vols (London: Kegan Paul, 1893).

12 For Bonner see Engen, *Dictionary of Wood Engravers*, pp. 26–7.

13 Engen, *Dictionary of Wood Engravers*, p. 27; Vizetelly, *Glances Back Through Seventy Years*, vol. 1, pp. 129–34.

14 G. and R. Cruikshank, *The Universal Songster*, 3 vols (London: n.p., 1825–26).

15 For Stiff, see King, *The London Journal*.

16 Engen, *Dictionary of Wood Engravers*, pp. 6–7; Houfe, *The Dictionary of British Book Illustrators and Caricaturists*, p. 219.

of licence in their work, Anelay's engravings were highly finished and painterly, bringing the sophisticated tonality and dense composition characteristic of oils into images cheaply produced for mass circulation. And indeed Anelay was a widely exhibited landscape painter, who showed at the Royal Academy for many years from the late 1850s on. Although unable to avoid the scorn of Vizetelly for his *Illustrated London News* work,[17] Anelay was an artist who was well known to both the middlebrow and artisan reading public, and would have given a substantial attraction to Reynolds's publications. In particular his painterly interest in finish and composition took the vignette away from its vernacular and vulgar associations and asserted the 'respectability' of Reynolds's works by combining gothic tropes of violence, melodrama and urban 'otherness' with the tonal and compositional finish of 'art'.

Frederick Gilbert, who illustrated *Agnes* (1855–57), *The Coral Island* (1848–49), *Ellen Percy* (1855–57) and *Mary Price* (1851–52), was, like Anelay, an exhibiting painter as well as an illustrator, although watercolours comprised his chosen medium.[18] He, too, worked widely for mass-circulation magazines, especially *Cassell's Magazine*. Gilbert was, equally characteristically, the subject of later Victorian contempt, described by Gleeson White as a 'facile understudy of [his brother] Sir John [Gilbert]'.[19] Edward Corbould, the illustrator of *Canonbury House* (1857–58), *Joseph Wilmot* (1853–55) and *The Rye House Plot* (1853–54), was more successful than Anelay and Gilbert in persuading both his contemporaries and later critics that it was possible to combine work for a range of mass-circulation literature with serious artistic productions and credentials. Described as a 'painter who occasionally drew on wood, also etcher and sculptor' by Engen,[20] Corbould had in fact moved directly from the Royal Academy Schools into book and periodical illustration, and seemed unconcerned at working for projects aimed at such different sectors of the market as S.C. Hall's upmarket *Book of British Ballads* (a key work of the early 1840s in establishing the aesthetic potential of, and collectors' market for, the wood engraving), the middle-market *Illustrated London News*, or the decidedly workaday *Churchman's Family Magazine*. As drawing master to the Queen's children for over 20 years, and with such a varied and impressive range of publications, Corbould clearly saw little shame in accepting jobbing work for Reynolds, and his painterly perception of the wood engraving brought aesthetic respectability to Reynolds's part-issued fiction. The use of painter-illustrators like Gilbert, Anelay and Corbould suggests the author's and publishers' interest in reaching a relatively sophisticated and aesthetically well-informed readership, and in to some extent gentrifying the wood-engraving form to give respectability to Reynolds's often maligned fiction.

---

17 Vizetelly, *Glances Back Through Seventy Years*, vol. 1, p. 238.

18 Houfe, *The Dictionary of British Book Illustrators and Caricaturists*, p. 315, Engen, *Dictionary of Wood Engravers*, p. 98.

19 Gleeson White, *English Illustration – 'The Sixties': 1855–70* (Bath: Kingsmead Reprints, 1970), p. 62.

20 Engen, *Dictionary of Wood Engravers*, p. 55.

written too in the afternoon, most likely just before she came out to go to Southampton Row. And another reason that made me anxious to get hold of her letter to Tom Rain, was that she did n't post it at the office where she received *his*, but took the trouble to go down to Holborn to put it into another box."

"I wonder why she did that?" said Mrs. Bunce.

"Oh! most likely to avoid exciting any suspicion or curiosity at the office in Southampton Row. Then there's another thing that puzzles me:—she was with Tom Rain last night—Jacob saw them together, and followed them home to Lock's Fields; and she is away from him to-day—writes to him this afternoon—and hopes to find a letter from him when she goes to Southampton Row this evening. One would think, by this, that they have been in the habit of corresponding together, and that the place in Southampton Row is where he directs his letters to her. So it's pretty clear that they do n't live together for good and all. But what perplexes me most is the sermon that she wrote him. It's plain she stole the diamonds, from what Jacob overheard Tom say to her when he gave her the ear-rings last night; and yet she does n't reproach herself a bit in the letter to him. She only tries to convert Rainford; and, to read that letter, one would think she was as innocent of a theft or such-like thing as a child unborn."

"Oh! I dare say she wrote the letter for some object or another which we can't see," observed Mrs. Bunce.

"I scarcely think so," returned Bones: "there was so much seriousness about it."

"But she's a precious deep one, depend on it," said Betsy. "Look how she got off about the diamonds. And, after all, perhaps her father had been talking her over; and so, if she wrote to Tom Rain in a serious way, the humour won't last very long."

"Well—we shall see," exclaimed Old Death. "I should like to secure her in my interests."

"What did you do with the letter she wrote to Tom Rain?" asked Mrs. Bunce.

"Put it back into the post," was the reply. "Fancy if Esther and Tom *did* get together again, and, on comparing notes, he found that the letter from her had miscarried, he might suspect a trick somewhere, and fix foul play on me. No—no: it was more prudent to let the note go, since I had gathered its contents."

9*

Fig. 14.5   Untitled woodcut by George Stiff, from Reynolds, *The Mysteries of London*, vol. III (1847), p. 65.

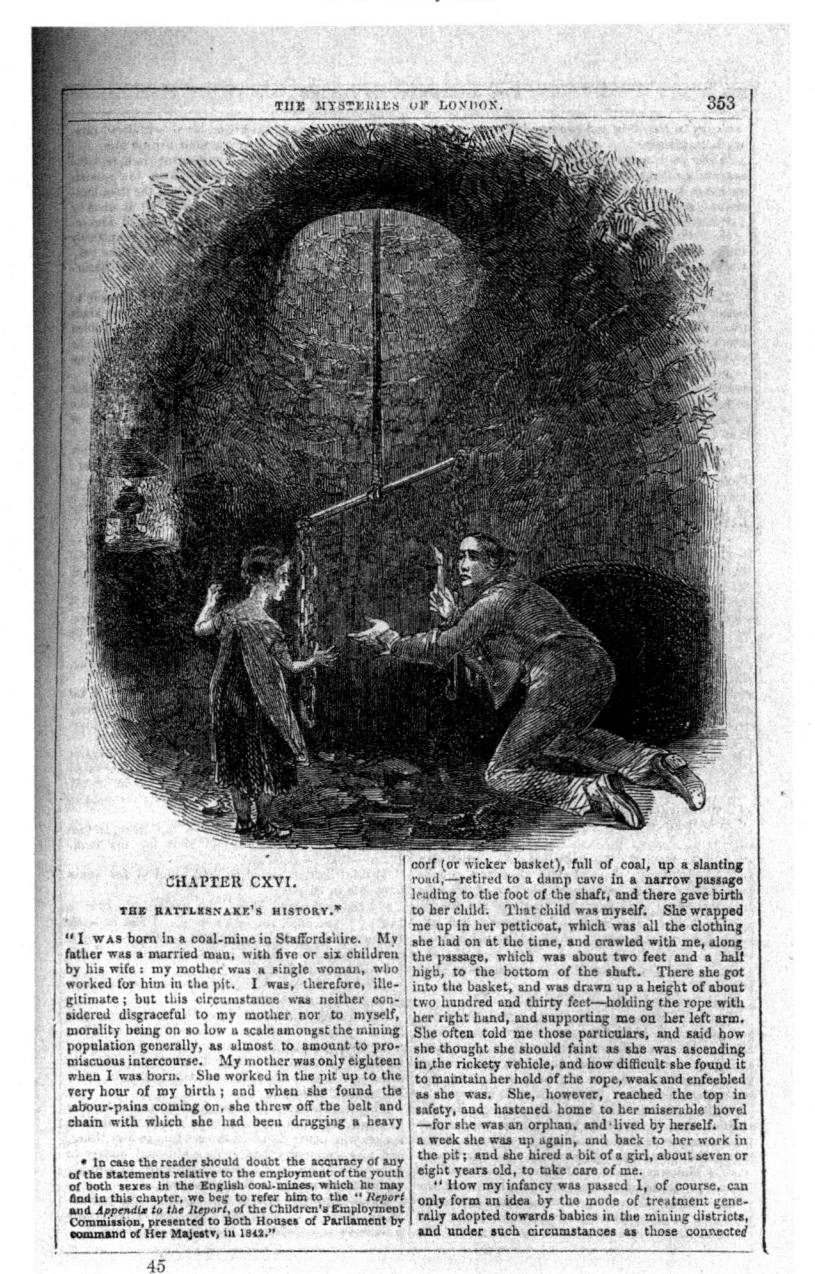

Fig. 14.6 Untitled woodcut by George Stiff, from Reynolds, *The Mysteries of London*, vol. 1 (1845), p. 259.

If the illustrations to Reynolds's texts had at least some aspirations to the aesthetic respectability that was beginning to gather round the wood engraving in the 1840s, their relationship with the printed text remains less easy to elucidate. Just as the illustrators were sometimes given title-page credit for their work but sometimes ignored and left to endure anonymity, the relationship between the text and its illustrations in Reynolds's novels was sometimes treated with considerable deference, but equally often left to chance. Obviously, the placing of the illustrations within the serial format is entirely dependent on the construction of individual issues – the wood engraving serves as a title to each issue as well as an enticement to become engaged in the subsequent narrative. Thus the scenes depicted in the illustrations did not necessarily sit alongside their textual 'place', but rather prefigured the text, offering tantalizing visual glimpses of what was to follow textually. Such a structure, of course, largely subordinates the significance of the illustrations to that of 'embellishment', with little narrative energy and more significance as advertisements for the text than as expositions of it. But internal evidence from the novels suggests that Reynolds was frequently concerned to ensure that readers *did* read the illustrations as forms of narrative exposition. The first volume of *The Mysteries of London* followed a common practice in providing a list of illustrations referring the reader to the precise textual moment that the wood engraving 'illustrated'. Certainly, in most of his volume reprints, Reynolds at least made sure that the illustration referred to the particular eight-page issue that succeeded it. Additionally, a number of the novels such as Reynolds's *The Young Duchess* (1857–58) included full-page wood-engraved portraits of central characters as well as the part issue title illustrations, suggesting that the author was trying to engage the reader closely in visualizing his text.

But, if there is considerable evidence that Reynolds and his publishers tried hard to ensure that their readers consumed texts and illustrations together, there are also indications of more careless, less integrated ways of managing the text/image nexus. The Dicks volume reprint of *Joseph Wilmot*, for instance, has, in chapter 32 on p. 97, an illustration that refers readers to events in chapter 20, thus firmly suggesting that the illustrations were largely conceived as a textual afterthought, and causing the reader to flit about the text in pursuit of graphic realizations of textual events. Such dissociation between narrative and image in Reynolds's work was at its most extreme in the early pastiche novels like *Pickwick Abroad* and *Master Timothy's Bookcase*, where the engraved full-page plates were offered largely as separate entertainments rather than as extensions of the narrative. Perhaps all that can be said on this issue of the relationship between text and illustration in Reynolds's work using the physical structure of the novels as evidence is that Reynolds seems to have been acutely aware of, if not always all that concerned about, the proximity between the visual and verbal. There is one of Reynolds's texts, however, where the relationship between visuality and fiction is deliberately exploited. *The Days of Hogarth* was built around 37 wood-engraved illustrations engraved after Hogarth by two obscure artisans, C.M. Gorway and Edwin Brett,[21] and offers a unique chance to consider further the reading experience of an illustrated serial text.

---

21 Engen records Brett, known as both Edwin and Edward, as belonging to a London wood engraving firm between 1864 and 1870 (Engen, *Dictionary of Wood Engravers*, p. 31)

The Days of Hogarth

Books that partially derived their structure from sequences of images were not unknown in the Victorian period, and it might be argued that three books where the illustrations, or the idea of illustrations, preceded or led the text, such as Pierce Egan, Sr's *Life in London* (1821–22), *Sketches by Boz* (1836–37)[22] and *Pickwick Papers* (1836–37), marked a distinct course from the picaresque and episodic to the realist narrative. But several other bestsellers in a number of different genres evolved as commentaries or narratives developed from a sequence of illustrations. *Seymour's Sketches* (1835–36), for example, had a considerable existence as a portfolio of comic engravings before being turned into a picaresque fiction by the addition of Alfred Forrester's [Crowquill's] text and reprinted on several occasions in that format.[23] In a different idiom, Kenny Meadows's series of portrait sketches, originating as a set of extra illustrations to *Nicholas Nickleby* (1838–39), were given extended popularity as *Heads of the People*, a series of urban archetypes or 'characters' accompanied by short essays by a range of well-known journalists and hack writers.[24] But *The Days of Hogarth* takes the use of visual sources to a new level through its engagement with Hogarth's best-known narrative sequences, sequences which had themselves been originally engraved in an attempt to bring serious and complex visual images to a range of consumers unable to afford oil paintings.[25]

The 37 wood-engraved illustrations used in *The Days of Hogarth* as title-pages for each of the serial issues were mainly reworkings of four of Hogarth's celebrated and widely known narrative sequences of engravings: 'A Harlot's Progress' (1732); 'The Rake's Progress' (1735); 'Marriage a la Mode' (1745); and 'Industry and Idleness' (1747). Five of the six plates for 'A Harlot's Progress' were used, six of the eight 'Rake's Progress' images, five of six 'Marriage a la Mode' illustrations and 11 of 12 from 'Industry and Idleness'. Additionally, the novel used all four 'Times of the Day' (1738), one of the 'Four Stages of Cruelty' (1750–51), 'Gin Lane' (one of a pair with 'Beer Street', 1750–51) and 'A Midnight Modern Conversation' (1732–33). Clearly some changes to the shape and presentation of Hogarth's engravings had to be made to meet the exigencies of Reynolds's text. While some of Hogarth's images translated

---

but cites none of his work. Gorway has entirely sunk below the level of available reference books.

22   See F.J. Harvey Darton, *Dickens – Positively the First Appearance* (London: Argonaut Press, 1933).

23   The bibliography of *Seymour's Sketches* is complex. First issued as five series of plates by G.S. Tregear in the 1830s, the *Sketches* with Forrester's text were reissued by Henry Bohn in 1841 and reprinted in various versions throughout the latter half of the century.

24   Everitt, *English Caricaturists and Graphic Humourists of the Nineteenth Century*, pp. 355–6.

25   I have used Joseph Burke and Colin Caldwell (eds), *Hogarth: The Complete Engravings* (London: Thames and Hudson, 1968) as the basic listing of Hogarth's prints, and all titles and dates are drawn from this edition. For Hogarth's influence on Victorian illustrated fiction see Harvey, *Victorian Novelists and Their Illustrators*. For a wider view of Hogarth's influence see Frederick Antal, *Hogarth and his Place in European Art* (London: Routledge and Kegan Paul, 1962).

easily enough to the portrait shape required by the layout of the novel's page, others, including 'Industry and Idleness', had originally been in a landscape format and required some horizontal compression to fit into the standard format of the serial issue front page. The 'Industry and Idleness' prints had originally been produced with elaborately engraved framing borders that included quotations from Proverbs. These were omitted in the novel. A number of the illustrations were printed in reverse from the Hogarth engravings, although deciding what the 'right' way round might be is considerably complicated by Hogarth's own reworkings of his oil-painted originals into prints, a process which sometimes involved reversing the original image. Clearly, while engravers were well accustomed to making images in reverse on their blocks, it would have been easier to redraw the original on to the block as a straightforward copy without reversing the image, and certainly some of the early images in the novel are the 'wrong' way round against their originals.

While the wood engravings in *The Days of Hogarth* were inevitably, given the limitations of the chosen medium and the need for cheapness, simplifications in both line and tone of Hogarth's originals, they do respect, and largely succeed in reproducing, the density of emblematic detail that characterized the earlier engravings,[26] as is seen in the woodcut to the first number (Figure 14.7). As this example illustrates, the woodcuts in Reynolds's serial closely followed Hogarth, so for subsequent references to Hogarth illustrations, the reader is directed to the original plates. Deference to Hogarth's emblematic method was crucial to Reynolds for two reasons. First, most obviously, Hogarth's moral preoccupations, and especially his critique of the behaviour of the rich, the dissolute and the corruptible, formed a necessary point of reference, or even framework, for Reynolds's more ambiguous and often prurient narrative engagement with metropolitan manners. Indeed, the invocation of Hogarth's name in the novel's title gave both a precedent and a legitimacy to the bursts of moral outrage that characterize Reynolds's text, as well as trading off the artist's famous attempts to democratize 'high art' and bring complex images concerned with moral judgement within the reach of a wider consumer base. But, less obviously, one of the central concerns, and presumably attractions, of Reynolds's novel was the detailed invocation of the textures, shapes and appearance of London in the earlier eighteenth century. *The Days of Hogarth* contains a considerable number of self-consciously declared, and somewhat applaudingly annotated, attempts to provide the audience with extremely precise information about 'things' and 'thingness' – a sustained fascination with commodities and fashions, especially dress, food and interior decoration, almost the equal of Hogarth's contemporary, Alexander Pope. Further consideration of this aspect of Reynolds's writing will be made later in this chapter.

---

26 G.W.M. Reynolds, *The Days of Hogarth* (London: John Dicks, [1850]). All subsequent references are to this edition, which was based on the collected penny-issue version [1848?]. Later editions reprint text and illustrations, but with a condensed layout and pagination (see Bibliography).

THE

DAYS OF HOGARTH:

OR, THE MYSTERIES OF OLD LONDON.

CHAPTER I.

THE PEER AND HIS SON.—THE MISER.

Our tale opens in the month of October, 1721; and we shall at once introduce our readers to a splendidly-furnished drawing-room at the Earl of Castleton's mansion in Lincoln's Inn Fields—at that period a fashionable part of the great metropolis.

It was about ten o'clock in the evening; and the crimson curtains were drawn over the windows, their rich gold fringes touching the thick carpet—then an article of comparative luxury, Kidderminster not as yet having sought to vie with Brussels or Tournay in their staple manufacture. The brilliant light of numerous wax-candles was reflected in the handsome mirrors, and gave effect to the fine polish of the massive and elaborately-carved furniture of mahogany —a material which had but recently come into vogue. On small but elegant side-tables were vases of porcelain, their rich colours bearing comparison with the hues of the flowers they contained; and on a larger table, in the centre of the room, were a few books bound in a style of elegance which showed that they were rather for ornament than use.

In this luxurious apartment were seated the Earl of Castleton and his only son, Viscount Langham.

The former was a personage of about fifty-eight— possessing a countenance that would have been con-

Fig. 14.7   'The Young Heir Takes Possession of the Miser's Effects', woodcut by C.M. Corway after William Hogarth, *The Rake's Progress* (1734–35), plate 1. In G.W.M. Reynolds, *The Days of Hogarth* (1848), p. 1.

Although all the illustrations to *The Days of Hogarth* were, allowing for omitted plates, printed exactly in the order of the original Hogarthian sequences, the individual sequences were at first carefully, but then more opportunistically, interleaved in Reynolds's text. The first five illustrations (on pp. 1, 9, 17, 25 and 33 in sequence with the eight-page part issues) comprised the first plates of five sustained Hogarthian sequences and each illustration introduced a key strand of Reynolds's narrative. As we have already noted, Reynolds's novel brings together Hogarth's best-known plates and narrative sequences, each providing different elements of the story. Thus the spendthrift Tom Ferrers is taken from 'The Rake's Progress', the procuress Mother Hayes and the dissolute Colonel Charteris come from 'The Harlot's Progress', while the contrasted apprentices, one of whom Hogarth actually calls 'Frank Goodchild', are based on 'Industry and Idleness'. 'Marriage a la Mode' provides the opportunistic and deceitful liaison between Viscount Langham and Amelia Johnson. Details from 'The Four Times of Day' reinforce the sense of eighteenth-century historical authenticity, as do the crowded details taken from Hogarth's narrative sequences. Structurally, Reynolds uses the moral import of Hogarth's retributive closures, such as the death and funeral of the Harlot, and the madhouse scene that ends 'The Rake's Progress', adding others of his own, including death by strangulation and burning at the stake.

While the Hogarthian sequences invoked by Reynolds's illustrations and texts did not continue in the orderly manner immediately suggested, the opening chapters of *The Days of Hogarth* offer a rather impressive, if somewhat complex, reading experience. Ingeniously, Reynolds has ascribed elaborate subplots in his text to each of the four main Hogarthian sequences he used as the principal sources for his illustrations, and brought them together in a single narrative. Such a process had a number of obvious merits. First, the narrative drive and closure of each of the Hogarthian sequences was both familiar and dramatic. Second, Reynolds has understood the key relationship between detailed naturalism and self-professed fictionality in Hogarth's prints. Third, Reynolds has grasped, and developed, the close relationship between prurience and moral outrage that informed Hogarth. Fourth, Reynolds has invoked the visuality of Hogarth as a key mode of apprehension of his text, and was prepared to spend much of the text glossing particular Hogarth plates in detail. The section of text that is spatially arranged around 'Morning', the first 'Four Times of Day' plate,[27] for example, gives a clear sense of the ways in which Reynolds both exploited the Hogarth-derived illustrations for his own fictional purposes and incited the reader to look at the plates with fierce attention. Reynolds began his account of this illustration by drawing attention to the visual contrasts so central to Hogarth's method in constructing his image. When introducing 'Noon' from 'The Four Times of Day', Reynolds remarks: 'The splendid apparel of the French gentlemen and ladies ... contrasted strongly with the miserable aspect of the neighbourhood' – and led the reader, by a series of rhetorical allusions, to examine the illustration in all its emblematic detail. 'Here', Reynolds explained, almost jabbing a finger at the detail of the image, 'a poor boy was seen roaring vociferously', thus

---

27 Reynolds, *The Days of Hogarth*, ch. 13, p. 33.

ensuring that the reader pays proper attention to the important details of the visual 'text'.[28]

But Reynolds's aim was more than merely to offer an exegesis of the image, and he moved on to use 'Morning' to demonstrate the historical authenticity of his own account of early eighteenth-century London: 'At noon in those times ... the poorer classes were accustomed to dine ... Hog-lane was at that period almost entirely peopled by French Huguenots.'[29] Mention of the Huguenots took the author off into another direction, a characteristic rant against intolerance: 'Oh! What diabolical tyranny has been perpetuated in this world in the sacred name of religion! ... And at the present day ... we still behold the most galling oppression practised in the name of the Church.'[30] Here, then, around an image not really intended to further the narrative drive of the novel to any great extent, we can see Reynolds exploiting what he saw as the great virtues of the Hogarthian narrative method: the intense focus on detail; the combination of such closely worked naturalism with broader emblematic signification; the moral intensity that allowed the narrative to rise into outspoken polemic; and the overarching intertextually present narratives of moral retribution implicit in the binaries found in the detailed textures of urban life.

While Reynolds maintained a close correspondence between text and illustration, expressed both spatially through proximity on the page and methodologically through the development of the various Hogarthian aspects of his narrative, his text promises the reader considerable rewards. Chivvying his readers towards Hogarth's reproduced images by constant reminders of the visuality of his text, such as 'the scene is crowded and interesting',[31] Reynolds as author took up a virtuously, and largely successful, Hogarthian persona. Such recognition of the virtues of Hogarth's aesthetic achievements and methods could be combined with the ingenious, perhaps even brilliant, perception that a melange of Hogarth's various 'progresses' would additionally provide a useful stock of dramatic narratives that combined low-life adventure with fervent moralism. The Hogarthian intertexts for *The Days of Hogarth* ought to have provided Reynolds with a structure and authorial stance from which to write a powerfully coherent historical novel. So what went wrong?

As the novel progresses, two disruptive characteristics begin to emerge. First, the text begins to lose both physical and narrative touch with the illustrations. Thus chapter 27 in part 12 of the novel[32] is entitled 'Another Scene in the Rake's Progress' and offers a detailed exposition of plate III of Hogarth's sequence, 'The Tavern Scene', described through the characteristically duplicitous manoeuvre Reynolds frequently used for his low-life interests: 'a scene of debauchery and dissipation which should find no mention in these pages, were it not necessary to point out the shoals and quicksands whereon the ship of youth is too liable to strike'.[33] But the illustration of Hogarth's plate is withheld until the next part issue, forcing the reader

28 Reynolds, *The Days of Hogarth*, ch. 13, p. 32.
29 Reynolds, *The Days of Hogarth*, ch. 13, p. 32.
30 Reynolds, *The Days of Hogarth*, ch. 13, p. 33.
31 Reynolds, *The Days of Hogarth*, ch. 10, p. 23.
32 Reynolds, *The Days of Hogarth*, ch. 27, p. 92.
33 Reynolds, *The Days of Hogarth*, ch. 37, p. 94.

to thumb backwards and forwards to find the visualization of what Reynolds claims to be reluctant to describe in words. Indeed, as the novel goes on, the narrative relationship between text and image begins to become increasingly strained. The illustration to issue 17 is a version of the third plate from 'Marriage a la Mode' – 'The Scene With the Quack'.[34] This image was never going to be an easy one to integrate into the narrative, a process not helped by the expository verbal description occurring four chapters previously.[35] In order to facilitate sustained exegesis of the image, Reynolds was forced into a number of transparent textual manipulations. A chance street meeting occurs between the arch-rake Sydney, Viscount Langham, and the ambiguously attractive rogue, Jem Raffles. Raffles explains his protracted absence from metropolitan society in terms of illness, to which Langham responds: 'talking of doctors – the scoundrels – puts me in mind of a diversion which took place yesterday',[36] and launches off into a detailed version of Hogarth's image.

Raffles hears him out, then remarks that Langham is 'quite graphic' in his description, which is a rather flat-footed prompt for the reader to head off through the novel in search of the relevant illustration, which only appears ten pages later. Langham responds that 'the place made a deep impression upon my mind – and I can recapitulate every feature' – which he does. When the reader reaches the relevant illustration, it is embedded in quite another narrative strand, the attempts of the procuress Mother Hayes to reinstate herself in the favour of her principal client, Colonel Charteris, by ensnaring a beautiful virgin for his pleasure. Here, as in several other places, the novel is forced to attend to its illustrations through heavily constructed plot devices rather than narrative necessity. In such instances, the lengthy exegesis of the illustration within the text is entirely redundant to the structure and plotting of the novel, and offers little beyond an isolated moment of urban picaresque adventure.

Second, Reynolds was ultimately not prepared to subordinate himself to the narrative discipline of his chosen visual sources. Instead he imposed on his text a characteristic framework of loosely linked fictional activities. As already suggested, one of these is a substantial claim for his text as not just a historical novel but as a serious attempt to describe the manners, textures and, especially, the criminal underworld of Hogarth's London with documentary accuracy. But against these impulses towards naturalism, Reynolds also insisted on the sustained fictionality of his novel not just through the highly elaborate and contrived plotting and the use of emblematic names drawn from Hogarth, but also through textual instructions. 'Let us suppose', he began his second chapter, 'that ten days have elapsed',[37] thus ensuring the reader acknowledges the constructed nature of his 'authentic' narrative. Later he announces that 'we do not bind ourselves in a tale of this kind to adhere too closely to facts ... the exigencies of our plot and of the groundwork of our story requiring an occasional deviation therefrom'.[38] Confusingly, a later chapter opens

---

34 Reynolds, *The Days of Hogarth*, ch. 50, p. 129.

35 Reynolds, *The Days of Hogarth*, ch. 46, pp. 118–19.

36 Reynolds, *The Days of Hogarth*, ch. 46, p. 118.

37 Reynolds, *The Days of Hogarth*, ch. 1, p. 4.

38 Reynolds, *The Days of Hogarth*, ch. 8, p. 21.

with: 'The rapidity with which incidents are made to follow one another in this tale, must not be deemed inconsistent with probability, nor at variance with the nature of everyday life.'[39] While in some ways a fitting response to Hogarth's blend of naturalism and emblem, Reynolds's text nonetheless oscillates between assertions of historical authenticity and a deliberate and declared fictionality in ways that subvert coherent reading.

In terms of plot, far too many of the opportunities offered by Reynolds's tightly knit sequences are taken up but ultimately resolved only by highly elaborate closures. Thus the novel is interested in disguise, origins, evil, social mobility and criminality, but reluctant to focus on any one of these issues as a means of consistent plotting. Instead, Reynolds continually delayed his narrative to launch into polemics, or even rants, about a miscellaneous variety of admittedly righteous topics – cruelty to women, fidelity, religious intolerance, religious fanaticism and its evils, war, taxation and so on. There are also interpellated picturesque narratives, notably the elaborate subplot about alchemy in a gothic Lancashire castle that occupies the central sections of the novel. Given this riot of competing possibilities, perhaps it was hardly surprising that Reynolds's good idea – a fiction based on a grand synthesis of Hogarthian visual narratives, with their combination of fascinated and precisely observed urban low-life manners and broader moral fabulism – was never entirely realized. Reynolds's *The Days of Hogarth*, along with many others among his novels, frustrated or disregarded the visual potential of its illustrations through the wilfulness of the narrative and the exigencies of serial publication. Despite the considerable evidence for the seriousness with which Reynolds and his publishers commissioned and deployed illustration in his novels, their narrative potential was never fully achieved.

39 Reynolds, *The Days of Hogarth*, ch. 30, p. 70.

PART V
Afterlife

Chapter 15

G.W.M. Reynolds: Rewritten in Nineteenth-century Bengal

Tagore's short story, titled *Tārāprasanner Kirti* or *The Achievement of Tārāprasanno* (1891), tells the story of the worldly failure of a Bengali intellectual who devotes his life to the composition of a scholarly treatise on Indian philosophy. The unintelligible jargon and incomprehensible content of Tārāprasanno's literary attempts are praised only by a certain section of critics who 'had not read anything apart from translations of Reynolds's *London Rahasya* [*The Mysteries of the Court of London*]'. Tagore comments: 'if instead of the trash that we (nowadays) get in the name of fiction, some serious books with this kind of theme were written more frequently, Bengali literature would have been richer'.[1] A later Bengali author, Rājsekhar Basu, supports this view of Reynolds's fiction widely held by Bengali intelligentsia:

> The works of Reynolds which once had flooded the market for fiction have disappeared without any trace.... I remember some of the general features of his works. [The novels contained] liberal doses of adventure and mystery, accounts of adultery, murders, burglaries, robberies, and portrayals of the luxurious lifestyle of the aristocracy. The heroes and heroines usually possessed incomparable physical beauty and unimpeachable moral characters.[2]

The disdain exhibited by two of its leading literary figures does not, however, reflect the high regard in which many of the Bengali public held George William MacArthur Reynolds and his brand of novels in the nineteenth century. Reynolds was not translated as semi-pornography, as intellectuals of the day imply. In fact all Reynolds's novels in the National Library, Calcutta, are from the collection of Sir Āshutosh Mookerjee, the second Indian Vice-Chancellor of the University of Calcutta, who was a graduate in Mathematics and Physics, and a High Court judge known as 'the Tiger of Bengal' for his fierce integrity. Among Reynolds's Bengali translators are the names of many respected nineteenth-century literary figures, proving that not all had a 'highbrow' reaction to Reynolds's sensationalism.[3] The

---

1   Rabindranāth Tagore, *Tārāprasanner Kirti* (1891), in *Galpaguchchha*, vol. 1 (Calcutta:Viswabhārati, 1993), p. 33. All translations are mine.

2   Rājsekhar Basu, *Galper Bāzār*, in *Parashurām Granthābali*, vol. 3 (Calcutta: M.C. Sarkar and Sons, 1986), p. 271.

3   One should remember that, ironically enough, only people who were English-educated could translate Reynolds from the original, and they were usually regarded as the cream of the society.

eminent poet Bihārilāl Chakrabarty translated Reynolds's *Loves of the Harem* (1855), with the title *Abarodh Prem*, in 1885. Bihārilāl was a highly regarded literary figure of nineteenth-century Bengal, and was also known as a blood relative of Tagore.[4] Another respected writer, Kāliprasanna Chattopādhyāy, was a veteran who had been commissioned by the publisher Ārya-Sāhitya-Samiti to translate 'standard' English novels for consumption by the Bengali reader.[5] Chattopādhyāy translated Reynolds's *The Young Duchess* (1857–58) as *Rāni Krishnakāmini* (1889), *Mary Price* (1851–52) as *Mary Prais* (1893), and *The Soldier's Wife* (1853) as *Sainik Badhu* (1895).

The popularity of Reynolds's novels with translators and readers was enhanced by the fact that in nineteenth-century India they were often read as moral tales. Reynolds's own impassioned self-defence at the end of the first series of *The Mysteries of London* confirmed this impression:

> If ... there be any who express an aversion to peruse this work, – fearful from its title or from fugitive report that the mind will be shocked more than it can be improved, ... – if, in a word, a false fastidiousness should prejudge, from its own suppositions or from misrepresentations made to it by others, a book by means of which we have sought to convey many an useful moral and lash many a flagrant abuse, – do you, kind reader, oppose that prejudice, and exclaim – 'Peruse ere you condemn!'
>
> For if, on the one side, we have raked amidst the filth and loathsomeness of society, – have we not, on the other, devoted adequate attention to its bright and glorious phases?[6]

This same sentiment is echoed in Haricharan Ray's *London Rahasya*,[7] one of the first vernacular versions of *The Mysteries of London*, published from the town of Berhampore in the district of Murshidābād, Bengal, in 1871. This is a translation of the first 12 chapters, marked by intricate, sanskritized language and accompanied by a plea to readers for subscriptions to enable him to pursue his labour of love without financial worry. Haricharan Ray's *bijñāpan* (advertisement/notice) reiterates

---

4   In his autobiography, Tagore eulogizes Bihārilāl's poetic capabilities, mentioning the fact that his own early poetic sensibilities were influenced to a large degree by Bihārilāl. See *Jivansmriti* (Calcutta:Viswabhārati Granthan Bibhāg, 1401 [Bengali year, corresponding roughly to 1995–96]), especially the chapter entitled 'Sāhityer Sangi', pp. 81–3. As an interesting footnote, Tagore's eldest daughter Mādhurilatā later married Bihārilāl's son.

5   There was a spate of Reynolds-inspired *guptakathās* (secrets/mysteries) in nineteenth-century Bengal. The concept of the urban mysteries/secrets was appropriated by native authors and applied to themes and issues entirely Bengali in essence. According to the noted critic Dr Priyaranjan Sen: 'In the intervening years between the death of Bankimchandra and the rise of Tagore as a novelist, i.e. during the eighth and ninth decades [of the nineteenth century], a particular kind of novel was being written which can be called "Rahasya".' This trend began with the publication of *Āmār Guptakathā* in 1871. Within a decade a veritable school of this kind of narrative grew up. See *Western Influence in the Bengali Novel* (Calcutta: University of Colorado Press, 1931). The *guptakathās* written in imitation of the Reynoldsian *Mysteries* therefore hybridized the native narrative mode and gradually incorporated the structure of the western novel into the traditional literary structures of Bengal.

6   G.W.M. Reynolds, *The Mysteries of London*, 1st series (London: George Vickers, 1846), vol. 2, p. 424.

7   The Bengali word *rahasya* literally means a mystery.

Reynolds's own claim that he has a moral purpose in writing the *Mysteries*, and is worth quoting at length:

> The tales of *The Mysteries of London* are vividly narrated, delightful, and incorporate moral messages; reading them elevates one's inner feelings, illuminates the mind with the light of *dharma*, and fills one's heart with pleasure. It portrays the customs, manners, and traditions of the European people. Great men regard *London Rahasya* as a piece of immoral literature without going deep into its narrative – our earnest request is that those people should read it in its entirety.... Perusal of this *rahasya* will enrich one with the knowledge of human psychology and morality ... with the realization that virtue is always triumphant, vice always defeated – virtue is capable of transporting one to heaven, vice takes one to hell – virtue is bright, beautiful, pure; vice low, dark, polluted.
>
> Almost all social scientists agree that exposure to social customs of different communities makes us civilized. The more we mix with different classes and peoples the better equipped we become to reform our own society. If there is truth in this saying, if there is need for reformation of our own society, then reading *London Rahasya* is obligatory for us; because this book acquaints us with different social structures, different kinds of people, different communities.... Some have condemned *London Rahasya* as stimulator of sensuality, breeder of malice, contributor to lowly desires. This condemnation is partial and wrong. The mystery which repeatedly makes the reader aware of the ugliness of vice can never be guilty of the above-mentioned charges. The mystery which projects the path of virtue as the source of all happiness, the only escape from all kinds of danger, is of force the inspirer of our nobler feelings.[8]

Haricharan's defence is significant. The fact that his translation was published from remote Murshidābād, and not one of the cheap presses of Battalā[9] in Calcutta, testifies to the fact that Reynolds's readership was not confined to Calcutta but spread over wide areas of Bengal. Reynolds was not read, adapted or translated solely for an urban readership, for his combination of sensation and moralizing gave his work a general appeal. It is evident that Haricharan himself hoped to emulate Reynolds's success with serialized 'penny dreadfuls'. At the end of the first (and, sadly, only) instalment, he informs the reader:

> *London Rahasya* is going to come out in this form every month from now on. The subscription charges inclusive of postal charges will be ten ānnās; the non-subscriber will have to pay twelve ānnās; only those paying for three months in advance will be regarded as subscribers.

---

8   Haricharan Ray, *London Rahasya* (Murshidābād: Printer Rāmnāth Tālookdār, Bangābda 1278, Bengali year roughly corresponding to 1871–72).

9   Battalā (the word literally means the 'shelter under a banyan tree') was a locality in the northern part of Calcutta with a concentration of cheap presses that catered for native readers who had not been initiated into more refined western literature. Battala books became synonymous with dirty stories, contemporary scandals, cheap paper and poor print. With their robust content and language, their popularity challenged the artificial and anaemic Bengali literature created by western-educated 'gentlemen'. Interestingly, Battala literature flourished in the neighbourhood of Sonāgāchhi, the best-known 'red light' area of nineteenth-century Calcutta.

Reynolds's *Mysteries* series found still other translators. From 1883 Nagendranāth Bandyopādhyāy serialized translations of *The Mysteries of London* and *The Mysteries of the Court of London* with the imaginative title *Prabāhini*,[10] a cross between a translation and an adaptation with indigenized characters. The title is interesting in that the Bengali word *prabāhini* means a 'flow' (of water), and more specifically a 'stream'. It therefore has a dual connotation, approximating to the English word 'serial' and also indicating that the translator interpreted Reynolds's work not simply as a collection of sensational episodes, as did many translators, but saw apparently unconnected events as part of a broader whole. Between 1884 and 1886, Bhairabi Mohan Bandyopādhyāy translated the first volume of *The Mysteries of the Court of London* as *London Rahasya* in six parts from 65 Cross Street, Calcutta. The first two volumes of Reynolds's *Mysteries* were also translated as *London Rahasya* by an anonymous translator in an edition from the Uchit-vakta Press, Calcutta, in 1885. Translations continued to the end of the century. In 1900 the Bengal Library Catalogue records an untitled translation of *The Mysteries of the Court of London* (second series), published from an obscure press on '17 Nanda Kumar Chaudhuri's Second Lane, Calcutta', and yet another *London Rahasya*, translated by B.C. Mitra and P.C. Pal, published from 68 Balarām De's Street.

These translations and adaptations are noteworthy not so much for the texts themselves as for their translators' approaches. It is a pity that few thought it necessary to explain their motives. Perhaps some did but in prefaces no longer attached to the damaged surviving copies. An exception is Kāliprasanna Chattopādhyāy's translation of *The Soldier's Wife*. Reynolds's novel tells the story of Lucy, a simple village girl whose betrothed Frederick is forcibly enlisted in the army, and records the sufferings they undergo, concluding with the military execution of Frederick and the death of Lucy and her child. Reynolds's story had a reform agenda, protesting against the harsh corporal punishment used to discipline common soldiers; but the translator found the pathos of Lucy's situation more appealing. It is understandable that in a country like India, where the figure of the suffering Sitā is revered as the ideal of womanhood, the theme of Lucy's unquestioning devotion to her husband should form the focus of the story. If in Reynolds's novel Frederick and Lucy were given almost the same space, Kāliprasanna weighs the scale in Lucy's favour. The translator's introduction pleads:

> Dear Reader, the unfortunate Lucy is the resident of alien shores – will she be able to draw your sympathy? Will you take pity on little Freddie, the child unhappy since his birth? – I entreat you – nay, I beg you to shed a single tear in the memory of these two unfortunate souls.
>
> I have not been able to hold back my tears at the moving narrative by Reynolds; I could not help crying even when I was actually translating the work; ... please show your appreciation for my labour by shedding a tear at the suffering of Lucy. That will be my reward – a single tear.[11]

---

10 *A Checklist of Translations of European Texts in Bengali: 1800–1900* (Calcutta: Department of English, Jadavpur University, 1996).

11 Kāliprasanna Chattopādhyāy, 'Introduction', in *Sainik Badhu*, 2nd edn, ed. Sābitriprasanna Chattopādhyāy, (Calcutta: Kar, Majumdār and Co., Cornwallis Buildings,

If this tips the scale excessively towards pathos, it is also rational, considering that many of the issues raised in the English original would have seemed remote to a Bengali readership. Kāliprasanna went one step further: he indigenized certain proper names and systematically listed specially coined words. To give a few examples: Obadiah Bates is turned into Abodh Betas (*abodh* in Bengali means 'ignorant, insensible', *betas* means 'cane'). Langley becomes Lānguli. *Lāngul* is a Sanskrit word meaning 'tail'; the addition of the suffix -*i* not only signifies Langley has the nature of a tailed creature, but also brings the name in line with the common Bengali surname Gānguli. Fleecewell turns into Fichel: in Bengali *fichel* means 'a cunning person', thus retaining the moral stereotype of the English original. The village of Oakleigh is transformed into the more Indian Dārupalli, *dāru* meaning 'tree' and *palli*, 'village'. Kāliprasanna bridged the distance between the alien dominant culture and the native scene in two ways. He identified the universal in Reynolds's moral types, and gave them native names. By focusing on the pathos of Lucy's situation, he drew on the appeal of pity, which transcends the boundaries of culture. While reshaping Reynolds's work, he gave his translation an appeal that would have matched that of its original.

The person most responsible for making Reynolds a household name in nineteenth-century Bengal was Bhubanchandra Mukhopādhyāy, now largely a forgotten figure (much like Reynolds himself), but one who in his own way tried to contribute to the slowly emerging Bengali prose literature. The title-page of the translation of *The Empress Eugenie's Boudoir* (1857), published by Basumati Sāhitya Mandir with the title *Rāni Iujini-r Baithak* (1924), describes Bhubanchandra as *Bānglā-r Reynolds*, the Reynolds of Bengal.[12] This points to the nature of Bhubanchandra's achievement: his original works often followed Reynolds's formulae of melodrama, spicy intrigue and near pornography, plus comment and moralizing on current affairs quite outside the narrative. Bhubanchandra's version of Reynolds provides the perfect example of what translation studies theory terms 'horizontal translation'. The text of his work totally avoids the intrusion of dominant culture sensibility into the language of the colonized. Bhubanchandra was a prolific and eclectic writer and seemed to have been at home with almost all literary genres, including poetry, fictional and non-fictional prose, social sketches, historical narratives, biography and travel accounts. But his forte was the translation of contemporary English sensational literature in general, and the work of Reynolds in particular.

Between 1871 and 1873 Bhubanchandra was part of a polemical Bengali literary group that adapted Reynolds's *Joseph Wilmot* (1853–55) under the strange title *Ei Ek Nutan! Āmār Guptakathā!!* (*This is a New One! My Secrets!!*). It was

---

1921). The introduction by the author carries the Bengali year 1302, which roughly corresponds to 1895/1896.

12   It was common practice in nineteenth-century Bengal to identify successful native authors writing in the vernacular with the European authors or poets whose characteristics they were seen as sharing. Bankimchandra was known as the 'Scott' of Bengal, the poet Madhusudan as the 'Milton' of Bengal, Saratchandra as the 'Dickens' of Bengal and so on.

published under the patronage of Rājā Asimkrishna Deb of Shobhābājār Rājbāri.[13] In 1887 Bhubanchandra adapted Reynolds's *Sister Anne* (1840), a translation of Paul de Kock's *Soeur Anne*, with the title *Bhāratiya Rahasya: Āmār Mahishi (The Mysteries of India: My Consort)*.[14] From 1888 to 1889 *Joseph Wilmot* again makes an appearance in his straight translation *Bilāti Guptakathā*;[15] and later in the guise of a Bengali Haridās in a reworking of *Ei Ek Nutan!, Haridāser Guptakathā* (1904). Bhubanchandra translated Reynolds's *Rosa Lambert* (1853–54) as *Bilāti Swarnabāi bā Sāheb-Bibi-r Guptakathā* (1910),[16] and from 1912 to 1914 the first 15 numbers of *The Mysteries of the Court of London* (1848–55), a task continued by Dinendra Roy. In 1924 he translated *The Empress Eugenie's Boudoir* as *Rāni Iujini-r Baithak*.

Bhubanchandra occupies a significant place in the history of literary translation in nineteenth-century Bengal, not only because of the sheer volume of his work but also for the way his own interpretation fused with the spirit of his originals. Hilaire Belloc, in *On Translation*, writes that the essence of the art is 'the resurrection of an alien thing in a native body',[17] but Bhubanchandra lets the text remain alien. He revels in the subversive nature of the original, and recognizes the elements that caused Reynolds to be regarded with suspicion in England. At the same time, Bhubanchandra sees Reynolds not as an author to be translated reverentially but as a kindred soul – almost a brother in arms in their shared anti-establishment stance. Their common reaction to the establishment goes beyond mere mechanical competence. Bhubanchandra's maturity as a translator is also evident in the prefaces and introductions he appends to most of the translated works.

Bhubanchandra's most important translation was Reynolds's *Joseph Wilmot*. The original text, of 104 numbers, was first published between 1853 and 1855. This picaresque novel tells the story of the orphaned Joseph Wilmot, who as the result of a complicated conspiracy is left to fend for himself in a hostile world, armed with nothing but his native intelligence. As in most of Reynolds's novels, the hero's experiences in the course of his struggles come to illustrate the evils of contemporary society and of human nature, in whose goodness Reynolds never had much faith. The novel has a fairytale ending, as Joseph is discovered to be the heir to a title and fortune, but this does not lighten the novel's pervasive grimness of tone. In spite of the multiplicity of subplots, the common bane of serialized novels, the work's basic structure, whose appeal to fiction-reading Bengalis inspired a

---

13 The Deb family of Shobhābājār, in north Calcutta, became rich through the munificence of the East India Company for services rendered, and were awarded the title Rājā by the British. Later this family came to exercise a great influence in nineteenth-century Bengali society, including the cultural and religious fields.

14 It had been rewritten as one of the three stories making up *The Empress Eugenie's Boudoir* (41 penny numbers, 1857–58): in the 'Preface' Reynolds declared that the story was the *raison d'être* of the novel itself.

15 October 1900 saw the publication of Bhubanchandra's *Thākurbārir Daptar*, a translation of Eugène Sue's *Le Juif Errant*; from 1903 to 1904 he translated Marie Corelli's *The Sorrows of Satan* with the title *Santapta Shaitān*.

16 Literally translated, the title reads *The English Swarnabāi or the Secrets of the White Lords and Ladies*. Swarnabāi was a famous courtesan of nineteenth-century Calcutta.

17 Hilaire Belloc, *On Translation* (Oxford: Clarendon Press, 1931).

succession of translations, is a simple one, appearing first in the above-mentioned adaptation of 1871–73, *Ei Ek Nutan!*, later renamed *Haridāser Guptakathā*. The hero of the Bengali adaptation is a precocious orphan boy called Haridās. The name, interestingly, is a typical Bengali proper name that literally means 'the servant of God/Lord Krishna', and is an ironic cross-reference to the subtitle of Reynolds's novel, *The Memoirs of a Man-Servant*.

For generations of Bengalis from the late nineteenth to the middle of the twentieth century, *Haridāser Guptakathā* came to embody the ultimate adult experience, to be read and enjoyed in secret. The word *Memoirs* in the original title was transformed into a more spicy *guptakathā*. *Gupta* means 'hidden, secret', referring both to the secrets surrounding Haridās's birth and inheritance and to the mysteries that he stumbles upon inadvertently, the unashamed exposure of the domestic vices of the Hindu household; *kathā* means 'narrative'. Haridās turns unwittingly into a voyeur, his experiences giving the lie to the concept of the purity of the family *andarmahal* ('inner sanctum') and revealing that no relation, whether social or determined by blood-ties, whether aunt, nephew, uncle, niece or even brother or sister, is resistant to the temptations of the flesh.[18]

Haridās, like his alter ego Joseph Wilmot, is a great traveller and traverses the length and breadth of the Indian subcontinent from Assam and Tripurā in the east to Gujarat and Rājputānā in the west. Haridās touches Calcutta very rarely, once early in the course of his escape from the clutches of his villainous pursuers and later when he is well settled in life. In this also he resembles Joseph Wilmot, who rarely if ever comes to the English metropolis, his adventures taking him to the remoter areas of England, Scotland and the continent.

> In Bhubanchandra's adaptation the sociocultural transference is effected so smoothly that there is no awkwardness in his description. The English and European landscapes are replaced by descriptions of purely Indian ones. Haridās has nothing but infinite contempt for the city of Calcutta; he adopts a high moral tone in his condemnation of what he sees as the chief symptom of the moral turpitude of the city:
>
> The location of the red light areas in the city shocks one's moral sensibilities. Brothels are everywhere – in respectable residential areas, by the dispensaries of doctors … they flourish right beside the Brahmo-samāj mandirs.… English-educated gentlemen openly admit, 'prostitutes are an integral part of urban civilization. City life means greater number of prostitutes, higher consumption of alcohol, more vice, even more so in the capital. Vice rules the capital city. These evils are necessary evils. No metropolis can function without these vices.'

---

18 That the portrayal of these vices was not merely a product of Bhubanchandra's fertile imagination is borne out by the fact that Bengali social reformers like Rāmmohun Roy and Iswarchandra Vidyāsāgar were passionate about female literacy, the abolition of child marriage and the remarriage of Hindu widows, who were often the victims of the lust of the males of their own family. Saratchandra Chattopādhyāy, who more than any other author was seriously involved with the question of the misery of Hindu women, in his novel *Bāmuner Meye* ('The Brahmin's Daughter'), as late as 1920 shows the sexual exploitation of a young widow by the husband of her sister, and her subsequent abandonment after she becomes pregnant.

I think if a civilization cannot survive without these vices, it deserves to be destroyed. I hated the city. I decided to leave it as soon as I could.[19]

But Haridās is not against western education; he is advised by one of his wellwishers to study English, and he takes the advice unquestioningly, for,

Englishmen now are the rulers of the country, so [one] should take English lessons...[20]

Haridās also is a strong believer in traditions: he is a conservative and accepts the Hindu caste division as a matter of course. Being an orphan he is unaware which caste he belongs to, but he makes sure that he is given food cooked by a Brahmin. When at the end of the narrative he decides to get married, his exchange with the girl of his choice is worth noting:

Amarkumāri sadly said, '...I don't want to hear anything regarding marriage ... I am past the age of marriage. I cannot even dream of marrying.' ... I interrupted her, 'Dear Amar, why do you repeat the same words? Why do you think you have crossed the marriageable age? ... It is true that you are a little past the age for marriage for Bengali girls.... But your nobility, innocence ... are qualities found only in the *avatars* of *Satya Yuga*, you do not resemble the women of *Kali Yuga*.... Moreover you as a woman can find happiness only in a marriage sanctified by the scriptures. If you go against this norm you will be committing a sin'.'[21]

The exchange explicitly reveals Haridās's attitudes to caste and marriage.

In 1887 Bhubanchandra's novel *Bhāratiya Rahasya: Āmār Mahishi* carried an advertisement for a soon-to-be published novel called *Bilāti Guptakathā*:

Ei Ek Nutan! Bilāti Guptakathā!! Atibaro Nutan Āscharya!!! ('This is a New One! The Mystery of England!! The Unsurpassed Wonder!!!') You have already met the Bengali Haridās in *Haridāser Guptakathā*, and you will soon be meeting the Bilāti [i.e., English] Haridās in *Bilāti Guptakathā*. The English Haridās is much braver, more intelligent, better able to fight the arrows and slings of life.... The same Bābu Bhubanchandra Mukhopādhyāy is the translator of this narrative into Bengali.... *Haridāser Guptakathā* was partially inspired by *bilāti Joseph Wilmot*, whereas *Bilāti Guptakathā* will present the undistorted story of *bilāti* Wilmot in the Bengali language.[22]

Haridāser Guptakathā was singularly free of political comments. It contained almost no remarks on the current political situation, no observation on the colonial

---

19   Bhubanchandra Mukhopādhyāy, *Haridāser Guptakathā* (Calcutta: Biswabāni Prakāshani, 1987), p. 86.

20   Mukhopādhyāy, *Haridāser Guptakathā*, p. 31.

21   Mukhopādhyāy, *Haridaser Guptakathā*, p. 643. According to Indian mythology the temporal cycle can be divided into four segments, *Satya Yuga* being the earliest one characterized by nobility and innocence, whereas *Kali Yuga* is the last stage when creation is pushed towards destruction for the excess of corruption in every aspect of life.

22   Mukhopādhyāy, *Bhāratiya Rahasya: Āmār Mahishi*, vol. 1. (Calcutta: Saradāprasād Neogi, Māniktalā Street, 23 Jugalkishor Dāser Lane, 1887), p. 109.

administration – in short, the adaptation is very unlike Reynolds in this aspect. There is a portrayal of contemporary society as well as an accurate and informative geographical description of the regions Haridās travels through to lend authenticity to the account, but he seldom exhibits any political consciousness. Haridās seems to be on a journey of self-discovery – anything larger in scope than his own interests and his immediate surrounding escapes him. *Bilāti Guptakathā*, the straight translation of *Joseph Wilmot*, is on the other hand replete with political observations. The title that Bhubanchandra gave the novel is interesting; it is no longer the memoirs of a single individual but, rather, the more comprehensive *Bilāti*, which can be loosely translated as *The Mysteries* or *Secrets of England/Europe*.

Bhubanchandra takes full advantage of the exposés that Reynolds uses to hook his readers. He takes no liberties with his interpretation and does not interfere with the text of the novel. Rather, he uses Reynolds as his ally, emphasizing the emotional tone of the original and involving his readers in the narrative rather than leaving them lost in the wilderness of a foreign culture. The title *Guptakathā* politicizes his translation of *Joseph Wilmot* from the start with its implicit reference to *The Mysteries of London*, a title not only better known than *Joseph Wilmot* but also Reynolds's most directly political novel. Bhubanchandra declares:

> My endeavour is to contrast with complete impartiality the different manifestations of the English civilization in its native country and in the colonies. English imperialism is trying to reform alien civilizations, criticizing the customs and manners of Hindu society, urging us to reform our national and social traditions by adopting the norms of an alien culture whereas in their own country some of the so-called 'civilized' Englishmen are polluting their society by their immoral actions.[23]

Bhubanchandra develops his closeness to Reynolds by weaving the fictional accounts into the history of colonial India. As with Reynolds's novels, fiction gains legitimacy by being yoked to reality. This furnishes the rationale for choosing to translate Reynolds's novel.

> Dear readers, Joseph Wilmot is born in the year 1820. He attains happiness twenty-three years later in the year 1842.... The year 1842 is not such a long way off; England had already become the ruler of the Indian subcontinent. At the time in question the Englishmen were in India on a divine-inspired mission to reform our country. Think of the year 1842; – within the space of the next seven to eight years India saw such improvements! – great men like Lord Auckland, Lord Ellenborough, Lord Hardinge succeeded one another, mindful of the responsibility of improving the destiny of Indians enabling them to live in peace. They were trying earnestly with the support of scriptural authority to reform the moral character of the Indians, to *civilize* them by teaching them to adopt the right kind of customs and manners.[24]

---

23 Mukhopādhyāy, 'Falasruti [Preface]', *Bilāti Guptakathā* (Calcutta: Basumati Sāhitya Mandir, 1889), vol. 2.
24 Mukhopādhyāy, 'Falasruti [Preface]', *Bilāti Guptakathā*, vol. 2, my italics. Lord Auckland was the Governor General of India from 1835 to 1842 and was responsible for the first Anglo-Afghan War, 1838–42 (often called 'Auckland's Folly'). Lord Ellenborough was his successor and annexed Sind to the British Empire in India. Lord Hardinge was responsible

Bhubanchandra's sarcastically expressed implication that the British 'reform' of India was a mask for imperial aggression reveals his pungent political awareness, and the 'Preface' continues to remind readers of the history of British belligerence:

> Think of the year 1842.... The British administration was not oblivious of its responsibility to ameliorate the condition of poor Indians even before the arrival of the great Lord Dalhousie in 1848. The Anglo-Afghan War, the Burmese War, the Anglo-Sikh War in the Punjab, the conflagration at Bharatpur – these were some of the examples of the untiring attempts by the great British military generals to ensure uninterrupted peace in India.[25]

In the Preface the larger-than-life Englishman, a morally superior image projected by the colonial administration,[26] is a contrast to the avaricious, vice-ridden English characters of the type Reynolds exhibited in his novels. The 'mystery' that Bhubanchandra uncovers in his translation is in fact the moral inferiority of the supposedly superior imperial race, a baseness that violates both the traditions and customs of the colonizers and the natural feelings of common humanity.

Bhubanchandra's radical Preface, however, could also express a conservative stance when addressing social issues in nineteenth-century Bengal.

> Child marriage is prohibited in almost all parts of Europe.... The results of this custom might be beneficial in the European social scenario, but sometimes they lead to undesirable ends. First, consider the effect of the unrestrained liberty enjoyed by English women; they do not need to take the consent of their parents when they marry; – in their youth or late youth they might fall in love with any Tom, Dick and Harry and get married without considering the possible consequences. The results occasionally are happy, but most bring unhappiness.... Widow remarriage is recognized in England. Even then examples of cheating ... [and] different kinds of sufferings [happen] as the events in the life of Joseph illustrate.[27]

Here Bhubanchandra expresses the anxiety, shared with many of the Bengali elite, that the emancipation of women promulgated by western reformers could lead to social anarchy. Instead, he focuses on the deprivation suffered by the orphan Joseph. He uses Joseph's innocence to expose the corruption of colonial society, and his exploitation establishes the vulnerability of the colonial subject. This creates an implicit bond between the hero and the oppressed native reader. However, this bond is compromised by the fact that Joseph in fact belongs, however loosely, to the *bilāti*

---

for the first Anglo-Sikh War that started in 1846. Interestingly, *RN* (20 September 1857) carried a letter to the Editor by 'Gracchus' with the heading 'Aristocratic Imbecility in India', where the three above-mentioned Governors General as well as Lord Dalhousie were held responsible for the injustices meted out to the natives.

25 Mukhopādhyāy, 'Falasruti [Preface]', *Bilāti Guptakathā*, vol. 2.

26 In his 'Minute on Indian Education' dated 2 February 1835, Macaulay expressed the opinion that a single shelf of European literature was worth more than the whole body of oriental literature. As literature is the expression of a nation's ethos, it establishes the superiority of the European culture.

27 Mukhopādhyāy, 'Falasruti [Preface]', *Bilāti Guptakathā*, vol. 2.

upper social class, and, unlike the common reader, is finally admitted within its fold.

As noted above, in 1887 Bhubanchandra published *Bhāratiya Rahasya: Āmār Mahishi*, his translation of Reynolds's *Sister Anne*. Apart from the fact that it carries the ubiquitous *rahasya* ('mysteries') in its title, there is no indication of any debt to Reynolds until well into the narrative. The plot roughly follows that of *Sister Anne*. The story in de Kock/Reynolds traces the fortune of an unlettered village girl called Anne (in Bhubanchandra's version Buni-didi), who falls in love with an aristocratic young man but becomes separated from him when she is carrying his child. She later goes out in search of the lost lover, is given shelter by the unsuspecting second and lawfully wedded wife, and is reunited with the object of her quest by the intervention of a *deus ex machina* in the shape of a raging fire.

But Bhubanchandra transforms the European melodramatic tale of a deaf and mute girl into a rich tapestry of adventure and contemporary social reality by adapting the setting to a Bengali cultural context. The different endings highlight the social, cultural and religious differences. In the European version, Sister Anne recovers her ability to speak after the shock of the fire but dies. In the Bengali version she survives the fire and is embraced into the household of the errant husband with the respect due to a wife. Sister Anne's tragic death reflects the nineteenth-century European refusal to condone sexual liaisons outside wedlock. Her early hermit-like state as a deaf-mute before meeting her lover sets her isolation, and her survival after her moral lapse would have offended against the ideals of female chastity that ruled in both fiction and society: her death literally and symbolically closes any possibility of social acceptance. Bhubanchandra's Buni-didi, on the other hand, has entered *Gāndharva Vivāha* (a relationship recognized by the Hindu society in which lovers can take marriage vows without sanctification by a priest), so there is no stigma attached to her motherhood. Her acceptance in the family of her husband is also due to the fact that in nineteenth-century India, polygamy was still an acceptable social practice.

There are many other instances of Bhubanchandra radically adapting his source to India. Like Reynolds, he makes social comments unrelated to the plot, scathingly criticizing the colonial administration. In one of these he refers to the effect of the dreaded Contagious Diseases Act, which by a special amendment came to be known as Act XIV in 1868, and was applied to the prostitutes of the city of Calcutta.[28] During her search for her lost husband Buni-didi has to save herself not only from dacoits and possible rapists, but also from the police who, empowered by Act XIV, are on the prowl with the intention of arresting unaccompanied females:

> Not so long ago when the prostitutes of Calcutta were being persecuted by Act XIV, the Calcutta police exploited the situation to the full.... One Governor General was not

---

28   This legislation allowed the police to arrest prostitutes in ports and army towns and bring them in for compulsory checks for venereal disease. If the women were suffering from sexually transmitted diseases they were placed in the Lock Hospital until cured. It was claimed that this was the best way to protect men, particularly the soldiers of the British army, from infected women. Many of the women arrested were not prostitutes but were still forced to go to the police station to undergo a humiliating medical examination.

willing to let the prostitutes be outside the pale of the benevolent British legal system....
This law has been responsible for the harassment and humiliation of quite a large number
of Bengali widows belonging to respectable families in the hands of the police.[29]

In other passages he rants against British rule in more general terms:

> When our nation was under the Islamic rule, our earning from business, from tax
> – or revenue earned from other sources, used to remain inside our country; ships did not
> carry it outside our own land. Now we are doing more business with the outside world,
> and [producing] more goods. There has been a corresponding rise in corruption.... The
> British are out to destroy our religion. Everybody knows that our sugar, candy, flour are
> adulterated with powdered bone.... Just a few days back Calcutta rocked with the rumour
> that 'ghee' [butter oil] was being adulterated.... In the autumn of [the Bengal year] 1293,
> during the Durgā Pujā many Hindu households had to refrain from using 'ghee' as a
> cooking medium.[30]

Such fragments of miscellaneous information, found throughout the adaptations
and translations of Reynolds's fiction, played their part in fostering his popularity
with his native translators and readers. However slight these details might seem today,
they contributed to the imaginative restructuring of a society seething under the rule
of foreign power. They helped readers identify with Reynolds's narrative technique,
his social and political attitudes and his alienation from the British educated middle
classes that formed the pillars of the colonial policy. The Indian readership could
sympathize with the sufferings of the repressed classes in Reynolds's novels and feel
by implication that he was also championing their cause. His work had a liberating
effect on the literary scene of nineteenth-century Bengal, freeing translators and
readers from the imaginative, political and aesthetic inhibitions of the colonial
experience.

---

29 Mukhopādhyāy, *Bhāratiya Rahasya*, vol. 1, p. 308. Surveys in Bengal during the
1870s revealed a large influx of rural women into Calcutta's brothels. These included girls
from lower castes sold by parents in acute financial crisis, girls kidnapped or falsely lured
and sold to the brothels, and daughters of professional prostitutes who left their villages and
moved to the metropolis in the hope of a better income. Yet among these, one group of women
puzzled the officials and embarrassed the Bengali gentlemen. They were the upper-caste
Hindu widows who, often out of a desperate need to be free of their social restrictions, fled
their village homes.

30 Mukhopādhyāy, *Bhāratiya Rahasya*, vol. 1, p. 147.

Chapter 16

Modernity, Memory and Myth: *Reynolds's News* and the Cooperative Movement

Ian Haywood

On 14 May 1950, *Reynolds's News and Sunday Citizen* proudly declared that on the following Tuesday (16 May) it would be holding a 'Century Party' at London's Albert Hall. This gala, for which memorabilia still exist, was to be a celebration of the centenary of the newspaper and its progression to a 'Second Century' (though in the event the paper only survived for less than 20 years). The glitziness of the event was reflected in the fact that high-profile guests included leading Labour politicians such as Herbert Morrison, Hugh Dalton, Manny Shinwell and Hugh Gaitskell (all architects of the post-war welfare state) and a smattering of film stars and theatre celebrities including Richard Attenborough and Joan Greenwood. But the bulk of the guests were drawn from staff of Britain's 800 shareholding Cooperative societies. The reason for this was that the gala had a dual purpose. It was a public celebration of two closely related radical institutions whose foundational historical 'moment' was the 1840s: the mass-circulation popular radical press, represented by its sole intact survivor, *Reynolds's News*, and the Cooperative movement, which commenced with the creation of the Rochdale Pioneers in 1844.[1]

These two traditions fused formally when the Cooperative movement purchased *Reynolds's News* in 1929, the year of the Wall Street Crash and the onset of the interwar crisis of capitalism. By 1950, the year of its centenary, *Reynolds's News* had a new, expanded name (the republican-sounding moniker 'Sunday Citizen' matched boldness with nostalgia), a circulation of almost 700,000 (though some commentators thought it should be larger) and the backing of a thriving radical organization whose identity looked both backwards and forwards.[2] The Cooperative

---

1 I have used the term Cooperative movement to refer to the national organization which, by the twentieth century, represented the collective will of hundreds of local Cooperative societies.

2 The circulation figures are from W.E.B. Camrose, First Viscount, *British Newspapers and Their Controllers* (London: Cassell, 1947), p. 143. Camrose is impressed that the paper is a 'brightly edited and active organ of Socialist opinion' but comments that the 'unlimited resources' of the Cooperative movement mean that the circulation is 'surprisingly small for a journal, which is the only, avowed Sunday paper of its particular opinions'. Given that the Cooperative movement had almost seven million members in the 1930s (see F. Hall and W.P. Watkins, *Cooperation: A Survey of the History, Principles, and Organisation of the*

movement's self-fashioned 'vision of the press' (to borrow a resonant phrase from the title of Mark Hampton's recent book, a study I will return to in a moment) was to represent *Reynolds's News* metonymically as an emblem of cooperation's twin virtues: looking backwards, a steadfastness rooted in core socialist values and working-class consciousness; looking forwards, a vigorous and dynamic modernity. This mutually reinforcing composite of synchronic and diachronic signifiers can be seen in the mottos which blazoned Cooperative propaganda for the paper: 'World's Oldest Cooperative Newspaper' and 'Press Power for the People', an echo of *Reynolds's News* socialist subtitle, 'Government of the People by the People for the People' (Figure 16.1). Though the paper had existed for 79 years before its purchase by the Cooperative, the effect of this recoding was to assimilate the paper into the history of cooperation and to imply that the teleology of *Reynolds's News* was inscribed in its original support for cooperative principles.

Fig. 16.1 'The World's Oldest Cooperative Newspaper'; 'Press Power for the People'. Publicity posters for *Reynolds's News*, 1946.

As a mode of production, a political cause and an alternative socioeconomic reality, cooperation supplied the ideal collectivized identity for the paper and its imagined community of readers. Though *Reynolds's News* was indelibly stamped with the individual identity of its founder, cooperation represented the next stage of the paper's evolution. At its most idealistic, this metonymic logic could interpret

Cooperative Movement in Great Britain and Ireland [Manchester: Cooperative Union, 1934], p. 32), Camrose may have a point.

the shift from entrepreneurial to collective ownership as a confirmation of the wider socialist transformation of the public sphere. In this chapter I want to reflect further on the implications of the *Reynolds's News* centenary for our understanding of the function of the discourses of modernity and memory in the culture and history of the radical press. In order to do this, I focus on the representation of the anniversary in the special 'Centenary Souvenir' that appeared in *Reynolds's News* on 5 May 1950. But that analysis should be prefaced with some comments on the significance of the anniversary.

The first point to note concerns the most conspicuous marker of the celebrations: the centenary dates 1850–1950. There is a notable recurrence of these dates in the period of press history chosen by Mark Hampton for his book *Visions of the Press in Britain, 1850–1950*.[3] In Hampton's chronology, these dates bracket the progress (or regress) of the press between the Stamp Duty Commission of 1850 and the Royal Commission on the Press of 1947–49. Whereas the former was a response to the liberal and radical demand for the end of 'taxes on knowledge' (the stamp duty was abolished in 1855), the latter enquiry reflected, ironically, broad anxieties about the commercial concentration of press ownership – in other words, there was a concern that the pendulum had swung too far the other way. Though the Royal Commission resisted recommending regulatory intervention, it nevertheless, according to Hampton, brought to a head 'the clash between labour and the capitalist press'.[4] Hampton's provocative characterization of this moment of cultural class war provides a useful context in which to place the centenary of *Reynolds's News*, a paper devoted precisely to the 'clash' between labour and capital. Indeed, the Cooperative journal *The Millgate* declaimed that

> The press has become merely another instrument in the possession of the great capitalist groups, used mainly for commercial ends as an integral part of the selling machinery of modern business, and having for its unavowed object the stifling of all opinion that does not accord with the views these newspaper owners take of their own interests, political aims, and the significance of popular movements.[5]

Seen from this perspective, the mobilization of radical origins in the anniversary of *Reynolds's News* carried two contrasting but ultimately reinforcing political messages. On the one hand, the centenary marked the culmination of a century of agitation for a more democratic and equitable society: in this sense the celebrations were emblematic of the wider post-war reconstruction of Britain. On the other hand, the paper's longevity was evidence that the 'clash' of labour and capital remained an ongoing struggle which gave the radical press a vital role as the fourth estate, the banner-bearer and voice of democracy, getting a grip on the future (Figure 16.2). So the memory of 1850 – personified by Reynolds himself – functioned diachronically as a guarantor of radical pedigree and synchronically as a talismanic reminder of the

---

3   Mark Hampton, *Visions of the Press in Britain, 1850–1950* (Urbana and Chicago: University of Illinois Press, 2004).

4   Hampton, *Visions of the Press in Britain*, p. 173.

5   Cited in Alan Burton, *The British Consumer: Cooperative Movement and Film 1890s–1960s* (Manchester: Manchester University Press, 2005), p. 64.

continuing class struggle.[6] It is this dual purpose of the memory of Reynolds which I call the Reynolds 'myth' – that he was both the founding father and the presiding deity of the newspaper's continuing life.

Fig. 16.2   'Get a Grip on the Future by Reading the Cooperative Press.' Publicity poster for *Reynolds's News*, undated.

---

6   According to Martin Conroy, the popular press has to be understood not only 'synchronically in terms of contemporary power struggle' but also 'diachronically in relation to longer traditions of folk, people's cultural experience and the modes and styles of their articulation' (*The Press and Popular Culture* [London: Sage, 2002], p. 84).

This myth found its first expression in the jubilee celebrations of 1900, and there are some striking similarities in the newspaper's construction of radical memory in the two anniversary events.[7] On both occasions the paper included a short résumé of Reynolds's life and achievements (including, importantly, a portrait), and on both occasions readers were invited to send in personal recollections of the paper's importance in their lives. The latter device allowed readers to express their devotion to the paper (and, by extension, to Reynolds himself), while also giving readers a stake in the historical construction of the paper's identity. The first page of the 'Centenary Souvenir' included both of these features, and its layout shows clearly the patriarchal relationship between Reynolds and his contemporary readers. From his elevated position in the top right-hand corner of the page, Reynolds looks down serenely on his modern followers. If the page is scanned from bottom to top, it looks as if the readers are personally recalling not just the newspaper but that 'young man in revolt'. Unlike the 50-year celebrations in 1900, when some readers recalled buying the very first issue of the paper, in 1950 the personal memories of readers only just stretched back to the Victorian period. But this historical gap is disregarded by the upbeat tone of the editorial comments which introduce these foot soldiers' letters:

> There is no mistaking the pride with which hundreds of veteran readers, many of them acclaiming *Reynolds's News* as their first introduction to Socialist thought and action, have delved into their store of memories to recall the stirring battles which this newspaper waged as the 'Champion of the Underdog'.[8]

The important emphasis here is on origination: by a series of metonymic links, the readers' 'first introduction' to democracy is a newspaper phenomenon which 'all started with' Reynolds. Significantly, the biographical sketch describes another dramatic 'start': the moment when Reynolds 'in one single afternoon' in March 1848 spoke for the first time to a Chartist meeting in Trafalgar Square, and as a result 'swept into national leadership of the Chartists'. The mythical essence of what the readers are recalling is the foundational moment of the paper's conception, but this moment is also a dramatic intervention by Reynolds into collective radical history. Notice that in the layout of the page, the movement from the present to the past (from reader to Reynolds) is mediated by the centrally situated image of marching Chartists. While the portrait of Reynolds is placid and beneficent (and in itself this is a direct challenge to conservative propaganda which portrayed him as a demagogue and rabble-rouser), the image of the Chartist demonstration of 10 April 1848 (which was called to support the presentation to Parliament of the third and final petition) is clearly an icon of class struggle. The visual patterning produces a flow of political energy from Reynolds through the collective agency of the Chartists to the cluster of contemporary readers.

---

7 See Ian Haywood, 'Encountering Time: Memory and Tradition in the Radical Victorian Press', in Laurel Brake and Julie F. Codell (eds), *Encounters in the Victorian Press: Editors, Authors, Readers* (Basingstoke: Palgrave, 2005), pp. 79–82.

8 'Centenary Souvenir', *RN*, 7 May 1950, p. 2.

Fig. 16.3   Front page of the 'Centenary Souvenir', *Reynolds's News*, 7 May 1950.

The 'mythic' meaning of this configuration of images is that Reynolds inspired the Chartist struggle, which in turn spawned later generations of activists. The Chartist image is therefore a reminder that 'stirring battles' remain in the present, and it is worth noting that Reynolds's face appears underneath the contemporary date of 7 May 1950 rather than the foundational date of 5 May 1850. Moreover, the centenary date is only one signifier of the present day: modernity is also represented by those Futurist symbols of advanced technology, modern forms of transport. The symbolic or 'mythic' logic at work in this second configuration of images provides another idealized vision of the radical press: Reynolds's 'dream' (his newspaper) has delivered a much wider Utopian 'dream', the transformation of society into modern technological marvels. As will shortly be shown, this vision fits neatly into the Cooperative movement's promotion of itself as a symbol of a modernity produced by and for the masses. But the other message that is implicit in the symbolic composition of the masthead of the 'Centenary Souvenir' is that sublime modernity (or the modernist sublime) cannot be taken for granted: just as the paper has spent a century 'fighting for the people', so the central image of the page is of the people fighting, and a nation in 'revolt'.

Despite the triumphal rhetoric, therefore, a stern message emanates from the face of Reynolds – 'it all started with a young man in revolt'. As the text puts it:

> He never lost faith in the common people. His vigorous, sometimes brutal writing had been an inspiration to millions of them – literally millions, for in the early years most copies of the 300,000 circulation of *Reynolds's News* passed through several hands.[9]

In this hyperbolic epic narrative, Reynolds is the single-'handed' patriarchal author of Victorian class struggle. The modest group of post-war readers is the inheritor of his 'vigorous' and 'sometimes brutal' journalistic potency. The phallic connotations of radical productivity are also evident in the Cooperative poster 'Get a Grip on the Future' (see Figure 16.2), in which the rolled-up copy of *Reynolds's News* is brandished in revolutionary manner by the metonymic 'hand' of the masses. (Notice that the rolled-up newspaper is given the nostalgic appearance of a tribunite scroll.)

Another conspicuous hand that requires some comment is that of Doctor Johnson, the figure who is waving amicably in the bottom left-hand corner of the page.[10] Although his literary authority is being harnessed to embellish an advert for the Bowater Paper Corporation, his 'mythic' narrative function is to place *Reynolds's News* in the longer liberal and radical struggle for press freedom and the establishment of the Habermasian public sphere. Reynolds's handiwork is therefore a spectacular illustration of the role of the press in diffusing enlightenment. But there is another, covert, historical narrative at work in this advertisement. The specific mention of 1765 surely evokes the period of 'Wilkes and Liberty', a seminal moment of popular radical agitation which achieved a significant breakthrough for press freedom when the government allowed parliamentary reporting for the first time. So behind Samuel Johnson is the ghost of John Wilkes, another 'vigorous' and much-maligned radical populist. In a clever piece of sleight-of-hand, the nostalgic allusion to the paternal Doctor Johnson may actually propose the 'brutal' libertine Wilkes as a model for the sensationalist Reynolds.

But as noted earlier, the Reynolds 'myth' is the story of the transformation of individual 'revolt' into the collective cause of socialism. Any appeal to a cult of personality (a risky rhetorical strategy in the post-war period) is tempered by a combination of nostalgia and historical process in which the patriarchal entrepreneur 'inspires' the democratic cause. Moreover, the teleological logic of this mythic narrative makes it clear that the engine of modernization is not only the spirit of Reynolds reincarnated in the labour movement. A more potent source of radical energy is the Cooperative movement, the institution which functions as the ideological and cultural self-consciousness of *Reynolds's News*. In the review of the newspaper's history that follows on from the brief biography of Reynolds, we are informed that the lowest ebb in the paper's fortunes came in the Edwardian period, when the paper was purchased by the Liberal MP Henry (later Lord) Dalziel. This transfer of ownership was regrettable for two reasons. Firstly, it moved the

---

9   'Centenary Souvenir', *RN*, 7 May 1950, p. 1.
10   As in Figure 16.3. In another edition he is on the right hand.

control of the paper out of the reach of the presiding spirit of its founding father: Dalziel bought the paper from the family of John Dicks, 'George Reynolds' original publisher'.[11] Secondly, Dalziel was a Liberal not a socialist, and his dilution of the political radicalism of the paper represented a period 'when policy veered'.[12]

Fortunately, all was not lost, and the day was saved by the heroic intervention of the Cooperative movement. Where Dalziel was 'a business man and a politician rather than a newspaper man' (Reynolds, of course, was all three), the Cooperative Press (the Cooperative's publishing arm) represented 'a federation of nearly 900 Cooperative Societies'. While Dalziel represented an outmoded brand of establishment politics, the Cooperative movement injected new life into the paper and ensured that it 'regained its old fighting spirit'. The souvenir programme of the Albert Hall centenary gala put this point in rather quainter language:

> We welcome our guests. We thank them for all they have done to give a new lease of life to a grand old newspaper since it became the property of the grandest of the people's movements.[13]

In order to revitalize its reputation and give it a new 'lease of life', the Cooperative movement gave the paper a new 'vision' of itself, including a new, republican name (*Sunday Citizen*) and a new editor of whom Reynolds could have been proud, the 'vigorous' Sydney Elliott, a man 'shaped and hardened in the great Socialist nursery of the Clydeside'. With these changes, the Cooperative movement had equipped the paper for a 'new era' in its history:

> There was no more searching the skyline for the mirage of a Liberal revival, no more marking time halfway between political democracy and economic democracy. *Reynolds's News* became the Sunday advocate of a full-blooded Socialist programme and the outspoken advocate of Cooperation as the most efficient and most democratic system of supplying the home.[14]

The takeover of the paper by the Cooperative movement in 1929 was therefore both a restoration and a modernization.[15]

This account of the paper's relationship with the Cooperative movement is a story of kinship, reciprocity and mutually beneficial ties; tropes of fidelity, allegiance

---

11   'Centenary Souvenir', *RN*, 7 May 1950, p. 2.

12   Bob Clarke notes that by the turn of the twentieth century 'the popular halfpenny papers' had abandoned their roots in 'the subversion and sedition of the popular radical and unstamped papers' (*From Grub Street to Fleet Street: An Illustrated History of English Newspapers to 1899* [Aldershot: Ashgate, 2004], p. 266). Clarke does not cite *RN*, which may have bucked this trend.

13   This programme and other memorabilia can be seen in the Cooperative Library, Manchester.

14   'Centenary Souvenir', *RN*, 7 May 1950, p. 2.

15   According to Johnston Birchall, the rest of the press was 'almost uniformly hostile to the Movement' at this time. See Birchall, *Co-op: The People's Business* (Manchester: Manchester University Press, 1994), p. 128. So *RN* may have helped to rescue the reputation of the Cooperative movement, another example of reciprocity.

and fulfilment construct a model narrative of enduring friendship and support. Three examples of this can be cited, all drawn from the second page of the 'Centenary Souvenir'. In the first example, we are told that the new paper resisted jingoism and 'remained faithful to the internationalism that had marked it from the first issue'.[16] This aspect of the paper's original political vision is complemented by the statement that the Cooperative movement is the 'only great international movement of the people that has not been torn apart by the conflicts of our time'.

The second example of reciprocity is taken from a short feature which presented examples of the paper's consistent advocacy of cooperation. A quotation from a *Reynolds's News* article of 1894, declaring that 'Cooperation seems to possess the germs of the speediest and most effective form of emancipation', is followed by an apposite comment: 'With this tradition of support of the Cooperative Movement behind it, the transference of the paper to Cooperative ownership in 1929 represented no change of policy.'[17]

The third example of the idealization of the union of *Reynolds's News* and the Cooperative movement is a particular gem, as it produces in a very literal way a new image of the paper. The second page of the 'Centenary Souvenir' contained a small congratulatory address by the 'C.W.S.', the acronym for the Cooperative Wholesale Society. As the announcement shows, the C.W.S. and the paper are very closely related: 'It was a mere thirteen years after the first issue of "Reynolds" that the C.W.S. – a natural outcome of the Cooperative Movement's early growth – was founded.' The paper is personified in nostalgic, heroic terms that 'recall' its founder's battle against the raw exploitation of the Victorian mode of production:

> *Reynolds's News*, fearless, outspoken, inspired by true democratic principles, fought tirelessly against exploitation, injustice, and tyranny.[18]

---

16 'Centenary Souvenir', *RN*, 7 May 1950, p. 2.

17 'Centenary Souvenir', *RN*, 7 May 1950, p. 2. Peter Gurney gives a slightly different narrative of the takeover in *Cooperative Culture and the Politics of Consumption in England, 1870–1930* (Manchester: Manchester University Press, 1996). In Cooperative congress debates about the purchase of *RN*, there was some expression of unease which reflected, according to Gurney, a puritanical attitude among many cooperators towards popular culture. One delegate, for example, stated that he wanted a 'cleaner paper' and added, 'If I want horrors I can always go to the "Pictures"' (p. 235). Gurney notes that *RN* 'had attempted, with considerable success, to hold together "high" and "low" elements within working-class culture since the mid-nineteenth century,' but after the Cooperative takeover the circulation 'plummeted' (pp. 234–5). As cited above, circulation was less than a million in the 1940s, a decline from the historic peak in the late nineteenth century, but 'plummeted' may be an exaggeration.

18 'Centenary Souvenir', *RN*, 7 May 1950, p. 2.

The C.W.S salutes a great newspaper

on attaining its century in the service of the people. Reynolds News, fearless, outspoken, inspired by true democratic principles, fought tirelessly against exploitation, injustice, and tyranny.

It was a mere thirteen years after the first issue of " Reynolds " that the C.W.S— a natural outcome of the Co-operative Movement's early growth — was founded. It has now become Britain's biggest business, owned and controlled by the consumers themselves. The C.W.S is proud to associate itself with Reynolds News ; from both, the people have gained so much.

ANNOUNCEMENT OF CO-OPERATIVE WHOLESALE SOCIETY LTD.

Fig. 16.4   Cooperative Wholesale Society announcement in the 'Centenary Souvenir', *Reynolds's News*, 7 May 1950.

By way of contrast with this heroic rhetoric, the C.W.S. represents the ideal realization of this 'tireless' agitation: 'It has now become Britain's biggest business, owned and controlled by the consumers themselves.' The supposedly unique achievement of the Cooperative movement – the socialization of the capitalist mode of production – is contained in the movement of the prose in this one sentence. But the final tribute that the C.W.S. pays to *Reynolds's News* takes the form of a new 'vision' for the paper. At the foot of the announcement is an image of the paper's centenary which could have become a delightful new modernist logo for the paper (see Figure 16.4). Unlike the conventional radical format of 'Get a Grip on the Future' (Figure 16.2), this image – in which the paper resembles a giant birthday card, or indeed a 'Centenary Souvenir' – evokes a stylish and sophisticated modern image of the radical press. The image's confident modernism eschews any reference to class struggle or conflict of any kind (unless, that is, one assumes that a black-and-white view of the world is being signified, but that seems a tenuous interpretation of the image's use of monochrome). The aesthetic appeal is founded on elegant symmetry and geometrical simplicity, a visual statement of the final sublimation of the Reynolds 'myth' into a transcendent realm of pure radical beauty. And though it is possible to interpret the human figure in the design as an allusion to Reynolds himself, now recast in elegant contemporary garb, this identification is submerged, and the point of the image is to denote the paper's new socialist and Cooperative identity. So far as I am aware, this image was not widely reproduced, but it remains an intriguing example of a radical appropriation of modernist aesthetics.

The argument so far has been that the 'Centenary Souvenir' of *Reynolds's News* presented a mythical narrative in which the Cooperative movement functioned as the ideal destiny for Reynolds's original 'dream'. Of course, there is an obvious cautionary point to make about the use of the 'Centenary Souvenir' as a historical document: all anniversaries produce self-serving, morale-boosting propaganda rather than disinterested history. But as press historians such as Mark Hampton, Aled Jones and Stanley Harrison have shown, the self-fashioned image of the press has always been an important factor in determining its cultural authority.[19] Moreover, as Fredric Jameson demonstrated in *The Political Unconscious* (1981), all history takes a textual form.[20] If this poststructuralist insight is applied to the centenary of *Reynolds's News*, it highlights the manner in which the anniversary constructed history out of a combination of personal and institutional memory. There is a clear parallel between the readers who 'delved into their store of memories' and the paper's centenary display of highlighted campaigns drawn from its archive of past issues. As the introduction to a reprinted article about the agricultural trade unionist Joseph Arch states: 'From the files of *Reynolds's News* in our Centenary Year we are retelling the story of men and women who challenged the overpowerful and the overprivileged to win us the rights

---

19   Hampton, *Visions of the Press in Britain*; Aled Jones, *Power of the Press: Newspapers, Power and the Public in Nineteenth-century England* (Aldershot: Ashgate, 1996); Stanley Harrison, *Poor Men's Guardians* (London: Lawrence and Wishart, 1974).

20   Fredric Jameson, *The Political Unconscious: Narrative as a Socially Symbolic Act* (1981; London: Methuen, 1983).

we enjoy today.'[21] These highlights of Victorian class struggle and radical reportage included the dockers' strike of 1889, the campaign against flogging in the army and a scathing eyewitness report from 1868 of the last man to be publicly executed in England (a Fenian called Michael Barrett, whom the paper believed was convicted on flimsy evidence). Other reprinted centenary pieces displayed the paper's wider popular appeal in its coverage of sport and fashion, though these cultural interests are not put forward as the central components of the paper's identity.

The cumulative effect of these reprinted stories is to turn the 'Centenary Souvenir' into a mini-archive of press history, a celebration and exhibition of the paper's textual and visual triumphs, and a powerful statement of the importance of maintaining a store of 'files' as usable radical history. The columnist Tom Driberg (who worked for the paper in the 1940s and 1950s) even used his own foray into the paper's 'old files' to dissent from the 'Souvenir's' general narrative of progress and to contrast the 'vigour' of Reynolds with the 'squeamish' standards of much modern reporting:

> In all the pages of these old files, indeed – in police court news, in Parliamentary reports, in animadversions on the Royal Family – there is a note too often lacking in our better-groomed modern newspapers: a note of racy, unsqueamish vigour and expansive critical freedom.
>
> To some extent, no doubt, this was a hangover from the Georgian era. The blight of Victorian bourgeois Puritanism had not descended fully on England. To a considerable extent it must be because the journalists of a century ago were not cramped and frustrated as their successors are by laws of libel whose interpretation by judges and juries is quite unpredictable (except that the verdict will usually go against a Socialist litigant).[22]

This diatribe characterizes the 1950s as still suffering from the 'hangover' of the 'puritanical' Victorian morality which the career of Reynolds did so much to challenge. Paradoxically, it was at the point when British society entered a new era of freedom of expression and permissiveness – the 1960s – that the paper finally expired. This may have been due to the fact that, after all the paper's attempts to reconstruct its identity, it still could not find a form in which to combine its traditional radicalism with new modes of popular desire and consumption. Even the mighty collective power of the Cooperative movement could not halt the closure of the paper in 1967.[23] The 'Centenary Souvenir' was therefore much more than an exercise in self-regarding exhibitionism. It was an object lesson in how to *do* press history. In the words of one of the paper's 'old friends', 'Your "Century Souvenir" is of unique historical value and will be treasured by all lovers of liberty'.[24] Ironically, in the absence of a proper history of *Reynolds's News*, the 'Centenary Souvenir' remains one of the best overviews of the paper's distinctive contribution to the British press and radical tradition.

---

21 'When the Village Awakened', *RN*, 14 May 1950, p. 5.

22 'Centenary Souvenir', *RN*, 7 May 1950, p. 3.

23 According to Arnold Bonner, Cooperative membership in the late 1960s was a staggering seven million, but the movement was inept at promoting *RN* to its own members (*British Cooperation: The History, Principles, and Organisation of the British Cooperative Movement* [1961; Manchester: Cooperative Union, 1970], p. 377).

24 'Centenary Souvenir', *RN*, 7 May 1950, p. 3.

A Bibliography of Works by G.W.M. Reynolds

Prepared by Louis James

It is impossible at this date to compile a complete and accurate bibliography of Reynolds's fiction. First editions of his novels were not lodged in deposit libraries, his works were constantly reprinted in undated editions, and printed on cheap paper in ephemeral form, most copies of his huge output were read to destruction. This bibliography lists the first known appearance of each title. But it gives no indication of their constant republication over his lifetime. The cumulative total of copies would have been in the millions.

From 1844, all Reynolds's fiction was published in weekly penny issues, featuring a woodcut on the first page: these were resold, gathered into monthly parts, and finally as one or two volumes. Where a title had first appeared in the *London Journal* or *Reynolds's Miscellany*, on its conclusion it was reissued in this format. In 1857 *Reynolds's Newspaper* was advertising 'A New Edition of the Works of G.W.M. Reynolds', almost certainly the single volumes at sixpence each that formed the basis for later collections of Reynolds's works, printed in a smaller format (down from 24 x 16 cm to 21 x 13.5 cm), keeping the original text and illustrations, but with a condensed layout and pagination. From 1864 they were being issued by John Dicks in his 'Standard English Novels' series, and from 1876 as 'The Complete Novels of G.W.M. Reynolds'. The John Dicks Press at 8, Temple Avenue EC published a further undated 'People's Edition', with attractive coloured wrappers from 1909.

Reynolds's works were also pirated, often with altered titles, in the United States. T.B. Peterson of Philadelphia was a particularly persistent publisher of such editions. E.F. Bleiler, in the Dover Publications reprint of G.W.M. Reynolds's *Wagner the Wehr-Wolf*,[1] lists some 44 American pirated editions, some of which were issued in separate parts under different titles. Most of these were ephemeral, but at least 20 (undated) volumes of an expensively produced American edition of *The Mysteries of the Court of London* and *The Works of G.W.M. Reynolds*, with fine steel engravings by Frank T. Merrill, carry the imprint of either 'The Oxford Society [New York?]' or 'The Burton Ethnological Society, Boston'. As neither body appears to have existed, the imprint may have been invented to give respectability to Reynolds's racy narratives for upmarket buyers.

---

1 (New York: Dover, 1975), pp. 153–60. We are pleased to acknowledge our debt to Mr Bleiler in compiling this bibliography.

I. Novels

Where Reynolds's novels are listed as first appearing in periodicals, it can be assumed that on their conclusion they were reissued in penny issue and volume form by John Dicks: this list only records this subsequent publication where there was a change in the title.

The Youthful Impostor, 3 vols (Paris: G.G. Bennis, Librairie des Etrangers, 1835). Reissued, revised and enlarged in weekly parts as *The Parricide, or, A Youth's Career of Crime* (London: John Dicks, 1847). Translated by A.J.B. Defauconfrêt as *Le Jeune Impostor* (Paris: E. Renduel, 1836).

The Baroness – a Novel, by 'Parisianus' (almost certainly Reynolds), seven chapters (unfinished) in the *Monthly Magazine*, August to November 1837.

Pickwick Abroad; or the Tour in France, with 40 steel engravings by 'Crowquill' (Alfred Henry Forrester) and 33 wood engravings (1838–39). The first 25 chapters appeared in the *Monthly Magazine*, from December 1837 to June 1838, after which it was probably withdrawn under pressure from the disapproving proprietors of the *Monthly*. Sherwood, Gilbert and Piper (London) simultaneously published the novel in 20 monthly parts from January 1838 to August 1839, when it was issued in a single volume. Other editions appear under the imprint of G.H. Willoughby (London, [n.d.]) and of Thomas Tegg (London, dated 1839 but probably published later). G.H. Bohn reused the well-worn stereotype plates for a shoddy edition in 1864.

Alfred de Rosann (1838). First published in the *Monthly Magazine*, July to December 1837, where it took over as the lead serial from *Pickwick Abroad*. Published with 13 illustrations by T. Phillips as *Alfred, or the Adventures of a French Gentleman* (London: Willoughby and Co., [1838?]) and reissued by John Dicks (London, [n.d.]). Bleiler records a 'slightly abridged' American version, *Life in Paris, or the Adventures of Alfred de Rosann in the French Metropolis*.

Grace Darling, or the Heroine of the Fern Islands (London: George Henderson, 1839).

Robert Macaire in England, 3 vols (London: Thomas Tegg, 1840). Republished as *Robert Macaire; or the French Bandit in England* (London: John Dicks, [n.d.]).

The Steam-Packet. A Tale of the River and Ocean (London: Willoughby and Co., 1840); another edition (London: John Dicks, [n.d.]). (A weak derivative of *Pickwick Papers*, with a 'club outing' on water rather than land.)

The Drunkard's Tale. In *The Teetotaller*, 27 June–28 November 1840. Republished as *The Drunkard's Progress* (London: George Henderson, 1841) and serialized under this name in *Reynolds's Miscellany*, 9 February–20 April 1850.

Master Timothy's Bookcase, or The Magic Lanthorn of the World (London: W. Emans, monthly parts, 1841–42); a collection of short stories, reissued, with some variation in the content, as *Master Timothy's Book-case*, 22 numbers (London: Office of *Reynolds's Miscellany*, 1847) and as *Master Timothy's Book-case; or, the Magic Lantern of the World* (London: John Dicks, [n.d.]).

The Mysteries of London, 1st series. Weekly penny issues, (?) October 1844–26 September 1846 (London: George Vickers). For a useful abridged edition of this series, with an introduction and selected illustrations, see G.W.M. Reynolds, *The*

Mysteries of London, ed. Trefor Thomas (Keele: Keele University Press, 1996). An unabridged, annotated version, with illustrations, edited by Dick Collins and Lee Jackson, is to be published by Valancourt Books: Kansas City (forthcoming).

Faust, a Romance. In the *London Journal*, 4 October 1845–18 July 1846. The penny issue edition was retitled *Faust. A Romance of the Secret Tribunals* (London: George Vickers, 1847); a later edition was published as *Faust. A Romance* (London: John Dicks, [n.d.]).

The Mysteries of London, 2nd series. Weekly penny issues, 3 October 1846–16 September 1848 (London: George Vickers).

Wagner, the Wehr-Wolf, a Romance. In *Reynolds's Miscellany*, 6 November 1846–24 July 1847; republished as *Wagner, the Wehr-Wolf* (London: John Dicks, [n.d.]). Reprinted with an introduction, bibliography and notes by Dick Collins as *Wagner the Werewolf* [sic] (London: Wordsworth Editions, 2006).

The Days of Hogarth, or The Mysteries of Old London. In *Reynolds's Miscellany*, 29 May 1847–29 April 1848. The wrapper of 'Dicks' English Novels' edition (*c.*1864) bears the alternative title, *Old London*.

The Coral Island, or The Hereditary Curse. In *Reynolds's Miscellany*, 15 July 1848–31 March 1849.

The Mysteries of the Court of London, 1st series. Weekly penny issues, 9 September 1848–17 August 1850 (London: John Dicks). Translated (no translator given) as *Les Mystères de la Cour de Londres*, 8 vols. (Paris: A. Faure, 1866-68).

The Pixy, or the Unbaptized Child, published in a green paper cover as a miniature imitation of Dickens's Christmas books (London: John Dicks, 1848); reprinted in *Reynolds's Miscellany*, 27 April–25 May 1850.

The Bronze Statue, or The Virgin's Kiss. In *Reynolds's Miscellany*, 31 March 1849–14 March 1850.

The Seamstress: a Domestic Tale. In *Reynolds's Miscellany*, 23 March–10 August 1850. Chapters 1–13 bear the title *The Slaves of England*. Reprinted as *The Seamstress, or The White Slave* [sic] *of England* (London: John Dicks, [n.d.]). 'Imité' by Azur Dutil as *Les Prolétaires deLondres et les Martyrs du Travail* (Paris: Azur Dutil, 1862).

Pope Joan, or The Female Pontiff. In *Reynolds's Miscellany*, 10 August 1850–15 January 1851.

The Mysteries of the Court of London, 2nd series. Weekly penny issues, 24 August 1850–(?) May 1852 (London: John Dicks).

Kenneth, a Romance of the Highlands. In *Reynolds's Miscellany*, 25 January–27 December 1851.

The Necromancer, a Romance. In *Reynolds's Miscellany*, 27 December 1851–31 July 1852. Ed with a Biographical sketch and Afterword by Dick Collins as *The Necromancer* (Kansas City: Valancourt Books, 2007).

Mary Price, or The Memoirs of a Servant-Maid. Weekly penny issues, 1 November 1851–7 October 1852 (London: John Dicks).

The Mysteries of the Court of London, 3rd series. Weekly penny issues, 1 May 1852–23 December 1853 (London: John Dicks).

The Massacre of Glencoe, a Historical Tale. In *Reynolds's Miscellany*, 31 July 1852–18 June 1853; reissued as *The Massacre of Glencoe* (London: John Dicks, [n.d.]).

The Soldier's Wife. Weekly penny issues, 12 November 1852–(?) June 1853.

The Rye House Plot, or Ruth, the Conspirator's Daughter. In *Reynolds's Miscellany*, 18 June 1853–19 August 1854.

Joseph Wilmot, or The Memoirs of a Man Servant. Weekly penny issues, 29 July 1853–4 July 1855 (London: John Dicks).

Rosa Lambert. Weekly penny issues, 4 November 1853–(?) October 1854 (London: John Dicks).

The Mysteries of the Court of London, 4th series. Weekly penny issues, 30 December 1853–5 December 1855 (London: John Dicks).

May Middleton, The History of a Fortune. In *Reynolds's Miscellany*, 19 August 1854–6 January 1855.

Omar, a Tale of the Crimean War. In *Reynolds's Miscellany*, 6 January 1855–5 January 1856.

The Loves of the Harem, or A Romance of Constantinople. Weekly penny issues, 3 February 1855–7 (?) July 1855 (London: John Dicks).

Ellen Percy, or The Memoir of an Actress. Weekly penny issues, 21 July 1855–September (?) 1857 (London: John Dicks).

Agnes: or Beauty and Pleasure. Weekly penny issues, 12 December 1855–January (?) 1857 (London: John Dicks).

Leila, or The Star of Mingrelia. In *Reynolds's Miscellany*, 5 January–5 July 1856.

Margaret, or The Discarded Queen. In *Reynolds's Miscellany*, 5 July 1856–11 July 1857.

The Empress Eugenie's Boudoir. (The title is a framework for a sequence of separate narratives.) Weekly penny issues, 4 February 1857–March (?) 1858 (London: John Dicks).

The Young Duchess, or The Memoirs of a Woman of Quality. A Sequel to Ellen Percy. Weekly penny issues, 17 June 1857–9 June 1858 (London: John Dicks).

Canonbury House, or The Queen's Prophecy. In *Reynolds's Miscellany*, 11 July 1857–1 May 1858.

Mary Stuart, Queen of Scotland. In *Reynolds's Miscellany*, 14 May–24 December 1859.

The Young Fisherman, and Other Stories (London: John Dicks, [1864]).

II. Short Stories

A complete list of Reynolds's short fiction is beyond the scope of this bibliography. Many short stories are embedded in his novels, and Reynolds had no scruples about recycling tales, sometimes under changed titles. In his bibliography to *Wagner the Wehr-Wolf*, E.F. Bleiler also points to the extensive piracy of Reynolds's stories, often disguised, in the United States. This selection can offer but a sample of a significant category of Reynolds's oeuvre.

'The Baroness', *Monthly Magazine*, September 1837. Republished as 'The Baroness of Grandmanoir', in *The Young Fisherman, and Other Stories* (London: John Dicks, [n.d.]).

'The Father', *Monthly Magazine*, September 1838. Republished as 'The Mysterious Manuscript', in *The Young Fisherman*.

'Mary Hamel', *Monthly Magazine*, October 1838.

'The Sculptor of Florence', *Monthly Magazine*, November 1838. Republished as 'The Broken Statue', in *The Young Fisherman*.

'Noctes Pickwickianae', *The Teetotaller*, 27 June–8 August 1840.

'Pickwick Married', *The Teetotaller*, 23 January–19 June 1841.

'The Assassin', *London Journal*, 29 March 1845.

'Margaret Catchpole', *London Journal*, 5 April 1845.

'A Tale for Christmas', *Reynolds's Miscellany*, 26 December 1846.

'The Matrimonial Advertisement', *Reynolds's Miscellany*, 30 January 1847.

'The Castellan's Daughter', *Reynolds's Miscellany*, 22 and 29 June 1850.

'The Greek Maiden, or The Banquet of Blood', *Reynolds's Miscellany*, 27 July 1850.

'The Janizary, or The Massacre of the Christians', *Reynolds's Miscellany*, 2 and 9 November 1850, republished in *The Young Fisherman*.

'The Prophecy, or The Lost Son', *Reynolds's Miscellany*, 7–21 December 1850.

'The Young Fisherman', *Reynolds's Miscellany*, 5 October–9 November, 1861, republished in *The Young Fisherman*.

III. Journalism

London and Paris Courier, Paris. January–August 1838. Part owner, literary editor.

Monthly Magazine of Politics, Literature, and the Belles-Lettres, London. 1837–38. Editor. While Reynolds's name never appeared as editor, and even his contributions remain unsigned, from August 1837 to December 1838 the *Monthly*'s content is dominated by his style and radical, pro-French attitudes. From January 1839 a 'New Series' publicized Abraham Heraud as editor, and stridently signalled the *Monthly*'s return to conservative views.

The Teetotaller, A Weekly Journal Devoted to Temperance, Literature and Science, London. 27 June 1840–25 September 1841. Editor, part owner.

London Journal and Weekly Record of Literature, Science and Art, London. March 1845–November 1846. Editor.

Reynolds's Miscellany of Romance, General Literature, Science and Art, London. 7 November 1846–19 June 1869, when it merged with *Bow Bells* (see below). Editor, proprietor or part proprietor.

Weekly Magazine, London. 1 January–1 July 1848 (amalgamated with *Reynolds's Miscellany*). This extremely rare halfpenny periodical was published from Reynolds's office, but may have been edited by Reynolds's wife Susannah, who published her novel *The Poacher's Daughter* in its pages.

Reynolds's Political Instructor, London. 10 November 1849–11 May 1850. Editor and proprietor.

Reynolds's Weekly Newspaper, London. 18 August 1850–19 June 1879. Editor and proprietor until 1862, when he may have become part proprietor.

Bow Bells, London. 12 November 1862–22 February 1897. Reynolds was probably editor of the 'new series' from August 1864 until some time in 1868.

IV. Translations and Miscellaneous Works

The Errors of the Christian Religion Exposed, by a Comparison of the Gospels of Matthew and Luke (London: R. Carlile, 1832).

Songs of Twilight (Paris: Librairie des Etrangers, 1836). A translation of Victor Hugo's *Chants du Crépuscule*.

The Modern Literature of France. Chapters 1–9 were first published as *The Modern School of French Literature* in the *Monthly Magazine*, April–December 1838. Completed in 2 vols (London: George Henderson, 1839); revised and enlarged, 1841.

The Catacombs of Paris, manuscript acting copy, *c.*1838. The title-page states: 'a melodrama in two acts by G.W.M. Reynolds. Founded on an original tale from part xiv of *Pickwick Abroad*'. The drama may be by Reynolds himself; if not, he is its effective inspiration.

The Last Day of a Condemned (London: George Henderson, 1840). A translation of Victor Hugo's *Le Dernier Jour d'un Condamné*.

Sister Anne (London: George Henderson, 1840). A translation of Paul de Kock's *Soeur Anne*. Later incorporated in part into *The Empress Eugenie's Boudoir* (see Novels, above).

The Anatomy of Intemperance (London: United Temperance Union, 1840). Planned as comprising eight weekly parts. Parts 1 to 4 exist, but it is not known whether the work was completed.

The History of the Ottoman Empire, Part 1. Announced as 'nearly ready' in *The Teetotaller*, 3 October 1840. It is, however, questionable whether it was ever published. 'The Foundation of the Ottoman Empire', in *Reynolds's Miscellany*, 18 and 25 February 1854, may be a portion of this.

A Sequel to Don Juan (London: Paget and Co., 1843).

The French Self-Instructor (London: John Dicks, 1846).

Reynolds's Diagram of the Steam Engine, with a Popular Description (London: John Dicks, 1854).

The Self-Instructor (London: John Dicks, 1861). Compiled from *Reynolds's Miscellany*.

Bibliography of Selected Secondary Materials on G.W.M. Reynolds and his Works

Prepared by Helen Hauser

I. Books

Altick, Richard, *The English Common Reader: A Social History of the Mass Reading Public, 1800–1900*, 2nd edn (1957; Columbus, Ohio: Ohio State University Press, 1998).

Andrews, Alexander, *The History of British Journalism*, 2 vols (London: Richard Bentley, 1859).

Baldick, Chris, *In Frankenstein's Shadow: Myth, Monstrosity, and Nineteenth-century Writing* (Oxford: Clarendon Press, 1987).

Biagini, Eugenio, *Liberty, Retrenchment and Reform: Popular Liberalism in the Age of Gladstone* (Cambridge: Cambridge University Press, 1992).

Bleiler, E.F. (ed.), *Wagner the Wehr-Wolf* (New York: Dover, 1975). Includes the first comprehensive list of Reynolds's publications, in chronological order, and discusses the myriad problems of compiling such a bibliography.

Bourne, H.R. Fox, *English Newspapers: Chapters in the History of Journalism*, 2 vols (London: Chatto and Windus, 1887).

Chevasco, Berry Palmer, *Mysterymania: The Reception of Eugene Sue in Britain, 1838–1860* (Oxford: Peter Lang, 2003).

Clark, Thomas A., *A Letter addressed to G.W.M. Reynolds reviewing his conduct as a professed Chartist* (London: Thomas Clark, 1850).

Dalziel, Margaret, *Popular Fiction One Hundred Years Ago: An Unexplored Tract of Literary History* (London: Cohen and West, 1957). A central text, one of the first to consider Reynolds as a sophisticated writer. See 'The Most Popular Writer of Our Time', pp. 35–45.

Denning, Michael, *Mechanic Accents: Dime Novels and Working-class Culture in America* (London: Verso, 1987).

Dicks, Guy, *The John Dicks Press* (published by the author, GuyDicks@msn.com, 2005).

Dix, John Ross, *Lions: Living and Dead, or Personal Recollections of the Great and the Gifted* (London: Tweedie, 1852), pp. 282–6.

Finn, Margot C., *After Chartism: Class and Nation in English Radical Politics, 1848–1874* (Cambridge: Cambridge University Press, 1993).

Gallagher, Catherine, *The Industrial Reformation of English Fiction, 1832–1867* (Chicago: University of Chicago Press, 1985).

Haining, Peter (ed.), *The Penny Dreadful; or, Strange, Horrid & Sensational Tales!* (London: Victor Gollancz, 1976).

Harrison, Stanley, *Poor Men's Guardians: A Record of the Struggles for a Democratic Newspaper Press, 1763–1973* (London: Lawrence and Wishart, 1974).

Haywood, Ian, *The Revolution in Popular Literature: Print, Politics, and the People, 1790–1860* (Cambridge: Cambridge University Press, 2004). Sourcebook for history and analysis of Reynolds's publishing and critical reception, both current and contemporary, as well as his involvement in Chartism.

Himmelfarb, Gertrude, *The Idea of Poverty: England in the Early Industrial Age* (London: Faber and Faber, 1984).

James, Louis, *Fiction for the Working Man, 1830–1850: A Study of the Literature Produced for the Working Classes in Early Victorian Urban England* (London: Oxford University Press, 1963; revised and corrected, Harmondsworth: Penguin, 1974). Includes extensive bibliography of contemporary and secondary sources on Reynolds.

James, Louis, *Print and the People* (London: Allen Lane, 1976). Includes extracts from Reynolds's writings.

Joshi, Priya, *In Another Country: Colonialism, Culture, and the English Novel in India* (New York: Columbia University Press, 2002).

Joyce, Patrick, *Visions of the People: Industrial England and the Question of Class, 1848–1874* (Cambridge: Cambridge University Press, 1991).

Kallikoff, Beth, *Murder and Moral Decay in Victorian Popular Literature* (Ann Arbor: University of Michigan Press, 1986).

Leavis, Q.D., *Fiction and the Reading Public* (London: Chatto and Windus, 1931). The first serious recognition, albeit brief, of the social significance of *Reynolds's Miscellany.*

Maccoby, Simon, *English Radicalism, 1853–1886* (London: Allen and Unwin, 1938).

Maxwell, Richard, *The Mysteries of Paris and London* (Charlottesville: University Press of Virginia, 1992).

Meisel, Martin, *Realizations: Narrative, Pictorial and Theatrical Arts in Nineteenth-century England* (Princeton, NJ: Princeton University Press, 1983).

Mitchell, Charles (ed.), *The Newspaper Press Directory* (London: Charles Mitchell, 1846).

Neuburg, Victor E., *Popular Literature: A History and a Guide* (Harmondsworth: Penguin, 1977).

Pearl, Cyril, *Victorian Patchwork* (London: Heinemann, 1972).

Punter, David, *The Literature of Terror*, 2 vols (New York: Longman, 1980). See vol. 1, pp. 145–63.

Reynolds, David S., *Beneath the American Renaissance* (New York: Knopf, 1988).

Reynolds, G.W.M., *The Mysteries of London*, ed. Trefor Thomas (Keele: Keele University Press, 1996). An introduction to biography, reading approaches and publication history; also includes a useful bibliography on the time period and generic approaches.

Shattock, Joanne and Michael Wolff (eds), *The Victorian Periodical Press: Samplings and Soundings* (Toronto: University of Toronto Press, 1982).

Summers, Montague, *A Gothic Bibliography* (London: Fortune Press, 1941; repr. New York: Russell and Russell, 1964). The entry on Reynolds includes a broadly comprehensive survey of the various publications of Reynolds's *Mysteries*.

Taylor, Antony, *Down with the Crown: British Anti-monarchism and Debate about Royalty since 1890* (London: Reaktion Books, 1999).

Taylor, Antony, *'Lords of Misrule': Hostility to Aristocracy in Late Nineteenth- and Early Twentieth-century Britain* (Basingstoke: Palgrave Macmillan, 2004).

Vicinus, Martha, *The Industrial Muse: A Study of Nineteenth-century British Working-class Literature* (London: Croom Helm, 1974).

Webb, R.K., *The British Working-class Reader, 1790–1848* (London: George Allen and Unwin, 1955).

Williams, Raymond, *Culture and Society, 1780–1850* (New York: Columbia University Press, 1958).

II. Articles and Chapters in Books

Maha Atal, 'G.W.M. Reynolds in Paris 1835-6: a New Discovery', in *Notes and Queries* (forthcoming).

Berridge, Virginia, 'Popular Sunday Papers and Mid-Victorian Society', in George Boyce, James Curran and Pauline Wingate (eds), *Newspaper History from the Seventeenth Century to the Present Day* (London: Constable, 1978), pp. 247–64.

Burt, Daniel S., 'A Victorian Gothic: G.W.M. Reynolds's *The Mysteries of London*', *New York Literary Forum*, 7 (1980): 141–58.

Diamond, Michael, 'Charles Dickens and Villain and Hero in *Reynolds's Newspaper*', *The Dickensian*, 68/457 (2002): 127–38.

'Dips into the Diary of Barrabas Bolt, Esq.', *The Man in the Moon*, vol. 3, no. 17 (1848), pp. 235–44. A satire of Reynolds's politics with caricatures of Reynolds.

Gough, Harold, 'G.W.M. Reynolds at Herne Bay', *Bygone Kent*, 6/5 (May 1985): 272–83.

Guivar'ch, Jean, 'Deux journalistes anglais à Paris: G.W.M. Reynolds et W.M.T.', *Etudes Anglaises*, 28/2 (1975): 203–14.

'G.W.M. Reynolds', *Saturday Review*, (6 February 1886): 199.

'G.W.M. Reynolds and Penny Fiction', *Times Literary Supplement*, (24 January 1924): 56.

Hargreaves, Ian, 'George W.M. Reynolds and "The Trafalgar Square Revolution": Radicalism, the Carnavalesque and Popular Culture in Mid-Victorian England', *Journal of Victorian Culture*, 7 (2002): 23–59.

Haywood, Ian, 'George W.M. Reynolds and the Radicalization of Victorian Social Fiction', *Media History*, 4/2 (1998): 121–39.

Haywood, Ian, 'Encountering Time: Memory and Tradition in the Radical Victorian Press', in Laurel Brake and Julie F. Codell (eds), *Encounters in the Victorian Press: Editors, Authors, Readers* (Basingstoke: Palgrave Macmillan, 2005), pp. 69–87.

Humpherys, Anne, 'G.W.M. Reynolds, Popular Literature and Popular Politics', *Victorian Periodicals Review*, 16 (1983): 79–89.

Humpherys, Anne, 'The Geometry of the Modern City: G.W.M. Reynolds and *The Mysteries of London*', *Browning Institute Studies*, 11 (1983): 69–80.

Humpherys, Anne, 'Popular Narrative and Political Discourse in *Reynolds's Weekly Newspaper*', in Laurel Brake, Aled Jones and Lionel Madden (eds), *Investigating Victorian Journalism* (New York: St Martin's, 1990), pp. 33–47.

Humpherys, Anne, 'Generic Strands and Urban Twists: The Victorian Mysteries Novel', *Victorian Studies*, 34/4 (Summer 1991): 463–72.

Hunter, J.V.B.S., 'George Reynolds', *Book Handbook*, 4 (1947): 225–36.

Jacobs, Edward, 'Bloods in the Street: London Street Culture, "Industrial Literacy", and the Emergence of Mass Culture in Victorian England', *Nineteenth-century Contexts*, 18 (1995): 321–47.

James, Louis, 'The View from Brick Lane: Contrasting Perspectives in Working-class and Middle-class Fiction of the Early Victorian Period', *Yearbook of English Studies*, 11 (1981): 87–101. Compares Dickens and Reynolds in terms of form, style and content.

James, Louis, 'The Trouble with Betsy: Periodicals and the Common Reader in Mid-nineteenth-century England', in Joanne Shattock and Michael Wolff (eds), *The Victorian Periodical Press: Samplings and Soundings* (Leicester: Leicester University Press, 1982), pp. 349–66.

James, Louis, 'Reynolds, George William MacArthur', in H.C.G. Matthew and Brian Harrison (eds), *Oxford Dictionary of National Biography: From the Earliest Times to the Year 2000* (New York: Oxford University Press, 2004), vol. 46, pp. 536–8. The most complete biographical information.

James, Louis and Saville, John, 'G.W.M. Reynolds', in Joyce Bellamy and John Saville (eds), *Dictionary of Labour Biography* (London: Macmillan, 1976), vol. 3, pp. 146–51.

James, Sara, 'Eugene Sue, G.W.M. Reynolds, and the Representation of the City as "Mystery"', in Valeria Tinkler-Villani (ed.), *Babylon or New Jerusalem? Perceptions of the City in Literature* (Amsterdam: Rodopi, 2005), pp. 247–58.

Jay, Frank, 'Peeps into the Past', *London Journal*, 26 October, 23 November, 30 November 1918. Online at: geocities.com/justingilb/texts/PEEPS.htm.

Kausch, Donald, 'George W.M. Reynolds: A Bibliography', *The Library*, 5th series, 28/3 (December 1973): 319–26.

Kelly, Patrick, 'G.W.M. Reynolds', in Ira B. Nadel and William E. Fredeman (eds), *Victorian Novelists Before 1885* (Detroit: Thomson Gale, 1983), pp. 248–51.

McWilliam, Rohan, 'The Mysteries of G.W.M. Reynolds: Radicalism and Melodrama in Victorian Britain', in Malcolm Chase and Ian Dyck (eds), *Living and Learning: Essays in Honour of J.F.C. Harrison* (Aldershot: Scolar, 1996), pp. 182–98.

McWilliam, Rohan, 'The Melodramatic Seamstress: Interpreting a Victorian Penny Dreadful', in Beth Harris (ed.), *Famine and Fashion: Needlewomen in the Nineteenth Century* (Aldershot: Ashgate, 2005), pp. 99–114.

Martin, David, 'Reynolds, George William Macarthur', in A. Thomas Lane (ed.), *Biographical Dictionary of European Labor Leaders* (Westport, CT: Greenwood Press, 1995), p. 836.

Maxwell, Richard, 'G.M. Reynolds, Dickens, and *The Mysteries of London*', *Nineteenth-century Fiction*, 32 (1977): 185–213.

'Mischievous Literature', *The Bookseller*, 1 July 1868, pp. 445–9.

'Mr. G.W.M. Reynolds', *Glasgow Examiner*, 8 November 1845; repr. *London Journal*, vol. 1 (1845), p. 191.

Neuburg, Victor E., 'Reynolds, G(eorge) W(illiam) M(acarthur)', in *The Popular Press Companion to Popular Literature* (Bowling Green: Bowling Green State University Popular Press, 1983), pp. 165–6.

Obituaries, *Reynolds's Newspaper*, 22 June 1879, p. 1; *The Bookseller*, 3 July 1879, pp. 600–601.

Plunkett, John, 'Regicide and Reginamania: G.W.M. Reynolds and *The Mysteries of London*', in Andrew Maunder and Grace Moore (eds), *Victorian Crime, Madness and Sensation* (Burlington: Ashgate, 2004), pp. 15–30.

Powell, Sally, 'Black Markets and Cadaverous Pies: The Corpse, Urban Trade and Industrial Consumption in the Penny Blood', in Andrew Maunder and Grace Moore (eds), *Victorian Crime, Madness and Sensation* (Burlington: Ashgate, 2004), pp. 45–58.

Reynolds's Newspaper, Jubilee issue and supplement, 27 May 1900.

Reynolds's News, 'Centenary Souvenir', 7 May 1950.

Rosenman, Ellen Bayuk, 'Spectacular Women: *The Mysteries of London* and the Female Body', *Victorian Studies*, 40/1 (Fall 1996): 31–64.

Springall, J., '"A Life Story for the People?" Edwin J. Brett and the London "Low-life" Penny Dreadfuls of the 1860s', *Victorian Studies*, 33/2 (Winter 1990): 223–46.

Summers, Montague, 'G.W.M. Reynolds', *Times Literary Supplement*, July 4, 1942, p. 336.

Sutherland, John, 'Reynolds, G(eorge) W(illiam) M(acarthur)', in *The Stanford Companion to Victorian Fiction* (Stanford: Stanford University Press, 1989), pp. 531–2.

Taylor, Antony, '*Reynolds's Newspaper*, Opposition to Monarchy and the Radical Anti-Jubilee: Britain's Anti-monarchist Tradition Reconsidered', *Historial Research*, 68 (1995): 318–37.

Thomas, Trefor, 'Rereading G.W. Reynolds's *The Mysteries of London*', in Alice Jenkins and Juliet John (eds), *Rereading Victorian Fiction* (New York: St Martin's, 2000), pp. 59–80.

Tindall, S.J., 'Victorian Popular Fiction and the Condition of England Question', *Publications of the Mississippi Philological Association* (1987): 154–63.

Williams, Raymond, 'Radical and/or Respectable', in Richard Boston (ed.), *The Press We Deserve* (New York: Routledge and Kegan Paul, 1970), pp. 16–23.

Williams, Raymond, 'The Press and Popular Culture: An Historical Perspective', in George Boyce, James Curran and Pauline Wingate (eds), *Newspaper History from the Seventeenth Century to the Present Day* (London: Constable, 1978), pp. 41–50.

Williams, Raymond, 'Forms of English Fiction in 1848', in Francis Barker, John Coombes, Peter Hulme, Colin Mercer and David Musselwhite (eds), *1848: The Sociology of Literature* (Colchester: University of Essex Press, 1978), pp. 277–90.

III. Dissertations

Benford, Criscillia Ann, 'The Multiplot Novel and the Dynamics of the Victorian Social Order' (Stanford University, 2004).

Berridge, Virginia, 'Popular Journalism and Working-class Attitudes, 1854–1886: A Study of *Reynolds's Newspaper*, *Lloyd's Weekly Newspaper* and *The Weekly Times*', 2 vols (University of London, 1976).

James, Sara, 'Capital Tales: The Urban Mysteries of Eugene Sue and G.W.M. Reynolds' (Birmingham University, 2001).

May, Ronald Hamilton, 'Unrestrained Women and Decadent Old Aristocrats: The Nineteenth-century Middle-class Struggle for Cultural Hegemony' (Louisiana State University, 1999).

Shirley, Michael H., 'On Wings of Everlasting Power: G.W.M. Reynolds and "Reynolds's Newspaper", 1848–1876' (University of Illinois, 1997).

Index